JOINING THE GLOBAL PUBLIC

SUNY SERIES IN CHINESE PHILOSOHPY AND CULTURE

Roger T. Ames, editor

JOINING THE GLOBAL PUBLIC

*Word, Image, and City
in Early Chinese Newspapers, 1870–1910*

EDITED BY

RUDOLF G. WAGNER

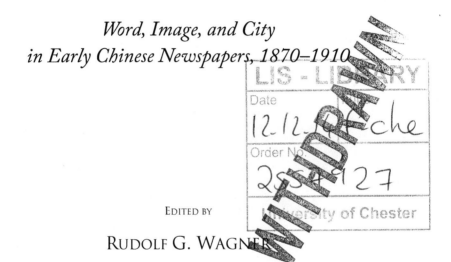
STATE UNIVERSITY OF NEW YORK PRESS

Published by
STATE UNIVERSITY OF NEW YORK PRESS
ALBANY

© 2007 State University of New York

For information, address
State University of New York Press
194 Washington Avenue, Suite 305, Albany, NY 12210-2384

Production, Laurie Searl
Marketing, Anne M. Valentine

Library of Congress Cataloging-in-Publication Data

Joining the global public : word, image, and city in early Chinese newspapers, 1870–1910 / [edited by] Rudolf G. Wagner.
    p. cm. — (SUNY series in Chinese philosophy and culture)
Includes bibliographical references and index.
ISBN-13: 978-0-7914-7117-3 (alk. paper)
ISBN-13: 978-0-7914-7118-0 (pbk : alk. paper)
    1. Chinese newspapers—China—History. 2. Newspaper publishing—China.
3. China—History—1861–1912. I. Wagner, Rudolf G. II. Title: Word, image, and city in early Chinese newspapers, 1870–1910.

PN5364.J65 2007
079'.51—dc22   2006021967

10 9 8 7 6 5 4 3 2 1

Contents

List of Illustrations

Preface

This volume presents some fruits of the work of members of an informal research group, Structure and Development of the Chinese Public Sphere, established in Heidelberg in 1993. It provided a forum for a broad range of independent research projects linked by this focus; subjects ranged from the rhetoric of late Qing editorials to the administration of the national memory through PRC archives; from the acculturation of the newspaper to Chinese preferences to the development of professional journalists; from studies of Ernest Major, the founder and manager of the most important early paper, the *Shenbao*, to studies of Li Boyuan, the man who set the standard for the Chinese entertainment papers; from the implied addressee of advertisements to the rise of the modern star.

The German Research Foundation DFG programs Transformations of the European Expansion and Theatricality have supported years of research, and the two conferences organized by the group have received funding from the German Research Foundation and the Chiang Ching-kuo Foundation. This support is gratefully acknowledged. A list of the publications of the research group and other relevant information will be found at http://sun.sino.uni-heidelberg.de.

The research group has now run its course, and while most of us still work in this field, many members are now continuing their careers elsewhere. Working together over the years was an amazingly uncomplicated and altogether gratifying experience for all of us.

Introduction

Rudolph G. Wagner

The 1989 translation into English of Jürgen Habermas's 1962 study, *The Structural Transformation of the Public Sphere* in Europe has provoked a debate among China scholars about the viability of concepts such as public sphere and civil society in China.[1] In a pathbreaking study independent of Habermas's work, Mary Backus Rankin has documented the gradual coagulation of local public spheres in Zhejiang into a regional Lower Yangtse Valley and even a national public sphere between 1860 and the end of the Qing in 1911.[2] She pointed to the increase of "public" activities by new elite groups only loosely connected to the state apparatus, to a growing self-awareness of these groups, and a concomitant growth in cultural articulations, ideological claims, and social links. She saw the *Shenbao* newspaper in Shanghai as an important link between them, and even as their voice. Although her focus was not on the press, she often used the *Shenbao* as a source. In another important work, William Rowe also focused on Jiangnan local elites,[3] but with a more "China-centered" approach. He saw a "civil society" developing in late imperial Chinese cities independent of foreign impact. While his Hankow merchants, as Frederic Wakeman pointed out, were mostly compradors of foreign firms in Shanghai and got the news about their own city from the foreign-owned *Shenbao*[4]—also a key source for Rowe himself—the "foreign" media have no place in his argumentation.

With the Habermas discussion, these works were reset into a larger context. Habermas's focus was on the communication within the public sphere rather than the familiar social basis of its development. His sociological study could draw on a wide range of empirical studies done by historians. In Chinese studies, such historical studies are still in the first stages. Without them, broader conceptualizations have a weak foundation. The present volume is an effort to help strengthen this base.[5]

Habermas had linked the public sphere with a distinctly European enlightenment agenda of a society speaking with its own voice independent of the state and with a critical edge against manipulation by modern monopolized media. In the 1990 Preface to a new German edition of his book, he revisited some of his earlier pessimism. The developments in Central and Eastern Europe seemed to show that even after decades of a fully monopolized propaganda press and certainly without being a "population used to freedom," people were able to use niches to craft the elements of a civil society strong enough to delegitimate a seemingly all-powerful authoritarian state.[6] To restrict the public sphere concept to Western Europe seemed too narrow. The PRC events in 1989 called for similar reflections.[7]

Habermas followed the Scottish enlightenment in defining civil society and the public as well as the public sphere of its deliberations in contradistinction to the state.[8] The state is the object of, but not a subject in, the debate. The state was not treated as an actor in the public sphere. The Chinese case here may serve to highlight a blind spot in this approach. Long before the first Chinese newspapers had made their appearance, the court had regularly released approved information and documents to the public. Although managed by private print shops, the resulting *Peking Gazette, Jingbao,* had to reproduce the entire release—and this without changes or addition of other texts. The early *Shenbao* editorials from the 1870s about the function of newspapers were quite right in saying that the *Peking Gazette* format reduced the flow of communication between high and low, between state and society, to a top–down dispensation. The flowering of Chinese-language newspapers in Shanghai since the 1870s, their distribution throughout the country, and their gradual but evident acceptance by a broad readership did not mean that the government gazette dwindled into insignificance as it did in many parts of Western Europe. The Chinese state continued to have a loud say in the Chinese public sphere. Whenever a central government had the actual strength to reduce legitimate public articulation to the state's voice, it did so, and it has done this most effectively since 1949. In China, the government gazette as well as other government media have been and are in fact the mainstream of public articulation; the existence of a multivocal press is perceived as the hallmark of a weak government unable to unify the minds of the nation. The elimination of the state from the public sphere seems also unsupported by the European record. Roger Chartier's work *The Cultural Origins of the French Revolution* (1990) shows to what extent the French state was active not just negatively as a censor, but proactively as a publicist, historian, polemicist, editor, and journalist.[9] In the Chinese case, things are even more complicated. Since the discovery of the newspaper as a tool of advocacy and propaganda by Liang Qichao in the last years of the nineteenth century, one generation after another of Chinese reformers and revolutionaries has followed in his footsteps. The claim that a newspaper is only the "tool of a class" such as the bourgeoisie, or of a power, such as an imperialist country, makes the notion of a free press into the camouflage of hostile intentions and has justified the use of this "tool" for CP proletarian propaganda and the advocacy of the interests of the "suppressed" country China. The official articulations in the PRC thus claim the combined authority of the voice of the state and that of the successful revolution. The ensuing elimination, within China proper, of "imperialist" public sphere enclaves such as Shanghai has effectively blinded the country, including its leadership, to its own situation. The costs have not been negligible. The worst man-made famine of the twentieth century was that of the Great Leap Forward in 1958–1961; as Amartya Sen has observed, one of the causes was the fragmentation of the information about "problems," so that no aggregate picture of the disaster could emerge. Another was the utterly surrealist reports in the papers about the ever more amazing breakthroughs in agricultural and industrial production.

Taking up some of the arguments made by China scholars since the early 1990s about the need to recognize the role of the state in the public sphere, I would suggest that we formalize this concept and reduce it to its functional value in a constellation not bound by a "bourgeois society."[10] In this sense, the notion "public sphere" conceptualizes the space in which state and society as well as different segments of society articulate their interests and opinions within culturally and historically defined rules of rationality and propriety. The existence of a public sphere is a key constituent of a social order whose members do not resort to violence in each instance when conflict occurs.

In this formalized sense, a public sphere did exist in premodern China not only in fact but also in the social imaginaire of how things could be, should be, and had been in the utopian past when sages had ruled the land. It appears in such notions as the "thoroughfare for articulation," *yanlu* 言路, the way for open articulation to the emperor by society and lower officials of critical opinions concerning the state and its officials. It was a standard remonstrative figure of speech that this thoroughfare had to be kept open so as to prevent dynastic collapse. In the opposite top–down direction it is operative in the notion of *hua* 化, the moral 'transformation' and resulting spiritual unification of the people through the *acta, verba,* et *gesta* of the emperor and his officials. The broad acceptance on the other hand, during the late Qing and Republican periods as well as in Taiwan since 1988, of a multivocal press signals the presence at least of conflicting cultural values concerning the public sphere in the Chinese world. In this respect, the study of the initial phase of Chinese-language newspapers is far less antiquarian than it seems.

As different forces tried to fashion this sphere and their own role in it after their own aspirations, dramatic shifts occurred. The Opium War, and with it the establishment of the treaty ports, especially of Shanghai and the crown colony of Hong Kong, mark such a shift. In these exclaves, a Chinese-language press developed which offered a platform for articulation in the wider Chinese public sphere. Eventually, Shanghai also became *the* haven for the formation of nongovernmental social organizations such as political parties, unions, or chambers of commerce. These enclaves were hybrid spaces, populated by people who would describe themselves as Chinese, and run by people who would not. Eventually, they adopted a joint identity as Shanghairen/Shanghailander that was based on their operating in the same urban space and mode, not their ethnic, linguistic, or cultural background. In the interaction between the two groups, a new structure for the public sphere arose that drew on both traditions. The studies presented here explore this new structure.

Testing the viability and validity of the public sphere concept in late nineteenth-century Shanghai and China highlights still other aspects that have been overlooked in the European case. Three additional areas could be marked as follows.

The public sphere:

1. is not coterminous with the nation but essentially transnational and international.

2. is not homogenous, but shows marked spatial differences in the degree of openness and "civilized rationality."

3. does not restrict articulation to a high and rational range of discourse and the segments of society able to generate it. It makes use of the entire span of forms of articulation and behavior at the disposal of different segments of society, of different "publics."[11]

Habermas, for one, treats the public sphere as being coterminous with a community within national borders. By any standard of volume, importance, quality, or influence, however, the overwhelming majority of Chinese public sphere articulations in any medium between 1870 and the Second World War was, and could only be, published in a foreign-run exclave on Chinese soil, Shanghai. With the 'liberation' of Shanghai in 1949 and the self-enclosure of China into the socialist bloc through internal measures and external boycott, the internal Chinese public sphere collapsed into a unified party articulation supervised by the Communist Party Propaganda Department. Since then, Hong Kong as well as foreign-based radio stations continued—albeit in a greatly reduced form—to play the role of Shanghai. The information and opinion provided in these exclaves, however, are—and remains down to the Internet and World Wide Web of our days—a core ingredient of the Chinese public sphere. A look back to eighteenth-century France shows the same structure. Without reference to Habermas's work, Robert Darnton has demonstrated that nearly all the works considered important indicators and even harbingers of the French Revolution, from Diderot's *Encyclopédie* to little porn pamphlets against Marie Antoinette, have been printed in Neuchâtel or Leiden beyond the French borders.[12] It is no accident that all the newspapers discussed in this volume, and these are indeed the most important for their genre and time, were published in either the Shanghai Foreign Settlement or in the British crown colony of Hong Kong; and that most of the key players were either bona-fide foreigners or Chinese with strong links to and protection by the outside world.

This globalizing public sphere again is not without its particular structures. Since the middle of the nineteenth century, China has been decentered. The trajectory to be followed, today called modernization, was defined in centers far beyond its borders. Chinese knowledge about these distant centers was generally shallow, which made for an essentialist, dehistoricized, decontextualized, and utilitarian perception. The very institution of the newspaper came in this package of successful modernization as a core ingredient promising information flow in society as well as rational and effective handling of conflict. The internationality of the emerging 'modern' Chinese public sphere is thus not just a matter of its core being situated in Shanghai and, to a lesser degree, Hong Kong, its being manned by a special brand of internationalized actors, and its inclusion of foreign news as relevant for Chinese foreign relations as well as models for China's development. The very institutions of the modern public sphere such as newspapers or civic associations together with their rationales have initially been brought in from outside (and to a degree have kept this foreignness to this very day). Within the Qing territory, we might see the formation of regional elites in different regions—even their gradual merger into a cohesive network—but the locus of their communication was to an overwhelming degree Shanghai. Shanghai at the same time had the largest concentration of members of these new elites. Seen from the media and social association side, it makes little sense to speak of a Chinese public sphere during the late Qing. Shanghai was not just the place from which the media emanated; it was at the same time the locus of Chinese modernity.[13] Media coming from Shanghai could and did bank on this prestige of the town, whether they dealt with high politics, courtesan entertainment, or proposals for social and institutional change. The modern Chinese public sphere spread from Shanghai and retained an extremely uneven density for many decades to come.[14] This uneven distribution came with great differences in handling conflicts. The openness of the *Shenbao* pages for different opinions privileged a "rational" and nonviolent debate.

The enlightenment and/or propaganda agenda in studies of newspaper history has for many years led to a neglect of popular but no less influential and important forms of articulation. While this misbalance has gradually disappeared in studies of Western newspaper history—probably in reaction to the evident impact of the modern tabloids—there is little of this in Chinese studies. The emphasis has been to this day on the advocacy press, which is seen by PRC authors as the legitimate ancestor of the modern Party papers. This emphasis began with the first propagator of this type of press, Liang Qichao. In his view, there is no Chinese press to speak of before 1895 because what was there before was purely commercial and furthermore under the financial control of foreigners. As a consequence, neither the commercial papers nor the large entertainment press has received more than cursory attention, and, if so, exclusively under a political perspective. In this reading, the early *Shenbao* can only be an instrument of reactionary imperialist interference into China's internal affairs. The standard proof is the critical attitude of Huang Xiexun, the editor of the *Shenbao* during the Hundred Days Reform in 1898, toward one of the leaders, Kang Youwei, a man now officially sanctioned as having been at the time a progressive bourgeois reformer. During harder phases of class struggle in the PRC, even the bona-fide Chinese proprietor and editor of the paper during the 1920s, Shi Liangcai, became a bourgeois reactionary.[15] The illustrated paper *Dianshizhai huabao,* in its turn, is reduced to an archive of illustrations of social and political scenes depicted from an often politically questionable perspective. And the plethora of small-format tabloids of the late Qing and Republican era, *xiaobao,* is neglected to the point that, to this day, just one single article in Chinese provides some overview.[16]

The founding decades of Chinese-language papers before 1900 have been written out of Chinese history by Chinese writers; because these papers have been written in Chinese by Chinese, and were read by Chinese, they have not found a place in the studies on the Western presence in China either. A classical case is the figure of Ernest Major, whose role was pivotal since 1872 in making Shanghai the media and print capital of China for the next seven decades. Still, this has not earned him even a modest place in either Chinese or Western handbooks of knowledge.

Given the size and importance of the work still to do in mapping the structure of the Chinese public sphere with its historical changes, revolutions, cataclysms, and varying densities, the contributions the studies in this volume will be able to make is modest enough. They will not all of a sudden create a rich, solid, and specific basis for broad and daring new conceptualizations. What they do, however, is probe the viability of different methodological approaches in the study of this exceedingly voluminous and difficult material; map some of the core features of the newspapers in the decisive initial phase when the basic parameters were set; and open the view to the broad spectrum of public articulations in this period through the inclusion of research about the illustrated and the entertainment press. They set out to open up a rich, diverse, and fascinating record of archival and printed, textual and visual, Chinese and Western sources, most of which are introduced and presented here for the first time in any language.

The new media had to be given a place in a Chinese order of things acceptable to the implied readers so that they had the necessary cultural cachet to legitimately claim attention and secure a place on the market. This place in the social imaginaire was secured through argumentations on the highest rhetorical level, ideally in the form of editorials and prefaces, as well as through strategies of cultural packaging, which retained the thrill of the new and global while presenting it in a more or less familiar garb.

It might be argued that readers really only cared for the news, the pictures, and the gossip in the *Shenbao,* the *Dianshizhai huabao,* and the *Youxibao,* and not for these rhetorical exercises. The repeated efforts at situating these papers in the Chinese imaginaire tell another story. In the case of the *Shenbao,* editorials set out to prove that the paper was the modern technical facilitator of the old Chinese ideal of unimpeded communication between high and low, the court and the people, state and society; in the case of the *Dianshizhai huabao,* the introduction advocated a realist turn in the use of graphic arts to illustrate strange things from all over the globe; and in the case of the entertainment papers, the texts offered an indirect reflection on social ills through the depiction of the Shanghai courtesan world to fill out the new leisure space in the weekly timetable of the city's inhabitants.

The cultural packaging was no less important. The evidence again are the constant changes in the ever renewed attempt to get the better fit, whether in format, use of calendar, language levels, rhetorical devices, handling of relationships with readers, or engaging in societal affairs such as the *Shenbao*'s long-standing attacks against the use of opium, the *Dianshizhai huabao*'s collection of money for the victims of a flood, or the *Youxibao*'s organization of the first "democratic election" in China—that of the most attractive courtesan voted on by the habitués of the Shanghai courtesan houses. These newspapers operated as individuated actors in the Chinese public sphere with all the nervousness and attention paid to their public image and acceptance as affecting their market success.

Barbara Mittler's chapter puts a strong emphasis on the analysis of the argumentative, rhetorical, and cultural strategies involved in setting up the first Chinese newspaper deserving this name. The idealizing language about the purport and role of newspapers in nineteenth-century European encyclopedias is introduced into China and recontextualized into an equally idealized picture of Chinese antiquity, but with a marked difference. While all over Europe the press was in fact subjected to a variety of constraints from censorship to market competition and financial control, the Shanghai City Council had no such institutions whatsoever. The only laws applying were the libel statutes in the law books of the different nations with consulates in Shanghai, but this was a dull instrument and it was hardly ever tried. In the Shanghai exclave existed, institutionally spoken, the freest press altogether, and this in a country where the court claimed the most exclusive monopoly in discussing state affairs. The problem the *Shenbao* had to deal with was not censorship, but gaining acceptance by Chinese readers without abandoning the thrill and promise of the new media.

Natascha Gentz Vittinghoff's prosopographic chapter of the first generation of Chinese journalists proceeds along the lines of historical sociology. It takes on the standard tropes claiming that there was a lack of interest and respect for newspapers before 1895, and that these were effusions by people of little quality who, having failed to succeed at the imperial examinations, offered their services to foreigners to vent their frustration through slanders against Chinese scholars and officials. This study shows a first new 'modern' class in the forming, a class of intellectuals and journalists, of educated people who shared a common background of some connection with missionary or other foreign-related institutions and schools, and would link up regionally and eventually nationally independent of their place of origin in the sojourner cities of Shang-hai and Hong Kong. These people have education, knowledge, and social sta-tus. They were the first to realize the new options coming with the change in the polity and the relentlessly growing global involvement of China.

Wagner and Kim deal with the first and superbly important Chinese member in the world league of illustrated papers, the *Dianshizhai huabao* (1884–1897), another product of Ernest Major's *Shenbao* company. Using a cultural studies approach, Wagner traces the origins of this paper in the con-text of a general and global shift toward the image as the core feature of the media, a shift in aesthetic preference toward the specific, and a valuation of common folk as potentially newsworthy items. Elements of this new visual empire are such things as lithograph forerunners of national emblems and propaganda posters. The development of a stable group of newspainters with compatible style and focus around this paper shows features similar to the journalists studied by Natascha Gentz.

Kim's study refuses to accept the selective perspective on the *Dianshizhai huabao* as an archive for a particular view of late Qing social history. It oper-ates with the assumption that knowledge of an order of magnitude, even if no exact numbers might be available, is infinitely more than nothing; it proceeds to effectively map out a highly specific profile of this first and most successful illustrated paper, of its thematic and regional selection, implied readership, and graphic strategies. A mentalité of the implied reader emerges that is infinitely more complex and less reducible to urban rationality than studies have hitherto been willing to take into account. The study directly links the implied reader with the real historical reader. This link is not, in itself, a given. In the particu-lar case, however, it is the market that forms the link. The implied reader of the text and illustrations must be a close relative to the real reader because only this could provide the motive for the latter to buy the *Dianshizhai huabao*. The paper's market success and duration are proof that this is what readers did.

Catherine Yeh offers a highly contextualized cultural study of the new and specialized entertainment papers developing in Shanghai after 1895 with a focus on the *Youxi bao* (Entertainment) and the *Shijie fanhua bao* (World Vanity Fair). This press started to blossom as an ironical comment on a time that saw the flourishing of the Shanghai culture of leisure against the back-ground of the Sino-Japanese War and the efforts at, and the failure of, the reform of 1898. The new entertainment papers and their success signal that the grand concerns of the nation, which our history books tell us were the only concerns of all relevant figures at the time, had to settle into an uneasy accom-modation with concerns about the best way to spend the new urban leisure time, and with the news that the four top courtesans had agreed on a day to highlight the beginning of the fall season by donning new hats. Li Boyuan, the editor putting these seemingly light papers together, figures with his novels, some of which he serialized in his papers, as one of the fiercest social critics of the time; at the same time his papers become the media through which the Shanghai courtesan and the opera singer get on their way to become public and national stars—and this years and even decades before the first political personalities would rise to comparable levels.

Altogether, the chapters share an agenda of offering broadly based empirical research. They do not shy away from presenting falsifiable translations of their key evidence to provide the basis for an informed disagreement and show the way in which the topics under consideration were discussed and narrated. They try to avoid being hampered by fashion in either source evaluation or argument, to make the best of approaches developed in other fields of the humanities, and to arrive, in a controlled and falsifiable manner, at broader conceptualizations.

NOTES

1. Jürgen Habermas, *Strukturwandel der Öffentlichkeit: Untersuchungen zu einer Kategorie der bürgerlichen Gesellschaft,* Frankfurt: Luchterhand, 1962; id., *The Structural Transformation of the Public Sphere: An Inquiry into a Category of Bourgeois Society,* translated by Thomas Burger with the assistance of Frederick Lawrence, Cambridge, Mass.: MIT Press, 1989. The French translation came at about the same time. Jürgen Habermas, *L'éspace public: archéologie de la publicité comme dimension constitutive de la société bourgeoise,* traduit de l'allemand par Marc B. de Launay, Paris: Payot, 1988. F. Wakeman, "The Civil Society and Public Sphere Debate: Western Reflections on Chinese Political Culture," *Modern China,* 19.2 (1993), pp. 108–138, and other articles in the same issue. R. Wagner, "The Role of the Foreign Community in the Chinese Public Sphere," *China Quarterly* 142 (June 1995) argues for the transnationality of the "Chinese" public sphere. Thomas Metzger, *The Western Concept of the Civil Society in the Context of Chinese History,* Hoover Essay #21, Stanford: Hoover Institution, 1998, argues that twentieth-century Chinese elites have not accepted the "bottom-up" notion of a civil society capable of order and morality without the strong guidance of the state. The theoretical discussion "Civil Society and China" was introduced to Chinese audiences in a journal edited by PRC scholars in Hong Kong. *Zhongguo shehuikexue jikan* (Hong Kong) 3 (1993), pp. 5–62.

2. Mary Backus Rankin, *Elite Activism and Political Transformation in China. Zhejiang Province, 1865–1911,* Stanford: Stanford University Press, 1986.

3. William Rowe, *Hankow: Commerce and Society in a Chinese City,* Stanford: Stanford University Press, 1984; id., *Hankow: Conflict and Community in a Chinese City, 1796–1895,* Stanford: Stanford University Press, 1989.

4. F. Wakeman, "The Civil Society and Public Sphere Debate: Western Reflections on Chinese Political Culture," *Modern China,* 19.2 (1993), pp. 108–138.

5. For other studies from the Heidelberg group, see Andrea Janku, *Nur leere Reden: Politischer Diskurs und die Shanghaier Press im China des späten 19. Jahrhunderts,* Wiesbaden: Harassowitz, 2003; Natascha Vittinghoff, *Die Anfänge des Journalismus in China (1860–1911),* Wiesbaden: Harassowitz, 2002; Barbara Mittler, *A Newspaper for China? Power, Indentity, and Change in Shanghai's News Media, 1872–1912,* Cambridge: Harvard University Press, 2004. For recent studies on post-1900 developments, see also Terry Narramore, "Making the News in Shanghai. *Shenbao* and the Politics of Newspaper Journalism 1912–1937," unpubl. Ph.D. dissertation, Australian National University, 1989; Joan Judge, *Print and Politics: Shibao and the Formation of the Public Sphere in Late Qing China,* Stanford: Stanford University Press, 1996.

6. Jürgen Habermas, preface to the 1990 German edition of his *Strukturwandel der Öffentlichkeit,* Frankfurt: Suhrkamp, 1990, p. 47. The Central European developments of the 1980s again are radically different from those in China. See David L. Wank, "Civil Society in Communist China? Private Business and Political Alliance, 1989," in John A. Hall, ed., *Civil Society: Theory, History, Comparison,* Cambridge: Polity Press, 1995, pp. 56–79.

7. David Strand, "Protest in Beijing: Civil Society and Public Sphere in China," *Problems of Communism,* May–June 1990, pp. 1–19. The development of "private" enterprise and NGOs in the PRC since the 1990 has prompted similar forays. Gordon White, *In Search of Civil Society: Market Reform and Social Change in Contemporary China,* Oxford: Clarendon, 1996; Timothy Brook and B. Michael Frolic, eds., *Civil Society in China,* Armonk: M. E. Sharpe, 1997.

8. The German term "Öffentlichkeit" means both—the public sphere as well as its actors, the public.

9. Roger Chartier, *Les Origines Culturelles de la Revolution Française,* Paris: Seuil, 1990. English edition 1991. This public nature was questionable not just for China, but also for Europe. Reinhart Koselleck, *Kritik und Krise: ein Beitrag zur Pathogenese der bürgerlichen Welt,* Freiburg: K. Alber [1959], shows the importance of the secretive Rosicrucian lodges as a forum of the public. Literary associations and private correspondence played a similar role in nineteenth-century China.

10. For a similar point with different arguments, see Philip Huang, "'Public Sphere'/'Civil Society' in China? The Third Realm between State and Society," *Modern China* 19.2 (April 1993), pp. 216–240. On the premodern Chinese public sphere, see R. Wagner, "The Early Chinese Newspapers and the Chinese Public Sphere," *European Journal of East Asian Studies* 1(2001), pp. 1–34.

11. Habermas hinted at some of these points in his Preface.

12. Robert Darnton, *The Literary Underground of the Old Regime,* Cambridge, Mass.: Harvard University Press, 1982.

13. Followed in importance by Hong Kong, Tianjin, and later Japan and the Huaqiao communities.

14. In many third world countries, a "dual economy" has developed that concentrated the "modern" sector in one internationally linked place. In this sense I speak of a "dual public sphere" in China.

15. See Feng Yaxiong, "*Shenbao yu Shi Liangcai*," in: *Wenshi ziliao xuanji* #17:156–165. See also "*Dui* << *Shenbao>> yu Shi Liangcai*" *yi wen buchong he dingzheng* in: *Wenshi ziliao xuanji* #23:244.

16. Zhun Junzhou, "*Shanghai xiaobao de lishi yange*" (The historical development of Shanghai tabloids), *Xinwen yanjiu ziliao* 42:163–179; 43:137–153; 44:211–220 (1988).

CHAPTER 1

Domesticating an Alien Medium: Incorporating the Western-style Newspaper into the Chinese Public Sphere

Barbara Mittler

China did not have newspapers in the Western sense of the word before foreign missionaries and merchants published their first Chinese-language papers
in China. Thus, the developing Chinese press also shared the particular features of its Western counterparts.[1] And yet, for these paper to be operative in
the new environment, they had to change.

This chapter will analyze this process of change. Starting from the normative late nineteenth century Western and Chinese discourse of what a paper
should be, it will turn to an exploration of what such an early Chinese paper
actually *could be.* It will argue that the process of domesticating the newspaper in China involved a number of ironic twists, which radically changed its
function and status. These twists made the medium into a rival rather than a
simple copy of the Western model.

WHAT IS THE NEWSPAPER? THE FOREIGN VIEW

By the time the press medium was introduced to China it already had become
a fixed institution in the West. The new profession of the journalist had
formed and consolidated, and as the self-confidence of this group grew, so did
their public projection of the benefits of the papers. The normative discourse
on newspapers at the time can be found in the great encyclopedias such as the
Grand Dictionnaire Universel du 19ième Siècle[2] and the *Encyclopaedia Britannica.*[3] Such works tend to reflect notions widely shared by the educated classes

at a given time and place. To flesh out the picture, I have added seminal quotations from editorial and inaugural statements from several newspapers.

While the history of the press is, over long stretches, the history of official publishing from official sources and under official supervision,[4] the ideal of the independent press has been emphatically evoked at least since Diderot's *Encyclopédie* (1751), in which the article dealing with the press states: "People ask if freedom of the press is advantageous or prejudicial to a state. The answer is not difficult. It is of the greatest importance to conserve this practice in all states founded on liberty. I would even say that the disadvantages of this liberty are so inconsiderable compared to its advantages that this ought to be the common right of the universe, and it is certainly advisable to authorize its practice in all governments."[5] Accordingly, encyclopedia definitions of the "true" press exclusively focus on the idealized form of the "free newspaper"[6] even though to this day the bulk of newspapers would not fit this rubric. Press laws and censorship are depicted not as legitimate supervisory instruments of the state but as unnatural curtailments of the "free press."

The idealized newspaper has, first, the ability to gather and spread a broad range of news. The *Encyclopaedia Britannica* thus cites the publisher of *The Daily Courant* (London) claiming in 1703: "The author has taken care to be duly furnished with all that comes from abroad."[7] Similarly, the inaugural issue of the *Universal Daily Reporter* stresses its efforts at diversity in 1785: "A News-Paper ... ought to be the Register of the times, and faithful recorder of every species of intelligence; it ought not to be engrossed by any particular object; but, like a well-covered table, it should contain something suited to every palate."[8] The idea of offering a broad variety of domestic and foreign, serious and entertaining news was among the earliest promises and purposes of newspapers. It appears prominently in the *Grand Dictionnaire Universel du 19ème Siècle* through a fine quotation from a rhymed gazette published in 1609:

> The Gazette in these verses/satisfies the brains:
> for from all over the universe/she gets her news
> The Gazette has a thousand runners/who live everywhere without a quarter
>   master.
> Everybody has to answer her/on her restless course
> Here and there,/from Orient to Occident
> and all the parts of the globe/without leaving a single matter out
> be it edicts, or commissions, or wars/general indulgences or bulls.
> She relates also/difficulties and prosperities,
> and whatever it is, nothing is forgotten/for the Gazette multiplies
> without reposing postillions/and is fast like the eagles.[9]

With their range from Orient to Occident, from the texts of edicts to reports about wars, news publications are able to speedily satisfy their readers' curiosity. Their varied contents have a second function, too: educational value.

The press is "the most powerful means of spreading enlightenment,"[10] as stated in the *Grand Dictionnaire* or, as an 1830s editorial for the *New York Herald* claims: "A newspaper can be made to take the lead ... in the great movements of human thought and human civilization. A newspaper can send more souls to Heaven, and save more from Hell than all the churches or chapels in New York—besides making money at the same time."[11] The entries "presse" and "journal" in the *Grand Dictionnaire* claim that the press is "power because it is knowledge," it is "electricity applied to matters of the mind."[12] And therefore it is "perceived as an enemy by the old society."[13] In a third function, the educating press is thus both a tool and a manifestation of modernization.[14]

Moreover, a paper offers room for the presentation of different views, for discussion, and for pondering things. It provides a record of popular feeling, and is responsible for the "shaping of public opinion,"[15] and "while contributing to the development of intellectual life, (it) also teaches to be informed about and rationally judge everything that has to do with public life."[16] The encyclopedias thus establish a fourth function of the newspaper: to foster the formation of public opinion.

And as newspapers inform and criticize, as they teach judgment to those above and below, they may even exercise control over the government. According to the *Grand Dictionnaire:*

> [The press] alone is capable of exercising, outside of the assemblies set up for this purpose, a supervision over the government. It alone is capable of keeping the citizens informed about public matters and of enlightening them with regard to their own interests. It alone, finally, is capable of making known to that sovereign judge, the public, the claims a citizen might have against particular representatives of the government.[17]

In the entry "journal," this encyclopedia even speaks of the press as "a weapon of opposition."[18] Governments have to read the newspaper to keep abreast of public opinion[19] because it "keeps the government informed about the concerns, thoughts, opinions, discussions, and grievances of society, and also about developments in other nations,"[20] and "quite independent of its being right or wrong, imposes itself on those who make a profession of despising it."[21] It thus becomes an important channel of communication between rulers and ruled.[22]

The language employed for describing the press in these encyclopedias is congratulatory throughout. The historical record certainly would support a rather different view as state authorities continuously and actively intervened to use this potentially "dangerous instrument" for their own purposes by putting journalists and publishers on their payroll, establishing censorship procedures, and publishing official newspapers. The potential to use the press for state (or other) propaganda is recognized, but it does not dominate the standard discourse.

WHAT IS THE NEWSPAPER? THE CHINESE VIEW

The core elements of the normative European discourse on the press reappear in programmatic Chinese statements. This section matches evidence from editorial and inaugural statements of the most important early Chinese-language paper, the *Shenbao,* with definitions by Chinese literati and statesmen. While surfacing only slightly later in encyclopedic works, these were, nevertheless, widely read and reflect shared beliefs and concepts. Founded in Shanghai in 1872 by a group of British businessmen, the *Shenbao* was managed by one of them, Ernest Major. Its staff was almost exclusively Chinese. Defending itself against occasional charges of being pro-Western,[23] it claimed that as a paper for a Chinese readership, it was written in Chinese for Chinese by Chinese[24] according to Chinese customs.[25] The inaugural editorial on April 30, 1872, proclaims that the transmission of news is the primary purpose of the paper: "Today there are a great many things in the world that could be transmitted, yet all too often [such things] are lost and never mentioned . . . which is perhaps due to the fact that no one is interested in recording them" (L.1). It will be the business of the *Shenbao* to record all these matters from China and abroad. A few days later, an editorial on "The origins of the *Shen(jiang xin)bao*"[26] repeats this point and argues that China, being one of the greatest countries in the world, certainly had a huge amount of news that until now would often have been suppressed or only submitted to the court, but would never have reached those living in far-off villages. The paper set out to remedy this situation.

Another 1872 editorial "On the difference between the official gazettes and the newspaper"[27] stressed the international news coverage: "Generally speaking, the Western newspapers transmit the affairs of all countries. Any deed, any word, any capacity, anything, be it from the court above, or from the smallest hamlet below, be it beautiful or ugly, fine or coarse, will be recorded in the papers" (L. 15–17).[28] Different explanations are given for the public appreciation of such a variety of news: " . . . those who read it (the newspaper) don't have to fear boredom. And how would they despise something which is able to deepen their opinions and broaden their knowledge?" ("The origins of the *Shen(jiang xin)bao*" L. 15–16). While offering entertainment, the *Shenbao* stressed its educational value much like its Western counterparts. An article in 1873 compares the newspaper with the "explanations of the grand historian," Sima Qian (145~90 BCE), who would critically comment on every biography of his *Records of the Grand Historian* and thus give it real didactic flavor.[29] To attain this goal, the *Shenbao* stressed from the outset the need for a clear and easily understandable newspaper language. Major admonished the staff "not to use extravagant and pompous vocabulary." A new (and unsuccessful) *Shenbao* venture, the "People's Paper," *Minbao* 民報, was specifically addressed to poorer people and women with low literacy levels, promising them that by regularly reading this interpunctuated newspaper in a simple language they would eventually master those "words, which they had hitherto not understood" and then "perfect wisdom will suddenly open up to them."[30] For similar educational reasons, the *Shenbao* editorialized in 1895 that illustrated newspapers would help "increase their (the readers') knowledge and experience and broaden their thoughts and intentions."[31] The *Shiwubao* 時務報 advertised in May 1898 that, like its Western models, it was interested in providing knowledge and broadening horizons. And as late as 1905, the *Shenbao* mentions, "Everyone knows that newspapers are capable of opening the door to knowledge."[32]

By stimulating public interest in current affairs, newspapers would serve as a "guide"[33] to their readers, educating humble citizen and high official about things foreign and Chinese.[34] The educational potential of this "modern" Western-style medium made it into the privileged instrument for propagating change and modernization in China.[35] In an editorial of 1905, a just rejuvenated *Shenbao* would stress: "The world progresses, new ideas make their appearance every day. Our strategy is not to hold on to the old and continue what has been there for eternities" (L.8–9).[36]

The contents of editorials appearing in the first few months of the publication some thirty years before already bear out this agenda with articles featuring railways, irrigation systems, Western medicine, steamships, and the cruelty of foot-binding.[37] In its promise of the newest and most up-to-date knowledge,[38] the *Shenbao* from early on distanced itself from Chinese antiquarian tendencies.[39] Newspapers brought to the reader "what he has never heard of before" in a manner technically accomplished (printed in movable letters) and with high speed. In describing the press in its breadth and accessibility, its presumed enlightened (and enlightening) content as well as its technical modernity, these editorials spell out the third function of newspapers: they are tools as well as manifestations of modernization.

The editorials also characterize the paper as a forum for opinion and discussion. While this fourth and pivotal aspect is only fully developed in *Shenbao* statements such as "newspapers are the general expression of public opinion" (baozhizhe yulun zhi gongyan ye) and "the newspaper is the mouth of the citizens" in articles of 1909 and 1910,[40] the idea can be traced back several decades.[41] The *Shenbao* editorial of August 18, 1873, "On the establishment of newspapers in different countries," argues: "The reason why private persons make such newspapers is that everything can be openly discussed there, *the most gigantic profits and losses of the court above, and the most minute blessings and sufferings of the hamlets below*" (L. 20–21). Thus, the newspaper serves as a platform for public discussion and medium for open criticism: "To exhort the state and to cause it to do away with its blemishes and to hope for its prosperity, that is what our company considers the proper way of being loyal to one's country" (L: 7–8).[42]

This type of newspaper critique is not only necessary, but also beneficial to the prosperity of the state:

The first rule for a newspaper-company is to honor the ruler. But to honor the ruler does not just mean to praise his achievements. . . . Everything that is of use for the country should be reported in detail, clarity, and depth. Everything which is bad for the country should be reported with a clear voice and without excuse for harsh words, and without fear to offend the ears. . . . Once (so) done the (state's) power will flourish daily more, and this has been so in every Western country which has used this (method). (L. 5–7)[43]

The press here appears as a transmission belt for public opinion(s). While informed and critical participation in policy discussions in China was associated with an ideal polity, it was decidedly not established procedure.[44] Papers such as the *Shenbao*, on the other hand, made the official Peking Gazette, the *Jingbao*, widely available by reprinting it in their news sections, and would also publish articles taking issue with these official emanations. In this manner, government decree and critical opinion met on the same public page. In a potentially upsetting way, the press impressed on those above to "reign according to [the views and opinions of the people]" and thus claimed to "supervise the government,"[45] as a *Shenbao* editorial in May 1872 argued:

It is quite curious but the court prints all the edicts, which it issues, and all the memorials, which it receives, in the court gazette to create a standard for the people. But not a single event or a single piece of news from the people reaches the ruler by this means. . . . Now as concerns the court gazette, it can be used to understand the views and opinions of the state, but (presumably) the citizens also have ideas. If the views and opinions of the people have no way of reaching the above, how could those above reign according to them? (L. 19–21)[46]

This capacity to connect ruler and ruled is elaborated on in "On the establishment of newspapers in different countries" of 1873: "If someone wishes to have a word (*you yan*) with the ruler, there are many inconveniences since one cannot avoid that ruler and ruled are separate. But if (the trouble) is mentioned in the newspaper, the situation of those below immediately reaches those above" (L. 11–12). Another editorial, "On the use of newspapers," explains that this is so because a ruler who reads the newspaper "can get to know about the true circumstances in his territory in the most complete manner and can thus rule and lead it to the greatest benefit" (L. 21).[47] The *Shenbao* sees this as the main merit of Western papers: "The basic thought in the establishment of newspapers by Western countries was set on connecting the affairs of those above and those below . . . if one wishes to read something about the situation of the people, nothing is as good as the newspaper" (L. 29–31). In the upbeat-language of *Shenbao* editorials, the Chinese newspaper lives up to its ideal form. It fulfills all the five functions contemporary European common opinion assigns to the press.

Because the *Shenbao* was a commercial enterprise under foreign ownership and management until 1905, it may seem natural that its descriptions of the use and function of the newspaper would correspond with those current in the West. If the *Shenbao* alone had proposed these functions of the press, one could argue that it was actually just a Western paper in Chinese disguise. Other papers at the time, however, took a similar position. The *Xinbao*,[48] for example, which was initiated by the Shanghai *Daotai* (Circuit Intendant) in 1876, described itself in its inaugural editorial as informative, educational, progressive, and interested in all that concerned those above and those below. [49]

> It is necessary that both Mandarins and Merchants should be kept well informed of all that is going on in the world. . . . There are affairs of state in the Capital itself, the changes and appointments of officials in the provinces, the politics of Western nations, and the state of commerce generally, the prospects of agriculture all over the country, the fluctuations in foreign goods, shipping intelligence, in fact, whatever may constitute the news or the rumour of the day all are matters in which officials and commercial men are alike interested, and which, therefore, should not be overlooked. . . . Matters of lesser importance, affecting the interests of the people generally, will also have a place in our newspaper, so that those who stay at home will be as well posted as if all the occurrences were written in the palms of their hand. . . . The articles (of special interest) will also be translated into English, so that foreigners may be able to read them and well-educated Chinese see for themselves the similarity between the two languages.[50]

Similar, too, are the views of two influential and widely read statesmen and intellectuals, Liang Qichao and Zhang Zhidong, from the late 1890s.[51] Their writings show that some of the rather daring positions propagated in the *Shenbao* and other early newspapers had by then become generally accepted.

Zhang Zhidong's (1837–1909) *Encouragement to Study* (*Quanxue pian,* 1898), was circulated, by order of the Emperor, in several million copies and enthusiastically received.[52] The section on newspapers[53] begins with a quotation from the *Laozi* (ch. 47): "Without leaving one's own house, one knows about the world"[54] to illustrate the breadth of information available from newspapers. They also help in instructing and creating "forward-minded" literati and officials.[55] As the educational tool of change and modernization, the paper allows for discussions and is thus the link between those above and below. Only in China, where there are few newspapers, are the people not allowed to know what is happening, and "even if they know something, they do not dare to talk about it in detail."[56] Zhang concludes this section with two historical exempla. Zhuge Liang (181–234), he says, "had been looking for someone who would harshly attack his weaknesses. Zhouzi (Duke Huan) had been very unhappy about the fact that it was withheld from him that a disease was destroying his body. The ancients said, 'The wise have friends who remonstrate with them.'"[57] These well-known positive paragons from history bear witness to the need of a ruler to get information and be confronted by criticism. Newspapers could perform both functions.

Zhang's arguments echo Liang Qichao's seminal August 1896 essay in his paper *Shiwubao,* "On the benefit of newspapers for state affairs" (*Lun baoguan you yi yu guoshi*).[58] Liang's reform writings were widely circulated for a few months in 1898 around the Hundred Days Reform when it was decided that officials would receive a copy of the *Shiwubao* with their order of the *Jingbao.* His views are representative of a larger group of officials pushing for reforms. In the article on newspapers, Liang warns of playing the "frog in the well":[59] "[In China] even the prefect and magistrate with their proximity to the citizens have no opportunity to know of all the affairs of the citizens over whom they reign, let alone the court."[60] This situation is contrasted with the state in the West where

> newspapers report the proceedings of parliaments, national budgetary records, death and birth rates. . . . and the employment conditions of the people . . . (as well as) legal reforms, new scientific theories and mechanical inventions. . . . Thus those who are responsible do not need to fear that anything could be obstructed from them or held back from them. . . . The more the people read the newspapers the more educated they become, the more newspaper companies are established the stronger the country becomes. And I say this is so only because of the communication [between high and low established by the papers] (*wei tong zhi gu* 為通之故).[61]

This succinct paragraph summarizes the core functions of a newspaper: it records all affairs of the people and the state and thus increases the knowledge and enlightens both ruler and ruled. By providing a channel through which communication and even critical dialogue between ruler and ruled is possible, it becomes the key factor in strengthening and thus modernizing the country.

It is evident that both Liang and Zhang praise in newspapers those very (alien) virtues that have become well-established tropes in Western normative writings. The uses and benefits of a free press are thus acknowledged in distinctly Western terms not just by Western-style newspapers such as the *Shenbao,* but by Chinese newspapers such as the *Xinbao* and by Chinese statesmen, too. Both Liang and Zhang were not advocating the alien medium for its own sake. Indeed, Liang Qichao was highly critical of scandal-mongering and partisan Western (and Chinese Western-style) papers.[62] Both men were promoting the alien medium only out of patriotism and in order to strengthen their country. For this reason, they remained within the same argumentative trajectory of advocacy as the very press products they criticized.

The pattern set by the *Shenbao* editorials is thus echoed in the two men's vocabulary for the *imaginaire* of newspapers in China. Liang and Zhang elaborated on the *Shenbao* arguments and, while they fashioned them according to their own liking, they never left their argumentative frame. This shows that the *Shenbao* rhetorics were foundational and typical for the late Qing. Within these rhetorics, the medium retains its alien guise. No one contested what the *Shenbao* first declared in its introductory announcement on April 30, 1872,

"Benguan gaobai": "The making of newspapers has been started by Western-ers and since has spread to Chinese lands." (*Xinwenzhi zhi zhichuang zi xiren chuan yu Zhongtu* 新聞紙之制創自西人傳與中土) (L. 7–8)[63]

DESIGNING A NEWSPAPER FOR CHINA

The normative descriptions and assumptions previously cited above provide us with a general view of what a newspaper *should be:* an alien medium. It remains to be questioned, however, whether the newspaper really *could be* such an alien medium in China. In a country with a well-established tradition of Sinifica-tion of alien rulers, institutions, and paraphernalia alike, it would be hard to envisage that the newspaper was able to march in seriously as an alien product that Chinese political culture simply had to accept. Taking a closer look now no longer at the normative, but at the "form-ative," the exterior and interior formal makeup of Chinese newspapers, I will turn to answering the question of what a newspaper *could be* in China.

The missionaries who first made use of the Western-style news media in China since the 1810s were interested in them as means for spreading Chris-tian beliefs and modern knowledge.[64] The merchants, on the other hand, who became involved in publishing Chinese-language newspapers in the second half of the nineteenth century, were primarily interested in them as profit-making enterprises. For different reasons, both groups must have felt that they would be more successful if they played their foreign game on Chinese terms. Much like later advertisers who would try to insert their foreign products into the value structure and iconography of their audiences, these early actors on the Chinese (print) market attempted to decrease the apparent foreignness of their dispensations.[65]

Many of the missionaries most active in this field read and wrote Chi-nese with ease. These men saw themselves as amateurs of Chinese culture. And such an attitude was not restricted to missionaries. For Ernest Major, too, the merchant's wish of "selling Chinese civilization to China" (Cochran) was directly intertwined with an honest interest in,[66] and a true love for, Chinese culture.[67] Thus, these men began to publish like Chinese in Chinese, [68] and they made efforts to find the right Chinese tone, the right idiom, or *kouqi* 口 氣, in order to communicate with their readers.[69]

There were many different ways of tuning into Chinese *kouqi*.[70] The motto, an almost integral part of the title page of any Western newspaper, was a good place to begin. The first Chinese-language newspaper, the *Cha shisu meiyue tongji chuan* 查世俗每月統記傳 (A general monthly record, containing an investigation of the opinions and practices of society) published in Malacca 1815–1821[71] by Robert Morrison and William Milne of the London Missionary Society, com-bined two quotations from the *Analects* on its title page into a motto: "The Master said: Listen to many things, distinguish the good and follow it."[72] Wal-ter Henry Medhurst used another quotation from the *Analects* ("The Master said: Everyone may tell his wishes") for his *Texuan zuoyao meiyue jichuan* 特選撮要每月記傳 (A monthly record of important selections) of 1823–1826 that came out in Batavia.[73] Karl Gutzlaff of the Netherlands Society found still another quotation from the *Analects* for the front page of his *Dongxiyang kao* 東西洋考 (Inquiry into Eastern and Western Oceans):[74] "If one does not think about what is far away, one will get into difficulties very close by."

Over the years, the use of such classical mottoes became common practice.[75] Similarly, some newspaper titles allude to or quote from Chinese works.[76] The locus classicus for the title *Liuhe congtan* 六合叢談,[77] for example, a short-lived (1857–1858) but influential monthly published by Alexander Wylie, is to be found in a passage of the *Zhuangzi* chapter "Qiwulun" that deals with the sages' willingness to talk of and discuss things within and beyond the known universe (*liuhe*).

The use of these allusions and quotations representing canonical values served to legitimize the Western merchant and missionary product. It was convincing to appeal to the authority of the canonical texts, to invoke the classics (*yinjing*),[78] however much one had to bend them for the purpose. The "Qiwulun" passage, for example, associated with *liuhe* from *Liuhe congtan*, runs: "What is outside the cosmos the sage locates as there, but does not talk about. What is within the cosmos the sage talks about, but does not assess." The entire passage evinces a certain skepticism toward the use and even the possibility of talking of, discussing, and understanding the workings of the universe, a skepticism quite typical of the *Zhuangzi*. Wylie's choice of title, however, shows that his own attitude is completely at variance with that of the *Zhuangzi*. Despite the *Zhuangzi*'s skepticism, Wylie's publication is indeed devoted to talking of and discussing (*congtan*) the universe (*liuhe*). Thus playing with the possible associations which a literate Chinese would have, newspapermen interested in introducing their product of change took license with the citations they used, going so far as to contradict them through insertion into a new, at times antithetical, context.[79]

Gutzlaff's *Lunyu* citation is evidence for yet another variation of this same method. Confucius here reminds his disciples of the necessity of forethought and precaution: "If one does not think about what is far away, one will get into difficulties very close by." By providing news from all over the world in his newspaper, Gutzlaff amplifies the meaning of Confucius's words. Confucius himself certainly could not have envisaged his disciples knowing everything about the world at large. But Gutzlaff implies that one who does not think about foreign countries will endanger the future of the mother country. Here again, without even changing the original citation, the passage acquires new and enlarged meaning.

This amplifying effect can also be seen in a line from the *Laozi* (ch. 47) in the inaugural statement of the *Shenbao* (which, incidentally, did not have a motto):[80] "Since newspapers have started appearing, everything can be transmitted and there is not one single matter that is not spread all over the globe.

Since the newspapers have started appearing, everybody who glances at it *can be [as the Laozi says] informed about the world without even leaving his house.*"[81] The *Laozi* line, read by most early commentators as a reference to the capacity of a sage to understand the principles underlying the world through introspection, had already been applied to the usefulness of an encyclopedia during the Tang; it is now used in praise of the usefulness of a newspaper in the *Shenbao* and later by Zhang Zhidong.[82] Both the Western manager of a Chinese newspaper and the Chinese advocate of such Western-style newspapers were aware of the power of allusions in legitimizing and thus domesticating the alien medium.

In 1909, the article "On newspapers" mentioned earlier still used this device.[83] To support the argument that the suppression of newspapers as the expression of public opinion would lead to the loss of prosperity and harmony in the state, it quotes a *Daya* ode from the *Book of Poetry*. "Male and female phoenix are singing on the high mast" there is part of a eulogy on a good ruler who brings about prosperity (signaled by the phoenix) and harmony in public articulation (singing out in full visibility from the top of the mast). A China in which public opinion can be expressed through newspapers will be as blissful. Again, pieces from the ancient canon are reread to justify and legitimize a modern claim: the call for an outlet for public opinion, the newspaper.

Chinese history is another source. The papers often provide Chinese historical antecedents for seemingly new Western things. The inaugural statement of the *Shenbao*, for example, sets the paper into the context of Chinese historical writings from dynastic histories and geographical studies to the great novels and the "stories about the miraculous."[84] During the great famine in the late 1870s, the *Wanguo gongbao* urges tax reductions and other economic incentives modeled on the Zhou dynasty next to long-term measures for the prevention of famine, including railroads, water conservancy, and irrigation projects.[85] In the *Shibao*, Liang Qichao links *Mengzi*'s "(assent by) the people as the root (of legitimacy)," *minben*, to the "rights of a citizen," *minquan*,[86] and traces the word for "public opinion," *yulun*, all the way back to the third century.[87] Montesquieu is compared to and explained by the virtues of Mengzi (cf. *Shibao* November 29, 1911), and Napoleon through the ancient kings (cf. *Shibao* January 19–20, 1908).[88]

The functions and abilities assigned to China's newspapers were identical to those attributed to their Western counterparts. In this sense, they retained their character as an alien medium. Nevertheless, not just on the outside, but also in content, the newspaper was reconfigured to secure its survival in the Chinese context. Missionary newspapers, commercial papers, and the political press all adopted similar devices in seasoning the Western medium to suit Chinese taste. They all won legitimacy not by insisting on being foreign and new, but instead by showing off being old and Chinese.

Their repeated claims of taking a Chinese stance and their manifold methods of Sinification described here and elsewhere are evidence of their deficit in intrinsic authority (a problem exacerbated by many of them being published in treaty port settings). My discussion of their formal makeup, which drew heavily on well-established older Chinese conventions, is evidence of what they could only be in China: Western-style newspapers perhaps, but in Chinese guise. The style of the editorials points in the same direction.

WRITING AN EDITORIAL IN CHINA

The use of well-established literary conventions in Chinese newspaper prose may well have been simple routine, since everyone with a Chinese higher education had learned to use and appreciate them.[89] Some missionary publications already had started this trend, only to be taken to task by their Chinese readers for not using them properly.[90] The use of Chinese rather than Western patterns was yet another method of convincing Chinese readers to accept the Western-style newspaper.

I will go through an exemplary *Shenbao* editorial[91] to show how its literary form was modeled on (although certainly not an exact replica of) the "eight-legged essay," *baguwen*.[92] This literary form, which has a(n unjustly) dreadful reputation, had been mandatory in the civil service examination essays since 1487. In *baguwen,* the writer assumes the pose of an ancient sage. It ideally contains eight sections, each with a particular function: the preface (*poti*), which takes up the topic from the classics in the examination title; two opening sections (*chengti* and *qijang*); the four legs, usually abounding in parallelisms (*qigu, xiaogu, zhonggu, hougu*); and a conclusion (*dajie*).[93]

Why think of a *Shenbao* editorial in terms of *baguwen?* The topic of the 1873 editorial "On the establishment of newspapers in different countries"[94] is not a quotation from the classics. With its 1500 characters it greatly exceeds the usual 600 characters of a *bagu*-essay.[95] Some of the sections with the required parallel passages have been significantly extended by inserted phrases with or without parallel constructions.[96] But while there are still other differences, it will become quite evident that the bone structure of a *baguwen* appears in this editorial and helps the reader follow the argumentation.

The editorial opens with an assertion in parallels that everyone knows who the best and the worst rulers in Chinese history were, and then asks: "What is the reason for this?" This opening is in some ways a combination of a quotation given by an examiner and an attempt at *poti,* "breaking open the topic." The following section explains why the four exemplary emperors from antiquity were in fact so good: they consulted with others and corrected their mistakes. The proverbial villains, on the other hand, did not care what others said and since they did not have "critics at court and honest friends in the provinces" through whom they "could have known of their mistakes and have changed for the better," they were not able to improve. These two sections take the pose of affirming what the imaginary sage is saying. The editorial *chengti* explains the question posed in the *poti:* Good government encourages two-way communication; a good ruler is one who listens to criticisms from near and far.

The next section (similar to the *qijiang*) turns to different territory. It explains the functions and effects of the newspaper in the West (parallels are marked in italics):

> Whenever the court establishes a new policy, *the newspapers of this place would perhaps say it is not beneficial (wu yi) and the newspapers of that place would perhaps say that it is faulty (you sun)*. In making alterations (to the policy), the court will most certainly wait for the newspapers from all the different places to state that it is (now) excellent until it will implement it.

> Let us consider (the situation) a good 200 years ago: newspapers had not yet been established in all countries, and the(se countries) were also not flourishing (as they are) today. If we consider those countries most flourishing today, there is none like the four countries of England, the US, Prussia and France, and it is there that newspapers are most thoroughly developed, too.

In this passage, the constant repetition of *xinwenzhi* (newspaper), *xingwang* (flourishing), and *xinwen* (news) forms a kind of hypnotic staccato that induces the reader to acknowledge the close connection and interdependence—even the interchangeability—between them. This effect is strengthened by the fact that, next, the author—as is to be expected in the *qijiang*—appears on stage to answer the questions posed by a fictitious interlocutor who stands in lieu of an implied reader. Some more ridiculous opinions are articulated to make sure that a real reader would disclaim any notion of ever having shared them, while at the same buy the rest of the argument.[97]

> Someone said: "How strange your words are! The newspaper is so small, how could it be able to bring prosperity to a country?

> I said: "(But) have you never heard that all countries in the West in all they do draw their benefit from the newspaper?" (L. 10–11)

The author concludes with an ironic understatement: "And you can read (all these) news in this *thin* and *useless* paper" (L. 14). Hidden behind his patient explanations, the author has set up a bombastic argument: The newspaper alone is a guarantee for good government.

The next section, corresponding to the *qigu* in *baguwen*, contains three parallel paragraphs:

> The reason why private persons make such newspapers is that everything can be openly discussed there, *the most gigantic profits and losses of the court above, and the most minute blessings and sufferings of the hamlets below.* (L. 20–21)

> That the newspaper is beneficial for the world is indeed not mistaken. The Westerners have a saying: "Generally speaking, the rulers and those ruled are about equal in their wisdom and foolishness, their capabilities and ineptitudes.

The rulers are few, the ruled are many; (therefore,) *those above are bound to take benefits from those below and the few are bound to take profits from the many."* Yet if the situation exceeds the appropriate, then those citizens, who wish to make secrets or intrigues public, would use the newspaper. (L. 21–23)

Thus, the reason why one cannot do without newspapers is that they enable *high and low to be connected with each other, far and near to reach each other,* pressuring and admonishing each other for the benefit of the political affairs of the nation. (L. 23–24)

This *qigu*-like section spells out the topics alluded to in the editorial *qijiang*: the national benefit of having an informed public made up of rulers and ruled with equal rights and abilities, connected through the newspaper. From the somewhat hesitant "that the newspaper is beneficial for the world is indeed not mistaken," the author moves to the triumphant conclusion that the newspaper is "something one cannot do without."

The following is a *xiaogu* of sorts, as the *xiaogu* is expected to build on material from the *qigu* and has digressive function. This paragraph elaborates on the benefits of communication between ruler and ruled by way of the newspaper. While in the *qigu*-section the perspective of those ruled was emphasized, this time, the point of view of the rulers is emphasized:

Among all those who focus on the national economy and the livelihood of the people, there is not one who is not happy about the existence of newspapers and who does not often encourage the citizens to publish them everywhere. *Among all those who prohibit and stop this matter, there is definitely not one who has a true focus on* bringing benefit to the country and profit to the people; instead they wish to act out their selfish desires only fearing that the people may expose them. (L. 24–26)

Formerly, (some) rulers in Western countries, too, feared that (the newspaper) might not be convenient to them and wished to stop it. Someone made an analogy: "Compare it with flowing water. *The great Gun*[98] *built a dam and it overflowed, Yu* (his son, the founder of the Xia dynasty) *let the water go and it ran peacefully.* Now if you wished to stop up the spring and hinder its flow, then its power will become wilder and all the more worrisome. This is not as good as making it a strategy to clear the spring and guide the flow!" (L. 26–28)

The parallel passages culminate in the analogy—a well-established trope for the power of public opinion[99]—used to this day.[100] The potential threat for the ruler is downplayed by the suggestion that he should "clear the spring"[101] and "guide the flow" so as to let the public have its say and avoid an outburst of popular frustration. The use of the adjective clear, 清 *qing,* suggests a connection with the disinterested, "clear" official, the 清官 *qingguan,* hailed and heard by the good rulers, but muted and condemned for his remonstrations by the evil ones. This traditional idea of conveying disinterested truth, an idea strong in cultural capital, is now applied to the newspaper.[102] The reader must conclude that any ruler who attempts to block the newspapers is, by definition, not one of the sages but one of the brutal princes of the editorial's opening lines.

These two sections deal with the same topic from a different point of view, and they both use a comparison for purposes of elucidation, the first in the form of an authoritative Western saying (which may be traced back to Hume)[103] and the second in the form of an analogy from Chinese history. It is interesting that while in the *xiaogu* the Chinese water analogy is at first addressed to Western rulers who wished to eradicate newspapers, in the *qigu* the Western saying appears to be addressed to the Chinese in mirror. By using this cross-cultural argumentation, the universalist objective of the editorial, to state clearly that newspapers are a must in the *world* and thus in China, too, is effectively addressed.

The following section, corresponding to the *zhonggu,* applies the principles developed earlier to the Chinese present. China's newspapers are condemned for not publishing sufficient criticism, especially of local government policies and officials (L. 30). Why? The responsibility lies with China's officials who hate the newspapers and make the transmission of news into a capital crime (L. 32).

China has a great history and culture, but this praise only heightens the contrast with its desolate present. Even nowadays, scholars and officials immerse themselves in study and are quite aware who the sages and the arch villains were, but they do not take the good but the bad as their model (L.32–34). They go so far as to prohibit private correspondence and burn unofficial histories in which their mistakes may have been recorded (L. 34–35). Their depravity is such that they even forge their own biographies to make them sound flattering, while hating newspapers, harassing journalists, and wanting to burn publishing houses. But all their reversing, 反 *fan,* the methods of good government is to no avail: "In the end *they might be able to deceive their ruler, but they will not able to deceive their people; they might be able to deceive their own times, but they will not be able to deceive later generations"* (L. 35).

As is typical for a *zhonggu,* this section initially provides answers to the question posed in the beginning.[104] China is ruled by the likes of Jie and Zhou even though "everybody knows" how bad their government was. The outrage at this state of affairs is taken up in the editorial *hougu* with two effectively constructed parallel paragraphs. One may be able to prohibit newspapers in both Chinese and English, but it is impossible to suppress public feelings.

The following parallel paragraph goes back to the beginning by contrasting the negative present with a golden age when contact between ruler and ruled existed.

(aa) Moreover, as

(a ruler) can understand the fortunes and misfortunes of the people by having (their) songs submitted and (their) habits observed (c),

and (a ruler) can understand (his) own strengths and weaknesses by being keen on asking and by scrutinizing statements (from others) (d), (bb) in the olden days

the sage rulers considered it a special virtue to take heed of remonstrance (d), *and the good and virtuous officials considered it of broad benefit to collect thoughts (from people under their administration)* (c). (L. 38–39)

The four lines in this last argumentative paragraph are coupled in chiasmic twos by parallel construction (aa, bb), with the first stating the principle and the second its application in inverse sequence, which results in a frame-structure (c dd c). Getting to know the thoughts of the people by listening to their songs, observing their habits, and collecting their thoughts (c) forms the frame for the idea of the particular critical aspect contained in such emanations, the use of remonstrance by those in power to improve their selves (d). This effective arrangement has an affirmative function and leads persuasively into the concluding paragraph.

In a moderate polemic familiar from examination essays, the concluding *dajie* returns to the present situation and sums up the advantages of the newspaper. While experienced and broad-minded scholars ought to be aware of the benefits of remonstrance, they act otherwise. Why? The author cites a *Mengzi* passage (4B9) in which it is said: "What future misery have they and ought they to endure who talk of what is not good in others?"[105] (L. 40). By quoting this rather obscure passage,[106] he explains, and to an extent shows understanding for, the timidity of present-day newspapermen. Nevertheless, the article concludes with an exclamatory question: How could it not be of benefit for both sides if each acted out the Truth? (L. 41).[107]

The author uses a number of rhetorical strategies to persuade the reader of the necessity of introducing more newspapers to China and reforming those already in existence. One of these strategies is the constant mediation between the dubitable and the indubitable. Indubitably, he states, there is no one who does not know the good rulers from the bad; indubitably, anyone who wants to suppress news has selfish goals. Indubitably, newspapers are beneficial to the world; indubitably, China is a country of great cultural heritage; indubitably, reckless officials will not be able to deceive later generations. The frequent use of rhetorical questions supports this affirmative type of argumentation. And yet the author is always cautious not to overdo his case; his use of double negatives and questions at least apparently leaves room for doubt. It brings the reader onto the author's side.

The author's attempt at suasion also works through the structural makeup of the argument. In the fictional dialogues, questions of the (implied) reader are taken up. This device makes him and his arguments an integral part of the text while leading him to the author's conclusions. And last, the adherence to the bone structure of *baguwen*—equally familiar to reader and author from schooldays—helps create a certain sense of agreement between sender and receiver: the very choice of this form, envisaged to be written in the voice of the sages, provides the editorial and its logic with authoritative weight. The allusion to this form avoids the potential alienation that could have occurred if the author's bombastic arguments were proffered in another form considered less respectable or simply incomprehensible.

The author employs a number of arguments from a very particular part of Chinese tradition, which, although frequently invoked by martyrs, dissidents,[108] and rulers alike, was only seldom actually realized.[109] It is a critical tradition associated with the theories of 民本 *minben* "(assent by) the people as the root (of legitimacy)," 天听 *tianting* "heaven hears as my people hears," and the 天命 *tianming* "mandate of heaven,"[110] which argue that a ruler's legitimacy hinged on the heavenly mandate that could be withdrawn if the ruler lost his popular base by neglecting contact and communication with the people.

This critical tradition was theoretically connected, but practically irreconcilable, with another important philosophical dream, that of an ever-present harmony, unity, and stability throughout China—even a unity through force—an idea that had dominated Chinese thinking at least since the Qin.[111] These two form a potential and mostly latent dialectic within the mainstream of Chinese philosophical thinking. Chinese rulers may often have listened to their censors in ritual matters and may have gone through public rituals of self-accusation in order to be granted rain from a Heaven presumably enraged at their transgressions.[112] Nevertheless, Chinese rulers have also time and again, after having banned or even killed Confucian critics whom they charged with flouting orthodox standards, continued to govern in the name of the noble "demophile" tradition of *tianming*.[113]

To convince Chinese readers of the benefits of the alien medium, the editorialist uses a familiar method of employing history as precedent as well as the form into which it is embedded. It is self-evident that Western-style newspapers such as the *Shenbao*, situated as they were in Shanghai or one of the other treaty ports, were also tied into a process of Sino-Western interaction that prompted them to fulfill functions quite independent from the orthodox arguments proffered to explain them. However, the editorialists themselves saw an apparent necessity to put an emphasis on the Chinese nature of their products. They did that not just because they intended them to become nationwide publications but also because—even though the Chinese population in Shanghai was a particular and peculiar set of Chinese who had chosen to come to Shanghai and reside there due to a special affinity with the West and "things alien"—there are many signs that their consciousness, too, was geared to a Chinese view of the world—if only to keep their psychological stability.[114] Thus, by packaging a plea for the revival of China's critical tradition in the format of something akin to the examination essay, the Western-style newspaper takes on a heroic heritage, legitimizing itself "in the voice of the ancient sages."

The editorialist thus attempts to win authority not by insisting on the newspaper's being foreign and new, but instead by showing off its being old and Chinese. While Western concepts could have been used to describe what a newspaper should be, a semantic remake was necessary to integrate this alien medium into Chinese structures of the public sphere. At the same time, this semantic remake was the beginning of a creative process in which unforeseen things happened that would change the status and function of this medium altogether.

WHAT COULD THE NEWSPAPER BE FOR CHINA?

The *Shenbao* editorials as well as the statements by political reformists mentioned at the beginning of this chapter had concurred: there was no Chinese medium that could be called the predecessor of the newspaper. They said this despite the fact that the Chinese did have a thing called by some the "world's oldest newspaper."[115] Since the Han (206 BC–220 AD), so-called *di* officials transmitted the news of the court to the fiefs of the feudal princes (*di*) and vice versa. Their so-called *dibao* (announcements from the *di*) was renamed during the reign of the Yongzheng emperor of the Qing (1723) when it officially became the *Jingbao* (Peking gazette).[116] The *Peking Gazette* recorded the emperor's official activities, appointments, promotions and demotions as well as officially approved edicts and memorials.[117] When Chinese officials first became acquainted with Western newspapers, they equated them with the *Peking Gazette*. In a letter written in the 1830s, Wei Yuan (1794–1856), for example, advocates the (secret) translation of Western newspapers, and equates them with the court newsletter—in his view, both were written and circulated primarily for the purpose of disseminating information.[118]

I have shown, here and elsewhere, how Western-style newspapers in China adjusted both in their physical makeup and in their rhetorics to the expectations of their potential readers in order to be understood.[119] They would be printed in the manner of a Chinese book and written in the form of a Chinese examination essay, with their arguments framed in quotations from the Chinese classics. Moreover, they would reprint the *Peking Gazette* and imitate its format and methods of segmentation. Evidently, these papers were aware of the fact (and were making use of it) that the perception of their medium was determined by their audience's familiarity with the *Peking Gazette*. Why, then, given their efforts to indigenize their papers, did they not claim that their newspaper was really only the continuation of an indigenous Chinese tradition?[120]

Apparently, the makers of these new papers were concerned that this familiarity might harm rather than benefit the recognition of their new medium.[121] This is evident from several early *Shenbao* editorials especially devoted to the differences between the *Peking Gazette* and the new papers. From these articles, it is clear that the new medium had to labor to distinguish itself from the *Gazette*. An editorial of 1872 "On the difference between *dibao* and the new(s)paper *xinbao*" acknowledges that the *Peking Gazette* may well fulfill some of the same functions as the newspaper (L. 19–20), and gives many examples from Chinese history illustrating that the *dibao* had indeed served to spread information. The emphasis, however, is on the fundamental difference between the two: "The *dibao* is made to spread court politics and matters exclusively. It does not record abstruse and distant matters from the smallest hamlets. And that is why (among) those who read it, the majority are literati and officials. Peasants, workers, merchants and businessmen are not found among them" (L. 17/18).[122] There is a difference in principle. The new papers spread news by everyone from everywhere, whereas the *Peking Gazette* exclusively reported on official affairs for members of the elite. A year later the editorial "On the difference between the Chinese *Peking Gazette* and the Western newspaper"[123] contends that the restricted scope of news in the *Peking Gazette* is the reason why it finds ever fewer readers (L. 3–4).[124] The editorial then surveys the stages of Chinese history and explains that an increasing centralization of court and political information eventually peaked during the Manchu reign. It was supplemented by a system of rigid secrecy laws.[125] As a result, the *Jingbao*—apart from being restricted to court matters by its very nature—would get even of those only the most commonplace (and thus boring) parts (L. 22).

As the Western *xinbao* was a *bao* after all, and of *bao* there had once only been (different versions of) the *Peking Gazette* in China, the Western newspaper would be seen through such spectacles. The new papers would have had the chance of adopting a completely different Chinese word for their newspaper instead of using the term *bao* by analogy, but they did not. Thus, they rather consciously put themselves into the same league as the *Peking Gazette*, making use of its cultural capital and the prestige of its name, while at the same time portraying it as a degenerate product of dreadful unpopularity, which they were now to supersede. There is an ambiguity of purpose: while being plagiarized in format, text, and name, the *Peking Gazette* appears not as the predecessor or the model for but rather—if anything—as the negative foil to the Western-style newspaper *xinbao*.[126] The very use of *xin* (new) in the term for the newspaper (*xin bao* = new announcements) can be interpreted as a polemic against the old-style, outdated paper of court announcements (*jing bao* = capital announcements). Accordingly, in a commemorative editorial for the 10,000th issue of the *Shenbao* (February 14, 1901)[127] the writer goes back in Chinese history, tracing the Chinese *dichao* (another name for the *Peking Gazette*), but again emphasizes the importance of the influence from the Western medium newspaper in waking up a "China seemingly sound asleep, *hunhun ru mian zhi Zhongguo.*"

Stressing the similarities between *Peking Gazette* and newspaper would have made them rivals: how, if China had a flourishing tradition of newspaper making, would it be justified to introduce an alien medium to substitute for it? But was there, truly, an inherent difference between the *Jingbao* and the *xinbao?* The editorialists would argue that there was: The *Jingbao* drew exclusively on official news while the Western paper was open to the public to make an input.[128]

This reasoning shows that there is method behind selecting certain elements of Chinese descent for the legitimization of the new medium and discarding others: for as much as Chinese tradition is used discriminately, so is the Western tradition—equations between Western and Chinese institutions and conceptions have been allowed in the articles previously cited above only in reference to the ideal conception of the Western newspaper as the free press. This largely invented and idealized "tradition" was linked in these editorials to an equally idealized critical tradition in Chinese thought that played no role in the *Peking Gazette*. Liang Qichao compares the critical functions of the newspaper with those of Confucian *qingyi* (pure discussion),[129] and styles the *yanguan* (remonstrating official) into a predecessor of the journalist, not mentioning that many a journalist in the West worked not just on the payroll but under the orders of his ruler, too.[130]

The newspaper is credited in Chinese writings with facilitating the flow of information between ruler and ruled, while the fact is never mentioned that quite a number of Western newspapers served, exclusively, the ruler, and communicated only one way, that is, from top to bottom.[131] In Zhang Zhidong's "Encouragement for Study," intercommunication appears as a panacea in situations where one "*bu neng jin zhi zhi*" (could not know everything) and "*yi bu gan jin yan zhi*" (one did not dare to say everything).[132] Sun Jian'ai states in an 1898 memorial that during the golden times of Tang, Yu, and the three dynasties in antiquity, "it did not occur that [the ruler] was not in connection with the situation of the ruled, *wei you bu tongda xiaqing.*"[133] He concludes that it is not so bad if a country was weak, yet that it was unpardonable if the channels of communication were obstructed.[134] Liang Qichao had started his discourse on newspapers two years earlier with the aphorism "The strength or weakness of a country are dependent on the openness or obstruction (of the channels of communication), and today obstruction prevails."[135] This obstruction led, in his view, to a situation in which one had eyes, ears, a throat, and a tongue and yet did not have them because they could not be put to proper use.[136] Even the Hong Kong *Xunhuan Ribao,* which otherwise came in a format much more Westernized than the Shanghai *Shenbao,* went back to the great sage-rulers of antiquity in its programmatic editorials on the purpose of a paper.[137] The *Shenbao* editorial "On the difference between the Chinese *Jingbao* and the Western newspaper"[138] cited earlier puts great emphasis on the difference between *Jingbao* and *xinbao* on the one hand, but on the other gives several examples of intercommunication between high and low from China's golden age. These are not associated with the *Peking Gazette* but with the functions of the *xinbao:*

> The reigns of Tang and Yu and the three dynasties are (reigns) that were detailed in what they recorded and transmitted and thus distinguish themselves from later generations. Therefore, in the *Hongfan*[139] (Great Plan in the *Shangshu*) it is said (as advice to the ruler): "If you have important queries consult your heart, consult the officials and ministers, and consult the masses."

(And) in the *Wang zhi* (Kingly Rules)[140] of the *Liji* (Book of Rites) it is said: "The son of Heaven went on the imperial inspection tour once in five years. He held audience for the feudal princes and searched for those who were 100 years old to call on them. He ordered that the master of music (i.e., the Zhou Grand Tutor) present the songs and poetry so that he could observe the habits of the people. He ordered that the prices would be recorded on the market in order to find out what the people liked and disliked.[141] (L. 4–7)

This glorious Chinese past in which ruler and people were in close communication is juxtaposed with a miserable present in which all the ensuing benefits have been lost. And while this type of argumentation is rather hackneyed and has occurred many times before in Chinese prose calling for the opening of the 言路 *yanlu*, the channels of communication, the new twist in the argumentation is the invocation of the Western-style newspaper as the only new medium that could save the situation. The antithetical structure here serves to accentuate the equation between this new medium and the methods of the golden age. Shortly after having stated that the sagely emperors of antiquity had realized the necessity of intercommunication and benefits of receiving criticism, the editorial "On the establishment of newspapers in different countries"explains: "When the countries in the West first established newspapers they in fact had a deep and intuitive understanding of this virtue of our ancients" (L. 4).[142] In coming up with the new medium, the newspaper, Westerners are attributed with a deep understanding of an ancient Chinese practice, an understanding long lost in China itself. A *Shenbao* editorial of 1886[143] reiterates the catalogue of activities that had made communication between ruler and ruled possible during the Chinese golden age (L. 1–4. 22–23), bewails the loss of the speed and accuracy in reporting through the increasing obstruction of the channels of communication, and praises the newspapers as the best tool to get to know the situation of the people accurately again. This is followed by the despairing conclusion: "In the West they all use this ancient Chinese method. They let the matters of those below reach those above (and thus) ruler and ruled form a single body, and state affairs flourish daily more. Why is it that China alone cannot reach the perfect method of the ancient kings?" (L. 31–32).[144]

An interesting phenomenon emerges. It has been observed that innovations are often consciously acknowledged as imitations of foreign models while subconsciously they are contextualized through recourse to indigenous traditions.[145] In the present case, however, the adoption of this foreign model will allow the reestablishment of a feature that was crucial in bringing about the golden age in ancient China, and will be crucial for China's prosperity in the modern world.[146] The semantic remake of the Western-style newspaper in Chinese hands, including its idealized description, was the beginning of a creative process in which the status and function of the alien medium were changed in their entirety. This innovation, the Western medium, was elaborately (if selectively) described so as to correspond to equally selected features from the Chinese past.[147] This and other editorials introducing the newspaper are not just argued in a Chinese manner, presenting a foreign medium à la Chinoise. In both their form and content they serve to integrate the newspaper into a particular Chinese context, the "better part" of China's idealized tradition. The question of its alien background is no longer relevant.[148] The Western-style newspaper is accepted as an innovation, but it can function as an organic and integral part of the Chinese public sphere, and is rooted in China's best traditions. The article just quoted asks whether there is more to the fit between the new medium and the old ideal: "In olden times there is no mention of *xinwenzhi* (newspapers). When (the word eventually) appeared (it was said) that the newspaper had come from the West. It is not known, however, whether it was really created in the West or not" (L. 1).

CONCLUSION

The coming of the newspaper to China has been described as the introduction of an alien medium. The normative functions of the foreign-style Chinese-language newspaper are modeled on prescriptions given for the (idealized) versions of their Western counterparts. Nevertheless, I have shown that the *xinbao* was neither sold nor perceived as a pure foreign import. Instead, there was a strong tendency to indigenize and domesticate the medium for Chinese use and Chinese understanding. On its journey to the East, the medium adapted to its environment and took on a new, sinified disguise. It changed in its outer makeup as well as in its interior decoration. Both Western and Chinese newspapermen took recourse to selected elements from China's tradition to contextualize a Chinese newspaper. In explaining newspapers as an important ingredient of Western power (and thus potentially also of Chinese power), and in stating at the same time that something quite equal to the newspaper had for long been an integral part of the ideal Chinese polity, the newspaper was provided with a double legitimization and, what is more, journalists could thrive in the twofold pleasure of being the inheritors of traditional political legitimacy as much as of the secret devices underlying Western wealth and power.

   All these methods were interpreted in this study as ways of presenting a lump of sugar with the bitter medicine, as a device necessary to ensure the successful incorporation of the acrid alien medium into China's public sphere. The presence of these Chinese elements on the pages of the new medium served to indicate the very awareness (among those who produced and advocated it) of its foreign devilishness. On the other hand, the answer to the question "Was the newspaper really created in the West or not?" and the assurance that the newspaper was indeed an "ancient Chinese method" cry for a different interpretation. To use one indigenous argument while disregarding the other (the *Peking Gazette* was not considered a predecessor of the *xinbao*)—just as powerful (or potentially even more powerful)—is testimony for a rather strong agenda on the part of the writers of these articles. The conscious reappraisal and reinstatement of selected elements from Chinese tradition resulted from a fundamental (and perhaps intentional) misunderstanding of the Western innovation, a misunderstanding that indicates a lack of a historical and operational consciousness shared by foreign source and Chinese recipient—historically speaking, the Western newspaper, too, had existed for long times mostly in the form of court gazettes, but this point was not made in the Chinese texts. The traditional constructs with which the writers of these articles would propagate the new newspaper came to be more than mere rhetorical devices used to translate unknown Western inventions into familiar cultural language. These constructs indeed remained the advocates' own most enduring frame of reference, determining and at the same distorting their understanding of the nature of the Western newspaper. Indeed, the Chinese preoccupation with rediscovering their own tradition in these new media went so far that they completely lost sight of the (real) alien nature of the medium. They became convinced that China had discovered the world's oldest and best political framework for a state's peace and prosperity in the form of 上下之通 *shangxia zhi tong*, the free flow of communication between ruler and ruled; and that the newspaper developed in the West was an ideal and fitting modern tool to bring this ideal to life.

NOTES

Earlier versions of this chapter, which also in turn form small parts of the Introduction, chapter 1 and chapter 2 in my *A Newspaper for China? Power, Identity and Change in Shanghai's News Media, 1872–1912,* Cambridge: Harvard University Press, 2004, have been presented to the Public Sphere Group in Heidelberg and in Berlin in February 1995 to the interdisciplinary research group Transformation of the European Expansion (funded by the German Research Association). I am grateful for the suggestions and criticisms provided by members of both groups. All remaining faults in this chapter are, however, mine.

1. Cf. Roswell S. Britton, *The Chinese Periodical Press (1800–1912),* Shanghai, 1933, p. 85.

2. *Grand Dictionnaire Universel* (Pierre Larousse, ed.), Paris, 1865ff (*GD*).

3. *The Encyclopaedia Britannica: A Dictionary of Arts, Sciences, and General Literature,* 24 vols. London, 1875–1878 (*EB*).

4. The reader is reminded of the foundation of the *Gazette* under Richelieu in France (1631), the imposition of the stamp tax in England (1712–1855) or Bismarck's press law (valid as late as 1919), not to mention censorship and dictatorial press control in the twentieth century.

5. PRESSE (*Droit polit.)*" in: *Encyclopédie, ou dictionnaire raisonné des sciences, des arts et des métiers, par une societé de gens de lettres* (M. Diderot, ed.), Paris (first ed.

36JOINING THE GLOBAL PUBLIC

1751–1780); reprint: Stuttgart, Bad Cannstatt: Friedrich Fromman Verlag, 1966, Tome Treizième, p. 320.

6. I am here primarily interested in the ideal image of the press. Questions of censorship and the relationship between the state and the press in China have been taken up in chapter 3, "Making the Chinese State Go Public" in Barbara Mittler, *A Newspaper for China?*

7. *EB*, vol. 17, "Newspapers," p. 415.

8. Cited in Mitchell Stephens, *A History of News: From the Drum to the Satellite*, New York: Viking, 1988, p. 165.

9. My translation. Rhymes could not be reproduced. Cf. *GD*, vol. 9, "Journal," p. 1044.

10. *GD*, vol. 9 "Journal," p. 1037.

11. Quoted in Shelley F. Fishkin, *From Fact to Fiction: Journalism and Imaginative Writing in America*, Baltimore: Johns Hopkins University Press, 1985, p. 18.

12. V. Hugo and P. Limayrac are cited in *GD*, vol. 13, "Presse," p. 93.

13. *GD*, vol. 13, "Presse," p. 99.

14. The *Asahi Shimbun* was founded in January 1879 for this very reason: "The samurai technocrats of Meiji saw newspapers, under strict control, as part of the modernizing and educative process." (Martin Walker, *Powers of the Press: Twelve of the World's Influential Newspapers*, New York: Pilgrim Press, 1983, p. 192.)

15. *EB*, vol. 17, "Newspapers," p. 412. Cf. Stephens, *History of News*, p. 9.

16. *GD*, vol. 13, "Presse," p. 107.

17. *GD*, vol. 13, "Presse," p. 108.

18. *GD*, vol. 9, "Journal," p. 1037.

19. In *GD*, vol. 13, "Publique," p. 387, it is said that public opinion may "reverse and subject all kinds of despotism."

20. *GD*, vol. 13, "Presse," p. 110.

21. *GD*, vol. 11, "Opinion," p. 1385.

22. Albert Schäffer (1831–1903), *Bau und Leben des sozialen Körpers*, 1875–1879, also stresses that collective consciousness and public opinion are formed in the process of communication between ruler and ruled (quoted in Hanno Hardt, *Social Theories of the Press: Early German & American Perspectives*, Beverly Hills: Sage Publications, 1979, p. 60) with the press as the most powerful link (p. 65).

23. Cf., e.g., *SB* 9.9.1872 "Benguan zishu" (Self-explanation of our company), *SB* Oct. 8, 1875 "Lun xinbao ticai" (On the format of the newspaper), and Oct. 11, 1875 "Lun benguan zuobao benyi," esp. L. 5–6 for some defensive remarks. On this question, see Natascha Vittinghoff, *Die Anfänge des Journalismus in China (1860–1911)*, Wiesbaden: Harassowitz, 2003.

24. Ernest Major, who was famous for his Chinese proficiency, did at least pretend to write some of the early *Shenbao* editorials by signing them *Shenbao guan zhuren* (Manager of the *Shenbao* Company).

25. These arguments are mentioned in *SB* March 13, 1875 "Yu Shenbaoguan lun Shenbaozhi geshi bijian" (My unworthy view of the style of the *Shenbao* offered to the

Shenbao office), and *SB* Oct. 11, 1875 "Lun benguan zuobao benyi" (On the original purpose of our company in making a newspaper), L. 4–5.

26. "*Shenjiang xinbao yuanqi,*" *SB* May 6, 1872. *Shenjiang xinbao* was the long name of the *Shenbao*. On the choice and origin of this name, see the early article Shenbao shibian xiezu "Chuangban chuqi de 'Shenbao'" (The *Shenbao* during the time of its foundation), *Xinwen yanjiu ziliao* 1979.1:133–142.

27. "Dibao bie yu xinbao lun" (On the difference between the official gazettes and the newspaper), *SB* July 13, 1872.

28. Similar statements can be found in other articles on the function of the newspaper such as "Lun xinbao ticai," *SB* Oct. 8, 1875, or "Lun geguo xinbao zhi she" (On the establishment of newspapers in different countries), *SB* Aug. 18, 1873.

29. *SB* 18.7.1873 "Dibao bie yu xinbao lun."

30. The advertisement appears in *SB* May 19, 1876. For a more detailed discussion of the *Minbao* and its implied readership cf. ch. 4 on women as implied readers in my *A Newspaper for China?*

31. *SB* Aug. 29, 1895 "Lun huabao keyi qimeng," L. 17.

32. *SB* Feb. 2, 1905 "Benguan zhengdun baowu juli" (An itemized list of adjustments of the management of our company's newspaper), L.1–2.

33. For this programmatic description of the educational function of the newspaper, cf. the first editorial of the *Shibao* on June 12, 1904, which argues, "China needs a guide of the right kind."

34. In 1873, this news-gathering policy of the *Shenbao* could celebrate a first triumph: allegedly a *Shenbao* article on April 2, 1873, first alerted the Qing court to Japanese war preparations on Taiwan. A recently published study on the *Shenbao* (Xu Zaiping/Xu Ruifang, *Qingmo sishinian Shenbao shiliao,* Beijing: Xinhua, 1988, p. 125) concludes: "This may well be taken as testimony for the need to establish newspapers to ensure the modernization of China."

35. For this quote, cf. *GD,* "Presse," p. 93. For a similar interpretation of the *Shenbao,* cf. Xu/Xu, *Shenbao shiliao,* 42.44. Christian Henriot, "Le nouveau journalisme politique chinois, 1895–1911, Shanghai-Hong Kong" *Cahiers d'Études Chinoises* 1980.1:5–71, 5.64, shows that this modernizing potential was a feature attributed to all kinds of newspapers, whether commercial or political in nature.

36. *SB* Feb. 2, 1905 "Benguan zhengdun baowu juli."

37. For an overview of some of the editorials mentioned earlier, cf. Xu/Xu *Shenbao shiliao,* pp. 10–12.

38. *SB* April 30, 1872 "Benguan tiaoli." This text is again signed with Major's sobriquet.

39. *SB* June 6, 1872 "Shenjiang xinbao yuanqi." This text is again signed "Shenbaoguan zhuren."

40. Cf. "Shuo bao" (On newspapers), *SB* Sept. 19, 1909 for the first statement, and the speech at the first meeting of Chinese newspaper circles in Nanjing reported in the *Shenbao* on Sept. 7, 1909 for the second.

41. Since this critical aspect and the agenda of advocacy of newspapers can be traced back to these early *Shenbao* editorials and even earlier to missionary papers, I

would dispute the argument (often stated in newspaper histories from the PRC such as Fang Hanqi, *Zhongguo jindai baokanshi* (History of the modern press in China), 2 vols.,Taiyuan: Shanxi renmin chubanshe, 1981)) that only the reformers and revolutionaries discovered the paper as an instrument of political and social propaganda.

42. *SB* Oct. 11, 1875 "On the original purpose of our company in making a newspaper."

43. *SB* Aug. 11, 1886 "On the use of newspapers" (Lun xinwenzhi zhi yi). A similarly strong advocate of newspaper criticism is also *SB* Aug. 18, 1873 "Lun geguo xinbao zhi she." This editorialist complains that while China does already have newspapers, they do not really do their job—i.e., by being critical. This editorial is discussed and analyzed in detail in my *A Newspaper for China?* pp. 58–69.

44. Despite the prominence of discussants (*lunzhe*) and remonstrators (*yanzhe*) in the dynastic histories, as studied by R. G. Wagner, the late Qing court was extremely apprehensive toward *qingyi* debates by literati. See Lloyd E. Eastman, "Ch'ing-i and Chinese Policy Formation," *JAS* 1965.24/4: 595–611. For an estimate of the *Shenbao* readership and its public value, see Andrew Nathan, "The Late Ch'ing Press: Role, Audience and Impact," in: Zhongguo yanjiuyuan, ed., *Guoji Hanxue huiyi lunwenji*, Lishi kaoguzu Taibei, 1981, 1281–1308.

45. Cf. *GD*, "Presse," p. 108.

46. *SB* May 6, 1872 "Shenjiang xinbao yuanqi," L. 19–21. For a similar argument, cf. also *SB* May 7, 1872 "Zhaokan gaobai yin" (Searching for advertisements), which argues that the publishing of newspapers guarantees that the ruler will be informed about the conditions of the ruled. Thanks to Natascha Vittinghoff for pointing out the latter article to me.

47. "Lun xinwenzhi zhi yi," *SB* Aug. 11, 1886.

48. On the history of the *Xinbao* and some of its predecessors, the *Huibaos* and the *Yibao*, see Natascha Vittinghoff's chapter in this book and Rudolf G. Wagner, "The *Shenbao* in Crisis: The International Environment and the Conflict between Guo Songtao and the *Shenbao*," *Late Imperial China* 20.1(1999):107–138.

49. For very similar descriptions of the functions of another Chinese-owned newspaper, the Hong Kong *Xunhuan Ribao*, cf. Vittinghoff "Chinese Newspapers' 'Response to the West,'" unpublished paper, esp. p. 95. The *Jiaohui xinbao*, too, founded by Young J. Allen already in 1868, had very similar aims (cf. the inaugural address on Sept. 5, 1868, 3b–4 and an article appearing Sept. 3, 1870, 5b.).

50. Translation as it appears in the *NCH* 1.12.1876 "Prospectus of the Sin-Pao." I have greatly profited from Andrea Janku's thorough search for articles on the Chinese press in the *North China Herald*, which she has made available to me.

51. For Zhang's influence, cf. Britton, *Periodical Press*, p. 99.

52. Cf. Kuo Ping Wen, *The Chinese System of Public Education*, New York: Teachers College, Columbia University, 1915, p. 71.

53. This essay, "Yue bao," is reprinted in *Jiangxi cunshe congkan*, part 10, *Quanxue pian*, part 2, 6.

54. This quotation is also alluded to in "Benguan gaobai" (April 30, 1872), L. 21.

55. "Yue bao," L. 17–18

56. "Yue bao," L. 25–26.

57. "Yue bao," L. 31–32.

58. For Liang's influence, cf. the reminiscences by Hu Sijing quoted in *Shanghai jindai wenxue shi* (A history of modern Shanghai Literature) (Chen Bohai/Yuan Jin, eds.), Shanghai: Shanghai renmin chubanshe, 1993, p. 143. Similar reminiscences are quoted in Li Liangrong, *Zhongguo baozhi wenti fazhan gaiyao* (Important Elements in the Development of the Use of Style and Form in Chinese Newspapers), Fuzhou: Fujian renmin chubanshe, 1985, p. 33.

59. Liang Qichao, "Lun baoguan you yi yu guoshi" (On the use of newspapers for the affairs of our country), in: *Yinbingshi heji*, vol.1, Beijing, 1989, pp. 100–103, 102. The frog first appears in the *Zhuangzi*.

60. Liang, "Lun baoguan you yi yu guoshi," p. 102.

61. Liang, "Lun baoguan you yi yu guoshi," p. 101.

62. Cf. his bashing the shortcomings of the Western press in "Lun bao you yi," esp. L. 101–102. See also his tirade against the Chinese newspapers translated in Nathan, "Late Ch'ing Press," p. 1282.

63. The argument returns in *SB* March 28, 1877 "Xuan xinwenzhi cheng shu shuo" (On selecting from the newspaper to make a book). Similarly, an article from as late as 1905 states: "In olden times China did not have the newspaper business" (*SB* Feb. 7, 1905 "Benguan zhengdun baowu juli"). *SB* Aug. 11, 1886 is the first article to question this assumption; it starts, "Since the olden times there is no mention of the newspaper. Once it is mentioned, it is said that originally it came from the West, but it is not known in fact, whether it was really created in the West."

64. Milne wanted his magazine to "combine the diffusion of general knowledge with that of religion and morals." (Cited in Britton, *Periodical Press*, pp. 18–19.) John Fryer, *Shanghai xinbao* editor since 1866, meant "to make the newspaper work its way to do a great deal in enlightening China." (Cited in Jonathan Spence, *The China Helpers: Western Advisers in China 1620–1960*, London: Bodley Head, 1969, p. 145.)

65. For this method, see *A Newspaper for China?*, p. 45n.8.

66. Major's obituary in the *SB* March 29, 1908 confirms that he "was very adept at understanding Chinese language and written characters," a skill he had trained for his childhood days in England (cf. an unpublished manuscript on "Ernest Major" by Rudolf G. Wagner). His broad interest in things Chinese (cf. Xu/Xu, *Shenbao shiliao*, p. 338) helped in his book publishing venture. He fits very well into the picture of the broadly interested publisher in the West, as described in Elisabeth L. Eisenstein, *The Printing Revolution in Early Modern Europe*, Cambridge: Cambridge University Press, 1983, p. 177: "The prospering merchant-publisher had to know as much about books and intellectual trends as a cloth merchant did about dry goods and dress fashions; he needed to develop a connoisseur's expertise about type styles, book catalogues, and library sales. He often found it useful to master many languages, to handle various texts, to investigate antiquities and old inscriptions along with new maps and calendars."

67. This attitude was rather the exception among Westerners in Shanghai. William Somerset Maugham on a visit to Shanghai, in 1920, remarks that China appeared truly boring to all those China-bound people he met. They knew just as much as they needed to conduct business and were suspicious of everyone who learned the Chinese language. For this and similar views, cf. Folker Reichert, "'Ich bin in Shanghai! Unvergeßlicher

Tag!' Impressionen und Aussagen" in: *Shanghai: Stadt über dem Meer* (Siegfried Englert and Folker Reichert, eds.), Heidelberg: Heidelberger Verlagsanstalt, 1985, pp. 206–207; Albert Feuerwerker, *The Foreign Establishment in China in the Early Twentieth Century*, Ann Arbor: Center for Chinese Studies, 1976, 5.31; and Don D. Patterson, "The Journalism of China," *The University of Missouri Bulletin* 1922.23/34, p. 3.

68. Assuming a Chinese name and employing Chinese journalists and editors were ways to assume a Chinese stance. Milne worked together with Liang Afa in his early missionary paper, Allen made extensive use of Chinese letters to the editor in the *Jiaohui xinbao* (cf. Adrian A. Bennett, *Missionary Journalist in China: Young J. Allen and his Magazines*, Athens: University of Georgia Press, 1983, esp. ch. 4, pp. 101ff.) and in many of the commercial papers such as the *Shenbao* educated Chinese were in charge of day-to-day management and involved in editorial decisions. Fang, *Baokanshi*, p. 42, claims that the allegedly "objective" reporting in these papers was only a dissimulation of foreign profit making. For the *Shenbao*'s defense against such charges, which had already surfaced during its early years, cf. the earlier quotations. Cf. also Li Liangrong, "The Historical Fate of 'Objective Reporting' in China," in: *China's Media, Media's China* (Chin-Chuan Lee, ed.), Boulder: Westview, 1994, p. 225.

69. The expression appears in Fang, *Baokanshi*, p. 38. Vittinghoff, "Chinese Newspapers' 'Response to the West,'" p. 20, gives examples of attempts to adapt to the different *kouqi* from Chinese and Englishmen writing in Chinese-language and English-language newspapers.

70. See chapter 1 in my *A Newspaper for China?* (pp. 47–53) for elements in newspaper format and layout designed to enhance acceptance in China. The *Jingbao* was an important model.

71. The 1812 order prohibiting missionary activity on Chinese territory was revoked in 1837. The publishers of the newspaper had to rely on travelers for taking their paper back to China.

72. The quotation is taken from *Lunyu* II, 18 and VII, 22.

73. The motto appears twice in *Lunyu* XI, 24.

74. This paper came out in Canton between 1833 and 1837. It was due to Gutzlaff's formidable relationship with the Chinese that the paper could be printed in China despite the prohibition of missionary work. Cf. Britton, *Periodical Press*, pp. 22–24.

75. Missionary books such as Gutzlaff's novels also used such mottoes, cf. Wagner "Ernest Major."

76. *Dongxiyang kao* took its name from the well-known work by Zhang Xie (1618), which gave a geographical sketch of kingdoms having tributary trade relations with Ming China (cf. Britton, *Periodical Press*, p. 23).

77. On the influence of this newspaper, cf. *Shanghai jindai wenxue shi*, p. 139.

78. Quoting, often out of context, from the classics, *yinjing*, was established practice since pre-Qin times (cf. Karl S.Y. Kao, "Rhetoric," in: *Indiana Companion to Traditional Chinese Literature*, Bloomington: Indiana University Press, 1986, pp. 121–137, 134). For the use of classical quotations in newspaper editorials, cf. Li, *Baozhi wenti*, esp. p. 22 and ch.1 in my *A Newspaper for China?*

79. This practice is already found in the *Huainanzi* or the *Zhuangzi*; cf. Jean Lévy, "Quelques exemples de détournement subversif de la citation dans la littérature

classique chinoise" in: *Le Travail de la Citation en Chine et au Japon* (Karine Chemla, Francois Martin, and Jacqueline Pigeot, eds.), Paris: Presses Universitaires de Vincennes, 1995, pp. 41–65.

80. Before the *Laozi* quotation, this statement begins: "Since the world is extremely vast, matters are extremely diverse. But the people are spread in (many different) areas and cannot see each other. Who can see everywhere and know everything?" "Benguan gaobai" (*SB* April 30, 1872).

81. An expression very similar to this line appears in the sixtieth hexagram of the *Yijing.*

82. Zhang Zhidong's endorsement of newspapers takes up the late Tang scholar Li Han's use of this *Laozi* phrase to characterize the encyclopedia *Tongdian* 通典 (Comprehensive Documents) by Du You (732–812), and adds: "These words are almost such that they could have been said of the Chinese and Western newspapers of today." "Yue bao," L. 3–4.

83. *SB* Sept. 19, 1909 "Shuo Bao."

84. Similar observations for the *Xunhuan Ribao* in Vittinghoff, "Chinese Newspapers's 'Response to the West,'" esp. p. 95.

85. For a discussion of the issues at stake, cf. Bennett, *Missionary Journalist,* pp. 220ff.

86. For an elaborate discussion, cf. Joan Judge, "Public Opinion and the New Politics of Contestation in the Late Qing, 1904–1911," in: *Modern China* 1994.20/1:64–91, 73.

87. Cf. Judge, "Public Opinion," p. 64.

88. Cf. Judge, "Public Opinion," p. 75.

89. Cf., for instance, Li, *Baozhi wenti,* Chen Pingyuan, "Bagu yu mingqing guwen," *Xueren* 1995.7:341–372, 341, and chapter 2 in *A Newspaper for China?*

90. For the debates on the style of writing by Young J. Allen in his *Jiaohui xinbao,* cf. Bennett, *Missionary Journalist,* pp. 106 ff.

91. It is also discussed in my *A Newspaper for China?*, pp. 56–69.

92. Li, *Baozhi wenti,* p. 20, emphasizes the inadequacy of *baguwen* for editorials on contemporary subjects and acknowledges that journalists would eventually abandon it. Also cf. Xu/Xu, *Shenbao shiliao,* p. 17. The use of the *baguwen* is interesting in view of the common contention that during the late Qing "newly fashioned 'newspaper prose' became more popular than the classics themselves" (William H. Nienhauser, "Prose" in: *Indiana Companion,* pp. 93–120, 115; cf. also *Shanghai jindai wenxue,* esp. 138–164.). As will be shown, this newspaper prose was in fact to a considerable extent "classic."

93. In practice, this structure was not always followed. There also is no unified terminology for the *bagu* elements. I here follow Tu Ching-I, "The Chinese Examination Essay," *Monumenta Serica* 31 (1974–1975) pp. 393–406, and Angelo Zottoli, *Cursus Literaturae sinicae: neo-missionariis accommodatus,* 5 vols., Shanghai, 1879–1882. For more details see *A Newspaper for China?*, p. 57 n.50.

94. *SB* Aug. 18, 1873.

95. Andrew Plaks, "Pa-ku wen," in *Indiana Companion,* p. 641.

96. For a selection of original essays, cf. Zottoli, *Cursus*. Useful translations with analytical notes are also in Tu, "Examination Essay," Andrew Lo, "Four Examination Essays of the Ming Dynasty," *Renditions* 33/34 (1990): 168–181, and Wayne Alt, "The Eight-Legged Essay: Its Reputation, Structure, and Limitations," *Tamkang Review* 17.2 (1986):155–174.

97. This type of dialogue is found in argumentative texts such as *Lunyu*, *Zhuangzi*, or *Yantielun* since early times. Missionary newspapers also made use of it. In the Western press it can be found at least since the eighteenth century (cf. *EB*, vol. 18, "Periodicals," p. 540).

98. Gun, called to court by Emperor Yao, built dams to get the waters under control. This blocked up the water and led to huge floods.

99. For the historical background and further occurrences of this analogy, cf. Rudolf G. Wagner, "The Structure of the Chinese Public Sphere" (unpublished, 1981).

100. A vivid example is the section on floods in the television series *Heshang* (River Elegy) (1987).

101. The locus classicus for "clearing the spring" *qingyuan* in the sense of ordering radically is the *Xingfa* zhi in the *Han shu*, Beijing: Zhonghua, 1964, 23. 1112.

102. The argument is, of course, highly idealized. Rather than articulating facts and Truth alone, newspapers have often very clearly stood for the interests of particular social groups.

103. Cf. David Hume, *Essays: Moral, Political and Literary*, London: Oxford University Press, 1963, p. 29: "(Since) the many are governed by the few, ... nothing appears more surprising to those who consider human affairs with a philosophical eye than the easiness with which men resign their own sentiments and passions to those of their rulers. When we inquire by what means this wonder is effected, we shall find that ... the governors have nothing to support them but opinion."

104. Cf. Wang Kaifu, *Baguwen gaishuo*, Beijing: Zhonghua, 1991, p. 10.

105. Translation by James Legge, *The Chinese Classics*, vol. 1: *The Confucian Analects, The Great Learning, The Doctrine of the Mean, Mencius*, Oxford: Clarendon Press, 1892 ff, p. 321. D.C. Lau, *Mencius*, p. 129, gives "Think of the consequences before you speak of the shortcomings of others." This maxim may be one of the reasons why the journalist's profession took so long to be accepted among Chinese. Nathan, "The Late Ch'ing Press," p. 128, finds a very similar argument in Bao Tianxiao's reminiscences.

106. Zhu Xi assumes that it must have been coined under particular circumstances, but gives no details (cf. *Mengzi zhangju jizhu* [Mengzi in sections and with commentaries], Shanghai: Shanghai Shudian, 1986, p. 61).

107. The Chinese term for such a suggestive, exclamatory question would *jiwen* (cf. Kao "Rhetoric," p. 130)

108. Cf. Arthur F. Wright, "Introduction," in id. ed., *The Confucian Persuasion*, Stanford: Stanford University Press, 1960, pp. 13–18.

109. Cf. figures such as Yao and Shun, Qu Yuan and Hai Rui, next to Wang Mang and Wu Zetian.

110. Lin Yutang, *History of the Press and Public Opinion in China*, Chicago: University of Chicago Press, 1936, p. 2, mentions the locus classicus for this phenomenon

in the *Zhoushu* of the *Shujing:* "tianting zi wo minting" (Heavens hears as my people, meaning the wishes of the people are the will of heaven, cf. Legge, *Chinese Classics*, vol. 3, p. 292).

111. Cf. Arthur F. Wright, "Introduction," p. 4.

112. For some evidence on these rituals during the late Qing, cf. ch. 3 in my *A Newspaper for China?*

113. An example would be the Ming dynasty founder Zhu Yuanzhang, who made use of Confucian moral philosophy after having killed off those who had criticized him in the name of the same philosophy cf. Benjamin Elman, "'Where Is King Ch'eng's Civil Examination and Confucian Ideology During the Early Ming," *T'oung Pao* 79(1993): 27.

114. For evidence cf. ch. 5 in my *A Newspaper for China?*; Lucien W. Pye, "How China's Nationalism was Shanghaied," *AJCA* 1993.29:107–133; Ye Xiaoqing, "Shanghai before Nationalism," *East Asian History* 1992.3:33–52; and Wagner, "Foreign Community II," 11.15.

115. Cf. Henriot, "Nouveau journalisme," p. 5. Cf. also Patterson, "Chinese Journalism." For a general introduction to these early Chinese newspapers cf. Huang Zhuoming, *Zhongguo gudai baozhi tanyuan*, Beijing: Renmin ribao chubanshe, 1983; Lin Yuanqi, *Dibao zhi yanjiu*, Taibei, 1976; Flessel, "Early Chinese Newspapers (10th to 13th centuries)," *Collected Papers of the XXIX Congress of Chinese Studies*, Tuebingen: Tübingen University Press, 1988, esp. p. 62, and for a critical view on the particular nature and incompatibility of the Chinese and the Western press p. 67, fn.6.

116. The *dibao* also has many other, often interchangeable names. For a careful study, see Huang, *Gudai Baozhi*, and Liu Yongqiang, "Ming-Qing dibao yu wenxue zhi guanxi" (The *dibao* of Ming and Qing and their relationship to literature), *Xueren* 1992.3:437–464.

117. Because the memorials in the *Jingbao* often discussed controversial and important issues, foreign-language papers such as the *North China Herald, Celestial Empire*, or the *Shanghai Mercury* published translated selections. Since the *North China Herald* precedes the Chinese-language papers, one could argue that the model for reprinting parts of the *Jingbao* in a newspaper was again an alien one.

118. The letter is reprinted in Ge Gongzhen, *Zhongguo baoxueshi* (A history of newspaper-studies in China), (1926). Reprint: Hong Kong: Taiping shuju, 1968, p. 99, and translated by Britton, *Periodical Press*, pp. 30–31.

119. Cf. *A Newspaper for China?*, pp. 43–117; Abraham A. Moles, *Informationstheorie und ästhetische Wahrnehmung*, Cologne: Schauberg, 1971, p. 22, stressed that a message can be understood and received if it comes "from a 'repertoire' . . . characterized by features of the recipient."

120. As claimed in Xu/Xu, *Shenbao shiliao*, p. 14, and also in Flessel, "Chinese newspapers."

121. Cf. Dietmar Rothermund, "Kognitive Interaktion und die Hermeneutik der Fremde," Einleitungsreferat zum ersten Symposium des DFG-Schwerpunktprogrammes "Transformationen der europäischen Expansion vom 15. bis 20. Jahrhundert. Untersuchungen zur kognitiven Interaktion europäischer und außereuropäischer Gesellschaften," Heidelberg, 25.2.1993, 4.

122. *SB* July 13, 1872 "Dibao bie yu xinbao lun."

123. *SB* July 18, 1873 "Lun Zhongguo Jingbao yi yu waiguo xinbao" (On the difference between the Chinese *Court Gazette* and the Western newspaper).

124. One could of course argue, as I do in ch. 3 in my *A Newspaper for China?*, that the *Jingbao* reprints in the commercial papers, faster and of better quality than the traditional *baofang* editions, cut into the readership of the *baofang* editions. This, however, is not the editorialist's point. But he is hypocritical about the fact that his own paper will include this allegedly boring *Jingbao* exactly to attract readers.

125. For a very similar argument, cf. *NCH* Jan. 31, 1879, "Steamers and Newspapers in China," esp. p. 92.

126. Britton, *Periodical Press,* p. 15, agrees with this interpretation when he concludes: "The new Chinese press was a collateral development which leaned heavily upon the old press, and gradually absorbed and replaced it; [but it was by no means] . . . an organic progression from the old press."

127. *SB* Feb. 14, 1901, "Benguan diyi wan haoji" (Record of the 10.000th issue of our paper).

128. As Huang, *Gudai baozhi,* shows masterfully, all news in Chinese newspapers before the nineteenth century, even of papers in private hands, originated in official sources. On this point I argue with Flessel, "Early Chinese Newspapers," who simply equates Chinese and Western papers.

129. Eastman, "Ch'ing-i," p. 596, explains the meaning of *qingyi* for the late Qing as follows: (1) "Expressions of opinion by low or middle ranking officials, "and thus (2) "a political tool with which [these officials] . . . sought to advance their careers, to give some vent to animosities, or otherwise to advance narrow interests."

130. Judge, "Public Opinion," p. 67, shows that Liang was in disagreement on this point with some of the other *Shibao* editors and journalists who were not all convinced that the *yanguan* had been effective in Chinese history and should thus be used as a simile.

131. Wang Tao (1828–1897) mentions this in his essays on the evils of the time, cf. Paul Cohen, "Wang T'ao and Incipient Chinese Nationalism," *JAS* 26(1967): 565–566. A *Shenbao* editorial of 17.9.1898 on the evil of secrecy and lack of information among the bureaucracy (translated in Andrea Janku, *Der Leitartikel der Shenbao im Reformjahr 1898: Perspektiven eines neuen Genres,* unpubl. M. A. Heidelberg, 1995) also invokes the necessity of open communication between ruler and ruled. See also *Shibao* Dec. 27, 1907: "Even in the Zhou dynasty officials consulted the masses" (cf. Judge, "Public Opinion," p. 73)

132. "Yue bao," L. 26.

133. *Wuxu bianfa* (Jian Bozan ed.), 4 vols, Shanghai: Shenzhou guoguang she, 1953, here vol. 2, p. 432.

134. *Wuxu bianfa,* vol. 2, p. 432. In principle, these authors agree with Henriot, "Nouveau journalisme," p. 62, who concludes that there was a lack of proper "channels of communication throughout Chinese history capable of transmitting subversive political thought."

135. Liang, "Lun Baoguan you yi yu guoshi," p. 100.

136. Liang, "Lun Baoguan you yi yu guoshi," p. 100.

137. Cf. the discussion of the *Xunhuan Ribao* in Vittinghoff, "Chinese Newspapers's 'Response to the West.'" Interestingly enough, these types of equation are also used by Western-language papers. An example is a *North China Herald* article on Sept. 11, 1880 "The 'Censorate' at Shanghai" describing the two Chinese-language dailies as fulfilling the function of the old Chinese censorate, and modernizing engine: "Shanghai boasts the possession of a 'Censorate' of prodigious power; the Settlement is a fulcrum supporting two levers which are moving the Middle Kingdom to its periphery. These are the *Hsin Pao* (News Reporter) and the *Shenpao* (Shanghai Reporter), two daily Chinese newspapers."

138. *SB* July 18, 1873 "Lun Zhongguo *jingbao* yi yu waiguo *xinbao*."

139. The translation follows Legge, *Chinese Classics*, vol. 3, p. 337.

140. For this part of the *Liji*, see Michael Loewe, ed., *Early Chinese Texts*, Berkeley: The Society for the Study of Early China, 1993, pp. 293–297.

141. The translation generally follows Legge, *Chinese Classics*, vol. 3: *The Book of Documents*, p. 216 (except for the last sentence).

142. "Lun geguo xinbao zhi she," *SB* Aug. 18, 1873. A *Shibao* Sept. 21, 1909 editorial went so far as to suggest that "the establishment of newspaper offices was the original (if not realized) intention of the ancient sages." (Cf. Judge, "Public Opinion," 71, who points to a similar argument in *Shibao* Jan. 19–20, 1908.)

143. " Lun xinwenzhi zhi yi" (On the use of newspapers), *SB* Aug. 11, 1886.

144. For the frequency of such conclusions in newspaper editorials, cf. Li, *Baozhi wenti*, 23–24.

145. Irmela Hijiya-Kirschnereit, *Selbstentblößungsrituale*, Wiesbaden: Harassowitz, 1981, p. 33, describes this for the process of literary modernization in Japan.

146. The claim that foreign innovations were based on Chinese inventions was often made at the time. For some examples, cf. Kuo Heng-yü, *China und die "Barbaren,"* Pfullingen: Neske, 1967, pp. 73–74. Both Taipings and Christians used it to promote the adoption of Christianity (cf. Bennett, *Missionary Journalist*).

147. This conclusion answers the questions posed by Eisenstadt, *Tradition, Wandel und Modernität*, p. 185: "welche Tradition . . . die alte oder die neue—repräsentiert die wahre Tradition der neuen sozialen politischen oder religiösen Gemeinschaft? In welchem Maße kann die bestehende Tradition der neuen zentralen Kultur einverleibt werden? Haben die traditionellen . . . Strukturen Gültigkeit für die neuen Symbole und Organisationen?"

148. This portrayal is similar to what William Rowe suggests in "The Problem of 'Civil Society' in Late Imperial China," *MC* 1993.19/2:139–157, 154: "Did the monarchical West, for example, ever develop the ideal of the remonstrating official (*yanguan*), or the principle of guaranteeing popular livelihoods (*minsheng*) as early or as fully as did imperial China?"

CHAPTER 2

Useful Knowledge and Appropriate Communication: The Field of Journalistic Production in Late Nineteenth Century China

Natascha Gentz

Studies on the public sphere and political culture in general in late Qing China have only recently started to focus on newspapers and other print media. This was in part due to the influence of Habermas's study of the pivotal role of print media in the development of the public sphere in eighteenth- and nineteenth-century Europe;[1] it also resulted from the discovery that these materials—even if descried by historians as a "weak source"—do at the very least contain a lot of unintended information on the political culture and social communication of the communities in which they are circulating. Until recently, however, studies with this new focus have mainly concentrated on the development of the Chinese press after the beginning of the twentieth century. This emphasis follows the PRC periodization, which has a truly "native" press starting only with the reform papers in the mid-1890s. It finds further justification in the claim that the professionalization of journalism made headway only during the last years of the Qing, and developed only during the 1910s and 1920s. The elements described by occupation sociologists as marking a "profession" such as a specialized and institutionalized education, the formation of professional associations, and a defined ethical code had indeed not now developed during the first decades of Chinese-language newspapers.[2]

An analysis of the archival record and the newspapers themselves, however, will show that the early stages of a Chinese press in the Shanghai Settlements and the Hong Kong crown colony already display a rather advanced perception of the role of the press in political and social communication as well as a high level of organizational and intercommunicative structures among the people involved.

This chapter follows a sociohistorical approach. It will be assumed that the position of the papers and the statements of the agents can only be fully interpreted and grounded within the broader context of what Bourdieu calls the "field of cultural production." Cultural production emerges from an interaction of different institutions such as those for material production, distribution, reception, or symbolic production, and these institutions are again created or shaped by the agents in the field and their specific activities, networks, alliances, and so on. This allows for a flexible empirical approach that studies textual production mainly in a pragmatic context.[3]

For my analysis, I chose the two most important private commercial papers of the last half of the nineteenth century, the Shanghai *Shenbao* (申報, 1872–1949) and the Hong Kong *Xunhuan Ribao* (循環日報, 1874–1949), as well as two little-known semiofficial papers in Shanghai, the *Huibao* (匯報, 1874) and the *Xinbao* (新報, 1876–1882).

Using Western printing technology and quickly developing a national and international distribution network, *Shenbao* and the *Xunhuan Ribao* as the first important and successful enterprises of their kind circulated widely, found the most attention, and are justly reckoned as the most important and influential newspapers in Chinese of that time. The *Xunhuan Ribao* was established by Wang Tao (王韜, 1828–1897),[4] a prose writer of renown, with the claim of being the first Chinese newspaper operating under an entirely Chinese management. The *Shenbao*, in contrast, was a joint venture of four British merchants, with Ernest Major (1841–1908) as the manager and editor assigned a majority share in both profits and losses. The *Huibao* and its successors *Huibao* (彙報, 1874–1875) and *Yibao* (益報, 1875) were the first attempts by an interest group to establish a newspaper—Cantonese merchants in Shanghai with the support of a Chinese official, the District Magistrate Ye Tingjuan (葉廷眷); these short-lived papers were set up to counter the *Shenbao*. The Shanghai *Xinbao*, for its part, can be seen as an attempt by the Shanghai Daotai Feng Junguang (馮浚光, 1830–1877) to establish within a market environment what in fact was an official organ.

HISTORIOGRAPHY

Although for the period under consideration, none of the papers has been the object of close source-based studies, the differences in their treatment have more to do with present-day political concerns than historical realities.[5] The early *Shenbao* appears in Chinese newspaper histories already since the late 1920s in the main as a commerce-focused paper run by foreignerers for financial gain.[6] Historical accounts on the development of journalism theory in China tend to completely disregard the *Shenbao*—all its importance notwithstanding—while dealing extensively with the *Xunhuan*

Ribao.[7] As the first indigenous newspaper, the *Xunhuan Ribao* is portrayed as a nationalist and patriotic endeavor, motivated by the quest for liberation from foreign domination in the editorial boards. The assumed author of its editorials, Wang Tao, is characterized as "the first excellent political editorialist in the history of China,"[8] and is granted the title "Father of Chinese Journalism."[9] He is said to have created this paper primarily to disseminate his now famous pro-reform political essays (*lunshuo* 論說). As Roswell Britton puts it: "Liang Ch'i-chao rounded out the pioneer work of Wang T'ao. He did for the magazine press what Wang T'ao had done for the newspaper press."[10] In this way, Wang Tao became the forerunner of the type of political advocacy journalism that unfolded since 1895 with Liang Qichao as the main representative.[11]

If the *Huibao* and the *Xinbao* are even mentioned, the focus is on their commercial failure, not on their being efforts of Shanghai officials to join the public sphere with a print medium of their own.[12] Such efforts are said to have started only after the Sino-Japanese War in 1895 when the Chinese Foreign Office started its first short-lived official government paper, and to have culminated in the large-scale establishment of official gazettes (*guanbao* 官報) in 1901 after the Boxer incident.[13]

The oft-repeated story that the early Chinese newspapers were of no broader interest to either the public or government officials, and that they did not get involved in political matters until the key actors of the reform period entered the scene,[14] goes back to Liang Qichao's enormously influential essays on Chinese newspapers since 1902. In order to emphasize the importance of his own reform press, he downplayed the importance of the Chinese press of the preceding decades.[15] Academic studies on Chinese newspaper history often buttress this claim by reference to the musing of Lei Jin (雷瑾, 1871–1941)—a journalist of the *Shenbao* only since 1897[16]—in the 1922 Jubilee Volume of the *Shenbao* on the first years of this paper:

> At that time it was calm in the court and in the countryside, nothing happened in [our] corner by the sea [=Shanghai]. Persons involved in politics . . . were neither respecting the newspapers, nor did they loathe them excessively, but everyone with great talent in the entire society was infatuated with the examinations, and none of them was willing to make newspaper work his profession; only bohemian literati (*luotuo wenren* 落拓文人) and reckless students (*shukuang xuezi* 疏狂學子) would on occasion use the paper to give vent to their frustrated and dejected mood. The correspondents in the different [treaty] ports were of noble character, but the reports they put together were mostly street rumors devoid of broader importance. There was no way for them to pick up sophisticated statements about the grand politics and plans of the country. And even should they have gotten hold [of such statements] they would surely not have dared to write them down. As a consequence the paper's contents were mostly diffuse and banal.[17]

Lei Jin furthermore claims that "no income could have been lower" than that of the journalists at the time.[18] Another often-quoted account from 1928 claims that the angry charge by the high Qing official Zuo Zongtang that journalists criticizing his taking a loan from a foreign bank[19] were nothing better than "worthless literati [*wulai wenren* 無賴文人] from Jiangsu and Zhejiang who have made the newspapers their last abode" reflected a widespread opinion about journalists in general. The same account claims that newspaper boys had trouble collecting the subscription fees and were often equated with the bawdy hawkers of the *Court Gazette.*[20]

One of the most-quoted derogatory terms for journalists, "polished scoundrels" (*siwen bailei* 斯文敗類), does not come from the general public but from Empress Dowager Cixi's edict ordering the persecution of journalists in October 1898 after the Hundred Days Reform.[21] On this weak base, sweeping generalizations are made and repeated.

My reevaluation of the status and public role of early Chinese newspapers and journalists is organized in two parts. The first will do a prosopographic foray to establish who was involved with the four papers previously mentioned and who had a word in deciding their policy. Detailed information about the first journalists is scarce, but by joining together small pieces of disparate information a fairly complete sketch of these publishing houses can be drawn. The social background of the agents and of the mode and process of establishing the publishing houses may also provide initial glimpses into the motives for founding and running a newspaper. In addition, changes in the editorial boards, information about social interaction among the first journalists, and their participation in other cultural and charitable activities will help to answer the question whether we are dealing with independent individuals or a social network.

The second part concerns the newspapers in their social context and their interaction: their financial management and market strategies are examined to analyze the preconditions for their public role. Their commercial strategies and layout design will serve as pointers to their intended and potential readership. We will investigate the public role the papers claimed for themselves. In order to decode sometimes hidden or allusive meanings in the relevant programmatic statements, we must read them in the context of contemporary modes of public articulation.

This analysis will show that the first Chinese newspapermen chose from a variety of different options for the design of their papers, and that their strategies to claim a public role were quite different from what was (and still is) ascribed to them; that there was considerable official interest in the newspaper business; and that a fair number of the Chinese officials carefully followed the newspapers and ascribed great importance to them. The specific profile of the papers reflects the struggle for a leading position in the public sphere of social and political communication.

NETWORKS OF NEWSPAPERMEN

THE EDITORS OF THE FOREIGN-OWNED *SHENBAOGUAN*

Information on the early *Shenbao* editors is scarce. Among the best—but hitherto unused—sources are obituaries published in the *Shenbao* itself, regardless of the eulogistic character of the genre.

The *Shenbao* was set up in April 1872 by the British merchant Ernest Major in a joint stock company with C. Woodward, W. B. Pryer, and John Wachillop, each of the four contributing 400 *taels* to the enterprise. Major was a young businessman who had come to China with his brother Frederick Major during the 1860s. He already headed three companies when his comprador Chen Gengxin (陳庚莘, second half of the nineteenth century) suggested that he should set up a newspaper as a business venture. Chen's advice is said to have been prompted by the profits made by the *Shanghai Xinbao* (上海新報), the Chinese language paper published by the *North China Herald* since 1861.[22] The three other British merchants do not seem to have been directly involved in running the paper since they are never mentioned again either in the *Shenbao* itself, in any news on the *Shenbao* in the *North China Herald/North China Daily News* (1864), or other sources. That Major was well versed in Chinese is stated in his *Shenbao* obituary[23] and supported by the fact that articles in the *Shenbao* are signed with his studio name "Master of the Appreciate News Pavilion" (*Zunwenge zhuren* 尊聞閣主人).[24] Major was also called on by the Shanghai Mixed Court as an authority for solving disputes concerning certain expressions in Chinese.[25]

In editing the *Shenbao*, Major was assisted by four Jiangnan Chinese: Jiang Zhixiang (蔣芷湘, ?), Wu Zirang (吳子讓, 1818–1878), He Guisheng (何桂笙, 1840–1894), and Qian Xinbo (錢昕伯, 1833–?). Two more editors, Zou Tao (鄒弢, ?–1913,)[26] and Li Shifen (李土棻, 1821–1885),[27] are mentioned in connection with the *Yinghuan suoji* (瀛寰瑣記) literary magazine published by the Shenbao Company since November 1872, but there is no clear indication whether they were more than authors for this journal. Zou Tao is also from Jiangnan. With the founding of the *Minbao* 民報 by the *Shenbao* house in 1876, a paper with easy-to-read excerpts from the *Shenbao*, two more Jiangnan editors assumed editorial functions, namely, Cai Erkang (蔡爾康, 1852–1920), and Shen Yugui (沈毓桂, 1808–1898).[28]

Originating from Zhejiang and Jiangsu in the Jiangnan region around Shanghai, they were all newcomers to the Shanghai Foreign Settlements but not related to each other by bonds of common origin (*tongxiang* 同鄉). There is a great variance in their age, with Shen Yugui (64) and Wu Zirang (54) being the two seniors, He Guisheng (39) and Qian Xinbo (32) in the middle, and Cai Erkang (22) the youngest. We do not know how Major selected his staff, but as will be shown, many of these men had had contact with Wang Tao, who had fled to Hong Kong in October 1862; some had kept these contacts alive. Missionary institutions in Shanghai provide another link.

The least known is Jiang Zhixiang. A *xiucai* from Jiangnan, he served the *Shenbao* for twelve years until he received the degree of a *jinshi* and left the publishing house in 1884.[29]

A short obituary about He Guisheng from Zhejiang mentions his fame as an infant prodigy; he continued his career as a successful *xiucai*, but failed in the next examination step. Having just arrived in Shanghai after being driven from home by the Taiping rebellion, he is said to have been influenced by Feng Guifen (馮桂芬 1809–1874), who had cooperated with the missionary journalist Young J. Allen (1836–1907)[30] to set up the first foreign language school in Shanghai, the *Shanghai tongwen guan* (上海同文館 or *Guang fangyan guan* 廣方言館) in 1861.[31] He Guisheng first was a clerk at the *Shenbao*, and later became one of the editors. He was married, had two sons and two daughters. He remained on the editorial board until his death from illness in 1894. He also published some books of his own.[32] On the occasion of his fiftieth birthday, the *Shenbao* praises him as a renowned scholar with vast knowledge in the classics, historical books, philosophical writings, and literature. Visitors from Japan, Korea, or Vietnam would send him presents only to be allowed to pay their respects to him and ask for one of his famous poems.[33] During He's birthday banquet in the Zhang Gardens, Wang Tao gave a speech about their long-standing friendship and praised He as a model for literary circles in Shanghai.[34] He is said to have been fond of Peking opera and in close contact with famous actors. Being very shortsighted and only able to read with glasses, he was rumored to have installed himself behind the stage to listen to the singers and write his theater review for the next day.[35]

Qian Xinbo was another *xiucai* from Zhejiang; he, too, was connected to the missionaries in Shanghai, although there are few details. He is said to have met Wang Tao during the latter's time with the London Missionary Society Press in Shanghai, the *Mohai shuguan*. When Wang Tao fled to Hong Kong, he entrusted his daughter to the Qian family, who was then married by Qian Xinbo in 1868.[36] The intimate relationship between the two men is also expressed in the letters Wang Tao later wrote to Qian from Scotland where he stayed with James Legge (1814–1897).[37] Shortly after the founding of the *Shenbao*, Qian was sent to Wang Tao in Hong Kong to study the more advanced publishing techniques there; as a consequence he is also listed as editor in the *Xunhuan Ribao*.[38] Like He Guisheng, he was a fan of the Kunqu opera, but no articles or literary works by him have been identified.[39]

Wu Zirang, another friend of Wang Tao, is only rarely mentioned as part of the editorial board.[40] Yet after his death in July 1878, Major dedicated a full-length obituary to "Mr. Wu, bestowed with the honorific title of a Grand Master of Court Discussions, official deputy salt controller, nominal department magistrate in Zhili and subsequent County Magistrate." He expressed his deep affection and respect for this man, from whom, he said, "most of the general and comprehensive editorials of the last six years have come."[41] After having failed in the provincial examination, Wu traveled through many provinces until he finally joined the military staff of Zeng Guofan (曾國藩, 1811–1872).[42] He received posts and official titles ranging from rank 4b to 7a on the basis of his military success as Zeng's advisor, and thus allegedly contributed to the already substantial fame of his family. Wu came to Shanghai after Zeng's death in 1872 when he was offered an editorial post by Major. He remained in this position until his death from sickness in 1878. Wu is said to have met Wang Tao in 1860, and one source assumes their friendship to be the reason for his *Shenbao* appointment.[43] Hu Daojing claims that Major's comprador Chen Gengxin promoted Wu because they came from the same county.[44]

Except Jiang Zhixiang, all these men remained editors of the *Shenbao* to the end of their professional careers. In this respect, only the two *Minbao* editors Cai Erkang and Shen Yugui were different and both, their age difference of 44 years notwithstanding, maintained a a lifelong friendship .

Having spent some time as an official in Yunnan—Song Jun says he had been a teacher in the Eight Banners and a magistrate[45]—Shen Yugui had already come to Shanghai toward the end of the *Daoguang* era (1821–1851), and later became acquainted with the missionaries Young Allen, Alexander Wylie, Joseph Edkins (1823–1905), and Timothy Richard (1854–1919). After only three years as a *Shenbao* editor, Shen assisted Allen in establishing the Chinese-Western Publishing House (*Zhongxi shuyuan* 中西書院) in 1881.[46] In 1889, Young Allan hired Shen as a Chinese editor for his *Globe Magazine* (*Wanguo gongbao* 萬國公報). In 1892—he was then eighty-four years old—he asked to be relieved of this job in order to "fully devote the rest of his life to poetry and literature," and retired two years later. Shen is the only Chinese ever mentioned in the impressum of the *Globe Magazine*. Cai Erkang, whom he himself had recommended, became his successor.[47]

Before joining the Shenbao Publishing House in 1874 at the early age of 22, Cai Erkang had been a secretary for the missionaries, which suggests that he could understand spoken and written English.[48] Having failed in the provincial examination, the young *xiucai* Cai Erkang is said to have loathed the writing style required for the examinations. In Shanghai, he started the entertaining life of a "settlement intellectual," *yangchang caizi* 洋場才子, and habitué of the courtesan houses. He was good at finger games, fond of drinking, and had a great fancy for fashion.[49] In the Shenbaoguan he was mainly in charge of locating and editing books for Major's famous deluxe editions (*juzhenban* 聚珍版), but also did editorial work for its literary magazines as well as the short-lived *Minbao* and *Globe Illustrated* (*Huanying huabao* 環瀛畫報, 1877).[50] In May 1882, he left the company, some claim in anger,[51] to become the Chinese editor of the *Hubao* (滬報, 1882–1900), a Chinese paper then started by the *North China Daily News*. Soon after his move he tried to outmaneuver the *Shenbao* in sometimes unprofessional ways.[52]

Frequent changes characterize Cai's professional career. He left *Hubao* in 1892 to assist Timothy Richard and Young Allen in editing books for the Missionary Society *Guangxue hui* (廣學會); a year later he was editor-in-chief of the newly-established *Xinwenbao* (新聞報, 1893), but left again after five months—apparently because of a disagreement over the paper's policy—and from 1894 to 1901 he was Chinese editor of the *Globe Magazine* while complaining that he was merely a recording machine (*liu sheng ji* 留聲機) for Allen—"Allen's mouth, Cai's hand" (林之口, 蔡之手)[53]—and proclaiming that he would rather edit a daily newspaper.[54]

Cai also contributed to the establishment of journalistic standards and was a prolific book editor and writer. In 1877, Cai had compiled the first collection of news in Chinese newspaper history, *Anthology of News* (*Jiwen leibian* 記聞類編) excerpted from the *Shenbao*.[55] His preface suggests that already at this early stage the news and editorials of the *Shenbao* were regarded as historical material important enough to be collected and handed down.[56] While working for the *Hubao,* Cai serialized for the first time in Chinese publishing history a Chinese novel, *A Rustic's Idle Talk* (*Yesou puyan* 野叟曝言) in a literary supplement, thus anticipating this common practice of the early twentieth century by more than twenty years.[57] He copied the very successful illustrated magazine of the Shenbao Company, the *Illustrated News from Dianshizhai* (*Dianshizhai huabao* 點石齋畫報), by publishing a similar magazine named *Illustrated Magazine of Literature* (*Cilin shuhua bao* 詞林書畫報) in 1888.[58] Cai is also credited with having coined the transliteration "Makesi" (馬克思) for Karl Marx, which is still in use today.[59] He published more than twenty books together with Timothy Richard and Young Allen. Most prominent among them was the 1895 translation of Robert Mackenzie's *Nineteenth Century. A History* (1889),[60] which immediately became a best seller with more than 30,000 copies, was reprinted in many places, and was the most important Chinese source at the time on the rise of the European powers.[61] His coedited collection of articles, reports, and memorials on the Chinese-Japanese War (1894–1895), *The Whole Course of the War Between China and Japan* (*Zhong Dong zhanji benmo* 中東戰紀本末, 1898), which included his own articles, was also widely read, and was recommended by high officials such as Li Hongzhang (李鴻章, 1823–1901) and Sun Jia'nai (孙家鼐, 1827–1909).[62] He eventually became so prominent a reform figure that he was invited to become a teacher in the new school *Shiwutang* 時務堂 in Hunan or to coedit the *Xiangxue Xinbao* 湘學新報 (1897) together with Huang Zunxian (黃遵憲,1848–1905), Tan Sitong (譚嗣同, 1865–1898), and others, but he declined all these posts. In 1903, he became a reporter for the *Southern Gazette* (*Nanyang guanbao* 南洋官報), and nothing more is known to me about his further life until his death in 1920.[63]

Cai Erkang's lifestyle and career already ressemble the popular image of a modern professional journalist and Sun Yusheng calls him a "real hero in the press-circles of the time." According to Zheng Yimei, Cai used a name card that started with listing his pen names:

Cai Erkang from Shanghai, Jiangsu, *Cina-sthana*

Boy's Name: Lucky Child; Hao: Purple Embroidery; Old age Hao: Supporter of Buddha; Unofficial Hao: Master of the Steelpot, Immortal Historian of Intensive Aroma; after the abdication of the Qing emperor changed to: Old Man Plucking Fragrant Iris

Cina-sthana is a Buddhist Sanskrit term for China. These Buddhist and Daoist elements are often found in pen names of journalists of the time. They evoke the semantic field of retired scholars or officials, old men and hermits with an attitude of protest against a corrupt government at the core.[64] Under the heading "profession," Cai had listed his various positions at the publishing houses and gave the titles of his most famous books on the back of his card.[65]

This information allows us to sketch a picture of the members of the Shenbaoguan and their different tasks. Apparently, one group of editors was strongly interested in literature, poems, and opera such as He Guisheng, Qian Xinbo, and later Cai Erkang and Shen Yugui. They were most likely in charge of the great number of poems and bamboo twig-ballads (*zhuzhi ci* 竹枝詞) on Shanghai appearing in the paper. According to Sun Yusheng, both He Guisheng and Qian Xinbo held at some time the position of general editors (*zong bianzuan* 總編纂) in the *Shenbao*.[66] There was, again according to Sun, only one general editor, who was responsible for the content of the entire paper, decided on the selection of manuscripts, telegrams, excerpts from other papers, edicts and poems to be published, and would write comments on special articles. The other editors were assigned to certain columns in the paper and had to submit their articles to the general editor, who would read and correct them.[67] If we are to believe the obituary for Wu Zirang, he wrote a large part of the early editorials. Like Shen Yugui and Jiang Zhixiang, he had passed the examinations and had seen an official career. Although Jiang possessed the highest examination degree among the editors, he is not mentioned as a writer of editorials. From the tone of the obituary, it seems that Wu Zirang was closest to Major, and this might have made him such an important writer of editorials. Major himself was in charge of the management of the paper, including its finances. Given all the other business enterprises that Major maintained in Shanghai, it is rather unlikely that he had the necessary time to spend on daily editorial work.[68]

All these Chinese pioneers in the Shanghai press market had had contacts with the missionaries of the London Missionary Society (LMS), Young Allen, and Timothy Richard and were thus familiar with Western knowledge. Most of them had received a classical education or had even worked as officials. Many were also friends or acquaintances of Wang Tao. The editors in Wang Tao´s *Xunhuan Ribao* in Hong Kong share some of these features, but there also are major differences.

The Founders of the Chinese-owned *Xunhuan Ribao*

Sources for the early history of the *Xunhuan Ribao* are scarce, and often contradictory. Although, the *Shenbao* is accessible in reprint and microfilm, little survives of the *Xunhuan ribao*. Few scholars had actually seen copies of this paper until Zhuo Nansheng discovered copies from the first months (February to August 1874) in the British Museum Library. Later discoveries in the Hong Kong University Library and the Diet Library in Tokyo added a few months each from the years 1881 and 1883–1885.[69] No copies from before 1895 survive of the first decades of the *Huazi Ribao,* which was very important for the founding of the *Xunhuan Ribao.*[70]

Compared to the *Shenbao,* establishing the *Xunhuan Ribao* was a more complex process. Accounts differ as to the actual financiers of the paper, yet they agree that everyone involved in establishing, financing, and managing the paper came from the upper stratum of the emerging Chinese elite in Hong Kong with its Western-educated literati, compradors, and merchants. Professional bonds, commercial interests, and family kinship held their network of social relations together.

The *Xunhuan Ribao* was printed with equipment bought by the General Chinese Printing Office (*Zhonghua yinwu zongju* 中華印務總局) in 1873 from the Sino-British College (*Ying Hua shuyuan* 英華書院), the former printing house of the London Missionary Society (LMS) in Hong Kong. Set up by Wang Tao and his colleagues, this Printing Office also published books and sold letters, matrices, and chemical fluids. The claim that the LMS Printing House had been sold to Wang Tao and Huang Sheng (黃勝, also Huang Pingfu 黃平甫, 1825–1905)[71] is contradicted by the sales contract that is signed only by Chen Aiting (陳藹亭, alias Chen Yan 陳言),[72] for the Chinese side, and James Legge and Ernst Eitel (1838–1908) for the LMS. The equipment, which included one set of matrices and patrices as well as Legge's English types and presses, was sold for \$10,000 to be paid in three installments until April 1873. This allowed for the printing of fine editions in English and Chinese, and, more important, for the casting of type fonts.[73]

Wang Tao had moved to Shanghai in 1849 after his father's death. To secure him a living, he was given a position in the London Missionary Society Printing House, which had been founded in 1843. He frequently complained about having to rely on what he once called the "barbarian pigmies." On the other hand, he went to see (and praise) Doctor Hobson when he was sick, and even bought some of Hobson's furniture for his own house in Shanghai—which contradicts his alleged contempt for foreign things.[74] Wang Tao taught Chinese to William Muirhead (1822–1900), Joseph Edkins, and Alexander Wylie and helped with editing their *Shanghai Serial* (*Liuhe congtan* 六合叢談, 1857–1858).[75] Wang Tao's fine literary style is said to have been instrumental in the wide distribution of their joint bible translation.[76]

Wang's colorful life as a man of letters in Shanghai earned him notoriety as one of the "three Shanghai maniacs" (*Haishang san qishi* 海上三奇士).[77] When in the spring of 1862 he was accused of having cooperated with the Taiping rebels, the missionaries and the British Consul Medhurst came to his rescue by secretly shipping him to Hong Kong; in autumn 1862, he began an exile that was to last twenty-three years[78] in a place where he found the food bad, the people vulgar, the dialect ugly, and the courtesans lacking in education.[79] However, he very much enjoyed working with James Legge on his grand project of translating the Chinese classics. He praised Legge's scholarship and expressed gratitude for his friendship and help.[80]

The translation work with Legge left him enough time to coedit the journal *Jinshi bianlu* (*Contemporary Affairs*, 近事編錄, 1864–1883).[81] The *Shenbao* even mentions him as cofounder of the *Huazi Ribao*.[82] During his trip to Europe from 1868 to 1870, Wang Tao familiarized himself with Western printing techniques by visiting print shops, paper factories, and publishing houses. After his return in 1870, he stayed for a short period with the proprietor of the *China Mail*, Andrew Dixon, and was fascinated by its printing equipment.[83] His letters to officials and friends begin to mention the need for newspapers in China.[84] During his first years in Hong Kong, Wang Tao had not been very active or visible.[85] But after returning from Europe with his new knowledge, his literary production revived[86] and he became an elected member of the prestigious Committee of the newly founded Tung Wah Hospital.

Later accounts regularly describe Wang Tao as the most prominent among the *Xunhuan Ribao* editors. He was, however, surrounded by a group of exceedingly prominent Hong Kong figures, many also members of the Tung Wah Hospital,[87] who played important roles in the enterprise but are rarely mentioned.

One of them, Huang Sheng 黃勝—perhaps the first Chinese professional printer[88]—had studied at the Morrison Education Society School in Hong Kong, and was one of the first three Chinese students to be sent to the United States in 1847. After a printer's apprenticeship at the *China Mail*, he had switched to the LMS as a translator for the new *Chinese Serial* (*Xiaer guanzhen*, 遐邇貫珍, 1853–1856), the first Chinese-language magazine of the colony. In the same year, he became the general print manager of the *Ying Hua shuyuan* where he stayed until Wang Tao arrived. Huang was also very likely the founder of the *Zhongwai Xinbao* in 1858.[89] The *Ying Hua shuyuan* was only sold to Chen Aiting and Wang Tao shortly after Huang Sheng had left Hong Kong to set up a print shop for the *Tongwen guan* 同文館 in Beijing in summer 1872.[90] In 1873, Huang accompanied the second group of students in Rong Hong's (Yung Wing, 容宏 alias Rong Chunfu 容純甫, 1828–1912) Chinese Education Mission scheme to the United States; after returning to Hong Kong three years later, he was the second Chinese to be appointed to the Legislative Council in Hong Kong in 1884. According to Carl T. Smith, Chinese government officials had recommended Huang for an appointment, but he had refused to work for the Qing regime.[91] In 1844, Huang had bought a plot of land from European owners in the former Middle Bazaar area of Hong Kong; it increased ten times in value and made him rather wealthy.[92]

Chen Aiting, a baptized student from St. Paul's College as well as a class-mate and good friend of Wu Tingfang (吳廷芳, 1842–1922), first entered Hong Kong government service at the magistrate's court. In 1871, he became a reporter at the *China Mail,* and one year later started its Chinese-language supplement, the *Huazi Ribao.*[93] For this purpose, he bought another set of Chinese type fonts from the missionaries. Chen Aiting's involvement with the *Xunhuan Ribao* is a little puzzling. While still manager of the *Huazi Ribao,* he bought the LMS Printing House; as a consequence, the *Xunhuan Ribao* lists him in its first issues in 1874 as its general manager. One month later, how-ever, he was succeeded by another manager who was to remain in this posi-tion for many years while Chen Aiting himself continued as general manager of the *Huazi Ribao* until 1877.[94] No reasons are given for his moving in and out of the *Xunhuan Ribao,* or for his motives in buying the LMS print shop. We can observe, however, that the two papers engaged in a fierce competition right from the beginning. Chen Aiting later gave up his career as a journalist and joined the staff of the newly appointed Chinese ambassador in the United States; eventually he himself was appointed as consul general in Cuba.[95]

Wu Tingfang allegedly also supported the *Xunhuan Ribao* financially.[96] A son of a Chinese merchant in Singapore, Wu Tingfang had come to Hong Kong at the age of seven. After graduating from St. Paul's College in 1858, he started his career as a translator for the *Hong Kong Daily Press.*[97] Since 1861, he served as interpreter in the magistrate court but took over the general man-agement of the *Zhongwai Xinbao* from 1864–1873 together with his younger brother Wu Yaguang (吳亞光), who later succeeded him as general manager.[98] Wu Tingfang was married to the sister of He Qi (何啓, alias He Kai, 1859–1914), another man who is said to have assisted Chen Aiting with financing the *Xunhuan Ribao;*[99] his son married a daughter of He Qi.[100]

He Qi was the grandson of a woodblock-cutter for the press of the Anglo-Chinese College at Malacca. His father He Futang (何福堂 alias He Jinshan 何近善, 1818–1871)[101] became well acquainted with Legge, accompanied him to Hong Kong in 1843 as the first ordained Chinese pastor, and lived with his family in the prestigious LMS compound.[102] He also was a very successful land speculator, which allowed him to secure a good education for his sons to whom he left an estate rumored to be worth over $150,000.[103] After graduat-ing from Queen's College, He Qi had gone to study in England in 1873 at the age of fourteen, and received a degree in medicine and law. On his return in 1882, he took up the profession of a barrister and increased his father's wealth as financier. He Qi became one of the most illustrious and important personages in the Hong Kong society of his time. While is is not clear how the connection with the *Xunhuan Ribao* came about—in 1874, He Futang was already dead three years and He Qi was not only too young but also far away in Europe—it is clear that He family members were closely connected to the LMS, and that He Qi was closely associated with other prominent supporters of the *Xunhuan Ribao*.[104]

Among the the earliest members of the group involved in editorial, management, and financial matters mentioned in the commemorative issue for the sixtieth jubilee of the *Xunhuan Ribao* we find next to Wang Tao and Qian Xinbo also Hong Ganfu (洪幹甫, also Hong Shiwei 洪士韋), Feng Hanchen (馮翰臣), and the the translator Guo Zansheng (郭贊生).[105]

Hu Liyuan (胡禮垣, Guangdong, 三水縣, 1847–1916) joined the *Xunhuan Ribao* only in 1879 for two years as a translator, the métier he was to become famous for. The son of a Guangdong merchant who, like Wang Tao, had to flee to Hong Kong because of his association with the Taiping rebels, Hu had studied English with Wu Tingfang since the early age of ten. He enrolled at Queen's College, where he met He Qi in 1870, a man again connected to Wu Tingfang. Hu failed several times in his attempts to pursue an official career through the examination system. After his stint as a translator with the *Xunhuan Ribao* ended in 1881, he started his own paper, the *Yuebao* (粵報, 1883). His various business ventures were successful enough to finance a Western education for his sons.[106]

The *Xunhuan Ribao* strictly separated management and editorial functions. After Chen Aiting had left, Hong Ganfu continued as general manager. He was supported by the vice manager Wu Qiongbo (吳瓊波, Guangdong, 南海) who stayed for fifty years with the paper and took over its general management in 1881. For the General Chinese Printing Office, three additional managers are mentioned in an 1874 advertisement: Feng Mingshan (馮明珊), Liang Hechao (梁鶴巢), and Chen Ruinan (陳瑞南).[107] Two of them can be identified as compradors and members of the Tung Wah Hospital.[108]

Feng Mingshan (alias Feng Puxi 馮普熙 or Feng Zhao 馮照, d. 1898)[109] was a comprador for A. H. Hogg and Company and later for the Chartered Mercantile Bank. He might have been a classmate of Wu Tingfang's at St. Paul's College. Feng was one of the founders of the Tung Wah Hospital, and signed the petition in 1878 that led to the establishment of the Po Leung Kuk, another important charity organization in Hong Kong of which he became president with Wu Tingfang as his vice president.[110] Liang Hechao (alias Liang An, 梁安 or Liang Yunhan, 梁雲漢, d. 1890)[111] was a comprador for Gibb, Livingston and Company as well as the chairman of the founding committee of the Tung Wah.[112] Similar to the *Shenbao*, the early leadership of the *Xunhuan Ribao* had a distinctly regional flavor, in this case Guangdong province. In contrast to the *Shenbao*, the *Xunhuan Ribao* had a high and sometimes camouflaged leadership fluctuation. Wang Tao is noted as the general editor of the paper until 1883 at the bottom of each first page of the *Xunhuan Ribao*, while in actuality he had already transferred the position to Hong Ganfu in 1876.[113] Feng Hanchen stayed only for one year; the translator Guo Zansheng was succeeded by Zhou Chongsheng (周重生) in

1877. The *Xunhuan Ribao* drew less than the *Shenbao* on people who had passed imperial examinations and had been officials. Among these Cantonese editors, only Hong Ganfu's background as a *xiucai* is known. Before his arrival in Hong Kong, he is said to have served under the Vice Censor Jiang Yili (蔣益澧) in Guangdong.[114]

Most of the important cofounders of the *Xunhuan Ribao* such as Huang Sheng, Wu Tingfang, Wang Tao, Chen Aiting, and He Futang were members of the Tung Wah Hospital,[115] which is now "generally regarded as marking the beginning of a publicly recognized elite among the Chinese population in Hong Kong."[116] The directors elected were mostly heads of the important Hong Kong guilds or wealthy merchants, but also other respectable personages and could thus "justifiably claim to represent the whole Chinese community, and more importantly, to be recognized by the government as an élitist group."[117] Except for Huang Sheng, however, no one of the Xunhuan circle became hospital director because they were not representatives of guilds but individual merchants. Nevertheless, many of the other founding fathers of the *Xunhuan Ribao* also rose to fame and status in the Hong Kong community. Wu Tingfang was the first Chinese to be appointed justice of the peace. He Qi and Huang Sheng followed suit, with all three becoming members of the Legislative Council.[118] These appointments marked the first official recognition of Chinese opinion in British government decisions.

Far from being a venture of some stray failures in the imperial examinations, the *Xunhuan Ribao* involved some of the most important Hong Kong merchants who combined commercial interest with commitment to public matters. Since Hong Kong lacked a hinterland of the kind Shanghai had with the prestigious and large Jiangnan cultural elite, many of whom moved to its settlements, these new and successful Hong Kong merchants had little competition in assuming the role of local elite. Their frequent appearance in the official robes of the ranks they had bought and their practice of arranging splendid banquets shows at the same time that they were eager to emulate the lifestyle and status of officials and literati.[119] As will be shown, the statement of purpose of the *Xunhuan Ribao* also fits their assumed pose of the traditional scholar. Still, the collected data suggest that all persons involved had received their education from the Protestant missionaries, and many of them shared the experience of traveling to Europe or the United States, which shaped the lifestyle of this part of the new elite. The most extreme case might be He Qi, who returned from England with a British bride, and was the first Chinese to wear a Western suit in Hong Kong.[120]

THE FOUNDERS OF THE FIRST CHINESE SEMIOFFICIAL NEWSPAPERS

Most information about *Huibao* editors and managers comes from contemporary papers such as the *Shenbao,* the *North China Herald,* and the *Celestial Empire.* Additionally—and hitherto hardly used as a source on newspaper history—reports by officials of the British Shanghai Consulate stored in the Public Record Office in London provide further helpful information.

The founding of the *Huibao* was the result of a highly controversial debate in the *Shenbao*, a connection mostly ignored in the secondary literature.[121] The dispute began after Yang Yuelou (楊月樓, 1844–1890), a well-known Peking opera actor in the Shanghai International Settlement, had married the daughter of a merchant from Xiangshan county in Guangdong. The Xiangshan community, enraged at the link between a lowly actor and the daughter from a "good family," convinced the magistrate—also a Xiangshan man—to have the couple arrested, separated, and tortured. After the *Shenbao* published a letter criticizing the magistrate's handling of the case with indications that he had bowed to pressures from the Xiangshan community, a fierce debate ensued in the paper. The Xiangshan compradors felt they were singled out for discrimination and, after unsuccessfully defending themselves first in the pages of the *Shenbao*, they asked the Magistrate to ban the paper.[122] After having also failed in this effort, they decided to start the *Huibao* as their counterproject. While it is not surprising that all persons involved in the *Huibao* came from Xiangshan, it will be more of a surprise that these links to Guangdong would lead us to the Hong Kong press community around the *Xunhuan Ribao*.

The *Huibao* was organized in 1874 as a joint-stock company with the District Magistrate Ye Tingjuan and the businessman Tang Jingxing (唐景星 alias Tang Tingshu 唐廷樞, 1832–1892) as the main contributors.[123] The *Shenbao* stated in a polemical editorial that the officials had to finance the enterprise entirely with government funds because merchants and common people disapproved so that no other funds were forthcoming; this statement is repeated by contemporary observers and in secondary sources.[124] Ye Tingjuan had been involved in the establishment of the Canton Guang-Zhao association in 1872, the same year when he entered his post as magistrate in Shanghai. This association connected merchants from the cities of Canton and Zhaoqing. Tang Jingxing was among the founding members and one of the main promoters and contributors to this association in Shanghai.[125] Although Ye was depicted as a sternly antiforeign and conservative official in the *Shenbao* articles during the above-mentioned debate, he was still interested enough in Western things to donate $100 to the foundation of the first public library on Western sciences in China, the Chinese Polytechnic Institution and Reading Room (*Gezhi shuyuan* 格致書院), an institution headed by Wang Tao after his return from Hong Kong. Tang Jingxing and the Daotai Feng Junguang also contributed.[126]

Tang had entered the Morrison Education Society School in Hong Kong in 1841; he and Rong Hong had been schoolmates there. Switching to the LMS School in 1849, he became acquainted with James Legge and Huang Sheng. Huang Sheng succeeded Tang in his post as an interpreter of the magistrate court in Hong Kong, which Tang had held from 1851 to 1856. While he was working as an interpreter in Hong Kong, several charges had been leveled at Tang that were also made public in the papers. This might have prompted him to leave for Shanghai. Tang assumed a position in the Shanghai Maritime Customs; became a comprador for Jardine Matheson; and, in 1873, took over the general management of the China Merchant Steam Navigation Company on the recommendation of Li Hongzhang. In 1883, he went on a tour to Europe. He resigned his post at the Steam Navigation Co. in 1884, and later was connected with the Kaiping mines until his death in 1892.[127] Tang was a wealthy and well-connected figure. He was bilingual and had had long exposure to Westerners and Western institutions.

The *Shenbao* revealed that the *Huibao* was managed by none other than Rong Hong.[128] A student of the Morrison Education Society School in Hong Kong like Tang and Huang Sheng, Rong had been one of the first three students to be sent to the United States for study with the support of the missionaries and the editor of the *China* Mail, Andrew Shortrede. In 1872, Rong had become famous for his education scheme of having the Chinese government send great numbers of very young Chinese students to study in the United States. He personally led the first group of these students to Hanover, Connecticut. When the *Huibao* was founded in 1874, he had just returned. He had cut off his queue, had married the American Mrs. Kellogg, and had become an American citizen; all this was much discussed in the Shanghai papers.[129] Surprisingly, his autobiography neither mentions the *Huibao* nor his involvement in its founding.[130] As he returned to the United States soon after the *Huibao*'s start, he cannot have worked there for long.[131]

The statutes of the *Huibao* are said to have been written by another Xiangshan man, the prominent reformer Zheng Guanying (鄭觀應, 1842–1922);[132] after failing in the first examination, Zheng had come to Shanghai in 1859 and had become a comprador for Dent & Co. After studying English in the English-Chinese College with the missionary John Fryer, he first worked as a translator; in 1868, he set up his own tea business and afterward became comprador for Butterfield & Swire. From his letters to Timothy Richard we know about his contacts with the missionaries. He was an old friend of Tang Jingxing, who nominated him in 1883 as his successor in the China Steam Navigation Co.[133] He is one of the early promoters of Chinese newspapers and often referred to as one of the earliest press-theoreticians in Chinese newspaper history.[134]

The actual editorial work was done by less prominent men from Xiangshan. The main editor was Kuang Qizhao (鄺其照), who had studied in the United States, cooperated with Morrison in editing a English–Chinese Dictionary, and was affiliated with Zhang Zhidong (張之洞, 1837–1909), who was to rise to national prominence as a high official and advocate of educational reforms.[135] About ten years later, Kuang established his own paper in Canton, the *Guangbao* (廣報, 1886–1891), which was closely designed after the *Shenbao* model.[136] Other editors of the *Huibao*, Guan Caishu (管才叔), Huang Jiwei (黃季韋), and Jia Jiliang (賈季良), are also mentioned.[137]

The *Huibao* came to naught just a few months later. Consul Medhurst described the reasons as follows:

> I have been informed by one of the Chinese principally interested that this step has been decided upon in consequence of the troublesome censorship to which the paper has continually been subjected by the High Provincial Authorities, and which so hampered the shareholders in catering for the public that they found it impossible to make the paper pay.[138]

Other sources, however, maintain that the closure and new opening under foreign management had been nothing but a technical trick "to avoid fulfilling a certain contract with a foreigner, which was to stand good as long as the *Weibao* appeared."[139] The paper was reorganized and reappeared on September 1, 1874, under the management of the British subject Scott Gill with the new name *Huibao* (彙報). According to the *Shenbao,* stockholders as well as editors were in fact the same persons as before.[140] The *China Directory 1874* still lists Gill as the manager of the missionary Anglo-Chinese College, where Zheng Guanying had studied.[141] This Eurasian school for children with mixed European and Chinese parentage, founded in 1870, had meanwhile become a very successful charity institution in Shanghai.[142]

In July 1875, a new editor, Zhu Liansheng (朱蓮生), entered the stage, and the name of the paper was changed again; it was now *Yibao* (益報). Zhu was not from Xiangshan, but from Songjiang near Shanghai. The paper had been reorganized under the leadership of Ye Tingjuan, who at this point had already left his post.[143] *The Celestial Empire* initially welcomed this change in the hope of seeing a decrease in the negative influence of "the Cantonese,"[144] but soon afterward had to admit that "it is astonishing really, that so wealthy and influential a class of men as the Cantonese cannot manage to get up a better representative organ than the *I-pao*," which shows that the paper continued in the same track and with the old owners.

The *Yibao* quickly became the butt of entertaining stories in the Shanghai press,[145] and the new effort was abandoned in December 1875, when Zhu announced his intention to quit the editorial job "because of other serious business;"[146] his departure might have also been motivated by a angry letter from the Consul Medhurst to the Daotai Feng, requesting prosecution of Zhu Liansheng for publishing articles in the *Yibao* that literally encouraged the readers to kill foreigners traveling in the hinterlands.[147]

Less than one year later, another, this time more lasting, attempt to establish a newspaper was conducted by the Daotai Feng Junguang—the first Chinese newspaper set up on the private initiative of an official. This paper, the *Xinbao* 新報, which ran until 1882, was also organized as a shareholding company. *The Celestial Empire* speaks of a capital of 6,000 *taels,* "which ought to carry it on for a couple of years at any rate";[148] the paper itself even claimed a capital of 10,000 *taels* in two hundred shares of 50 *teals* each.[149] The whole project was said to have been financed from the official coffers of the Daotai, and it was even insinuated that Li Hongzhang himself was the actual owner of the paper.[150]

The Daotai Feng Junguang had been—like Wu Zirang—a clerk in Zeng Guofan's secretariat, and was—like the others persons involved in the *Huibao*—a Cantonese. He had been a coastal defense subprefectural magistrate and from 1865 to 1874 and managing director of the Jiangnan Arsenal in Shanghai before assuming his post as Daotai in Shanghai in 1874 at the age of forty-four.[151] Although he spoke no foreign language, he took great care in establishing and supervising the foreign language, department in the Arsenal.[152] He had a cooperative attitude toward foreigners and was an open-minded promoter of the *yangwu* current. He is described as "perhaps the only taotai before the Sino-French War who had some idea of economic modernization."[153] Concomitantly, he also stressed national sovereignty. While he is said to have been the first Shanghai Daotai to employ a foreign secretary, he was sternly opposed to the construction of the Woosung Railway.[154] Although he was publicly promoting a modernization along Western lines, he is said to have been privately a devoted Confucian moralist.[155] His selection of journalists for the new paper shows a clear preference for men with foreign language skills and direct experience of working with foreigners and foreign things.

Two editors of the *Xinbao*, Yuan Zuzhi (袁祖志,1827–1898) and Yang Zhaojun (揚兆均), were former translators and editors of the magazine *Recent News from Western Countries* (*Xiguo jinshi* 西國近事), a translation journal published by the Shanghai Arsenal since 1873.[156] *The Celestial Empire* mentions another man as editor, "a Cantonese of some reputation and cleverness and ability, named Yao, who was formerly connected to the *Wei-pao*."[157] Ma Guangren identifies him as Yao Fen (姚芬), a man who had been employed as a translator at the Jiangnan Arsenal.[158] The intelligence report of the British consulate in Shanghai for the first months of 1879 finally mentions that the "manager" of the paper is a "petty official" called Ts'ai (Cai), having two "editors" under him.[159]

Yuan Zuzhi was a grandson of Yuan Mei (袁枚, 1716–1798), a famous official and poet of the mid-Qing. The family fortunes had received a heavy blow from Taiping rebellion. Yuan Zuzhi's grandfather had been the owner of the famous *Suiyuan* garden near Nanjing, which was completely destroyed in 1853; Yuan Zuzhi's brother, a magistrate in Shanghai, had lost his life while defending the city against the Taipings in the same year.[160] When he joined the *Xinbao*, Yuan Zuzhi had behind him a career as an official and magistrate, and was almost fifty years old. He had become known for his prolific writings; he seems to have been on good terms with *Shenbao* journalists, and to have been good friends with Qian Xinbo.[161] In 1883, he accompanied Tang Jingxing on his tour to Europe and wrote down his observations. Ten years later, in 1893, he joined the newly founded *Xinwen bao* at the age of sixty-six and worked there with Cai Erkang for several months.[162] Nothing further is known to me about the manager Cai or about the "foreigner" who the intelligence report says was employed by the paper as a translator.

Feng is depicted as having strict control over the editorial work. When the foreign community began to ridicule the extreme banality of the paper's articles, Feng is said to have written a stern letter to the main editor, even threatening to resort to punishments.[163] As the "Censor of the paper,"[164] in the words of the Intelligence Report, he allegedly examined each single article before publication.[165]

The paper survived two changes in office of the Daotais, but was eventually closed—without any reason given in the paper—by the new Daotai Shao Youlian (邵友濂) in February 1882.[166]

It is evident from this overview that the *Xinbao* remained wedded to Cantonese, and especially Xiangshan interests, although these men had direct experience with the Jiangnan Arsenal, foreign missions, and foreign languages. New qualifications were required that were specific to the new profession, even if the paper was not able to live up to its own aspirations and was suffocated by the attentions of the Daotai.

Apart from personal friendship and professional contacts, individually or jointly written work may be another link between the persons involved in these early newspapers. Next to their usually anonymous newspaper articles, these men also published many reform-oriented essays and works on Western learning, quite apart from poetry and letters. Both the content of the works published and their publication dates show that they continuously engaged in debating and deliberating questions of China's future, and that they were maintaining their personal bonds over decades. Their past experience as journalists stood them in good stead and lent them some authority when in later years they would join the reform debate with major works of their own.

Wang Tao's untiring editing activities and the numerous essays from his own hand in his collections *Second Volume of Wang Tao's Essays (Taoyuan wenlu waibian* 韜園文錄外編),[167] *Taoyuan chidu* (韜園尺讀)[168] and so forth, are wellknown, and it may suffice here to only mention them. Less known are some of his works showing his continuous interest in Western learning.[169] He also continued to work as a translator—from English and also Japanese.[170] Cai Erkang published poems jointly with Qian Xinbo[171], besides editing a collection of poems submitted by readers of the *Shenbao* (*Zunwenge shixuan* 尊聞閣詩選) as well as translating the titles and inscriptions on a set of eighteen Western paintings published by the Shenbaoguan.[172] Almost all later publications by Cai, which I have found, were books related to international politics and Western learning co-authored with Timothy Richard and Young Allen.[173]

Yuan Zuzhi also was a writer putting all his efforts into the dissemination of Western learning in China by presenting different countries of Europe and explaining their governments, customs, defense systems, production, and so forth.[174] Kuang Qizhao published works on Taiwan and a geographical treatise next to the Chinese–English Dictionary,[175] and even the Daotai compiled two treatises on geography.[176]

Rong Hong and Zheng Guanying were well acquainted with Wang Tao and all supported their respective reform projects in their publications or through writing prefaces for each other.[177] They also jointly compiled books[178] and exchanged letters.[179]

In 1894, when the *Guangxue hui* organized a national competition involving the composition of essays on such topics as railways, tea and silk trade, or the prohibition of opium in Suzhou, Hangzhou, Beijing, Fuzhou, and Guangzhou, the judges to evaluate the 172 submissions were none other than Shen Yugui, Cai Erkang, and Wang Tao.[180]

Many more references for such connections and alliances could be given.[181] However, these examples might suffice to testify that we are dealing with a rather homogenous group of people who are connected to the most influential or most "progressive" institutions of the time, such as the publishing houses of the missionaries that had become important centers of cultural exchange for travelers coming from abroad or going abroad; the translation bureaus of the Shanghai Arsenal or the Chinese Polytechnic Institution and Reading Room; the translation schools like the *Guang fangyan guan* or societies like the *Guangxue hui*. People were moving in and out of these institutions. This suggests a rather constant flow of information among these journalists. New knowledge from and about foreign countries had gained importance for all agents in the field. They were collaborating with foreign colleagues, translating Western books and also traveling to Europe and the United States. They were a significant source of foreign knowledge in China.

WHAT IS A CHINESE NEWSPAPER: "NATIVE" AND "FOREIGN" PAPERS IN THE CHINESE VERNACULAR

Despite the transnational networks of the journalists and the global orientation of their writings, it was an important market strategy of all papers to present themselves as native and truly Chinese endeavours.

When the *Yibao* ceased publication in December 1875, the *Celestial Empire* expressed satisfaction, but still regretted that Shanghai would from now on again lack a medium able to transmit "the views the natives take of public questions." The *Shenbao*—although it was taking the lead in the Chinese press market in Shanghai—did not qualify for this role because "as is well known [it] is foreign owned and foreign controlled and of course is not expected to become acquainted with native views and prejudices."[182] The *Celestial Empire* welcomed Feng Junguang's *Xinbao* as the first paper that is "Chinese, and Chinese only,"[183] although the *Huibao* and its successors were all published under the formal editorship of Scott Gill. At the same time, the *Celestial Empire* continued to publish translations from the *Shenbao* under the heading "The Spirit of the Native Press," a form echoed by the excerpts from the "Native Press" in

The North China Herald. The *Xunhuan Ribao* in its turn tried to capitalize on its Chinese ownership to enhance its claims to an authentic representation of enlightened Chinese views, while the *Shenbao* found the editorials of the *Xunhuan Ribao* valuable enough to regularly reprint them for many years, something it never did with the editorials of the other Shanghai Chinese-language papers. Obviously, a justifiable claim to represent "native views" was crucial in the struggle for a leading position in the news market.

As in Shanghai, modern Chinese scholarship drew a line between Chinese and foreign-owned Chinese vernacular papers in Hong Kong and has praised the *Xunhuan Ribao* as the first truly "Chinese" paper. The evidence is, amazingly enough, a self-advertisement by the *Xunhuan Ribao* itself:

> ANNOUNCEMENT: The capital for this Printing Office was solely raised by us Chinese, and in this way we are different from all other publishing houses.... From our having, thanks to the support by scholars and merchants from Hong Kong and many Treaty Ports, already found numerous readers in different places, one can see that we Chinese stand solidly together."[184]

When the *Xunhuan Ribao* was founded in 1874, two other Chinese-language papers, the *Zhongwai Xinbao* (1858) and the *Huazi Ribao* (1872), were already on the market in Hong Kong, both published by the two major local British newspaper companies in Hong Kong.[185] The *Xunhuan Ribao* dismissed them as "set up by Westerners":

> When our company set up the *Xunhuan Ribao* at the end of last month, the initiative for this was entirely coming from Chinese. The General Manager is Chen Aiting, and the Editor-in Chief is Wang Ziquan [Wang Tao]. Both had been proposed by the colleagues [involved in the paper], and this from the exclusive motive of benefiting the Chinese. Newspapers in different places have recently also published Chinese editions, but as these were essentially set up by Westerners, there would, even when they engaged a Chinese as editor-in chief, unavoidably remain big differences when it came to the way and purpose of writing [in the paper]. Time and again [the Western proprietors] furthermore imposed restrictions so that [the Chinese] were unable to freely express their views. At the same time some of the [Chinese] literati writing [in these papers] possessed only a shallow knowledge of the West; they thus were unavoidably very detailed about things Chinese, and sloppy about foreign affairs. When one is searching for someone able to combine [knowledge about] China and the West in one hand, such people are rare indeed![186]

In reality, *Huazi Ribao* as well as *Zhongwai Xinbao* were largely independent units linked to their parent publications by financial contracts. These contracts stipulated that the Chinese partner would be independent in his management and editorial policies, and shoulder the financial risks. The foreign contractor would provide, against a monthly rent, space as well as printing material and equipment. In addition, he was guaranteed a fixed space for free advertisements.[187]

The foreign contractor could and did increase the rent if the Chinese partner seemed to prosper. At least in two cases, this prompted the Chinese partners to cancel the contract and set up their own newspaper. The reasons for dissolving these contracts were financial, not ideological.[188]

There is, moreover, an astonishing similarity in their self-definitions, whether they were owned or controlled by Chinese or foreigners. When the *Huazi Ribao* was founded in 1872, its advertisements in the [English language] *China Mail* emphasized in italic letters that "*it will be the first Chinese Newspaper ever issued under purely native direction.*"[189] The *Xunhuan Ribao* announced its publication in the same *China Mail* nearly two years later almost with the same words, adding, "it will on the one hand command Chinese belief and interest, while on the other deserve every aid that can be given to it by foreigners."[190] Thus, the *Huazi Ribao* also stressed its native direction whereas the *Xunhuan Ribao* saw no problem in asking for foreign support.

The *China Mail* had greeted the publication of the *Shenbao*[191] and now wrote about the two Hong Kong papers that both wished "to secure the support of the foreign public in their enterprises."[192] It praised the professional expertise of Chen Aiting, the editor of the *Huazi Ribao,* as a journalist "whose experience and competence have already been fully demonstrated."[193] The claim to be under native direction thus was a business and marketing device used by all while they remained very open to foreigners and, to a degree, relied on their support.

A fierce competition between the two Chinese newspapers developed in the first months of 1874. When the *Xunhuan Ribao* shifted to a daily rhythm, the *Huazi Ribao* followed only weeks later[194] and by March 1874 it also boasted a distribution network reaching as far as the United States and Australia that matched its competitor's. Ironically, British observers praised as "progressive" the same *Xunhuan Ribao* where "everything was under Chinese direction" for adopting the *Times* format and emulating the editorials of its British contemporaries in Hong Kong.[195]

Wang Tao's editorials make it abundantly clear that he was including foreigners into his implied readership and he even suggested that Chinese should publish newspapers in foreign languages in China itself or in the West.[196] Many articles dealt with Western items of marginal interest to the Chinese community, such as congratulations to a marriage bond between the English and Russian imperial families.[197] Quite often they reflected and supported the opinion held by the foreigners in Hong Kong rather than by Chinese officials.[198] Others praised the British government in Hong Kong for its administration of the colony.[199]

The rendering of the title *Xunhuan Ribao* as *Universal Circulating Herald* in the English-language Hong Kong papers emphasizes the envisaged worldwide news coverage and distribution network.[200] This use in titles of words implying the meaning of "global," "universe," or "international" was quite a fashion at the time; examples are Shenbaoguan magazines such as *Universal News Item* (*Yinghuan suoji* 瀛寰瑣記, 1872–1875), *Global New Items* (*Huanyu suoji* 寰宇瑣記, 1876), or *Global Illustrated* (*Huanying huabao* 環瀛畫報, 1877).

While the *Xunhuan Ribao* stressed its being open to the world, the *Shenbao* as a foreign-owned paper emphasized its promotion of the enlightened interest of the Chinese. Even its translation and printing of foreign news and discussion did in no way imply a pro-Western orientation of the *Shenbao*.

> As the machinery used is by and large Western, it is said that this [paper] is an affair of Westerners, but what is not known is that those wielding the brush are all Chinese. . . . If Westerners are discussing the pros and cons of their own affairs, Westerners will be informed about it, but once a translation is made, the Chinese will be informed as well! If the Westerners are discussing things acceptable and unacceptable in Chinese matters, the Westerners will be informed about it, but once a translation is made, the Chinese, too, will be informed![201]

The *Shenbao* thus claimed to represent Chinese interests as much as the *Xunhuan Ribao* did. The *Shenbao*'s alleged pro-Western stance is again disproved by the fact that it had to defend itself against repeated reproaches from Western papers of being too pro-Chinese, and, by implication, directed against the interests of the foreigners. In an article rebutting such charges from a "Western language newspaper," the *Shenbao* wrote:

> Something Westerners will definitely appreciate might be much to the displeasure of some Chinese. And in something that definitely fits the aspirations of the Westerners, there might be an element that goes completely counter to the aspirations of the Chinese. . . . Our company's newspaper in Chinese characters is a means to get to the eyes and ears of the Chinese, and to broaden acceptance [of this new medium] by Chinese. If we would not protect the Chinese, would the Chinese submit to the public-mindedness of [our] arguments, 議論之公? And if we would not put some praise on the Chinese, would the Chinese rejoice in the excellence of [our] reportages?[202]

British citizens and diplomats also criticized Major's lack of patriotism evident in the *Shenbao* translations of the queen's status and title and its failure to grant her the honorary spaces it reserved for the Chinese emperor.[203]

A statement by the *Shenbao* that it was a business venture designed to make a profit[204] has led scholars to characterize it as "purely commercial."[205] The context of this statement, however, is the defense against charges of pro-Western proselytizing with the claim that its commercial success hinged on acceptance by Chinese readers. At the same time, the statement claimed the legally secured lawfulness of British commercial enterprises in the settlements against the efforts by its semiofficial contemporaries, the *Huibao* and *Yibao* to have it closed down.[206] Major also marked the difference from the subsidized and proselytizing missionary publications that had recently come under criticism.[207]

The semiofficial papers only rarely described their editorial policies or their perceived role in the newspaper market. A general description of the *Huibao* by the Consul Medhurst (quoting one of his Chinese colleagues) reflects an opinion often expressed in the British newspapers.

> He [a Chinese employee of the Consulate] says [the Huibao] mainly consists of a rechauffé of *Peking Gazette* matter, with but a scanty addition of foreign scraps, mostly of an unimportant character, and that it does not come at all near the "Shenpao" in the quality or variety of its content.[208]

The most striking evidence that a newspaper owned by foreigners did not necessarily have to be pro-foreign is the fact that even the semiofficial papers like the *Huibao* and *Yibao* appeared under the name and protection of the foreign editor Scott Gill. In its turn, the *Yibao* was frequently criticized by its foreign contemporaries for its antiforeign spirit.

A lawsuit brought to light that the employment of a foreign editor was only to serve as a protective shield. Gill was hired by Kuang Qizhao not to make editorial decisions but to manage the foreign department of the paper, make translations of news, keep foreign accounts, and maintain contact with foreign advertisers. In the official announcements of the second *Huibao*, however, he is the only—and thus legally responsible—editor.[209] When Gill explained to the court that he had in fact no power or influence in the paper, the court still held him responsible for the paper as a whole because of this public announcement.[210]

There is a difference between treaty port Shanghai and the crown colony of Hong Kong. Hong Kong journalists would dissolve contracts with foreigners for financial reasons; the Chinese papers in Shanghai were seeking foreign "editorship" for legal protection. While this protection was as a rule granted, the legal responsibility of the foreign editor was also stressed.

The *Xinbao* emphasized the information needs of merchants and mandarins.[211] Its official character, however, is reflected in popular expressions; the Chinese would refer to it as a "newspaper of the official circles" (*Guanchang xinbao* 官場新報), the foreigners as "the Taotai's organ."[212] In 1877, there allegedly was a plan to actually rename it *Official Gazette* (*guanbao* 官報).[213] In contrast to the *Peking Gazette* (*Jingbao*), which, "as a rule," would not publish news about foreign countries or matters related to foreigners, even in China,[214] the *Xinbao* emphasized the need to be informed about the politics of the Western nations; the paper is said to have subscribed to the London *Times,* and to have been in close contact with the other papers in Shanghai and Hong Kong.[215]

The *Xinbao* tried a new tack compared to the court or provincial gazettes by inserting Chinese translations of Western articles and even English articles for foreign readers. The foreign community's reaction was bemused:

We have more than once referred to the extraordinary taste displayed by the *Sinpao* in the paragraphs it offers to its foreign readers. Not long ago it published a series of papers about "Inkstones" . . . and now it is giving us a number of "Items from History" which are about as appropriate as if we were to print a series of tales from Lempriere's *Classical Dictionary* in the place of the usual editorial and local paragraphs. . . . Could anything be more utterly absurd! . . . Seriously, we wish the *Sinpao* could be induced to give us more substantial food.[216]

The English inserts had disappeared by May 1877.

FINANCIAL MANAGEMENT AND MARKETING

Perhaps the most obvious proof of the *Shenbao* efforts to convey a China-friendly image is its practice of charging foreign firms higher rates for advertisements than Chinese.[217] The financial effects of these special prices for foreign advertisers in the *Shenbao* were not negligible. The *Xunhuan Ribao* did not distinguish between Chinese and foreign advertisers, but generally had lower prices due to its much smaller circulation numbers.[218] Still, it was much less successful in this business. Almost one-half of the advertisements in a random issue on February 5, 1874, came from the publishing house itself. The *Huibao* also did not distinguish between Chinese and foreign advertisers, and encouraged long-term advertising through big rebates. The *Yibao* apparently lost many of its predecessor's advertisers. In one of the last issues of the *Yibao* (December 2, 1875) it carried only eleven ads. The *Xinbao* used the same calculation for advertisements as the *Huibao*, and had about the same number of insertions. Because its advertisements had more text, the paper outdid its predecessors.

Since most advertisers in all the papers were foreign firms, the *Shenbao* with its special price system did best by a large margin. This dominance of foreign advertisers was not the result of policy but of the reluctance of Chinese merchants to use this device. The papers published articles explaining the benefits of advertising, but it was a difficult task; the *Shanghai Xinbao* (1862–1872) had never been able to solicit Chinese advertisers, although it specifically targeted Chinese merchants.[219]

Shenbao circulation figures, which had reached 8,000 to 10,000 copies a day by 1877,[220] were much higher than the 500, 600, or 800 copies sold by the *Xunhuan Ribao*.[221] Although the price of the *Shenbao* of eight *wen* per day (less than 2.5 dollars/year) was half that of the *Xunhuan Ribao*, its sales thus grossed 20,000–25,000 dollars/year against the 5,000 of its Hong Kong contemporary. The publishing house of the *Xunhuan Ribao* also sold chemical fluids, books, and type fonts; the latter had been the major source of income of the LMS Printing House, but no numbers are available.[222] The *Celestial Empire* once mentioned 120 subscribers of the *Xinbao*, which seems low given the fact that the paper was able to survive six years.[223]

NEWSPAPER	PRICE	ADVERTISEMENT PRICES	NUMBER OF ADS	INCOME PER DAY	CIRCULATION
Shenbao	8 *wen* (= 2,5$/year)	50 字 = 1$, +1 cent ad	19	30 $/day = 11,000$/year	8–10,000
Xunhuan	5$ year (= 16 *wen*/day)	100 字 = 1$; + ½ cent ad	15	19$/week 1000$/year	700–1000
Huibao	10 *wen* (= 3$/year)[226]	10 字 = 50 *wen*	31	11$/day 4000$/year	?
Yibao	10 *wen* (= 3 $/year)	1 字 = 5 *wen*	17	8,5 $/day 3000$/year	?
Xinbao	10 *wen*	10 字 = 50 *wen*	27	16 $/day 6000$/year	(120)

The routine of monthly payments for newspaper subscriptions was not easily introduced in either Shanghai or Hong Kong, and the *Shenbao* as well as the *Xunhuan Ribao* frequently had to exhort their readers and threaten them with cutting off delivery.[224] To ward off fake collectors, the *Xinbao* additionally admonished its readers only to pay boys provided with a certificate from the publishing house.[225]

Comparing income from advertisements and sales to expenses in the table, it is easily seen that the *Xunhuan Ribao* income could barely sustain the enterprise. The editors' wages alone—between 10 and 50 yuan per head and month—amounted to about $2300.[227] For a rough calculation of the expenses for printing, archival material on the LMS Printing House is of help. In 1872, Eitel calculated about $1100 per year for wages in the printing house. This included one print shop master, one assistant, two compositors, and two apprentices.[228] With a compositor composing about 4000 characters per day and the paper consisting of about 18,000 characters, the *Xunhuan ribao* alone must have needed four to five compositors.[229] Eitel's sum of $1100 is certainly at the low end.

The second largest cost factor was paper. Eitel calculated $1080/year for paper for his print shop; the *Yuebao* $1100/year for paper and ink.[230] The *Xunhuan Ribao* was larger than the *Yuebao* and printed its main edition on imported paper. A minor edition containing market news was printed on much cheaper Chinese (*Nanshanbei* 南山貝) paper. It is highly probable that the *Xunhuan Ribao*'s combined income of $6000 plus income from font, book, and chemical sales was unable to cover the costs once rent, capital amortization, and write-offs for machinery are included. It is thus very likely that the *Xunhuan Ribao* had been continuously subsidized to a modest degree by wealthy Hong Kong merchants. This did not prevent the *Xunhuan Ribao* from developing strategies to outdo its rivals, and to establish the newspaper as advertisement media on the Hong Kong market. During the first three weeks, the paper was delivered for free, and lower prices for advertising were offered.[231] Chinese merchants were encouraged to post the paper or ads for the *Xunhuan Ribao* in their shops. Advertisement customers of other papers were invited to switch to the *Xunhuan Ribao*, with lower prices guaranteed.[232] In addition, the paper developed a professional journalistic style in tune with the requirements of a modernizing merchant society: promptitude, punctuality, reliability, calculability, and precision. It was repeatedly emphasized that the paper would come out on time. Advance notice was given if the paper would not appear on a given holiday.[233] For the publication of certain very important news, special issues in smaller format were promised.[234] Corrections of mistakes were a regular feature, with a special column called "correction" (*jiaozheng* 校正).[235] All these measures directly spoke to a merchant readership and met the requirements of a capitalist business culture.

In a similar manner, the *Shenbao* developed its own and very effective strategies to broaden its readership. Apart from quickly building up a national distribution network, it kept the focus on making the paper culturally acceptable among members of the Jiangnan elite.[236] It regularly published their poetry, including the very popular bamboo twig-ballads (*zhuzhici* 竹枝詞),[237] organized literary competitions, and rushed to be the first in publishing the lists of successful candidates of the state examinations, with dramatic peaks in sales on such days as a result.[238] It advertised that it would publish interesting poems and literary pieces without charge.[239] For Shanghai literati, this offer was very attractive. The paper provided a free medium for a quick and wide distribution of their work and an avenue to literary fame and social status, even to newcomers. Even the literary flavor given to the titles of certain news items was intended to appeal to literati taste.[240]

In addition, the *Shenbao* would occasionally insert entertaining miraculous stories. While this has been attributed to the first editors' lack of experience,[241] and was criticized at the time by Westerners for stimulating superstition, Major responded that his readers were quite aware of the nature of these stories and as the Westerners also believed very strange and superstitious stories (in the Bible), they lacked the authority to judge the case.[242]

The *Xunhuan Ribao* also carried such stories, but they all appeared in the column "News from Canton" (*Yangcheng xinwen*), and were strictly separated from the "News from China and Abroad." Their content took after the romances of the "Scholar and Beauty" genre or depicted the literati milieu in an often humorous and satirical tone close to the novel *The Scholars* (*Rulin waishi* 儒林外史). A bunch of roaming scholars discovers a "butcher capable of writing poetry;"[243] a magistrate's son is caught at a presumably secret rendezvous with his neighbour's concubine, which turns out to have been a well-planned trap;[244] a courtesan manages to uphold virtue; and an evil landlord cheats peasants by relying on their superstition and credulity. However

entertaining these stories might be, they all end with the exclamation mark
of a moral exhortation:

> Those nowadays in high ranks and important positions only enjoy filling
> their stomachs and enriching their families. How would they still remember
> the fragrance of books and scrolls, and the friendship of the days when they
> had still lived in humble circumstances? They live in a dream day by day and
> no one knows when they will ever awake! What a shame!"[245]

Thus, instead of belittling these stories as the helpless beginnings of news
reporting, they have to be seen as literary and moral helpings for a merchant
readership in Hong Kong that liked to present itself in the gear of traditional
literati. The mere selection of such stories for publication on a news page
indicates that the editors earnestly strove for public acknowledgment of their
moral responsibility in issuing the paper.

To attract literati readers, the *Yibao* took an idea from Western papers
and offered prizes for the solution of word puzzles based on extremely short
quotations from the classics, which the literati knew by heart.[246] Readers also
were encouraged to send in their own puzzles. The promised prizes, however,
never seemed to have materialized. The *Celestial Empire* reported with glee
that the participants realized this and "on Thursday it ended in a *fracas;* during
which, if we are rightly informed, the editor was hauled from his sanctum to
the streets by his queue."[247]

All papers printed parts or all of the *Peking Gazette* at the beginning or
end of each issue. As the court regulations for the *Peking Gazette* required the
full and unabridged publication of all the edicts and memorials made public,[248] a random selection—such as the "Selections from the *Peking Gazette*" in
the *Xunhuan Ribao*—was an option only in the crown colony while the *Shenbao, Huibao* and *Yibao* in the Shanghai settlements published the *Gazette* "in
full" as *Jingbao quanlu* 京報全錄.

The placement of the *Peking Gazette* in these papers was neither an innocent nor an undisputed issue. The *Shenbao* was criticized for lack of respect when
squeezing the *Peking Gazette* between its own reports and the advertisements.
In its defense, it lamely argued that it had done so to avoid confusion of *Shenbao*—"news from Shen" (= Shanghai)—and "news from Beijing" (*Jingbao*).[249]
The *Yibao* continued to trounce the *Shenbao* as an immoral and traitorous paper;
immoral because it printed the imperial edicts right after the section with lasciv-
ious poems about courtesans and sing-song girls; traitorous because it reprinted
news and editorials of the *Xunhuan Ribao*, which was edited by the traitor Wang
Tao.[250] It also reproached the *Shenbao* for falsifying imperial edicts.[251] The
problem of typesetting errors—which frequently occur in any newspaper—was
intensified with the introduction of the telegraph and the ensuing decoding
problems. When the *Shenbao* published the first "telegraphically transmitted
edict" (*dianzhuan shangyu* 電傳上諭) on Jan. 16, 1882, Yuan Zuzhi of the *Xinbao*
chastized it for recklessly risking to have mistakes in the reproduction of the

imperial edicts.[252] To which the *Shenbao* replied that any delay in the publication of such important matter as imperial edicts had to be avoided.[253]

While the semiofficial papers printed the *Peking Gazette* at the beginning, they also tried to avoid becoming too officious by treating them, much like the other papers, as "news," occasionally even adding a header to a *Peking Gazette* item. Apart from the *Peking Gazette,* most papers also included official proclamations from the provincial Yamen, the *Yuanmenchao* (袁門鈔), or from the Taotai. In general, the semiofficial papers printed such extracts much more regularly and in more detail, thus emphasizing the importance of local news from official circles.

SELF-REPRESENTATION OF THE NEWSPAPERS

Apart from securing the financial viability and appealing content of their papers, editors were confronted with the more basic need to convince the readers of the necessity, advantages, and acceptability of the new medium and even get some of them to become contributors as news services and correspondent networks were still lacking. While the rapid growth of the *Shenbao*'s circulation may suggest that this process went smoothly, many conflicts suggest a rather dramatic dimension in this familiarization process. A few months after the founding of the *Shenbao,* Major asked for Consul Alabaster's intervention—apparently because the paper had criticized a certain family of the Chinese city of Shanghai, one of Major's typesetters had been beaten up on his way to the office and had then been taken to the magistrate's court on some trumped-up charge.[254]

For papers like the *Xunhuan Ribao,* there was no need for ideological justification before its merchant readership. While a purely professional and economic argumentation was acceptable in these circles, the paper met harsh criticism from the traditional Confucian spectrum, which perceived it as a challenge. In editorials that took the form of fictitious dialogues, these opponent were named clearly: they were the narrow-minded *Ru* scholars, ignorant of the needs of the time. "If they see someone discussing current affairs, they call him big-mouthed and impertinent. If they see someone commenting on foreign affairs, they call him seduced by the foreigners."[255]

To justify their new public role of disseminating useful information and communicating opinion, Chinese journalists of the late nineteenth century had recourse to the traditional political ideal of an easy flow of communication between high and low, and to the idealized institution of the censorate with its duty to criticize abuses of power. The *Peking Gazette* with its history of many centuries provided a positive or negative backdrop. On the side of the readers there were long-established practices of exchanging personal views on public issues in letters or expressing aesthetic comments in literary societies.

Both the *Shenbao* and the *Xunhuan Ribao* made sure to insert the new form of the newspaper into this idealized Chinese framework[256] by emphasizing that the function of the newspapers (*xinbao*) was to "bring high and low into communication" (*tong shangxia* 通上下)—that is, to inform the government about the situation and grievances of the people, and the people about affairs of the state.[257] They appealed to a shared understanding that the flow of information between high and low and remonstrance with the emperor were necessary to uphold a rightful government, and that the government in turn had to keep "open the avenues of expression" (*kai yanlu* 開言路).[258] Comparing themselves to Confucius, the editors expressed their loyalty to the government, but at the same time claimed for themselves the heritage of Confucius's obligation to notify the government about criticism among the people.[259] "The first rule of a newspaper is to respect the ruler. But to respect the king does not mean only to praise [his] success and virtue."[260]

At stake was the legitimacy to speak on state matters. To their opponents, the journalists' public expression of personal opinions on state affairs and even their collection of information from and about the people fundamentally challenged the authority of the court and the *Ru* as well as the principle of hierarchical communication. Quite in contrast to the actual content of his paper, Wang Tao defended himself in one *Xunhuan Ribao* editorial with the claim that he was quite able to handle the classical texts in the orthodox way, "taking the precedent from the past as evidence for the present" (*yuan gu zheng jin* 援古證今).[261]

Editors also met criticism for not being responsible enough in the fulfillment of their programmatic statements about the need to be outspoken in news reporting. Wang Tao's "guest" argues: "When writing on current events you have many scruples, when reporting on someone's evil actions you leave out the name. Are you not in this way violating the principle of truthfulness?" Wang Tao in his response goes so far as to belittle the significance of his articles, claiming that any mistake should be ignored, rebutted, or contested by similar projects from other scholars.[262] Moreover, all articles reflect individual opinions, which the guest, the reader, or the authorities are free to accept or reject.[263] But it was as impertinent to encourage the readers and authorities to select, form their own opinions, and even respond by setting up papers of their own. Ironically enough, if the Confucian opponents were to meet the challenge and issue their own pamphlets or newspapers, they would undermine their own clamor for more centralized authority. Thus, the medium newspaper not only disseminated—it was, in a sense, the message.

The *Shenbao* even went a step further. It also constantly quoted historical examples of successful or unsuccessful court policies. In emphasizing the moral and political standards of China's past, these editorials marked their neglect in the present by the Qing government and implicitly demanded a new and challenging position for the newspapers in the structure of political communication. They were to take over functions the government was not able to fill anymore, and to offer a public platform for the discussion of issues of national concern.

According to the *Shenbao*, the new Tang dynasty practice to keep military orders and edicts secret marked an important turning point in the communication between high and low. The official in charge would not even dare to talk to his colleagues about them or ask questions. The editorial continued, "the secretaries of the Great Council of today are like this scholar of the Tang."[264] The reference is to the system of secret memorials introduced by the Yongzheng emperor and not restricted to military matters. Qing officials were not allowed to communicate horizontally with each other, and even much "of the communication between magistrates and superiors was conducted through confidential documents"[265] sent to the court. Lack of transparency in governmental affairs and the consequent expansion of corruption were thus frequently mentioned as a sign of crisis.

A major obstacle for the papers was the uncooperative attitude of local officials. According to the *Shenbao*, they were mostly interested in closing down the newspapers, and prohibiting public discussions.[266] They branded the publication of items that the officials meant to keep secret as "libel" (*huibang* 毀謗) or "spreading rumors" (*zhuanwen* 傳聞). Conflicts with local officials mostly arose when the *Shenbao* published details on judicial questions or law cases, such as the cases of Yang Yuelou or Yang Naiwu (楊乃武, 1840/1841–1914).[267] The *Shenbao* argued that rumors only emerged if the practice of law and government was not transparent enough.[268] Again with reference to ancient times, the paper points out that the Chinese officials always had been reluctant to discuss in public those issues as yet undecided because they feared disturbance and chaos among the people.[269] If, however, the officials would publish the controversies as well as results of law cases to the "outsiders" (*wairen* 外人), people would not have to depend on private information any longer.[270]

In the European tradition, the notion of a public sphere (Öffentlichkeit) evolved from the legal sphere with the meaning of a guarantor of the adherence to legal standards and norms of procedure. Public activity was equaled to moral uprighteousness and legitimacy, and perceived as an opposite to secret and concealed actions.[271] In a similar way, the *Shenbao* saw the dichotomy of "the public" and "the private" as that between "public" and "secret." As the late Qing government tried to keep government affairs secret, the creation of rumors could be expected. Outsiders are those without access to esoteric forms of communication prevailing among the elite and exclusive official circles. The *Shenbao* thus attempted to open the narrow channels of communication and take over the task of informing the people about the government, and the government about the people. Studies on the politics of rumors in nineteenth-century Europe show that rumors emerge as a "black market of informations" in times when repressive conditions block the usual legal avenues of criticism via petitions, reclamations, and so forth, and when a public desires to understand but does not receive the information.[272] The *Shenbao* made efforts to verify its reports, but as rumors only emerged when the government failed to inform the people about its actions, the publication of things talked about "in the lanes and narrow alleys" was legitimate as long as they represented widely held opinions.[273]

The only programmatic item in the semiofficial papers appeared in the first issues of the *Huibao*. It emphasized that the paper's name—*Huibao* meaning "report on collected [news]"—was carefully chosen: it would just gather news and publish them, but would not be so presumptuous as to edit and comment in editorials.[274]

Before the first *Huibao* had come out, the *Shenbao* revealed that "they [the Xiangshan sojourners in Shanghai, N.V.] wish to set up an official paper in order to annihilate non-official ["commoners'"] papers is tantamount to sealing the mouths of the multitude so as to impose their own views." (*yu she guanbao yi mie minbao yi ru sai zhongkou er shicheng ji zhi* 欲設官報以滅民報亦如塞眾口而視逞己志). The *Shenbao* regarded the new medium mainly as a concealed official organ, not as the medium of a Shanghai interest group, which would have been an option since it was managed by representatives of the Xiangshan guild. Because Magistrate Ye had originally intended to name the paper *gongbao* (公報), the *Shenbao* asked what public interest (*gong* 公) a paper could represent that owed its existence to a controversial readers' debate.[275] Still, when the *Huibao* came out on June 16, 1874,[276] the *Shenbao* wrote a warm welcome, but it soon described it as an "official organ" that was unable to represent public opinion, but had as its only purpose to destroy the *Shenbao*. In contrast, the *Shenbao* presented itself as the newspaper of the people, a paper that welcomed every new enterprise so long as an equal exchange of views was possible.

In numerous articles, the *Shenbao* explained its own editorial policy and attacked the *Huibao* for not abiding by professional standards: criticism and polemics between newspapers were welcome and necessary, but the *Huibao*'s attacking a colleague by name was inappropriate;[277] the *Huibao* wantonly printed unfounded rumors with the result that innocent people were being punished; because of the improper conduct of the *Huibao* reporter in the Mixed Court, the magistrate barred all journalists from attending. Although this last item was interesting news, the *Shenbao* declared it had withheld it in order to protect the *Huibao* colleague. Newspapers were of great importance, and thus had a heavy responsibility. It was necessary to cooperate in making the newspaper business more prosperous.[278] Time and again, the *Shenbao* insisted even in the most adverse articles on the advantages of having many papers coexist, even if this meant competition; this seems to have been an article of faith.[279]

After the reorganization of the *Huibao* in September 1874, the polemics became fierce. Still, while the arguments, for example, about the introduction of railways in China were controversial, they were not entirely unreasonable. With the next reorganization and the beginning of the *Yibao*, a new editor took over: Zhu Liansheng, a man characterized as rather foolish and incompetent. The *Shenbao* went so far as to publish a seemingly innocuous news story "Swine Serially Farrowing" (豬連生 *zhu liansheng*) that was a pun on Zhu Liansheng's name and the rapid sequence of the birth of the papers *Huibao*, *Huibao*, and *Yibao*. An editorial dealt extensively with the barking of dogs— the *Huibao* had claimed that the *Shenbao* editorials were nothing better. In the view of the *Shenbao*, the *Yibao* now made it a principle to contradict the *Shenbao*, claiming that "everything the *Shenbao* says is false; everything the *Yibao* says is true." The *Yibao* reduced itself to spreading slanders, which were as annoying for the *Shenbao* reporters as for the *Yibao* readers.[280] It personally slandered Qian Xinbo, one of the *Shenbao* editors.[281] In reply to these affronts by the *Yibao*, which it felt threatened the credibility of the press at large, the *Shenbao* came out with programmatic statements on the need of mutual help, mutual protection, information exchange, and solidarity among journalists and publishing houses in China. Although they have never been dealt with in Chinese historical accounts, these statements were the first to develop the contours of a professional ethics code for Chinese journalists.

The focus of the *Xinbao* was on news from Beijing, from official circles, and on commercial matters. It promised: "no personal attacks arising from jealousy or ill-will shall be inserted."[282] According to Ma Guangren, the paper made it clear and public that neither discussion of governmental politics were to be printed nor supernatural and strange stories or societal news.[283]

The article "The Origin of Newspapers" in the second issue of the *Xinbao* was in a way a reply to "The Origin of the Newspaper" that the *Shenbao* had published in its fourth issue in 1872. The tension of "private" and "secret" versus "public" and "transparent" surfaced as well, but it was handled in quite a different way:

> As is known, the word "newspaper" [*bao*] means "*bai*," to speak. They take the contents of what is publicly divulged, *paobai*, and make it known in the empire. When the people of old were managing government affairs, there was no privately holding back. Every single action of every single [local] government office was altogether permitted to be divulged among the [local] people, and how could it then be that the great orders from the principal government center would not be made known in the entire empire in the utmost public manner?[284]

Informing the public is necessary, but communication here is a one-way street from above to below. Information is neither gained nor disseminated by outsiders—such as the *Shenbao*. An insider elite is instructing and informing outsiders. The paper's duty is to publish government documents and address the public. An articulation of public opinion not filtered by official institutions was not part of this program. The principle stated by the *Shenbao*, not to be partial (*bu piantan* 不偏袒) in reporting,[285] which meant to allow free discussion without interference by the editors, was taken up here with a quotation from the *Great Plan* of the *Shangshu* (尚書) as "not to be partial or factional" (*wu pian wu dang* 無偏無黨), but filled with another meaning: "'Without deflection, without partiality, broad and long is the Royal Path. Without partiality, without deflection, the Royal Path is level and easy.'[286] What our paper estimates highly is to expel the false [empty] and honor the true [full], to hide the bad and praise the good, and in this way to protect throughout justice and peace" (*yishou fu zhongzheng heping ye* 一守夫中正和平也).[287] The *Xinbao* thus advocated a selective, moralistic, and homogenous press. It presented itself as an elite paper largely serving its own purposes. It redefined the changing social world of the commercially exploding city in traditional terms of the kingly way, and addressed the new merchant community as new and potent actors in this world.

CONCLUSION

Most of the pioneers of Chinese journalism come from a similar background. Regardless of their affiliations with specific papers, they were well acquainted with each other. They pursued the same objectives to disseminate new and useful knowledge, but employed different strategies of communicating them to a new public. Different strategies evolved from different external circumstances, diverging readerships, and cultural habits, but they also involved a different assessment of the value of symbolic and financial capital.

In each of the three cases, the core group shared particular features. The Shenbao company assembled both former officials and young *xiucai* literati from Jiangnan who had failed in the higher civil service examinations. Like many others, they had been eager to leave behind the devastations of the Taiping rebellion and had been attracted by the new options offered by Shanghai. The newly emerging activism of local elites—an outcome of the Taiping rebellion as has been observed by Mary C. Wright,[288]—seems to have been motivated by the conviction that more could be accomplished outside the bureaucracy and through individual engagement in welfare and education than through government channels.[289] A starting point for such a career certainly was Shanghai.

While Hong Kong, too, received many Taiping refugees from the Pearl River Delta, they were not among the founders of the *Xunhuan Ribao*. Instead, it was the product of the joint efforts by a group of prominent merchant leaders of the Chinese community in Hong Kong who were striving for a stronger and institutionally secure influence on the colony's politics. As Rowe observed for the trade city of Hankow, wealth as a determinant of social rank was increasingly gaining importance in the trade ports.[290] In Hong Kong, this process was advanced enough to provide the necessary legitimacy for merchants—and for intellectuals associated with their enterprise—to operate in the public sphere as spokesmen for society. These merchants and Western-trained intellectuals set up welfare organizations such as the Tung Wah Hospital in seemingly traditional manner, but soon converted them into political institutions representing a broad spectrum of the Chinese elite in Hong Kong. In Shanghai, no such institution developed that could—if informally—represent the Chinese inhabitants, even though the *Shenbao* advocated its establishment with direct reference to the Tung Wah Hospital.[291]

The career paths of the Hong Kong and Shanghai journalists differed greatly. While most of the *Shenbao* editors remained in their profession, the Hong Kong journalists often switched to different—and usually much more prominent and profitable—ways of making a living. This might be explained by the different social composition prevailing in the two ports. The Shanghai literati elite was continuously replenished from Jiangnan and it soon was culturally and socially settled and accepted, while Hong Kong was never able to build up such a rich stratum of intellectuals. The appreciation of learning and scholarship was still prevalent enough in Shanghai to enable a man like Cai Erkang to print name cards documenting his unsteady life, rather than simulating some official career. While cultural capital continued to count in Shanghai, wealth became more and more the only standard in Hong Kong.

The journalists in the semiofficial papers in Shanghai were mostly linked by their common Cantonese origin. The local guilds and native associations no doubt played an important role in the formation of local identity and sense of community.[292] However, these papers apparently never became expressions of Cantonese interests in Shanghai, but were in the main an effort of Shanghai officials to counter the *Shenbao* short of closing it down or seeing it burn down.[293] The Cantonese were the most important and wealthy merchant group in Shanghai; the founder of the paper, Tang Jingxing, headed the prestigious China Steam Navigation Co. The *Xinbao* was promoted by the same circles in Shanghai; many of them had a connection to the Shanghai Arsenal and through it to Western machinery. Many of the cofounders of the *Huibao* shared the educational background of the *Xunhuan Ribao* founders, and were sometimes even known to them from their schooldays in missionary institutions in Hong Kong. Although these papers seem so different at first sight, they found a common interest in Western learning and new things in general as evident in later publications, which they sometimes even jointly authored. All this makes them appear as a rather homogenous group of new and open-minded men attempting to join the discussion about China's future through the new medium of newspapers.

In view of their educational and professional background as well as their later careers, it seems obvious to me that the later statements about the warped career paths and low social prestige of the first journalists, which have been taken at face value by modern Chinese scholars, have to be understood as polemics. Following the general May 4 routine, the journalists of the younger generation of the 1920s and 1930s dissociated themselves from their forebears whom they described as hemmed in by feudal thinking. The historical record, however, fails to come up—within these still undefined circles of first journalists—with the young adventurers who had failed their exams, or the corrupt and uneducated scribblers with no other way out. Instead, these early journalists were certainly well educated, and were among the most concerned, informed, daring, visible, and successful Chinese men of middle age in the late nineteenth century; among them were successful entrepreneurs, retired officials, and well-known popular writers. They all were looking for ways of pushing China into a new direction, with the newspaper (sometimes) being but one of them.

The multilayered networks and connections between these social actors were the basis for the transnational orientation of all the papers. A newspaper is, however, foremost a commercial enterprise; it attempts to sell texts on a daily basis, and marks, as Benedict Anderson has put it, the beginning of a print capitalism implying the conception of texts as goods for consumption whose ephemeral character is well calculated.[294] The papers therefore had to develop strategies to make their paper sell, and to establish a position on the new print market. Thus, the transnational character of the papers was matched by a simultaneous self-presentation as "purely Chinese" with an emphasis on patriotic commitment. This claim—made by Chinese-owned papers as well as by those under foreign ownership—has to be understood as a marketing label. That representing the national interest had become a sales pitch does not, however, mean that newspapers developed antiforeign attitudes.

These common features notwithstanding, each paper developed distinct characteristics fitting the perceived interests of its implied addressees. The *Xunhuan Ribao*'s main addressee was the merchant community in Hong Kong; its main focus, accordingly, was on Hong Kong and Macao, along with the Chinese communities abroad. For a Chinese paper located on the southern edge of the empire, the notion of being but one part of a much larger world was perhaps easier to develop. In view of the Western education and experiences of its journalists as well as their economic links with the Western community,[295] it is not too surprising that their paper would be most similar to Western papers in format and content. The presence of *Peking Gazette* excerpts and entertaining moralistic stories shows that their interests went beyond merely commercial issues and were also directed toward imperial China. Wang Tao's role as an editor of this paper remains ambiguous. While mainly serving a merchant community in theory, the paper nevertheless emphasized traditional Confucian obligations and responsibilities in its editorials, well in tune with fashion among the merchants to present themselves in literati and official guise. As an alleged traitor and political refugee, Wang Tao lacked the authority to assume quasi-official functions of public remonstrance in the Qing context. He thus had to emphasize his scholarly upbringing and Confucian values to legitimate his speaking out in public; the institutional and social environment of Hong Kong was instrumental in enabling him to assume his new role: as a member of a new representative organ he suddenly had regained a social status that provided him with enough authority to self-confidently raise his voice against the blind traditional scholars again. It should be kept in mind, however, that

Wang Tao nevertheless constantly petitioned for his return to Shanghai, which he in fact secured in the early 1880s.

The *Xunhuan Ribao* had an audience already used to Western-style papers. The commercial background of its founders and supporters notwithstanding, the paper itself never mentioned that it was there for profit, and, according to my calculation, it did not break even during the first years. Its ongoing existence thus meant ongoing subsidy. It must therefore be seen as the endeavor of an increasingly self-confident social stratum willing to support and subsidize this paper as a medium expressing their growing importance in Hong Kong society. As far as we can judge from the few issues left from the first years of the paper's existence, this voice is, however, not too frequently raised in order to articulate specific public criticism of officials. The editorials of the *Xunhuan Ribao* mostly retain a reformist tone explaining general issues of importance for strengthening the nation and enriching the country; the short stories in the local news section retain a standard moralistic bent in admonishing officials to be virtuous and good to the people. In terms of rhetorical pose, the editor is talking down to the readers, and the main function of the paper lies in informing the people, the merchants, and the British and Chinese officials.

In presenting itself as a "patriotic" paper with the objective interests of China and loyalty to the emperor at heart, Ernest Major's *Shenbao* went much further than the *Xunhuan Ribao*. It promoted Chinese interests in commercial and financial affairs, and charged foreigners higher prices for advertisements; it criticized actions by missionaries and British merchants, and annoyed its British contemporaries with supernatural and highly imaginative reports, an anathema to a "rational" press. Still, its reports, combined with its wide circulation, proved a constant irritant to Chinese authorities. The *Shenbao* reading of loyalty to the emperor included—well in tune with traditional Chinese concepts—open remonstrance, and its reading of the communication between high and low included—perhaps closer to the European tradition—the demand of transparency of governmental actions.

The *Shenbao* had no qualms in pointing out the governmental institutions that were defunct at present and had to be substituted by institutions such as the press and highlighting the pervasive official corruption and nepotism that hindered lawful procedures. Against this background, it explained the necessity of its own existence and the legitimacy of its activities. One of the paper's most important convictions, expressed in its editorials as well as in practical implementation, was the need for open articulation of divergent opinions. The *Shenbao* itself provided such a forum to its readers, but it also proclaimed an unconditional acceptance of other papers so long as they were adhering to the principles of fair, rational, and lawful discussion. The public and published debates and disputes were—at least theoretically—supposed to be conducted by all social strata of society, the literati, merchants, craftsmen, peasants—and even women. The features of the paper that made it most successful in terms of sales figures, however, were all directed toward an educated elite readership with its interest in government and world affairs, literature, and poetry; those outside the official class were lacking an institutional channel and public medium to articulate and test their opinions. The paper offered the opportunity and medium to make their voices heard—and eliminated the hitherto strictly hierarchical structures of such a communication. In contrast to the *Xunhuan Ribao*, which rather provided a medium for articulating opinions, the *Shenbao* emphasized debate and communication with its readers, whether literati, merchants, or officials. While the *Peking Gazette* was inserted without any negotiations with the central government, the local Chinese authorities of Shanghai ended up using the *Shenbao's* pages, too, to disseminate their opinions, proclamations, and decisions. Through the medium in which they appear, these public statements and proclamations by the authorities became objects of public discussion and could be criticized by any reader in the next issue. With its rapid rise of circulation and advertisement income, the *Shenbao* quickly became a profitable enterprise. Its competitor, the *Shanghai Xinbao*, folded in less than one year, although this had probably not been *Shenbao's* intention. The paper's financial independence was reflected in its content. Although advertisements from foreign companies were its main source of income, it felt free to criticize their practices or to defend the Chinese position in disputed issues. The *Shenbao's* commercial success, impressive as it was, does not seem sufficient reason to explain Major's continued engagement. There were certainly other promising ventures open to this already very successful merchant in Shanghai, ventures that would have spared him many of the troubles he predictably was to have with Chinese as well as British authorities.

Because models are never as strictly followed as the sketching of an ideal image would suggest, we can thus observe an ironic intertwinement: The *Xunhuan Ribao* came out as a truly Western-style paper in terms of design and formal programmatic policy, but maintained an editorial policy that ended up (though perhaps not intentionally) excluding discussions and critical debates among the readership. The *Shenbao* kept to more traditional forms in its design and its strategies in soliciting readership, but in its actual work did much more to implement the demands of a liberally inspired press by allowing comparatively free and unlimited discussion on its pages. In the same ironic vein, the *Xunhuan Ribao*, as a paper that emerged from and was strongly supported by financial circles in Hong Kong, is emphasizing its social responsibility and duties in Confucian literati terms. The *Shenbao*, quite to the contrary, with a number of Jiangnan literati among its editors, has no qualms in emphasizing the commercial character of the paper and bluntly stating that its main purpose was to make profits.

The short-lived semiofficial papers in Shanghai also carried a strong ingredient of international news and foreign affairs, although their news section concentrated on imperial China, most clearly through the prominently displayed *Peking Gazette* and *Provincial Gazette*. It directly addressed foreign readers in their own tongue with news about the imperial government of China, and had a sizable segment of translation of international news. The emphasis on informing rather than articulating opinions and participating in public debate was programmatically expressed in the self-description of the *Huibao* and led to their exclusion of public debates on their pages. While the *Huibao* did accept as a principle of Chinese antiquity the importance of government transparency, it preferred informing the people about the government's decisions rather than informing the government about the people's criticisms. Yet, while the *Peking Gazette* never contained a text dealing with its own role and function, the programmatic statements of these new semiofficial papers and their private initiative reveal a beginning awareness of the importance of the modern newspaper as well as a reflection about the proper role of this new medium in Chinese political culture. Even if these semiofficial papers never made much headway, they attest to the acknowledgment of the potential power of the press. For them, the difference between a newspaper and the *Peking Gazette* was more one of the technology used. They were proposing to employ this new machinery to propagate traditional virtue and moral uprightness. They had perhaps not anticipated the conceptual changes necessary once they entered a market situation.

At first sight, the design or commercial strategies of these papers did not differ much from those of the *Shenbao* and *Xunhuan Ribao*. From the outset—with the exception of the *Yibao*—they managed to solicit enough advertisers to make their business pay, which shows that they had found a market in the Shanghai community.

The most important innovation of the semiofficial papers is in their readership. While the *Peking Gazette* mostly circulated among officials, the new semi-official papers explicitly addressed the merchants as their potential readers, an open acknowledgment of the growing importance of this social stratum. Moreover, they also sought to reach the foreigners as part of their readership. This is especially clear in the case of the *Xinbao* and its inserted English translations of certain "important" articles. Still, these papers were not able to raise their initial capital from the merchants as had been intended, but depended on official coffers. The push for this paper was not coming from the merchants, but rather from officials with a strong regional link. Instead of the merchants clamoring for a forum to make their voice heard, the officials prodded them to contribute; and instead of expressing contempt for the merchant class in a conventional manner, these new businessmen are now invited to join in the discourse on ideological matters and national affairs.

The semiofficial papers in a way mark the beginning acceptance of a multivoiced public. While this acceptance might have been prompted more by treaty port conditions than by genuine appreciation, the result was a willingness to participate in the struggle for an authoritative voice in the urban public, rather than insistence on the traditional communication hierarchy.

NOTES

1. Jürgen Habermas, [1967], *Strukturwandel der Öffentlichkeit*, Frankfurt a.M.: Suhrkamp tb, 1990.

2. E.g., Howard M. Vollmer and Donald M. Mills, *Professionalization*, Englewood Cliffs: Prentice Hall, 1966.

3. Pierre Bourdieu, *Les règles de l'art: Genèse et structure du champ littéraire*, Paris: Seuil, 1992.

4. The best study on Wang Tao still is Paul Cohen, *Between Tradition and Modernity: Wang T'ao and Reform in Late Ch'ing China*, Cambridge: Harvard University Press, 1987; see also Henry Mc Aleavy, *Wang T'ao. The Life and Times of a Displaced Person*, London, The China Society, 1953; Lee Chi-fang, *Wang T'ao (1828–1897): His Life, His Thought, Scholarship and Literary Achievement*, unpubl. Ph.D. dissertation, University of Wisconsin, 1973; Zhang Hailin, *Wang Tao pingzhuan*, Nanjing: Nanjing daxue chubanshe, 1993. On Wang Tao's activities in Hong Kong, see Lam Kai Yin and Wong Man Kong, eds., *Wang Tao yu jindai shijie*, Hong Kong: Xianggang jiaoyu tushu gongsi, 2000.

5. Given that quite some time time has passed since the original writing of this chapter, I must apologize for not having been able to integrate recent important publications in Chinese and Western languages.

6. Ge Gongzhen, [1928], *Zhongguo baoxue shi*, Shanghai: Shangwu yinshuguan, reprint: *Minguo congshu*, Ser. II, Shanghai: Shanghai Shudian, 1990, vol. 49, p. 79; Fang Hanqi, *Zhongguo xinwen shiye tongshi*, Beijing: Zhongguo Renmin daxue chubanshe, 1992, pp. 322–324. Both list *Shenbao* under "foreign" newspapers, attaching primary importance to ownership rather than language, content, and readership.

7. Xu Peiting, *Zhongguo xinwen chuanbo shi*, Chongqing: Chongqing chubanshe, 1994; Hu Taichun, *Zhongguo jindai xinwen sixiang shi*, Taiyuan: Shanxi jiaoyu chubanshe, 1987.

8. Fang Hanqi, *Xinwen shiye*, p. 536.

9. Lin Yutang, *A History of the Press and Public Opinion in China*, Shanghai, Hong Kong and Singapore: Kelly & Walsh, 1934, p. 79.

10. Roswell Britton, *The Chinese Periodical Press, 1800–1912* [1933]. Reprint, Taipei: Chengwen, 1966, p. 86.

11. Zeng Xubai, *Zhongguo xinwen shi*, vol. I, Taibei: Taiwan shangwu yinshuguan, 1966, p. 196. Lee Chi-fang, "Wang T'ao and His Literary Writings," *Tamkang Review*, vol. XI, no 3 (1981, Spring), pp. 267–285; Fang Hanqi, *Xinwen shiye*, pp. 472–474; Zhuo Nansheng, "Zhongguoren ziban chenggong de zui zao Huawen ribao 'Xunhuan Ribao,'" *Xinwenxue yanjiu*, (Taibei), 48.1994.1, pp. 259–279; Liu Jialin, *Zhongguo xinwen shi*, Wuhan: Wuhan daxue chubanshe, 1995, 2 vols., vol. I, pp. 127–129. This periodization also structures another extensive study on Chinese journalism, which starts with a chapter on the Western missionaries, followed by one on Wang Tao, and a third on Liang Qichao. Lai Guangling, *Zhongguo jindai baoren yu baoye*, Taibei: Taiwan shangwu yinshuguan, 1987, 2 vols.

12. Ge Gongzhen, *Baoxue shi*, pp. 122ff., has eight lines on these four papers. See also Fang Hanqi, *Zhongguo jindai baokan shi*, Taiyuan: Shanxi jiaoyu chubanshe, 1991,

pp. 62–63; Fang Hanqi, *Xinwen shiye,* pp. 486ff: "Sange banbao de Shanghai Dao," in: Shanghaitong she, ed., *Shanghai yanjiu ziliao xuji* [1936]. Reprint, Shanghai: Shanghai shudian, 1984, pp. 322ff.; Zeng Xubai, *Zhongguo xinwen shi,* vol. I, p. 196. A more detailed description has only recently been given by Ma Guangren in his *Shanghai xinwen shi 1850–1949,* Shanghai: Fudan daxue chubanshe, 1996, pp. 74–81.

13. Li Siyi, "Qingmo 10 nian guanbao huodong gaimao," *Xinwen yanjiu ziliao,* no. 55 (1991), pp. 127–144. Again, Ma Guangren is the first to notice that Daotai Feng's efforts preceded these efforts by nearly twenty years. Ma Guangren, *Shanghai xinwen shi,* p. 81.

14. E.g., Andrew J. Nathan, "The Late Ch´ing Press: Role, Audience and Impact," *Zhongyang yanjiuyuan guoji hanxue huiyi lunwenji,* 3 vols., Taibei: Zhongyang yanjiuyuan, 1981, vol. III, pp. 1281—1308; esp. p. 1288. Leo Ou-fan Lee and Andrew Nathan, "The Beginnings of Mass Culture: Journalism and Fiction in the Late Ch´ing and Beyond," in David Johnson, Andrew J. Nathan, and Evelyn S. Rawski, eds., *Popular Culture in Late Imperial China,* Berkeley: University of California Press, 1985, pp. 360–395, esp. p. 363.

15. Whereas Liang uses the Western press as a negative foil to elaborate onto the journalistic standards in 1896, these negative characteristics are all transferred onto the early Chinese press from 1902 on, when Liang sketches a first "history of Chinese newspapers" in his famous article for the 100th edition of the *Qingyibao.* For a detailed discussion, see my "Unity vs. Uniformity: Liang Qichao and the Invention of a 'New Journalism' for China," *Late Imperial China* 23.1 (June 2002), 91–143.

16. Shanghai shi Songjiang xian difang shizhi bianzuan weiyuanhui, ed., *Songjiang xianzhi,* Shanghai: Shanghai renmin chubanshe, 1991, pp. 1031ff.; Lei Jin, "Shenbaoguan zhi guoqu zhuangkuang," *Zuijin zhi wushi nian: Shenbao wushi zhou jinian* [1922]. Reprint, Shanghai: Shanghai shudian, 1987. Section "Shijie xinwen shiye," p. 27b.

17. Lei Jin, "Shenbaoguan zhi guoqu zhuangkuang," p. 27a.

18. Ibid., p. 28b.

19. On this loan, see Liu Kwang-Ching and Richard J. Smith, "The Military Challenge: The North-West and the Coast," in Denis Twichett and John K. Fairbank, eds., *The Cambridge History of China: Late Ch´ing, 1800–1911,* Cambridge: Cambridge University Press, Pt. 2, 1980, pp. 238ff.

20. Yao Gonghe, *Shanghai baozhi,* Shanghai: 1928, reprinted in Yang Guanghui et al., eds., *Zhongguo jindai baokan fazhan gaikuang,* Beijing: Xinhua chubanshe, 1986, pp. 260ff. Quoted in Ge Gongzhen, *Baoxue shi,* p. 100; Hu Daojing, *Shanghai xinwen zhizhong de fazhan,* Shanghai: Shanghaitong zhiguan, 1935; Reprint: *Minguo congshu.* Ser. II, Shanghai: Shanghai shudian, 1990, vol. 49, pp. 4–5; Lin Yutang, *Press and Public Opinion,* p. 90. Also in the recollections of Bin Zhi, "Shenbao zhanggu tan, 3–4," in *Shenbaoguan guannei tongxun,* vol. 1, no. 4 (1947), p. 22. E.g., Xu Zaiping and Xu Ruifang, *Qingmo sishi nian Shenbao shiliao,* Beijing: Xinhua, 1988, pp. 14–15, have both quotations. Andrew Nathan and Joan Judge argue the same, with Nathan ("The Late Ch'ing Press," p. 1288) mainly quoting Bao Tianxiao, *Chuanyinglou huiyilu,* Taibei: Longwen chubanshe gufen youxian gongsi, 1990, pp. I-III, and Joan Judge (*Print and Politics,* pp. 15 and 34–35) referring to Nathan. Only Ma Guangren, *Shanghai xinwen shi,* p. 63, gives a new and diverging evaluation of the status and advantages of the new journalists. Yao Gonghe's comment that Zuo Zongtang's reaction tells us more about him than about the journalists has not been picked up.

21. Quoted in Zhongguo Renmin daxue xinwenxi ed., *Zhongguo jindai baokan shi cankao ziliao,* Beijing: Renmin daxue chubanshe, 1982, vol. I, p. 291. A similar attitude toward journalists may be found in nineteenth-century Germany. See Rudolf Oebsger-Roeder, *Untersuchungen über den Bildungsstand der deutschen Journalisten* (Wesen und Wirkungen der Publizistik Bd. 7), Leipzig: Marquard, 1936; R. Jacobi, *Der Journalist,* Hannover: Jänecke, 1902.

22. See Hu Daojing, "Shenbao liushiliu nian shi," in id., *Baotan yihua,* Shanghai: Shijie shuju, 1940; Qin Shaode, *Shanghai jindai baokan shi lun,* Shanghai: Fudan daxue chubanshe, 1993, pp. 23ff.

23. "Baoguan kaimu weiren Meicha shilüe," *Shenbao,* March 29, 1908, p.1.

24. The *Shenbao* house was named *Zunwenge,* "Appreciate News Pavilion." Bin Zhi in his "Shenbao zhanggu tan, 3–4," *Shenbaoguan guannei tongxun,* vol. 1, no. 4 (1947), p. 22, describes a board written in calligraphy by Wu Jutan 吳鞠譚 in the editorial office. Ernest Major used Zunwenge zhuren, "Master of the Zunwenge Studio," as signature, often juxtaposed with his seal "*meicha* [=Major]," see Wagner in this volume. Song Jun, "*Shenbao*" *de xingshuai,* Shanghai: Shanghai shehui kexueyuan chubanshe, 1996, p 21, however, assumes that *zunwenge zhuren* was the pen name of Qian Xinbo.

25. See "Law Reports," The *North China Herald,* February 18, 1875.

26. Shi He, Yao Fushen, and Ye Cuidi, eds., *Zhongguo jindai baokan minglu,* Fuzhou: Fujian renmin chubanshe, 1991, p. 368. Chen Yutang, ed., *Zhongguo jinxiandai renwu minghao da cidian,* Hangzhou: Zhejiang guji 1993, p. 394. An author of novels and essays, Zou Tao later joined the *Subao;* cf. Ma Liangchun and Li Futian, eds., *Zhongguo wenxue da cidian,* Tianjin: Tianjin renmin, 1991, p. 3072. For more details on Zou Tao, see Catherine Yeh, *Shanghai Love: Courtesans, Intellectuals, and Entertainment Culture, 1850–1910.* Seattle: University of Washington Press, 2006, pp. 190–194.

27. *Zhongguo jindai baokan minglu,* 1991, p. 368. Chen Yutang, ed., *Zhongguo jinxiandai renwu minghao da cidian,* Hangzhou: Zhejiang guji 1993, pp. 293–294. Li Shifen is said to have published poems on "Travels Afar" in the *Xunhuan Ribao.* Zhou Jiarong, "Zai Xianggang yu Wang Tao huimian—Zhong Ri liangguo minshi de fang Gang jilu," in Lam Kai Yin and Wong Man Kong, eds., *Wang Tao yu jindai shijie,* Hong Kong: Xianggang jiaoyu tushu gongsi, 2000, pp. 375–394. In 1901, Li Yuxian published the satirical magazine *Yuyanbao* (寓言報) Cf. *Jindai Shanghai da shiji,* 1989, Shanghai: Shanghai cidian chubanshe, p. 558.

28. There are, however, deviations from these accounts: a warrant of 1874 against the "Chinese writers" of the *Shenbao* office names the following four persons: Wu Tzujang, Chin tzu-cheng, Shen Tso-chun, and Chiang Tzu-chiang; FO 228/540 no 3. Enclosure 2; "Note from the Shanghai Daotai Shen to Mr Consul Medhurst," Jan. 24. 1874, pp. 135–136. Shen Yugui´s other names were: Shen Shoukang 沈壽康, Shoukang 沈壽康, Shen Zhuisou 沈贅叟, Shen Zhuiweng 沈贅翁 and Shen Jueji 沈覺齊. See Wang Kangnian, *Wang Kangnian shiyou laizha,* Shanghai: Shanghai guji chubanshe, 1986, 4 vols., p. 4066. Song Jun, "*Shenbao*" *de xingshuai,* p. 19, mentions him as Shen Dingnian 沈定年. Xu Zaiping, *Qing mo sishinian,* does not mention Shen Yugui at all. *The China Directory 1874,* Hong Kong: China Mail Office, Section "Shanghai," p. 30, lists apart from Zhang Zhixiang and Wu Zirang also Liu Hoh-pei [Liu Hebo] and Pan Yenyun. Liu Hebo accompanied Guo Songtao and Liu Xihong to England. Cf. J. D. Frodsham

(trsl. & annot.), *The First Chinese Embassy to the West: The Journals of Kuo Sung-t'ao, Liu Hsi-hung and Chang Te-yi,* Oxford: Clarendon Press, 1974, passim.

29. Xu and Xu, *Qing mo sishinian,* p. 24; Song Jun, "*Shenbao*" *de xingshuai,* p. 19.

30. Song Jun, "*Shenbao*" *de xingshuai,* p. 19. Adrian Bennett, *Missionary Journalist in China: Young Allen and his Magazines 1860–1883,* Athens, Georgia: University of Georgia Press, 1983, pp. 57–59.

31. Xiong Yuezhi, *Xixue dongjian yu wan Qing shehui,* Shanghai: Shanghai Renmin chubanshe, 1995, pp. 334ff.

32. The works mentioned in the obituary include "Fire-catastrophes" (劫火紀焚), "A title catalogue of *Dream of the Red Chamber* poems" (紅樓夢詞題名錄), "Notes of an Old Man" 齒錄, and "126 Essays" (一二六文稿)," which was not published. "Shanyin He jun Guisheng xiaozhuan," *Shenbao,* Dec. 8, 1894, p. 1.

33. Quoted without date in Xu and Xu, *Qing mo sishinian,* p. 35.

34. Again quoted without date from *Shenbao* in Xu and Xu, *Qing mo sishinian,* p. 34.

35. Sun Yusheng, *Baohai qianchen lu,* p. 25. This is a series of articles by the former editor of the *Xinwen bao* in the Shanghai *Chenbao* in early 1934 (quoted as such, e.g., in Fang Hanqi, 1992, passim). My copy has no date and location of publication.

36. *Xinwenxue da cidian,* Zhengzhou: Henan renmin chubanshe, 1993, p. 694; Xu and Xu, *Qing mo sishinian,* p. 24; Song Jun, "*Shenbao*" *de xingshuai,* p. 19.

37. Wang Tao, *Taoyuan chidu* (No place and publisher given), 1887, vol. 8, pp. 1a–2b.

38. Xunhuan Ribao ed., *Xunhuan Ribao liushi zhounian tekan,* Hong Kong, Xunhuan ribao, 1932, p. 14.

39. Sun Yusheng, *Baohai qianchen lu,* p. 25.

40. A short biography is in "Zhongguo xinwenjie mingren jieshao, (3)," *Zhongguo xinwen nianjian, 1985,* Beijing: Zhongguo xinwen chubanshe, 1985, p. 421; Song Jun, "*Shenbao*" *de xingshuai,* p. 20.

41. "Gaofeng chaoyi dafu yuntong xian Zhili zhou zhizhou yong Hubei ji bu xian Wu jun ailei," *Shenbao,* July 4, 1878, p. 1.

42. Charles O. Hucker, *A Dictionary of Official Titles in Imperial China,* Stanford: Stanford University Press, 1985, pp. 118, 599, 157, and 240.

43. Song Jun, "*Shenbao*" *de xingshuai,* p. 20. Unfortunately, Song gives no source.

44. Hu Daojing, "Shanghai de ribao," *Shanghaitong zhiguan qikan,* vol. 2 no. 1 (June 1934), pp. 243–244.

45. Song Jun, "*Shenbao*" *de xingshuai,* p. 19. Song speaks of a Shen Dingnian, though. See footnote 33.

46. *Xinwenxue da cidian,* p. 694. *Wang Kangnian shiyou laizha,* p. 4066. Xiong Yuezhi, *Xixue dongjian,* pp. 616ff.

47. Shen is even listed as Chinese editor long after Cai had taken over the editorial job. A farewell article by Young Allen in the *Wanguo gongbao* mentions Shen' dissatisfaction at the missionary magazine and his desire to retire because of age. "Ji shen xie kun," *Wanguo gongbao,* July 1891, p. 19.

48. *Xinwenxue da cidian,* p. 694; "Zhongguo xinwenjie mingren jieshao (1)," *Zhongguo xinwen nianjian, 1983,* Beijing: Zhongguo shehui kexue chubanshe, 1983, p. 569; Wang Huilin and Zhu Hanguo, eds., *Zhongguo baokan cidian (1815–1949),* Taiyuan: Shuhai chubanshe, 1992, p. 438.

49. Sun Yusheng, *Baohai qianchen lu,* p. 27.

50. For this magazine, see R. Wagner, "Joining the Global Imaginaire: The Shanghai Illustrated Newspaper *Dianshizhai huabao,*" in this volume.

51. Ma Guangren, *Shanghai xinwen shi,* pp. 86ff.

52. On conflicts between the two newspaper houses, see below.

53. Quoted without source in Fang Hanqi, *Zhongguo jindai baokan shi,* p. 29.

54. Cai Erkang, "Wanguo gongbao baijuan qingcheng ji," *Wanguo gongbao,* vol. 27, no 100. (= May 1897), p. 2. It not clear whether such statements should be taken at face value. Chinese journalists and translators had good reasons for belittling their cooperation with Westerners in introducing Western knowledge and ideas. I discuss them in "Protestanten, Presse und Propaganda in China: Strategien der Aneignung und Selbstbehauptung von chinesischen Journalisten im 19. Jahrhundert (Protestants, Press and Propaganda: Strategies of Appropriation and Affirmation of Chinese Journalists in the 19th century," Dietmar Rothermund ed., *Aneignung und Selbstbehauptung: Antworten auf die europäische Expansion* (Appropriation and Affirmation: Responses to the European Expansion), München: Oldenbourg, 1999, pp. 137–160.

55. The collection contains what he saw as the most important *Shenbao* news in the years 1872–1873.

56. Cai Erkang, *Jiwen leibian,* Shanghai: Shanghai yinshuju, 1877. Reprint: *Jindai Zhongguo shiliao congkan,* Taibei: Wenhai chubanshe, 1966–74, Ser. III, vols. 172–173. Similar compilations exist for the *North China Herald* and its *Peking Gazette* translations.

57. Both Zheng Yimei, *Shubao huajiu,* Shanghai: Xuelin chubanshe, 1983, p. 207, and Ma Guangren, *Shanghai xinwen shi,* p. 89, credit Cai Erkang for this innovative practice. Already in 1872, however, the journal *Yinghuan suoji,* whose successor, the *Siming suoji,* was managed by Cai Erkang since 1875, had begun serializing the translation of an English novel; see Rudolf G. Wagner, "China's First Literary Journals," unpubl. ms, pp. 16ff. Cai was thus the first to serialize a novel originally written in Chinese, and this in a daily newspaper. Several incomplete manuscript copies of *Yesou puyan* from the Qianlong period were in circulation. Already during Cai's time at the Shenbaoguan, he was sent to search for a complete copy, and the *Shenbaoguan* published a lithograph edition in 1882, which is considered the complete version. See Jiangsusheng shehui kexueyuan Ming Qing xiaoshuo yanjiu zhongxin, ed., *Zhongguo tongsu xiaoshuo zongmu tiyao,* Beijing: Zhongguo wenlian chubanshe, 1990, p. 501. Serialization in the *Hubao* started on June 12, 1882. This seems to have been an incomplete version, where Cai—as Ma Guangren states—had added some sections himself. The advertisements for the novel admit these changes, but give no name of their author. See *Hubao,* June 10 and 12, 1882, p. 1. Cai's attempt to compete with the Shenbaoguan is rather obvious. He also soon ran into other problems with the *Shenbao* when he was secretly—perhaps with the help of former colleagues—copying their news telegrams without paying for it. He was found out when the *Hubao* printed a dispatch with exactly the same decoding errors as the *Shenbao.* Ma Guangren, pp. 88ff.

58. Nothing seems to survive of this paper.

59. *Zhongguo baokan cidian (1815–1949)*, p. 438.

60. *Taixi xinshi lanyao* 泰西新史攬要 (Essentials of the Recent History of the West) Shanghai: Guangxuehui, 1895.

61. Xiong Yuezhi, *Xixue dongjian*, pp. 597–602.

62. Timothy Richard and Cai Erkang, eds., *Zhong Dong zhanji benmo*, Shanghai: Tushujicheng ju, 1898. Reprint: *Jindai Zhongguo shiliao congkan*, xuji, Taibei: Wenhai chubanshe, 1975, vols. 701–704. After the quick sale of the initial 3000 copies, a second edition followed. This enhanced Cai's fame in Shanghai. Ma Guangren, *Shanghai xinwen shi*, p. 165, and Xiong Yuezhi, *Xixue dongjian*, pp. 625–632.

63. For a more detailed biography of Cai Erkang, see my "Ein Leben am Rande des Ruhmes: Cai Erkang (1852–1920)" (A Life on the Margins of Fame: Cai Erkang), In: Neder, Rötz, and Schilling, eds., *Gedenkschrift für Helmut Martin*. Bochum: Projekt Verlag, 2001, pp. 195–205.

64. For a detailed analysis of the different groups of pen names and their meanings, see my *Die Anfänge des Journalismus in China (1860–1911)* (The Beginnings of Journalism in China, 1860–1911), opera sinologica 9, Wiesbaden: Harassowitz, 2002, pp. 128–131.

65. Quoted in Zheng Yimei, *Shubao huajiu*, pp. 207ff.

66. Sun Yusheng, *Baohai qianchen lu*, p. 25. Wang Tao is also mentioned as a main editor (p. 24). While the *Shenbao* does not mention Cai Erkang at all, the *Hubao* lists him as editor (p. 27).

67. Ibid., p. 3.

68. The *North China Herald* and documents in the Public Record Office indicate that Major often had to appear in front of the Mixed Court, which shows that he was engaged in a lot of different projects.

69. Wang Kangding, "Guanyu Wang Tao yu `Xunhuan Ribao´ de jixiang kaocha," *Xinwen chunqiu*, 1994, no 1, pp. 13–16.

70. A fire destroyed this publishing house in 1883 (Lin Youlan, *Xianggang baoye fazhan shi*, Xianggang: Shijie shuju, 1977, p. 80), or 1895 (Li Jiayuan, *Xianggang baoye zatan*, Xianggang: Sanlian shudian, 1989, pp. 8–12).

71. Transcriptions of Cantonese pronunciation differ widely. The writings for Huang Sheng include Wong Hsing , Wong Shing, Wong Ping-po, or Wong Tat-kuen. Liang Renfu (梁仁甫) is also mentioned as "director" 董事 and buyer of the Printing Office. See Li Jiayuan, *Xianggang baoye*, p. 14.

72. Also Chan Ayin, Chun Ayin, Chan Oi-ting, or Chen Axian.

73. A brief summary of the agreement as well as a signed copy of it can be found in the London Missionary Society Archive, South China and Ultra Ganges: Box 7, Letter from Eitel to Mullen, January 28 and February 5, 1873. The apparently very high price included two complete sets of Chinese type fonts as well as matrices and patrices (6000 characters) alone estimated to be worth $9000 (ibid., Letter from Eitel to Mullen, July 19, 1872), and one set of English letters. The printing equipment consisted of two flat-bed printing machines, estimated value $400 each; cf. *Xunhuan Ribao liushi zhounian tekan*, pp. 13 and 65.

74. Xiong Yuezhi, *Xixue dongjian*, p. 202. How his own statements have to be read in the context of his isolation and defense against reproaches by traditional Confucian

literati is convincingly shown by Catherine Yeh, "The Life-style of Four *Wenren* in Late Qing Shanghai," *HJAS* 17.2 (1997).

75. On the history and influence of this institution, see Xiong Yuezhi, *Xixue dongjian*, pp. 181–188. Fang Hanqi, "Wang Tao yu 'Liuhe congtan,'" *Baoshi yu baoren*, Beijing: Xinhua chubanshe, 1991, pp. 282–285; Bennett, *Missionary Journalist*, pp. 57–59. Zhang Hailin, *Wang Tao pingzhuan*, p. 471.

76. Lo Hsiang-lin, *The Role of Hong Kong in the Cultural Interchange Between East and West*, Vol. I–II, Tokyo: Center for East Asian Cultural Studies, Ser. No. 6, 1963, pp. 43–45.

77. Yu Xingmin, *Shanghai, 1862 nian*, Shanghai: Shanghai renmin chubanshe, 1991, pp. 415ff. Together with his friends Li Shanlan and Jiang, Wang Tao was quite notorious for loudly reciting poems and singing songs in the nightly lanes of the walled city of Shanghai or smashing cups and furniture into pieces in the guesthouses after consuming an excessive amount of wine.

78. It is generally assumed that he would have been decapitated by the Chinese authorities. A communication from Prince Gong, however, to the British Minister Bruce in Peking stated that he would not have been in danger had he been willing to repent. In that case, the Chinese government would have excused his fault and employed him—most likely as a spy among the Taipings. Wang Tao did neither repent—still in Hong Kong he was claiming his innocence—nor test the credibility of this statement. FO 228 /912, no 53, "Demanding Rendition of Wang Han, Teacher of Mr. Muirhead," Prince Gong to Bruce, July 1, 1862, pp. 149–151. For a detailed discussion of the documents see my "Why Did Wang Tao Go to Hong Kong? Some Preliminary Observations and Questions Raised by Some Unpublished Documents of the Public Record Office," *History and Culture*, no 2 (1999), pp. 60–68.

79. Wang Tao, "My Sojourn in Hong Kong," trsl. by Yang Qinghua, *Renditions: Special Issue: Hong Kong*, nos. 29 & 30, 1988, pp. 37–41.

80. Wang Tao, *Taoyuan wenlu waibian* [1883], Reprint: Shenyang: Liaoning renmin chubanshe, 1994, p. 315; Wang Tao, "*My Sojourn*," p. 40. Legge attested to the mutual character of this friendship in the preface to his *Shijing* translation. James Legge, *The Chinese Classics: The Shih Ching, or Book of Poetry*, Vol. 4, 2nd rev. ed., Taibei: Wenshizhe chubanshe, 1972.

81. Lo Hsiang-lin, *The Role of Hong Kong*, p. 43; Fang Hanqi, *Xinwen shiye*, p. 302.

82. "Benguan zishu," *Shenbao*, May 8, 1872, p. 1. However, two weeks later, the *Shenbao* gave Chen Aiting as editor. "Benguan zixu," *Shenbao*, May 20, 1872, p.1.

83. Wang Tao reports this in his diary *Manyou suilu*. Quoted and described by Su Jing, "Cong Yinghua shuyuan dao Zhonghua yinwu zongju: jindai zhongwen yinshua chuban xin jumian," in: Lam Kai Yin and Wong Man Kong, eds., *Wang Tao yu jindai shijie*, pp. 299–312.

84. Wang Tao to Ding Richang, *Taoyuan chidu*, vol. 8, pp. 3–7; to Feng Shunding, ibid., vol. 9, p. 12; to Tang Jingxing, ibid., vol. 9, pp. 15ff.

85. He had not given up his favorite leisure activities of drinking wine and visiting the brothels, as recorded by Hu Liyuan. Hu Liyuan, *Hu Yinan xiansheng quanji* [1908]. Reprint: *Jindai Zhongguo shiliao congkan*, xuji, Taibei: Wenhai chubanshe, 1975, vols. 261–266, p. 1577.

86. After his return he published his description of the Prussian-French War, the *Pu Fa zhanji*, as well as a flurry of other works, such as *Wengyou yutan* (Gossip from a Poor Man's Window), 1875; *Dunku lanyan* (Random Talks of a Man in a Hidden Cave), 1875; *Haizou yeyou lu* (Record of visits to Courtesan Houses in a Distant Corner by the Sea), 1878; *Huaguo jutan* (An Account of Sing-song Courtesans), 1878; and *Henghua guan shilu,* 1880.

87. Elizabeth Sinn, *Power and Charity, The Early History of the Tung Wah Hospital, Hong Kong,* Hong Kong: Oxford Univ. Pr 1989, pp. 56ff.

88. Huang Ronghui, "Xianggang zaoqi wenhua dabao," in Jin Yingxi, ed., *Xianggang Shihua,* Guangzhou: Guangdong renmin chubanshe, 1988, pp. 161–165. Li Jiayuan, *Xianggang baoye,* pp. 3 ff.

89. Many accounts credit Wu Tingfang with founding this paper, but at the time he was only 16 years old. See Linda Pomerantz-Chang, *Wu Tingfang (1842–1922), Reform and Modernization in Modern Chinese History,* Hong Kong: Hong Kong University Press, 1992, p. 29.

90. LMS Archive, South China and Ultra Ganges: Box 7, Letter from Eitel to Mullen, May 12, 1872. Huang Ronghui, "Xianggang zaoqi wenhua," pp. 161—165; Li Jiayuan, *Xianggang baoye,* p. 3; Lin Youlan, *Xianggang baoye fazhan,* p. 69.

91. Carl T. Smith, *Chinese Christians: Élites, Middlemen and the Church in Hong Kong.* Hong Kong, Oxford, New York: Oxford University Press, 1985, pp. 134–135, 147.

92. Chan Wai Kwan, *The Making of Hong Kong Society. Three Studies in Class Formation in Early Hong Kong,* Oxford: Clarendon Press, 1991, p. 75, fn. 3. G. H. Choa, *The Life and Times of Sir Kai Ho Kai. A Prominent Figure in Nineteenth Century Hong Kong,* Hong Kong: Chinese University Press, 1981, p. 19.

93. Carl T. Smith, *Chinese Christians,* p. 133.

94. Chen Aiting is mentioned as the manager besides Wang Tao in another pamphlet (attached to the microfilm in the British Library) of February 11, 1874. No title. Also in "Zhonghua yinwu zongju gaobai," *Xunhuan Ribao,* February 5, 1874, p. 4. This text also mentions the new manager Hong Ganfu (see below) from March on; see "Zhonghua yinwu zongju gaobai," *Xunhuan Ribao,* March 19, 1874, p. 4.

95. Ibid.

96. Zhang Hailin, *Wang Tao pingzhuan,* p. 474.

97. Carl T. Smith, "The English-educated Chinese Elite in Nineteenth-Century Hong Kong," *History of Hong Kong 1842–1984,* David Faure ed., Hong Kong & London: Tamarind Books, 1975, pp. 29–56, especially p. 36.

98. Carl T. Smith, *Chinese Christians,* p. 132.

99. Huazi Ribao bianjibu, ed., *Huazi Ribao qishiyi zhounian jiniankan,* Hong Kong: Huazi Ribao, 1934, p. 1. Because of his young age of thirteen years the support must have come from He Qi's father He Futang.

100. Huang Sheng is also said to be a relative of He Qi's, although their exact relationship is not known. The importance of family ties in the closely knit network of the Hong Kong elite is convincingly shown by Chan Wai Kan, *The Making of Hong Kong Society,* p. 115.

101. Ho Tsun-shin or Ho Fuk-tong.

102. Carl T. Smith, *Chinese Christians*, p. 122.

103. Linda Pomerantz-Chang, *Wu Tingfang*, pp. 22ff.

104. Chan Wai Kwan, *The Making of Hong Kong Society*, p. 75. G. H. Choa, *Sir Kai Ho Kai*, pp. 9 and 39. On He Qi´s social activities, see also Luo Xianglin, *Xianggang wenhua yu Zhong Xi wenhua zhi jiaoliu*, Xianggang: Zhongguo xueshe, 1961, Chapter 5.

105. *Xunhuan Ribao liushi zhounian tekan*, p. 14.

106. Tsai Jung-Fang, "The Predicament of the Comprador Ideologists: He Qi (Ho Kai, 1859–1914) and Hu Liyuan (1847–1916)," *Modern China*, vol. 7, no 2 (April 1981), pp. 191–225, esp. pp. 197–198.

107. *Xunhuan Ribao*, pamphlet of February 11, 1874. No title.

108. On the history of this important institution in Hong Kong, see Elisabeth Sinn, *Power and Charity;* Chan Wai Kwan, *The Making of Hong Kong Society*. Both studies draw much material from and frequently refer to Carl Smith´s study, *Chinese Christians*.

109. Fung Ming-shan, Fung-Pohai, or Fung Chew.

110. Carl T. Smith, *Chinese Christians*, pp. 126ff; Chan, *The Making of Hong Kong Society*, p 109.

111. Leung Hok-chau, Leon On, or Leung Wan-hon.

112. Carl T. Smith, *Chinese Christians*, pp. 125ff.; Chan, *The Making of Hong Kong Society*, p. 108.

113. Fang Hanqi, *Xinwen shiye*, p. 477.

114. *Xunhuan Ribao liushi zhounian tekan*, p. 14; He Qi and Hu Liyuan, *Xinzheng zhenquan* [1900]. Reprint: Shenyang: Liaoning renmin chubanshe, 1994, p. 1.

115. Elisabeth Sinn, *Power and Charity*, pp. 56ff.; p. 131.

116. Chan Wai Kwan, *The Making of Hong Kong Society*, p. 79.

117. Elizabeth Sinn, *Power and Charity*, p. 4. Access to the "society" was open to any Chinese who contributed at least $10. By 1873, it already had 830 members with a body of elected representatives headed by the board of directors (12). Chan, *The Making of Hong Kong Society*, p. 83.

118. Wu Tingfang was a member of the legislative council from 1880 to 1882, Huang Sheng from 1884 to 1889, and He Qi from 1890 to 1914. Chan Wai Kwan, *The Making of Hong Kong Society*, pp. 110ff.

119. When, for example, Sir John visited the Tung Wah Hospital in 1878, he was received by, among others, Wu Tingfang, Huang Sheng, Chen Aiting, Feng Mingshan, all of them dressed in mandarin costumes. Chan, *The Making of Hong Kong Society*, p. 123. William T. Rowe observes on Hankow that such emulation was not simply a pose by urban merchants, but was also stimulated by a serious interest in traditional learning and culture. William T. Rowe, *Hankow: Conflict and Community in a Chinese City, 1796–1895*, Stanford: Stanford University Press, 1989, p. 58.

120. Carl T. Smith, *Chinese Christians*, p. 131.

121. Only the missionary magazine *Zhong Xi wenjianlu* mentions the fact that this paper had been set up by Cantonese dissatisfied with the debates in the *Shenbao*. "Shanghai jinshi: xin she baoju," *Zhong Xi wenjian lu*, no 24 (July 1874), p. 33b.

The *Xunhuan Ribao*, which was normally supportive of the *Shenbao*, welcomed the new paper in Shanghai without special reference to its controversial background. "Shanghai Huibao chuangxing," *Xunhuan Ribao*, June 11, 1874. p. 3.

122. On the details of the Yang Yuelou case, its consequences for the *Shenbao* editorial policy, and the battle between the papers, see my "Readers, Publishers and Officials in Contest for a Public Sphere and the Shanghai Newspaper Market in Late Qing," *T'oung Pao*, 2001, no. 4–5. pp. 393–455.

123. "Shanghai qianshe xinwenguan," *Shenbao*, March 3, 1874, p. 2; "Shanghai xinwen ribaoguan shi," *Shenbao*, March 12, 1874, p. 1; also Fang Hanqi, *Xinwen shiye*, p. 486; *Jindai Shanghai da shiji*, p. 312.

124. "Shu Mojisheng lai xin hou," *Shenbao*, November 21, 1874, p. 1.

125. Shanghai also had *tongxiang* associations for the Nanhai and Shunde counties, the *Nanhai yiguan*, and the *Shunde yiguan*. Zhang Zhongli, ed., *Jindai Shanghai chengshi yanjiu*, Shanghai: Shanghai renmin chubanshe, 1991, p. 518. Song Zuanyou, "Yige chuantong zuzhi zai chengshi jindaihua zhong de zuoyong—Shanghai Guangqi gongsuo chutan" (The function of a traditional organization in urban modernization), ibid., pp. 415–431, p. 417; on the guilds in Shanghai, see the excellent study by Bryna Goodman, *Native Place, City and Nation: Regional Networks and Identities in Shanghai, 1853–1937*, Berkeley, Los Angeles and London: University of California Press, 1995. For the statutes of the association and its main contributors, see Peng Zeyi, ed., *Zhongguo gongshang hanghui shiliao ji*, Beijing: Zhonghua shuju, 1995, 2 vols., pp. 877–879.

126. Xiong Yuezhi, *Xixue dongjian*, p. 356.

127. Tang's elder brother Tang Tingzhi (唐廷植, 1828–1897) had to move to California because his reputation, too, had been damaged; this caused a newspaper to remark in an editorial: "members of the Tong family connected with the Hong Kong Government . . . have an unfortunate knack of getting themselves into scrapes." Quoted from the *China Mail* (September 4, 1856) by Carl T. Smith, *Chinese Christians*, p. 44. Tang Tingzhi, a classmate of Rong Hong, first took over his brother´s post at Jardine & Matheson, represented him at the Steam Navigation Co. while Tang was in Europe in 1883, and became president of the Canton guild in Shanghai. On the Tang Family, see Carl T. Smith, *Chinese Christians*, pp. 34–51.

128. "Shanghai xinwen ribaoguan shi," *Shenbao*, March 12, 1874, p. 1.

129. The discussion is reported in the *Celestial Empire*, January 28, 1875.

130. Yung Wing, *My Life in China and America* [1909], New York: Henry Holt and Company. Reprint: New York: Arno Press, 1978. "Shanghai qianshe xinwenguan," *Shenbao*, March 3, 1874, p. 2.

131. Ma Guangren, *Shanghai xinwen shi*, p. 75, assumes that a conflict in the editorial board must have prompted Rong Hong's early departure. The new statutes laid out by Zheng Guanying assigned all responsibilities to Kuang Qichao. The statutes are included in the first issue, which is not available to me. However, the *Shenbao*, too, states that the printed statutes were not the original ones, thus indicating a dispute in the editorial board. "Shu mojisheng laixin hou," *Shenbao*, November 21, 1874, p. 1.

132. Ma Guangren, *Shanghai xinwen shi*, p. 75.

133. Johannes Kehnen, *Cheng Kuan-ying: Unternehmer und Reformer der späten Ch'ing-Zeit*. Wiesbaden: Harrassowitz, 1975, pp. 18–34.

134. See the chapters on Zheng Guanying in Xu Peiting, *Xinwen chuanbo shi*, and Hu Taichun, *Jindai xinwen sixiang shi*. However, Zheng Guanying formulated these ideas rather late in his *Shengshi weiyan*. The forerunners of this text, his *Jiushi jieyao* 救時揭要 and *Yiyan* 易言, did not yet contain any special sections on newspapers.

135. *Xinwenxue da cidian*, p. 693.

136. Wu Baling, *Guangdong zhi xinwen shiye*, Zhongguo wenhua xiejinhui (no place given), 1940, p. 4.

137. Fang Hanqi, *Xinwen shiye*, p. 486. Ma Guangren, *Shanghai xinwen shi*, p. 75. The *Desk Hong List* of 1875, however, gives more and different names, which I could not identify: Hui Bao (Wai Bao): 18, Nanjing Road, H. Scott Gill, editor; Kwong Tsun Fuk, manager; Wong Ah Sui, writer; Kwan Choi Sui, do [= Guan Caishu?]; Wong Shu Hon. do; Yien Chuan Yu, do; Kah Tschee Leng, do [= Jia Jiliang?]; Chung Tai Shang, do. I wish to thank Rudolf G. Wagner for this information.

138. FO 228/541 no. 95. "Change of management of 'Huipao' newspaper," British Consulate to Wade, September 1, 1874.

139. *The Celestial Empire*, June 5, 1875.

140. "Baoguan geng ming," *Shenbao*, September 9, 1874, p. 2.

141. *China Directory 1874*, Hong Kong: China Mail Office, 1874.

142. "Eurasian School Report," *North China Herald*, May 29, 1872.

143. His tenure officially ended on May 25, 1875. *Jindai Shanghai da shiji*, p. 906. Ma Guangren, *Shanghai xinwen shi*, p. 77.

144. *The Celestial Empire*, June 5, 1875, and August 28, 1875.

145. See, for example, *The Celestial Empire*, August 7, 1875.

146. "Benguan gaobai," *Yibao*, December 4, 1875, p. 5.

147. FO 228/556, no. 100. Medhurst to Taotai Feng, October 9, 1875, p. 205.

148. *The Celestial Empire*, March 30, 1876.

149. "Particulars," *Xinbao*, November 23, 1876, p. 1.

150. This was suggested by *The North China Herald*, June 9, 1877.

151. Ma Guangren, *Shanghai xinwen shi*, p. 81.

152. According to Xiong, as directors of the Arsenal the Daotais were even personally interviewing the students and conducting the English examinations. Xiong Yuezhi, *Xixue dongjian*, pp. 337–341.

153. Leung Yuean-Sang, *The Shanghai Taotai: Linkage Man in a Changing Society. 1843–90*, Singapore: Singapore University Press, 1991, p. 99.

154. *The Celestial Empire*, June 2, 1877. Also, Leung Yuean-Sang, *Shanghai Taotai*, pp. 80–82.

155. Leung Yuean-Sang, *Shanghai Taotai*, p. 159.

156. Ma Guangren, *Shanghai xinwen shi*, p. 73. *Shanghai yanjiu ziliao xuji*, p. 322.

157. *The Celestial Empire*, Mar. 30, 1876.

158. Ma Guangren, *Shanghai xinwen shi*, p. 80.

159. FO 228/632, "Intelligence Report, January 1st to May 1st 1879," pp. 52–63.

160. Arthur W. Hummel, *Eminent Chinese of the Ch'ing Period. (1644–1912)*, Washington: US Government Printing Office, 1943, pp. 955–957.

161. Ma Guangren, *Shanghai xinwen shi*, p. 80.

162. "Jindai Zhongguo xinwen shiye shishi biannian, 1815–1919, (2)," p. 224.

163. *The Celestial Empire*, December 14, 1876.

164. FO 228/632, "Intelligence Report, January 1st to May 1st 1879," pp. 52–63.

165. *The Celestial Empire*, February 8, 1877.

166. *Shanghai yanjiu ziliao xuji*, p. 322; Fang Hanqi, *Xinwen shiye*, p. 491; Qin Shaode, *Shanghai jindai baokan*, p. 29. Ma Guangren, *Shanghai xinwen shi*, p. 81, assumes that the paper was terminated because of an ongoing dispute among government officials about closing the *Shenbao*. Instead of taking on the *Shenbao*, the Daotai, who had grown increasingly irritated by the newspapers, closed the *Xinbao*.

167. Wang Tao, *Taoyuan wenlu waibian*, pp. 323–325.

168. Wang Tao, *Taoyuan chidu*. The continuation of his letter collection is *Taoyuan chidu xuchao*, Wang Tao [1889], no publisher.

169. His *Investigations on Sino-Japanese Trade (Riben tong Zhongguo kao)* and *On Geography (Tan di ji)* are both included in the *Zhongwai diyu tushuo jicheng*, 130 vols., edited by Tong Kanglu 同康廬, Shanghai : Jishan shuju, 1894, vol. 22. *The Tribute System of the Ryukyu Islands (Liuqiu chaogong kao)* is included into the collection *Xiaofang huzhai yudi congchao*, collected by Wang Xiqi, Shanghai: Zhu yi tang, 1891, vol. 10. *Three Chapters on Western Learning (Xixue jicun sanpian)*, a handwritten copy of this publication is included into the collection *Zuile caotang congchao*, 591 vols. Copied and compiled by Shu Fenglü. (No date and place of publication given.)

170. See Wang Tao's translation of the six volumes of A. Wylie, *Xixue jicun liu zhong*, Shanghai: 1880; or of the *Chongding Faguo zhilüe*, 1890.

171. Qian Wei (= Qian Xinbo), *Xieyu Congtan shiqi pian*, in *Zuile caotang congchao*, vols. 11–17.

172. Ma Guangren, *Shanghai xinwen shi*, p. 86. For this album, see the chapter by Rudolf G. Wagner in this volume.

173. E.g., Cai Erkang and Timothy Richard, 1896, *Datong xue* (Theory of the Great Unity), Shanghai: Guangxue hui; Cai Erkang & Young Allen, 1898, *Xinxue huibian* (Collection on New Learning), Shanghai: Guangxue hui; ibid., 1899, *Bao Hua quanshu* (Encyclopedia on the Protection of China), Shanghai: Guangxue hui.

174. Yuan Zuzhi, *Tan ying lu* (Accounts on Foreign Countries), Shanghai: Tongwen shuju, 1885. His *Suiyuan suoji* (Anecdotal notes from the Suiyuan Garden) is included in the collection *Zuile caotang congchao*, vols. 562–563. *Chuyang xuzhi* (Essential Knowledge for Oversea Travel), *Xisu zazhi* (Miscellanea on Western Customs), *She yangguan jian* (My Humble Views on Western Things) and *Yinghai caiwen jishi* (Factual Reports on Western Things) are included into the collection *Xiaofang huzhai yudi congchao*, 1891, vol. 17. See also Catherine Yeh, *Shanghai Love*, pp. 197–198.

175. His *Wudazhou yudi hukou wuchan biao* (Matters of Geography and Population in the Five Great Continents) in *Zhongwai diyu tushuo jicheng*, vol. 4; *Taiwan fanshe kao* in *Xiaofang huzhai yudi congchao*, vol. 8.

176. His *Yudi lüe* (Brief Account on Geography) in *Xiaofang Huzhai yudi congchao*, vol. 1; *Rushui shuo* (On the Ru River) in *Zhongwai diyu tushuo jicheng*, vol. 15.

177. Wang Tao supported Rong Hong's projects in his collection of essays *Taoyuan wenlu waibian* and wrote the preface for Zheng Guanying's *Warnings in a Prosperous Time* (*Shengshi weiyan*, 1893). Zhang Hailin, *Wang Tao pingzhuan*, p. 476. Wang Tao also admired Feng Guifen and wrote a preface for his early reformist work *Notes of Protest from the Jiaobin Studio* (*Jiaobinlu Kangyi*, 1897): *The Whole Course of the War Between China and Japan*, published by the Guangxue hui had three prefaces, one each by Shen Yugui, Cai Erkang, and Wang Tao. Tang Jingxing wrote a preface for Yuan Zuzhi's *Accounts on Foreign Countries* (*Tan ying lu*).

178. Huang Sheng and Wang Tao compiled a book on gunnery, which was presented to Li Hongzhang in 1864, Wang Tao, *Taoyuan wenlu waibian*, p. 326, and Wang found Chen Aiting's support in writing his *The Prussian-French-War*, Hong Kong: Zhonghua yinwu zongju, 1873. This book was widely read and contributed much to Wang Tao's growing reputation; it was translated into Japanese in 1889. He Qi and Hu Liyuan jointly published the polemic pamphlet *True Meaning of Political Reforms* (*Xinzheng zhenquan*) [1900], against Zhang Zhidong's *Exhortations on Learning* (*Quanxue pian*) [1898]. Both treatises include an essay on the need to establish newspapers.

179. Letter to Tang Jingxing in *Taoyuan chidu*, vol. 9, pp. 15ff; ibid., vol. 11, p. 3.

180. Xiong Yuezhi, *Xixue Dongjian*, pp. 558ff.

181. For these connections between journalists and reformers in the new institutions of new learning, see my "Social Actors in the Field of New Learning in Nineteenth Century China," in Michael Lackner and Natascha Vittinghoff, eds., *Mapping Meanings: The Field of New Learning in Late Qing China*, Leiden: Brill, 2004, pp. 75–118.

182. *The Celestial Empire*, December 9, 1875.

183. *The Celestial Empire*, December 14, 1876.

184. "Ci zhi qi tie zai baohao bi jian wei dao," *Pamphlet*, March 1874. (Included in the *Xunhuan ribao* microfilm of the British Museum Library, London.)

185. Cf. W. H. Donald, 1908, "The Press," in Alexander Wright, *Twentieth Century Impressions of Hong Kong, Shanghai and Other Treaty Ports of China*, London: Lloyd's Greater Britain Publ. Co., 1908, pp. 343–367. The *Huazi Ribao* was the Chinese edition of the *China Mail*, founded by A. Shortrede in 1845; the *Zhongwai Xinwen* belonged to the *Hong Kong Daily Press*, founded by Murrow in 1857.

186. Pamphlet without title, *Xunhuan Ribao*, February 11, 1874, attached to the first weekly Reader's Digest of the *Xunhuan Ribao*.

187. The Chinese contractors were not necessarily journalists. One contractor of the *Zhongwai Xinbao* was Wu Tingfang's cousin Wu Zhisheng. His successor was Zhao Liangcun, a typesetter, who was followed by Feng Huanru (馮煥如), a translator. *Xunhuan Ribao liushi zhounian tekan*, 1932, p. 64.

188. One of them, the *Jinshi bianlu* (Contemporary Affairs), was edited by Ling Jichun in a contract with the Portuguese Publisher Noronha & Co. When Noronha increased the rent in 1879, Ling canceled the contract and set up his own *Reform Daily* (Weixin Ribao). The second was the *Huazi Ribao*. Manager Tan Yiqiao dissolved the contract with the *China Mail* after the rent had been raised, and set up the *Jiebao*.

Xunhuan Ribao liushi zhounian tekan, 1932, p. 64; Huang Nanxiang, *Xianggang suiyue,* Xianggang: Benma chubanshe, 1985, p. 283.

189. "New Publications," *China Mail,* April 2, 1872, p. 3.

190. Ibid.

191. *China Mail,* April 9, 1872, p. 3.

192. "New Publications," *China Mail,* April 2, 1872, p. 3; "Prospectus," *China Mail,* February 2 1874.

193. "The Chinese Mail," *China Mail,* January 26, 1874, p. 4.

194. "The Hong Kong China Mail," *China Mail,* March 12, 1874, p. 3.

195. "A native 'Press,'" *The North China Herald,* February 19, 1874.

196. Letter to Fang Zhaoxian, in Wang Tao, *Taoyuan chidu xuchao,* (no place and publisher given), 1889, vol. 4. pp. 15–17. As noted earlier, also in a letter to Tang Jingxing; Wang Tao, *Taoyuan chidu,* vol. 9, pp. 15ff. Newspaper editorial, quoted without title by Ge Gongzhen, *Baoxue shi,* p. 104.

197. "Sheng qi zhi jia," *Xunhuan Ribao,* February 5, 1874, p. 3.

198. E.g., on the blockade of Hong Kong: "Xiren lun xunzhuan zhi quan," *Xunhuan Ribao,* February 5, 1874, p. 3.

199. "Fudeng laizha: Xianggang Huamin zhengqusi shixian songci," *Xunhuan Ribao,* February 27, 1874, p. 3. The importance of foreign news is highlighted by the fact that the majority of articles in the weekly Reader's Digest of the *Xunhuan Ribao* dealt with foreign countries. The first and only extant edition of this Reader´s Digest is attached to the microfilms of the London British Library. First film.

200. Modern Chinese scholars often follow Ge Gongzhen's rather far-fetched suggestion that "Circle" (*xunhuan*) in the title suggested that the circle of revolution had to take another turn after the failure of the Taiping Rebellion with which Wang Tao had tried to associate himself. See Ge Gongzhen, *Baoxue shi,* p. 121. Others have speculated that it was an expression of Wang's general view of history as a never-ending circular development. Wang Kangding, "Wang Tao `Xunhuan lun´ yu `Xunhuan Ribao´ mingming shiyi ," unpubl. manuscript for the *95 Shijie Huawen baokan yu Zhongguo wenhua chuanbo guoji xueshu yantaohui 1995,* Wuhan-Chongqing, October 1995.

201. "Benguan zixu," *Shenbao,* September 9, 1872, p.1.

202. "Lun xizi xinbao lü bo *Shenbao* shi," *Shenbao,* December 13, 1872, pp. 1ff.

203. E.g., "Yingguo zhi boxing dalüe," *Shenbao,* May 13, 1872, pp. 3ff., resp. "Tai zhuan Zeng Wenzheng liezhuan," *Shenbao,* May 9, 1872, p. 3; "Shanggu lun," *Shenbao,* May 11, 1872, p. 1. As Mr. Hillier put it: "It is to be regretted that Mr. Major, a British subject, should make his patriotism subservient to what he no doubt considers his private interest, by invariably pandering to the prejudices of the Chinese." FO 228/632, "Intelligence Report, January 1st to May 1st 1879," p. 59. The proper address of foreign authorities in Chinese print media is related to the official acknowledgment of the equal status of the foreigners in China. I deal with this question of proper translations of international terms in my "'British Barbarians' and 'Chinese Pigtails'? Translingual Practice in a Transnational Environment in 19th Century Hongkong and Shanghai," Bryna Goodman, ed., Special Issue of *China Review,*" Transnational Dimensions of the Chinese Press," vol. 4 no. 1 (spring), 2004, 27–54.

204. "Lun benguan zuo bao benyi," *Shenbao,* October 10, 1875.

205. See Ge Gongzhen, *Baoxue shi,* p. 79; Fang Hanqi, *Xinwen shiye,* p. 323; Liu Jialin, *Zhongguo xinwen shi,* p. 125; Song Jun, *"Shenbao" de xingshuai,* p. 10. Leo Ou-fan Lee & Andrew Nathan, "The Beginnings of Mass Culture," p. 363.

206. Before Major started the *Shenbao* he had asked the British plenipotentiary Thomas Wade what he thought of the legal status of a Chinese-language newspaper under the treaties; Wade had said he considered it a "fair commercial enterprise." FO 671/88. Major to Davenport, April 4, 1879.

207. Paul A. Cohen, *China and Christianity: The Missionary Movement and the Growth of Chinese Antiforeignism 1860–1870,* Cambridge, MA: Harvard University Press, 1963. See also footnote 58.

208. Medhurst to Wade. June 24, 1874. FO 228 /540, no. 59, "A second Chinese newspaper established," pp. 294ff.

209. *North China Daily News,* September 1, 1874.

210. "Law report," *The North China Herald,* February 18, 1875. As I argue in my *Die Anfänge des Journalismus,* pp. 324–338, this practice to seek legal protection in the settlements originated in a first discussion on press laws in China in 1866.

211. "Benguan gaobai," *Xinbao,* November 23, 1876, p. 1.

212. *Shanghai yanjiu ziliao xuji,* p. 322.

213. *The Celestial Empire,* March 29, 1877.

214. FO 233 / 35. "Mr. Mayer and Shen, Tung, Chunghow, Chenglin and Hia, with the *tsungpan* Chow," 1.9. 1875. pp. 219–224.

215. *The Celestial Empire,* December 14, 1876.

216. "The 'Sinpao' and its foreign readers," *The North China Herald,* May 19, 1877.

217. For a detailed calculation of the financial situation of each newspaper house see my *Die Anfänge des Journalismus,* pp. 166–78. The prices for advertisements are listed in all the papers.

218. *Xunhuan Ribao* prices for one week: 1 dollar for 100 characters, half a cent for each additional character.

219. "Zhaokan gaobai yin," *Shenbao,* May 7, 1872, pp. 1ff. For an analysis of the medical advertisements in the *Shenbao* as an indicator for national strengthening, see Patrick Hess, *Anzeigen für westliche Heilmittel in der Shanghaier Tageszeitung Shenbao, 1872–1922,* unpubl. MA thesis, Institute of Chinese Studies, Heidelberg University, 1995.

220. Circulation figures: Without title, *Shenbao,* June 11, 1872, p. 1: 4500; "Lun benguan xiaoshu," *Shenbao,* February 10, 1877, p. 1: 10 000; "Benbao zishu jia pei," *Shenbao,* June 20, 1877, p. 1: 8–9000.

221. The *Huazi Ribao* claims a circulation of 3000 to 4000 copies a day when the paper was started, but gives the lower figure of 1000 copies two years later. ("New Publications," *China Mail,* April 2, 1872; "Notice," *China Mail,* February 24, 1874). Lin You-lan, *Xianggang baoye fazhan,* p. 13, generally states a number of 5–600 copies for the *Xunhuan Ribao.* The jubilee edition generally states that even the bigger Hong Kong papers would never exceed a circulation of 500–600, *Xunhuan Ribao liushi zhounian*

tekan, p. 65; the *Blue Books* of the Hong Kong Government, however, give rather detailed and different circulation figures of the *Xunhuan Ribao:* 1876–1878: 710 copies; 1879: 1087 copies; 1885: 1100; 1890: 1100 copies. In 1890, the *Huazi Ribao* is registered with only 500 copies, whereas the newly founded *Weixin Ribao* has a circulation of 1960 copies already in 1885. By 1902, the *Xunhuan Ribao* reached a number of 1200 copies—whereas the *Huazi Ribao* is said to surpass it with a circulation figure of 2000. See Great Britain Colonial Office, *The Hong Kong Blue Book for the Year 1875* (*resp.—1876, 1877, 1878, 1879, 1885, 1890, 1902).* Hong Kong: Noronha & Co.

222. See the numerous advertisements in the *Xunhuan Ribao* beginning in the first issue. For the LMS, see F. Turner to J. Mullen, October 28, 1867, LMS Archive, CWM Incoming Letters: South China and Ultra Ganges: Box 6.

223. *The Celestial Empire,* April 12, 1877.

224. See "Benju gaobai," *Xunhuan Ribao,* August 6, 1874, p. 2.

225. No title, *Xinbao,* December 1, 1876, p.1.

226. The price is given in Fang Hanqi, *Xinwen shiye,* p. 486.

227. In a calculation of the Hong Kong *Yuebao* from 1886 the following numbers are given: main editor (主筆), 50 yuan; editors (編輯), 30 yuan; translator (翻譯), 20 yuan; assistant editors (副主筆), 10 yuan; (*Xunhuan Ribao liushi zhounian tekan,* p. 65). The *Xinbao* in Shanghai paid between $20 and $30 per month (FO 228/632. "Intelligence Report, January 1st to May 1st 1879," p. 63); Lei Jin, "Shenbaoguan zhi guoqu zhuangkuang," gives variations from 10 to 40 Yuan a month for the first journalists, which is also stated by Bin Zhi. According to the latter, He Guisheng had earned $30 a month. "Shenbao zhanggu tan, 3," *Shenbaoguan nei tongxun,* vol. 1, no. 4, 1947, p. 21. The *Xunhuan Ribao* operated with two main editors, two subeditors and one translator.

228. E. Eitel to J. Mullen, July 3, 1873, LMS Archive, South China and Ultra Ganges: Box 7.

229. "Chinese Printing," *The Inland Printer,* vol. 29, no. 3 (June 1902), p. 447.

230. *Xunhuan Ribao liushi zhounian tekan,* p. 65.

231. "Benju gaobai," *Xunhuan Ribao,* February 25, 1874, p. 2, and "Changshe ribao xiaoyin," *Xunhuan Ribao,* February 5, 1874, p. 4.

232. "Ci zhi qi tie zai baohao bi jian wei dao," *Pamphlet,* March 1874.

233. "Benju jinqi," *Xunhuan Ribao,* February 14, 1874, p. 2; "Benju gaobai," *Xunhuan Ribao,* June 11 and 18, 1874, p. 2.

234. "Benju gaobai," *Xunhuan Ribao,* February 2, 1874, p. 3.

235. E.g., *Xunhuan Ribao,* March 7, 1874; March 26, 1874.

236. On the various sales strategies taken up by the publishing house Shenbaoguan, see Rudolf G. Wagner, "Commercializing Chinese Culture: Ernest Major in Shanghai," paper given at the AAS Annual Meeting in Honolulu, Hawaii, April 11–14, 1996.

237. A very fine collection was reprinted recently: Gu Bingquan, *Shanghai yangchang zhuzhi ci,* Shanghai: Shanghai shudian chubanshe, 1996.

238. Bin Zhi, "*Shenbao* zhanggu tan, 10," *Shenbaoguan nei tongxun,* vol. 1 no. 7, 1947, pp. 36–37.

239. See "Benguan gaobai," *Shenbao,* April 30, 1872, p. 1; "Ci zhi qi tie zai baohao bi jian wei dao," *Pamphlet,* March 1874. This might seem surprising nowadays, but literary publishing was still subsidized by the author or patron at the time, and the concepts of authorship, copyright, and manuscript fees only gradually developed.

240. Bin Zhi, "Shenbao zhanggu tan, 5," *Shenbaoguan nei tongxun,* vol. 1, no. 5, 1947, pp. 18ff.

241. See Ge Gongzhen, *Baoxue shi,* pp. 100ff.; Fang Hanqi, *Xinwen shiye,* pp. 390ff.; Madeleine Dong, "Communities and Communication: A Study of the case of Yang Naiwu, 1873–1877," *Late Imperial China,* vol. 16, no. 1 (June 1995), pp. 93–94. The editors are also said to have had to make up these stories for lack of "hard news," a process described in detail in *The Celestial Empire,* October 2, 1875. See also *The Evening Gazette,* June 16, 1874; *The Celestial Empire,* January 14, 1875 and August 26, 1876.

242. "Bo Xianggang xibao lun Shenbao shi," *Shenbao,* December 25, 1874, p. 2.

243. "Tuzhe neng shi," *Xunhuan Ribao,* February 5, 1874, p. 2.

244. "Tanguan bei pian," *Xunhuan Ribao,* February 5, 1874, p. 2.

245. "Mengzhong ti lian," *Xunhuan Ribao,* February 5, 1874, p. 2.

246. See "Deng mi," *Yibao,* July 17, 1875, p. 5.

247. *The Celestial Empire,* August 14, 1875.

248. Mayer quotes regulations from the censorate in Beijing of the year 1873, in which most emphasis is laid on the fact that the printers have to publish the full texts. W. F. Mayer, "The Peking Gazette," in *Translation of the Peking Gazette for 1874,* Shanghai: North China Herald, 1875, p. viii.

249. "Zhuke wenda," *Shenbao,* January 28, 1875, p. 1. On the insertion of the *Jingbao* into the *Shenbao,* see also Barbara Mittler, *A Newspaper for China? Power, Identity and Change in Shanghai's News Media 1872–1912,* Cambridge: Harvard University Asia Center, 2004, pp. 173–244.

250. "Yin bao ni bao," *Yibao,* November 11, 1875, p. 1.

251. "Lun Shenbao gai shangyu beimiu," *Yibao,* November 11, 1875, p. 1.

252. Reported in Ma Guangren *Shanghai xinwen shi,* p. 86. I could not find such an article in the *Xinbao.*

253. "Benguan gaobai," *Shenbao,* January 16 and 17, 1882, p. 1.

254. Major to Alabaster, June 26, 1872, FO 671/29, no. 78; Major to Alabaster, July 23, 1872, FO 671/ 29, no. 92; Major to Alabaster, July 24, 1872, FO 671/ 29, no. 93.

255. "Changshe Ribao xiaoyin," *Xunhuan Ribao,* February 5, 1874, p. 4.

256. For a study of the rhetorical devices in the editorials, see Andrea Janku, *Nur leere Reden: Politischer Diskurs und die Shanghaier Presse im China des späten 19. Jahrhunderts* (Just Empty Talk. Political Discourse and the Shanghai Press in Late Nineteenth-century China). Wiesbaden: Harrassowitz, 2003.

257. See "Benqu ribao tongqi," *Xunhuan Ribao,* February 5, 1874, p. 3. The article "Lun xinwenzhi zhi yi," *Shenbao,* August 11, 1886, p.1, explicitly states that this tradition is Chinese and the newspapers are not to be regarded as a foreign import.

258. The most thorough description of these traditions is to be found in Lin Yutang´s famous *A History of the Press and Public Opinion in China,* where he describes,

p. 2, the history of China as one "of the struggle between public opinion and authority in China." See also D.W.Y. Kwok, "Protesting Tradition and Traditions of Protest," *Protest in the Chinese Tradition*, University of Hawai'i at Manoa, Center of Chinese Studies: (Occasional Papers, no. 2.), 1989, pp. 1–8.

259. "Zhuke wenda," *Shenbao*, January 28, 1875, p.1.

260. "Lun xinwenzhi zhi yi," *Shenbao*, August 11, 1886, p.1.

261. "Benguan Ribao lüelun," *Xunhuan Ribao*, February 4, 1874. This article from the now lost first issue of the *Xunhuan Ribao* is reprinted in the first weekly edition of the *Xunhuan Ribao*, which was issued by the publishing house itself. It survives and is attached to the beginning of the microfilm.

262. "Benguan Ribao lüelun," *Xunhuan Ribao*, February 4, 1874.

263. "Ribao you bi yu shizheng lun," *Xunhuan Ribao*, February 6, 1874, p. 3.

264. "Lun Zhongguo jingbao yi yu waiguo xinbao," *Shenbao*, July 18, 1873, p. 1.

265. John R. Watt, *The District Magistrate in Late Imperial China*, New York and London: Columbia University Press, 1977, pp. 377f.

266. "Shanghai xinwen ribaoguan shi," *Shenbao*, March 12, 1874, p. 1.

267. The latter case is dealt with by Madeleine Dong, "Communities and Communication."

268. "Shen an zhuanwen," *Shenbao*, July 16, 1875, p. 1.

269. "Xuan xinwenzhi cheng shu shuo," *Shenbao*, March 28, 1877, p. 1.

270. "Yangshi an lüe," *Shenbao*, April 12, 1875, p. 2. The *Jingbao* published edicts and memorials only *after* their approval or a corresponding decision by the emperor.

271. Sandkühler, Hans Jörg, "Öffentlichkeit, Öffentliche Meinung," in *Europäische Enzyklopädie zu Philosophie und Wissenschaften*, Hamburg, 1990, 4 vols, pp. 594–600.

272. Andreas Würgler, "Fama und Rumor. Gerücht, Aufruhr und Presse im Ancien Régime," WerkstattGeschichte, no. 15, 1996, pp. 20–32.

273. "Shu dichao Wang siyu zou Zhejiang sheng da li cheng shen'an shu hou," *Shenbao*, April 7, 1877, p.1.

274. "Benju gaobai," *Huibao*, July 18, 1874. This item was apparently written by Zheng Guanying.

275. "Shanghai ribao zhi shi," *Shenbao*, May 12, 1874, p. 1.

276. "Shanghai qianshe *Huibao*," *Shenbao*, June 17, 1874, p. 2.

277. The Huibao had attacked the *Shenbao* journalist Qian Xinbo; see above.

278. "Shu huibang an lüe hou," *Shenbao*, February 17, 1875, p. 1.

279. "Shu Tongzhi shisannian *Shenbao* zonglu hou," *Shenbao*, February 4, 1875, p. 1.

280. "Lun xinbao ticai," *Shenbao*, October 8, 1875, p. 1–2.

281. "Lun *Shenbao* gai shangyu da peimiu," *Yibao*, November 20, 1875, pp. 1ff.; the *Yibao* attitude is clearly revealed in the titles alone: "The *Shenbao* commits a mistake" (*Shenbao* cuowu), *Yibao*, August 20, 1875, p. 2; "The Mistaken Argument of the Shenbao" (Shenbao li lun zhi fei), *Yibao*, September 9, 1875, p. 2.; "Yingbao nibao," *Yibao*, November 22, 1875, p. 1.

282. "Particulars," *Xinbao,* November 23, 1876, p. 1.

283. Ma Guangren, *Shanghai xinwen shi,* p. 80.

284. "Xinbao yuanqi shu," *Xinbao,* November 24, 1876, pp. 2–3.

285. See "Benguan quanxi Xiangshan ren lun," *Shenbao,* January 21, 1874, p. 1.

286. Cf. James Legge, *The Chinese Classics,* vol. III, Taipei: Southern Material Centers, 1985, p. 331.

287. "Xinbao yuanqi shu," *Xinbao,* November 24, 1876, pp. 2–3.

288. Mary C, Wright, *The Last Stand of Chinese Conservatism: The T'ung-chih Restoration, 1862–1874,* Stanford: Stanford University Press, 1957, pp. 68–95.

289. Mary Backus Rankin, *Elite Activism and Political Transformation in China: Zhejiang Province, 1865–1911,* Stanford: Stanford University Press, 1986.

290. William T. Rowe, *Hankow: Conflict and Community,* pp. 50–56.

291. "Ni Shanghai zujie fangzhao Xianggang tingqing Huashen huiyi difang ying banshi yi yi," *Shenbao,* August 27, 1973, p. 1.

292. William T. Rowe, *Hankow: Conflict and Community;* Bryna Goodman, *Native Place, City and Nation.*

293. *The North China Daily News,* January 23, 1874.

294. Benedict Anderson, *Die Erfindung der Nation: Zur Karriere eines folgenreichen Konzepts,* Frankfurt a.M.: Campus, 1989, p. 41.

295. Tsai Jung-fang, "The Predicament of the Comprador Ideologists," p. 212, states that by the late 1890s forty mio taels of Chinese capital had been invested in foreign enterprises and Chinese merchants held shares in almost all large foreign firms.

CHAPTER 3

Joining the Global Imaginaire: The Shanghai Illustrated Newspaper *Dianshizhai huabao*

Rudolf G. Wagner

THE WORLD CONTEXT

The nineteenth century saw a vast expansion of the reading public in Europe and North America through public education; of reading time through the introduction of gas and electric lamps; and of reading occasions through extended leisure and railway travel. Paper manufacturing was greatly enlarged, and machine-driven presses sped up the printing process; the resulting higher actuality and lower prices made newspapers and periodicals interesting and accessible for a broader public.

One aspect of this print revolution is often neglected, namely, the printed image. Since the Renaissance, engraved reproductions of art works were widely available. Senefelder's accidental discovery of the lithography technique in 1798 eventually allowed for a photolithographic reproduction of a high faithfulness and low cost.[1] At the same time, the new printing presses were able to mechanically handle copper and woodblock engravings so that even in these two realms the obstacles to popularization were greatly reduced.

As a consequence, we see two print products flourish and enter into the homes of classes new to the market of quality images: the illustrated paper and the lithograph print. Since the 1820s, new illustrated papers such as *Harper's* and *Frank Leslie's Illustrated Newspaper* in the United States, *The Illustrated London News* and *The Graphic* in London, *Le Monde Illustré* and *Le Tour Du Monde* in France, and the *Illustrirte Zeitung* and *Die Gartenlaube* in Germany, to name but a few, successfully established themselves in the market and gathered enough subscribers to become profitable enterprises. At the same time, specialized publishers such as Currier and Ives in the United States[2] or the printers from Épinal[3] in France offered a wide array of hand-colored lithograph prints to decorate the home. (Color lithography was already known, but was not used by either.) While these papers and prints would also reproduce 'high art' and some of them, such as *The Graphic* (London) exerted considerable influence on the work of artist subscribers such as van Gogh, the subject matter and painting technique of the works reproduced here were generally geared toward the tastes of their new customers and the news media in which they were published. A new genre flourished—newspainting. With the growing importance of international developments, these media would visualize for their readers the sights of distant places and events. The Russian-Ottoman War on the Crimea (1876–1878) marked a turning point, as the *Illustrated London News* sent an illustrator to accompany its correspondent so that the pictures could claim on-site authenticity much as later news photography did. The entertainment aspect of these prints privileged the quaint and interesting, anecdotal and stunning image and information over a systematic or even strongly documented presentation.

The illustrated papers quickly formed something like a world community; they knew of each other, and they would reprint each other's illustrations and quote each other's articles as a way to improve and authenticate their international coverage.[4] We see the beginnings of a global imaginaire develop, in which images, perspectives, scenes, plot lines, and reader attitudes were increasingly shared, a development eventually finding its most cohesive expression in the universal grammar of the moving image later known under the name of the "Hollywood system."

The themes and styles of these illustrations reflect the efforts of the publishers to reach a new reading public, especially women, who were considered to be more attracted to easy and illustrated reading matter, as well as people from the newly emerging literate classes for whom a combination of image and word would provide easier access. In this growing importance of the image as a conveyor of information and entertainment, later developments in film and television are prefigured. The circulation numbers and longevity of these illustrated papers signal that they were profitable enough. These new media of "print entertainment," to take a term suggested by Catherine Yeh, did not come to the detriment of the more "serious" newspapers, which also saw a rapid expansion at this time. These serious papers continued to be geared toward a readership in decision-making positions for whom fast and reliable information on international, political, business, and social matters were at a premium. In fact, the illustrated press offered reading matter for the new type of leisure hours inserted into a strenuous working day and working week of these readers, quite apart from making paper reading a habit among the larger populace.

The new themes, the new technology, the new public, and the new market began to attract artists. While high art mostly shunned the new development, Baudelaire spotted its importance with his essay on the "newspainter."[5]

Although there had been earlier forms of art reproduction, Walter Benjamin's argument about a qualitative change technically, socially, and artistically still is plausible.[6]

In this print world, China was a frequent object of description and depiction, serving as a repository of the quaint and interesting, but it was not a subject. No Chinese illustrated paper was around to join the league and contribute Chinese perspective on things Chinese and foreign. While since the 1850s important translation projects for the Chinese classics were under way (by James Legge, L. Giles, S. Couvreur among others), no Chinese from that time managed to establish himself as a voice heard internationally beyond a narrow circle of diplomats. Chinese culture found itself decentered, and marginalized to a degree that Chinese literati were not even seen as reliable sources for the social, political, cultural, and economic realities of China itself, especially as far as the common people were concerned. The "physiological" (the term then for "sociological") interest awash among both readers and writers of the kind of Balzac, Dumas, Sue, or Dickens in Europe since the 1830s with its fascination with the strange and unknown lives of the metropolitan social types eventually also included distant peoples.[7] China missionaries found little to go by in Chinese works, and eventually published their own firsthand observation such as Justus Doolittle's *Social Life of the Chinese* (1865), Arthur Smith's *Chinese Characteristics* (1890), or Dyer Ball's *Things Chinese* (1903).[8]

One of the effects of this cultural marginalization of China was that the general trend was set, and continued to be set, in centers far beyond the Chinese cultural realm. Given the cultural power dynamics at the time, the question was not anymore whether China would join or not, the question was when and how.

THE CHINESE CONTEXT

It would feel good to insert China's joining the global imaginaire into a harsh context of imperialist expansion. The few PRC authors who actually had a look at the sources have found it hard to come up with evidence. In 1962, a former *Shenbao* journalist went through the early years of his paper. He ended up claiming that the English founder and owner of this paper, Ernest Major, "was truly a friend of China."[9] In 1988, Xu Zaiping did the same, with the same result.[10]

The decisive figure for the introduction of the illustrated paper in China as well as for lithograph reproduction of newspainting and art is Ernest Major. Born on February 15, 1841, with his twin brother Frederic into the modest circumstances of a third clerk in the War Office in London, he benefited from the eagerness of the father to give the boys a truly international education, including Chinese lessons; from the social connections of his uncle, a financier in the City; and, perhaps, from an openness to the outside world on the side of his mother who was born in Calcutta, the daughter of an East India Company clerk. The family seems to have belonged to a circle of Londoners with a marked and continuous interest in things Chinese, and an opinion—rare at the time—that in order to deal with this country and its people one would better know about its culture and institutions, and even speak the language. There was an element of Scottish enlightenment in their pursuit of improvement, their business acumen, and their cosmopolitanism.[11] They rejected what they saw as the tepid arrogance and ignorance of many of their countrymen who also were involved with China.[12]

The Major twins went to China in 1861; after various jobs and business ventures, Ernest moved to Shanghai where he is first mentioned in July 1870.[13] Here he now moved from trading to industry, and this with a truly amazing level of energy. Within the next five years, he founded, together with silent partners, what became the most important early Chinese newspaper, the *Shenbao* 申報 (1872); what was to become the most important Chinese language publishing house of the time, the Shenbaoguan; and a first national print distribution network with two stores in Shanghai and contracts with stores all over the country, the Shenchang Book Office, Shenchang shuju 申昌書局; later, after the printed image had been added to the product line, the Shenchang Book and Illustration Office, Shenchang shuhuashi 申昌書畫室. For all of these, he handled the day-to-day management. In addition, he bought a small chemical plant, which he expanded into a modern factory transforming the broken massive silver pieces, sycee, used for payment during the day, into standardized ingots during the night. His Kiangsu Chemical Works soon also began to turn out matches and chemical fluids for diverse purposes in a first step at import substitution. It is one of the earliest private modern industrial enterprises in China.

In 1878, Major spotted lithography as a way to produce cheap high-quality image reproductions, which will be the focus of this chapter. He bought hand-pulled lithograph printing presses and set up a further company within the Shenbaoguan framework, the *Dianshizhai* 點石齋 lithograph studio. He managed to hire the only experienced Chinese lithograph printer at the time, Qiu Zi'ang 丘子昂, away from the Tushanwan print shop the French Jesuits had set up in 1876 in Shanghai for religious material. To hire a Chinese printer was a policy decision; most printers at the time in Hong Kong as well as in Shanghai were multilingual Portuguese.

The new studio hit the market with reproduced paintings and books in 1879.[14] An illustrated volume on the wonders of Shanghai with fine lithograph illustrations (1884) shows Major's pride and appreciation of his role in creating the new Shanghai. Of the sixty-four illustrations by Wu Youru in this album, no less than four deal with Major and his Shenbaoguan.[15] Major was not shy either in praising the advantages of the new reproduction technique. The text accompanying the picture of the Dianshizhai office in this volume, (Figure 3.1), ran:

In olden times, the classical writings were all engraved in stone [for people to get rubbings]; the state of Shu [Sichuan] under the Meng [in the tenth century CE] was the first to change this by means of woodblock printing. Here now [in the Dianshizhai] comes another stunning innovation, even more extraordinary; again based on stone, it creates a new procedure. No need [anymore] for cutting and polishing [the stone slabs and woodblocks]; and none for engraving and carving them.

Red patterns [as the ones discovered by the Yellow Emperor on the body of the fish without scales which formed Chinese characters] and [texts written on] green bamboo [slips] are set [with lithography] in the wink of an eye; the craftsmen with the heavenly gift and the carvers with the uncanny skill [needed for carving the stone slabs and woodblocks] are gone without a trace.

The machine rolls over it, the stone shimmers wet, and collected tidbits [of writing] or official documents are transferred to the smooth stone.

The money to be made with lithograph [printing] is [so much that it is] impossible to calculate; and [the prints] will be [at the same time] a precious gift for the hundreds, the thousands, the tens of thousands, the hundreds of millions of later born.[16]

點石成金何足算，一嘉惠百千萬億之後人

The last line—enthusiastically breaking through the rigors of the two-times-seven character pattern of the other verses to make room for the multitude of the later born readers—reads like a program for the entire Shenbaoguan enterprise. It was a business undertaking, and it was there to make money, but it strove to integrate this clear purpose with a cultural mission of high valor: namely, to preserve and make available to later generations with this new, cheap, and high-quality technology the 'precious gift' of the rich inheritance of Chinese writing and graphic arts that had suffered so much from the recent civil war. This last phrase, rather than being an indicator of a hunger for profit, is rather an invitation to other—Chinese—businessmen to join in this profitable and meritorious enterprise to preserve Chinese culture.

In his book venture, Major had shown an acute sense of the importance of cultural compatibility for the success of a new product.[17] He made sure to insert his new lithography venture into a deep Chinese context. The idea of supplementing a written text with illustrations, charts, maps, and graphs was not new in China, but in text illustrations, so Major noted in a well-informed programmatic article, the image was always secondary to the text.[18] Already a Song scholar had noted that illustrations might be "most to the point" and "easy to grasp" while writing was "extensive to the extreme," and that "the scholars of old had emphasized learning, and thus had put the illustration to the left and the writing to the right," while the later born had "given up illustration and focused on writing [only]."[19] However, we still find illustrations in government-sponsored technical handbooks for agriculture and in the grand encyclopedia *Gujin tushu jicheng*. From the Song dynasty on, illustrations also depicted human action, and since the late Ming some of the illustrators of novels used this approach. Many of the morality books such as the *Taishang ganying pian* were illustrated with scenes emphasizing the core points, and so was the imperial antidote for these books, the *Illustrated Sagely Sayings, Shengyu xiangjie*.[20] The only areas in which illustrations of contemporary scenes with some claim to realism could be found were either commissioned from Western artists, such as those about the Kangxi emperor's campaigns and his southern inspection tour that were following the tradition of Western military painting, or were to be found on popular newssheets, which again can be traced to the same tradition. The illustrations previously inserted by Protestant missionaries into many of their Chinese publications had been made from reused Western copper engravings of weak remaining definition.[21]

For quite a few famous Chinese books, a typeset edition would be forbiddingly expensive because either the fine calligraphy of the original would be lost or one would have to deal with a combination of text and illustrations. Here a lithograph reprint would get very close to the original and could cut down on bulk by reducing size without losing in precision. The *North China Herald* noted this advantage in 1899:

> "The cheapness of the books thus produced is a great recommendation in a country where reading is a common accomplishment. Another advantage is that the beauty of good writing is better preserved on stone [with lithography] than on carved wood."[22]

Art reproduction also had a long Chinese tradition. Beyond the handmade copies of famous paintings, works were reproduced with woodblock printing, rubbings were made of inscriptions, and an entire trade of woodcarvers and printers specialized in cheap prints with scenes from the stage, images of gods, and symbolic matter for seasonal and family occasions. In the reproduction of Chinese ink paintings and calligraphy, lithography also had a clear edge—copies were undistinguishable from the original, and could even improve on it by being printed on better or cleaner paper.

Lithography would allow Major to stay within the confines of established taste, but do so with a technical innovation that cut costs and gave luster to print products cherished by the cultural elite as well as by nouveau riche merchants aspiring to this status. In and beyond Shanghai, a large and wealthy market loomed for lithograph goods.

By 1879, the Shenbaoguan had become a highly respected cultural hub of communication for literati in Shanghai and beyond.[23] The Dianshizhai could bank on Major's expertise in the mechanics of the Chinese book market and on his large clientele. The lithography products would be sold through Major's managerial innovation, a national distribution network for print products, the first of its kind for industrial goods in China. The *Shenbao* was used to advertise them and they were distributed with the paper and the typeset books. By

1889, his competitors had followed suit, setting up branches and depots for lithographed works in Peking, Canton, Chongqing, and elsewhere.[24]

MAJOR'S FIRST FORAYS INTO
THE MARKET OF THE PRINTED IMAGE

At first, Major, too, saw no other way but to print images from foreign matrixes on imported paper. In May 1876, two years before setting up the Dianshizhai, he came out with a set of copper reproductions of eighteen paintings done by "famous English painters," entitled *Huanying tuhua,* 寰瀛圖畫 (Universal Illustrations). The *Shenbao* advertisement gives an idea of this set, which I have not located.

> Our company recently bought from abroad paintings by famous English painters of a variety of Chinese and foreign scenes such as the Great Sacrifice at the Altar of Heaven, *Tiantan daji* 天壇大祭, in Peking; the comings and goings of merchants at the southern port; the eternal ice on the north seas; newly-made armored warships; and battles between the English, French and Russians [on the Crimea].
>
> On these paintings there are people, houses, trees, and instruments as well as all sorts of scenes. Even among Chinese drawing artists there is not one who draws in such delicate detail. Altogether these are 18 illustrations.
>
> Our company has written up short [Chinese] explanations for them so that the readers will at once know what they are about. We used top quality white foreign paper, bound them into volumes and added a blue cover ... Each volume is two *jiao.* These are extremely important foreign object painters, and the people who engraved [the copper plates] are all famous in our time. Because the [painters] came to China for the first time, they only took a small fee in order to get their name known here.[25]

We see a double agenda. In terms of content, themes of the Chinese dynasty's national grandeur are linked with disquieting images showing strong nations at war with modern weapons, alluring images of merchants trading in Canton, and some tourist sites. In terms of technique, the realism and precision of the foreign paintings are praised and shown as being superior to what Chinese painters could do, and therefore foreign paintings had to be used. The volume was considered the first issue of a journal with illustrations depicting "the world" that was to become the *Huanying huabao* (Globe Illustrated). To top the "national" agenda, a large print of an image of the Great Wall was folded into the volume to take out, mount, and hang on the wall.[26]

The Great Wall was at this time already famous and much depicted in the West, but it had not become a national symbol in China, where it was rather remembered as the place of wasted corvée days. Major's insert is the first to depict the Great Wall as such a symbol. Its grand career in this role only started in the early 1920s.[27] Waldron has shown that it was the Western image of the Great Wall that gradually percolated into China and helped it assume the grand role. We are here at the very beginning of this percolation. Major's Great Wall is the mother of the modern national propaganda poster in China, which eventually developed into a major industry for the "public" patriotic or revolutionary decoration of people's private quarters.

The cost of the paintings and of the foreign engravers drove the price to a high two *jiao*. Still, Shanghai buyers picked up the volume so fast that the *Shenbao* had to apologize twice for delays in shipments to outside subscribers.[28]

In this optimistic mood, the Shenbaoguan in quick succession published two more images. The big sensation of 1876 was the Wusong Railway, a narrow-gauge track between Shanghai and Wusong far beyond the settlement's limits. Many Chinese merchants had supported the scheme,[29] the *Shenbao* had published lively discussions and had editorialized in favor, while the *Huibao*, a paper set up in 1874 by merchants from Xiangshan in Guangdong together with the Taotai to do away with the *Shenbao*, had blasted away at this disturbance of the *fengshui* of the region and infringement on the livelihood of transport workers.[30] Assuming that many people had no real idea what this new thing was and therefore might have objected to its introduction, the *Shenbao* decided on its standard course—make the information available. Besides the articles, it now offered, for one *jiao*, a real photograph of the Wusong Railway, matching the newness of the train with that of the photograph reproduction technology, which had recently become available. This photograph print seems to have been the first to go on sale in China. They had "especially asked a photographer, *zhaoxiangzhe* 照相者," to take the shot so that even "women and children and people living far away can for the first time see this railway" by which Shanghai "travelers go everyday," "which is the first in China," "and never has been seen in other districts."

A few weeks later, the next sensation on the illustration market came with a hand-colored copper-engraved *Map of East Asia*, the *Yaxiyazhou dongbu yudi quantu* 亞細亞洲東部輿地全圖.[31] With a height of 110 and a width of 155 cm and meant to be hung on the wall, this was the first map of East Asia done on the basis of geographic surveys with a modern projection technique and all the place names in Chinese.[32] It would enable *Shenbao* readers to locate the places mentioned in the news; to get an optical impression of China's place in a segment of the world called Yaxiya dongbu, East Asia; to see the world cut up into nation-states with rigid borders; to travel through East Asia with the eyes and fingers—and all this without needing any English.[33] Major reacted to complaints about the high price of 1.5 *jiao* by explaining that the map was extremely detailed, the names were done carefully enough to be clearly legible, and it was hand-colored. The labor costs for the engraving alone had amounted to 1000 *yuan*. Compared to the prices of Western maps, this one was quite reasonable.[34]

With its mixture of Chinese and Western, national and tourist themes, the *Huanying tuhua* volume was to be a big opening and test for a regular illustrated journal containing items from the London illustrated papers with Chinese commentaries. These were to be written by Cai Erkang, whom Major had hired in 1874 to take care of editing his periodicals *Yinghuan suoji* 瀛寰瑣記 (Universal News Items, 1872–1874) and then *Siming suoji* 四明瑣記 (Global News Items, 1874–1876). The title of this new illustrated paper, *Globe Illustrated, Huanying huabao* 寰瀛畫報, which was started in 1877, linked up with the "global" orientation visible in the other titles.[35] A Ying already noted that it marked a profound shift by emphasizing the image rather than the text. It was in fact China's first "illustrated paper" to properly speak of.[36] A British consular official reported that, for a regular supply of images, Major had made a direct arrangement with the *Illustrated London News*.

> A Chinese illustrated paper has been started, issued nominally by the Shen Pao office. The sheets come from London with the illustrations printed by the Illustrated London News Office from their old blocks. It has been got out by Mess. Ingram of the *London Illustrated News,* and Murray, lately of the Hongkong and Shanghai Bank in Shanghai, and no one here has any pecuniary interest in it, only one number has as yet appeared, an enormous number of copies of which were distributed gratuitously. Number two will shortly appear, an edition of 20,000 copies having been sent out from home. The sketches are good, but the subjects are not well chosen, and the descriptive letter press is wretched: Her Majesty the Queen is spoken of as 英王 [the English leader/prince]. I append a copy of No. 1.[37]

The images were woodblock prints based on illustrations drawn by Westerners, printed in London, and shipped to Shanghai.[38] The only known surviving set of this journal shows that, of the fifty-three illustrations altogether published in the *Globe Illustrated,* several actually came from the *Graphic* rather than the *Illustrated London News.*[39] Major ordered runs of particular illustrations from both, and perhaps also from still other journals. The 20,000 copies refers to the number of illustrated sheets. The first as well as the second issues contained eight illustrations each. This gives roughly 2500 copies for the second issue.

The comment on the "wretched letter press" refers to the old quarrel of the consulate with Major's "pandering" to his Chinese readers by failing treat the queen on a par with the Chinese emperor. The title *ying wang,* 'English prince,' puts the queen into a slot reserved for imperial relatives and some higher tribal chieftains. According to the report, the selection privileged Chinese and East Asian matters as well as Western things known from news in the *Shenbao.* By this time, the *Shenbao* might have sold around 6000–7000 copies a day;[40] the decision to distribute the first issue for free and then print the second issue in 2500 copies signals Major's optimism that he would break new ground. He might have been encouraged by reports of Chinese interest for the *Illustrated London News.*[41]

Both Cai Erkang and Major wrote introductions for the *Globe Illustrated*. The "Small Preface for the *Globe Illustrated*" by Cai Erkang for the first issue in the fourth month of 1877 ran:[42]

> When people of old transmitted that the "three superlatives 三絕" [on the gifts presented to the Tang emperor] by Zheng Qian 鄭虔 were poetry, calligraphy, and painting, [this means that] illustration was definitely [still] on par with poetry and calligraphy, and [like them] was transmitted forever. Gentlemen in the West who are amateurs of learning have traveled in all directions with their pen in their bags, and forthwith noted down whatever they were the first to see or hear; and if there were things their pen was unable to transmit [with words], they would communicate it through an illustration. [The sage emperor] Yu of the Xia Dynasty [in antiquity] did not consider it beyond him to cast [bronze vessels] of the *ting* type with representations of [the hundred] things [so as to inform the people how these looked]; [does this mean] that [today only] the West is still practicing the way of [China's] olden times?
>
> [Journals such as] the *Globe Illustrated* are already circulating in the West for quite a while. The Master of the Zunwen Studio [= E. Major, R. W.] has had them posted to China, and [had them] printed and bound for publication.
>
> Among the people considered excellent painters, Wang Youzheng (Wang Wei 王維) ranks highest. After him came Jings (Jing Hao 荊浩, Wudai period) and Guans (Guan Tong 關仝, Song dynasty) in great numbers who in similar manner were capable of drawing mountains and rendering rivers by way of depicting their inner spirit. The Western gentlemen are their match in this method, and have fully grasped it. But to the [Western painters'] drawing with utter precision, and the meticulousness of their highlighting and shading, even the high skills of a Li Longmian (= Li Gonglin 李公麟, Song dynasty) in outline drawing are no match.[43]

From the catalogue of the books published by the Shenbaoguan in 1877, written by Cai Erkang on the basis of conversations with E. Major, we learn about the contents.

Huanying huabao, 1 j.

> These illustrations, *tu*, have been drawn by famous English painters and come with a legend by Cai Erkang. They are altogether nine in number. 1. The English old palace Windsor Castle of imposing grandeur and with imposing tombs, depicted as if one was eye to eye with this site. 2. The English crown prince on the steamer Aspen (?). The painted ship plying through the waves and the embroidered sails gleaming in the sun are as if they were right before one's eyes. 3. The new Japanese official dress. 4. Japanese ladies sightseeing in a carriage. They are [depicted in a] fine and clear manner, their manners [are shown] with great likeness, resembling the excellence of Li

Longmian's 李龍眠 (= Li Gonglin 李公麟) outline drawings. 5. Old royal tombs in Bijapur in India. Together with the first illustration this will be of interest to the archaeologist. 6. Fashionable English ladies' dress with the finest bracelets and rings. 7. A train made in India without the use of metal. 8. A train going into a tunnel. The sophistication [of this device] surpasses the work of Heaven, and its ingenuity reaches as far as the axis of the earth. In addition there is the Great Sacrifice at the Temple of Heaven. The officials in full dress are all very solemn, beautiful and lifelike. This picture is too large to be inserted, thus it was appended [in a folded format].

Those who look at [these pictures] will have the impression that they are directly connected to the localities and peoples of the different states, quite better than the 'Record of a Dream Travel' [written up] by Zong Shaowen [from the fifth century]. The price is 1 foreign jiao per issue.[44]

Cai is less concerned with subject matter than with another emblem of "modernity," painting style. By the late Qing, illustration, which had reached such a high point late in the Ming, had greatly deteriorated in quality. The new journal was to reinvigorate and change this tradition. The first step was to give illustration a status equal to that of text and calligraphy. The Chinese sages of old had seen the uses of realism, but today only the Westerners were adhering to these old ideals. The new journal would challenge the Chinese painting tradition by confronting it with Western painters who matched it in terms of characterization and catching the essence, but were superior in realistic detail.

The preface is not opportunistic. It does not offer the Chinese reader the quaint technical exertions of illustration craftsmen from abroad as had been done a century earlier, but boldly claims their overall superiority. The subject matter of the paintings was broadly selected and included a share of sights Chinese. The inverted perspective of seeing Chinese sights depicted and appreciated by foreigners was more than just curious. It showed that Westerners took great care to accurately render things as far beyond their own border as the sacrifice at the Temple of Heaven in Peking. They saw China as part of the world, and quite a dignified one. A China that wanted an honored place on this globe would have to make efforts to become familiar with herself and the rest of the world in a similar open-minded manner in which realism was combined with the quest for the essence. This was what the journal would help to achieve.

The Great Sacrifice at the Temple of Heaven painting is recycled here from the earlier volume to take out, mount separately, and hang on the wall. It continues the mass production of paintings of a national if not outright propaganda character begun with the Great Wall, although again no propaganda language is attached.

For the second issue, Major himself wrote the introduction.

Since antiquity the curious in events and things, in form and color 事事物物 形形色色之奇 has been made known by word of mouth, but as in this manner it could not endure, it ended up being transmitted in writing. Those things that could not be exhaustively rendered through writing ended up in being transmitted through illustrations. Thus there are clear directives since olden times with the story on the left and the illustration on the right. Looking at our times, however, Chinese books [are so many] as to make the oxen [pulling the cart with them] sweat and the rafters [of the house in which they are stored] bend, and no one is able to describe all the subtle curios and bold extravaganzas 幽奇俶詭 [contained in them]. But as to illustrations, there hardly are any.

That a reader will know the name but cannot figure out the shape [of the object in question]—that is the reason why it is so hard to be broadly learned.[45]

The studies in the West go after the real principle and not after empty names [so that] the books circulating there are able to crack the innermost secrets and shed light on the key factors. As they are furthermore concerned that people might not understand their explanations, they make the greatest efforts to insert fine illustrations, and rest only when the winds and the clouds, the sun and the moon, the mountains and the stones, the palaces, what flies and what dives, what moves and what grows have been depicted in finest detail. The readers follow the names [in the text], get the real thing [in the illustration], and with one glance they understand. Is not this great effort for the benefit of students something truly profound!

As to the daily papers, these definitely are an excellent Western device. With discussions of state policies above and reports about the life of the common people below as well as the successes and failures of different nations, they give to the ruler and the high officials the wherewithal to grasp models [to be followed] and warnings [to be heeded], and to the common folk they give the wherewithal to understand trends [in state policy] that are still hidden.

On this single hair [of the newspaper] a thousand catties are hanging, about comparable [in its importance] to [announcements] hung up at the Palace door where not a single character might be added or deleted.

Recently we also have set up an illustrated paper that is distributed all across the land. The first volume has already been brought into China with its captions translated, and those with a wide horizon proudly proclaim that they have never received anything comparable. We now have put together another volume and have appended [the picture] of a paddlewheel ship reaching the Changjiang; as a second supplement several items in Western script 西字之論數則(?) have been added. One does not have to be concerned that there is superfluous talk, as they all focus on what is essential. These [last-mentioned] items have been translated with special care and this translation has been appended for reference so as to enable one to enlarge what one has heard and seen. As to the subtlety and refinement of the illustrations anyone with eyes [to see] will appreciate them and will not depend on my making big words about them. As the translation [of the subtitles] is already done, I add these few words by way of a short introduction. 1877, tenth month, the Master of the Zunwen Studio [= Ernest Major].[46]

Major does not repeat Cai Erkang's points. Combined with writing, illustrations are useful and economical means of communication. The content is not reduced to the instructive or scientific, but all that is *qi*, curious and interesting, "in events and things, form and color." *Qi* is at the core of Shanghai's marketability.[47] Seen from the actual contents of the later *Dianshizhai huabao*, it includes all things that might evoke interest from a battle raging to the birth of a deformed child, from an underwater bicycle to the features of a celebrity. Into the traditional hierarchy, given in the philosophical part of the *Book of Changes*, of the spoken, the written, and the intended meaning, Major inserts the illustration as an additional and equally important device; he deplores the disproportion between the plethora of elusive Chinese books and the dearth of illustrations in them. His eulogy on the tight and focused empirical argumentation and painstaking illustration in Western publications is one of the strongest statements of the aesthetic agenda driving his engagement with the visual media.

In these few phrases, the harbingers of a dramatic new development can be seen. Equal status for the image is claimed, and practical steps are taken to develop a publishing enterprise that will focus on the image. This inserts Shanghai, and through it, China, into a strategic and global shift in communication media where the image starts its rise to supremacy. Major's enterprise did more than spot a market; it set out enhance the status of the image as a prop for "real" and realistic modern communication.

He links the illustrated paper to the daily paper rather than to illustrations of novels. The newspaper, however, is for him the key instrument of communication between high and low, and is the source from which the statesman learns what to do and what not, and the people learn to understand the direction in which things are moving. The importance of the paper is elevated to match that of imperial edicts of which not a word can be changed, certainly a strong claim for the dignity of the press.

The *Globe Illustrated* readers were special, they were "those with a wide horizon *hui yanjie zhe* 恢眼界者," who were able to appreciate its specific depictions of real things and events from all over the world. They were even willing to consider that there were flaws in a part of Chinese cultural pride, painting. The figure of thought that modern Western forms of communication only made into a graspable reality what had been envisaged by the sages of the Chinese past had already been used by Major in a *Shenbao* editorial about the purpose of newspapers.[48]

The supplements came without surcharge. The free supplement had been a perk already used by the *Shenbao*, which had inserted as free gifts maps and photographs, and would, in 1889, insert the first illustrated Sino-

Western calendar.[49] Free supplements were to be a key feature in the later *Dianshizhai huabao* (*DSZHB*).

The preference for clear and "physiological" depiction is also visible in Shenbaoguan books as well as in the language used in the *Shenbao* to describe contemporary affairs. Still, there remains a strong difference from the other publishing ventures of the Shenbaoguan. These focused on the high-quality prints of major Chinese works that combined Chinese cultural authenticity with modern Western printing techniques. With the illustrations came the claim that they were from Western hands because there was no comparable Chinese tradition alive. The paper's sales points were its foreignness, its "global" presumptions, and its insertion of incipient Chinese "national" themes. The second issue sold 2500 copies at 20 cents a copy, which, according to a contemporary, "must be considered a success, when we reflect that 20 cents is thought a considerable sum by a Chinese. The [third, R. W.] number which is now advertised contains fewer pictures, but is advertised at 10 cents, and the reduced price will no doubt result in increased sale."[50]

In September 1878, the Shanghai daily *Celestial Empire* had come out with a bold appeal for a Chinese illustrated paper on quite a different scale.

> One of the great requirements of China is an illustrated newspaper.... The Chinese are very anxious to acquire information, and their curiosity is very inadequately supplied by the papers now in circulation. They want to see for themselves and to get at the truth about this wonderful outside world which, whenever it comes in contact with their world, exercises such a disturbing influence upon it and creates so much irritation and hubbub.... We have very great hope that an illustrated paper would produce good effects and be a very widely useful instrument in arousing the native mind. There have been attempts made in this direction on a small scale, of which perhaps the best is the Child's Paper, but we should like to see larger capital invested in the undertaking and an attempt made on a wide and liberal scale.... The general scheme is very easily sketched out. The paper should contain a sufficient number of well executed pictures, and these should represent conspicuous objects of nature and art. There should be views of celebrated mountains and remarkable waterfalls, of great buildings and beautiful statues. The Chinaman above all knowledges craves a knowledge of geography, and nothing could be more beneficial than to give him such a practical acquaintance with the habitable globe as could be gleaned from faithful wood engravings. These would awaken his attention.... Ethnological subjects and objects of natural history, too, should be freely represented on the pages of the paper, and the manners and customs of men and the habits of animals, wild and domestic, would be brought to his attention. New inventions of a practical character would also be depicted, and scenes which have formed epochs in the history of the great nations of the earth would not be omitted, if the task of educating the Chinese through the eye was to be effectually carried out.... We should like to see some philanthropist with capital start an Illustrated News in China. He

would do more lasting good by spending his money in this direction than by employing it in any other way we can think of.[51]

The *Celestial Empire* kept a clear distance from the Shanghai missionary community, as did Major. It mapped out a philanthropic rather than a commercial enterprise; it was to use "faithful wood engravings"; it was to be centered not on China but on things global and foreign (from a Chinese perspective); and while it should have the task of "educating the Chinese," the idea of entertaining the Chinese does not occur.

A conceptual discussion about a Chinese illustrated paper did take place in China, but I see no evidence for any independent Chinese participation in it.

The *Huanying huabao* died mid-1880.[52] With five issues in five years it cannot have been too great a success.[53] All the thrill of seeing how Westerners would depict things could not in the long run obviate the necessity of coming up with newspaintings by Chinese painters and a stronger Chinese content. Major's publishing enterprise was increasingly informed by the insight that Western books and images would not sell in China but only works that combined a strong China focus, a "modern" agenda, and the best Western technology.

After the experiments with different types of illustrated print products had shown their market potential, and had indicated the preferences of Chinese buyers as well as the limits of what they were willing to spend, Major moved to a systematic exploration of this market. The techniques used hitherto, the copper engraving and the photograph, were exceedingly expensive. They wore off (copper engravings) or could not (now) be printed on regular paper at all (photographs).

Lithography offered the way out.[54] Late in 1878, Major bought the equipment, set up the Dianshizhai studio, and hired his Chinese master printer; from May 1879 on, the *Shenbao* advertised the products of the new press.[55]

Because Dianshizhai lithography art reproduction deserves a closer study, I will only sketch the barest outline here. The studio at first reproduced upscale paintings, calligraphy, and other artwork, not newspaintings.[56] Major had to get the originals for this purpose, and he seems to have mostly borrowed or bought for reproduction paintings by Jiangnan painters such as Li Gonglin 李公麟, the Northern Song painter already praised for the precision of his sketches,[57] Tang Yin 唐寅 (1470–1523), Yun Nantian 惲南田 (Yun Shouping 惲壽平 1633–1690), and Fei Xiaolou 費曉樓 (Fei Danxu 費丹旭 1801–1850). He also managed to get hold of—at least temporarily—famous pieces of calligraphy (or preciously crafted copies thereof) by Wang Xizhi (303–361), Shi Kefa 史可法 (1602–1645) and Mao Yixiang 毛意香.[58] "There is not the slightest difference from the original calligraphy," Major wrote in February 1879. "If you want to buy the originals, even dozens or more gold pieces will not get them."[59] And his prices were 2 *jiao* a piece, a fifth of a single silver dollar. He also commissioned paintings from famous Jiangnan contemporaries with the rights to reproduce them. Among these painters were luminaries such as Ren

Xun 任勳 (1835–1893) and Ren Bonian 任伯年 (1840–1896) as well as lesser-known painters such as Wang Lanfeng 王蘭峰 or Zhao Zi'ang 趙子昂. For special occasions such as the New Year's of 1884, Major would commission Ren Bonian to do a painting with "pines and four specified gods," which was "quite different" from what people normally would get, and was offered with different mountings and hand colored.[60] We know nothing of Major's patronage of contemporary Jiangnan painters, but this type of publicity through reproduction certainly helped to spread the national fame of these painters and increase their market standing. Already in June, the studio claimed that "the calligraphy reproductions of the Dianshizhai have already spread far and wide."[61] By the ninth month it was offering reproductions of sixteen calligraphies, fifteen *duilian* (parallel sentences to attach to the sides of doors), and twenty paintings.[62] It remained active in the area of lithographic art printing. An advertisement in 1884 lists 11 maps (among them at least three copper engravings), 32 paintings, 41 reproductions of rubbings, 9 calligraphies, and 32 *duilian* inscriptions—altogether 125 items without counting the various specifications offered such as hand colored or mounted.[63] This might not be a match to the Currier catalogue with its well over 300 items on sale in 1860, but the focus was not on popular prints but on high-register cultural items. The year 1879 also saw the last of the Shenbaoguan photography publications. On the occasion of the visit of the former U.S. president Ulysses Grant—a wildly popular affair in a Shanghai now craving for international status—the *Shenbao* made no less that 10,000 prints of his photo (which *Shenbao* readers got for free), running into terrible delivery problems again because the humid weather prevented the prints from drying.[64]

Very soon, the Dianshizhai studio also began publishing books in lithograph print, starting off with a very handy reduced-size *Zihui* 字彙 dictionary, an *Introduction to English, Yingzi rumen* 英字入門, and a reprint of Medhurst's *English and Chinese Dictionary* 華英字典 with a new Chinese preface by Ernest Major himself. Lithograph reprints avoided the high costs of typesetting with both Chinese and English characters or of reproducing fine illustrations such as those inserted into the travelogue *Hongxue yinyuan ji* 鴻雪因緣記,[65] or the agri- and sericultural handbook *Gengzhi tu* 耕織圖, both of which also came out in summer 1879. Compared to the Shenbaoguan, the Dianshizhai published few books, with only nine by the fall 1879. However, the real blockbuster book of the entire Shenbaoguan enterprise was the lithograph print of the *Kangxi Dictionary* (1882), which is said to have sold over 100,000 copies.

Lithography was a technical and cultural success in Shanghai and China altogether. Within a few years, other publishers such as the *Tongwen shuju* 同文書局 of the Xu brothers from Guangdong (1881) began to compete in the area of lithography book reproduction, reportedly starting off with no less than twelve machines and five hundred workers, and emulating the competitor by publishing the same titles such as the *Kangxi Dictionary*.

While also convinced of the viability of an illustrated paper in China, Major's eventual strategy went in the opposite direction in all four points suggested by the *Celestial Empire*. His enterprise was to be commercial, would print with state-of-the-art lithography, was to combine things Chinese and foreign, and it was to be entertaining. But were there Chinese artists who could fill a truly Chinese illustrated paper with newspaintings?

A CHINESE ILLUSTRATED PAPER FOR CHINA

By 1884, the Dianshizhai studio was the leader in the publication and nationwide distribution of lithography books and art reproductions. Together with the Shenbaoguan, it had taken on such mega-projects as a reprint of the entire richly illustrated *Gujin tushu jicheng*, a print known to this day as the Major Edition, Meicha ban. It was now a major industrial enterprise; an 1884 illustration of a large part of the Dianshizhai studio shows fifty-five people at work there on no less than ten different machines[66] (Figure 3.1). It seems that, very much like in Europe, private modern industrial enterprise in China began with printing and publishing, and that the Shenbaoguan played a key role in this development.[67]

Figure 3.1. The Dianshizhai print shop. Lithograph. From *Shenjiang shengjing tu,* Shanghai, Shenbaoguan, 1884, 1.60.

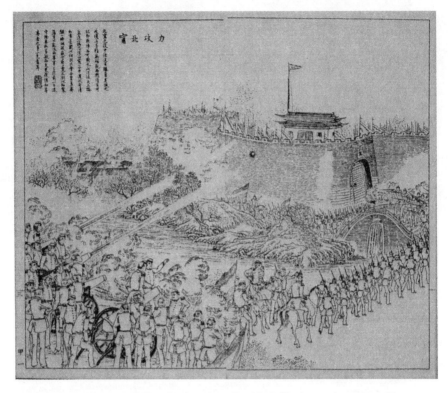

Figure 3.2. Wu Youru, "Forceful Attack on Bac Ninh." Lithograph. *DSZHB*, Jia 1, no. 3, 1884.

In April 1884, the studio suddenly came out with a lithographed illustrated paper, the now famous *Illustrated News from the Dianshizhai, Dianshizhai huabao* 點石齋畫報. Two factors prompted Major to go for a Chinese illustrated paper at this time: a perceived heightened interest in such a publication by the Chinese audience and the discovery of Chinese illustrators capable and willing to work as newspainters.

A glance into the first issue shows both factors at work. The issue illustrates the battles around Bac Ninh in the Sino-French War just raging (Figure 3.2). This War had brought humiliating defeats for the Qing army,[68] but it also had created a new hero. General Liu Yongfu (1837–1917), a former Taiping officer who had found refuge in Vietnam with his Black Flags, had sided with the Qing. His battle successes publicly proved that there was more to China than the obsequious Manchu and Han-Chinese officials. Illustrated newssheets touting his exploits were all over the place. Here was a moment of heightened public interest, a popular newspainting medium, and a crowd of capable newspainters. Major launched his new illustrated paper right at this juncture, and with this war as the first focus.

The French intended to overrun Son-Tay on the way to take Liu's fortress at Bac Ninh. In the Son-Tay battle (December 13–14, 1883), Liu's forces had stood their ground until they ran out of ammunition. They came back a few hours later with renewed energy. A correspondent of the *North China Herald* managed to get to the site. His detailed report describes the effective resistance put up by Liu's Black Flags. They managed to inflict losses of 200 men and twenty-two officers in the first half-hour of fighting onto the Turkish, Algerian, and Foreign Legion troops of the French.[69] From newspapers in Hong Kong and Shanghai, this stirring news about the singular successes of Liu spread among the Chinese "imagined community." Quickly, illustrated newssheets, *xinwen zhi* 新聞紙, made their appearance. While no such illustrations of the many routs of the Qing are known, the heroization of the outlaw Liu Yongfu certainly implied a harsh criticism of the court and a patriotic identification with this Han hero. These newssheets had both a news and a propaganda purpose. Some are included into PRC publications that otherwise quite openly excise illustrations glorifying resistance to forces considered "revolutionary," such as the Nian or Taipings.[70]

One such woodblock print, "Complete Depiction of the Great Success of Liu [Yongfu's] Army Getting Control Over Son-Tay," shows Liu's Black Flag army successfully ambushing a French contingent at Son-Tay.[71] No publisher is indicated. While later than the newspaper reports, it evinces little knowledge of the different types of troops the French used.

Other such prints deal with the subsequent battle for Bac Ninh.[72] The French news blockade, the grandiloquent reports by Chinese officials,[73] and the profuse rumor mill, however, all cooperated in obfuscating events so that it is hard to identify the battle. One woodblock print from Shanghai was discussed in the *North China Herald*.[74] At a price of about 5 *fen*[75] it shows the Black Flags holding out heroically even against the superior armament of the French, with one fallen Black Flag soldier fighting and a French officer being led into captivity.

A February 1884, Shanghai woodblock print directly refers to a French attack on Bac Ninh on February 4, more than a month before the French eventually occupied it. The numbers of French soldiers put out of action given in the text are as proud and romantic as the depiction itself. In a ruse, the French have been allowed to enter Bac Ninh, and through a sudden attack are now forced to flee into a well-prepared ambush. The strategy is familiar from the famous play *The Ruse of the Empty City*. Time and again the loss of a town was explained in Chinese communications in terms of this strategy.[76] The text claims that the French Commander-in-Chief Coubert lacked the manpower to take Bac Ninh alone and therefore used 4000 Annamese soldiers to supplement his forces. The Annamese, however, secretly contacted Liu Yongfu with the result that three thousand French soldiers were put out of action in the ambush laid by Liu's eldest son while Liu's daughter and his second son attacked the town, putting another three thousand out of action and forcing Coubert to flee. Coubert is seen leaving Bac Ninh through the city gate. Only seven or eight hundred French soldiers got away with their lives. The leading figures are highlighted through such name tags as "Heroic Great General Liu Yongfu" and "French Commander-in-Chief Coubert." The print had been occasioned by the report in the foreign papers during the previous days that the French commander Millot planned a further attack on Bac Ninh with a combined force of 12,000 soldiers.[77] This had prompted this "newspaper office" to quickly publish this print to mobilize public opinion in support of the Black Flag heroes. A late April, 1884, print on Liu's defense of Bac Ninh was reproduced in *The Illustrated London News* (Figure 3.3). These newsprints were thus combining information derived from newspapers, including Western newspapers, with rumors, wishful thinking, and propaganda. Their audience was a public already accustomed to modern ways of getting information from outside official channels.

Another print (Figure 3.4) presents a naval battle, "Up-to-date Illustration How in the River Battle for the Control of Bac Ninh/Hanoi Liu [Yongfu's] Army Scored Victory 克復北寧河內水戰劉軍的省新圖." It is an undated copperplate print of good quality published by a "newspaper office" in Hong Kong.[78] Another depiction of the same battle, this one from Tianjin, has a similar overall arrangement and shows that engravers of such illustrations would take hints from each other.[79] The reference seems to be to the battle at the paper bridge near Hanoi on May 19, 1883, during which the French commander, Captain Rivière, was killed and his contingent routed. This triumph of Liu Yongfu's must have served as patriotic propaganda once the war got under way in earnest. I therefore think that this poster came out at about the same time as the others when Liu Yongfu was lionized as a commander of a type needed to save China. Among the Hong Kong Chinese, national feelings seem to have provided a market even for such relatively refined and therefore probably more expensive newspaintings. The French side is clearly outnumbered in boats and personnel. In terms of cannon, both sides are equal, while the French have better firearms. Still, Liu's army has the upper hand as only French soldiers are in the water. The illustration manages to convey its information with minimal text through a very dramatic confrontation between the two naval forces in the center of the picture.

The term *xinbaoju* 新報局 "newspaper office" is not listed in dictionaries. Because both the publishers of the Shanghai and the Hong Kong prints used it, it must be a generic term linked with a place name to identify the publisher. It is not clear whether these "offices" were permanent.

Battle newspaintings are known both from the court and the popular level. The name tags for persons and places on the prints take after the paintings ordered by the court—sometimes from Western artists—to commemorate meritorious officers.[80] On the popular level, we find them in illustrations for novels such as the *Fengshen yanyi,* the *Shuihu,* the *Xiyou ji,* or the *Sanguo* as well as newsprints on actual events such as the Taiping and Nian wars.[81] Compared to their underlings, the key figures are often oversized.[82]

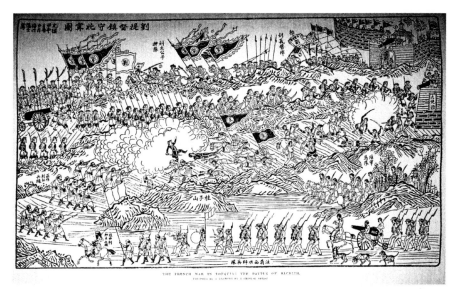

Figure 3.3. "Illustration of the Defense of Bac Ninh by General Liu," April/May, 1884, woodblock, reproduced in *The Illustrated London News*, May 17, 1884, p. 477. Woodblock print.

Figure 3.4. Xianggang xinbao ju, "Up-to-date Illustration How in the River Battle for the Control of Bac Ninh/Hanoi Liu [Yongfu's] Army Scored Victory." Woodblock print. Hong Kong, 1884. Public Record Office MPK 441/123.

The existence of papers such as the *Shenbao* ensured that this Vietnam war was the first public war in Chinese history. They enabled the emerging Chinese "public" to be informed on short notice about the war itself and the political deliberations surrounding it, including, on occasion, secret documents leaked to the papers. The *Shenbao* published the first-ever Chinese firsthand journalistic accounts of the battles by a Russian specially dispatched there, so that once "Franco-Vietnamese incidents occur, all that had to do with China would be reported to the paper, which would print these reports."[83] The new telegraph lines helped to speed up communication. A lithograph map of Vietnam was inserted into the Shenbao as a free supplement to help locate places mentioned in the news.[84] Soon *Shenbao* editorials began disputing the wisdom of continuing the war.[85] By contrast, the reports by the officials in charge of the war banked on the old communication structure that would take months to check their veracity. As a result, the resounding Chinese victories reported in the *Peking Gazette* were shown by the paper to be as much thin air as the victory reports of the French, and, oddly, the court itself ended up turning to the newspaper to find out what actually was going on.

This was an auspicious moment to launch a Chinese illustrated paper. The war would secure instant and high attention in the core markets and allow the paper a good initial run. With the Dianshizhai, Major had the equipment and the technical manpower to react quickly. The newssheets had shown that there were realistic Chinese newspainters. The paper would sweep the market opened by the illustrated newssheets and China would join the global trend toward news illustration.

Major was to compete with print publishers who were covering the entire span from the opera to the New Year to the latest news. From the outset, therefore, his new illustrated paper would not just illustrate big politics, but include the quaint, the timely, the sensational, and the beautiful. An emphasis on the core markets in Jiangnan around the new Shanghai was advisable. From the professional organization the *DSZHB* had since the first issue, it seems probable that such a venture had been in the planning and that Major had been waiting for the right moment to launch it. It was now crucial to find painters of enough skill and experience to fill the pages.

WU YOURU

PRC studies routinely describe Wu Youru 吳友如 as the man in charge of the *DSZHB*. Their evidence is weak. A short biographical note in the gazetteer of his home district (1933) begins his "progressive" career. Despite his fame due to an invitation to the court to paint the Qing victories over the Taipings, he did "not appreciate renown and fame" and directly returned to Shanghai.[86] The introduction to a 1958 selection of *DSZHB* newspaintings claims that *DSZHB* painters were not divorced from reality like their "formalist" contemporaries and had opened a new direction in painting, and elevates Wu Youru to the "chief responsible for the painting work" in the journal.[87] A 1959 *Wenwu* article added that Wu came from a poor family and had studied making drawings for woodblock prints. The imperialist [British] affiliation of the *DSZHB* notwithstanding, some of the illustrations showed "a certain progressive tendency" by reflecting the historical background and social situation of its time. The 1958 selection had been based on this criterion. In tune with the more rigid political criteria dominating in 1959, the article pointed to Wu's willingness to paint the suppression of the "revolutionary" Taipings as a sign that he was still under the influence of feudal forces; it claims that he eventually abandoned his newspainting orientation.[88]

Wu Youru's regular name was Wu Jiayou 吳嘉猷, but he signed his paintings and drawings Wu Youru 吳友如, Youru 友如, or Wu You 吳猷. Belonging to the lowly class of illustrators, newspainters, and *nianhua* painters, little information about him is available. Although Wu and other *DSZHB* painters also painted in more traditional styles, even the Dianshizhai studio itself never reproduced and sold their works separately. Efforts to determine Wu Youru's life dates and circumstances mostly relied on external and anecdotal evidence; often a dose of "anti-imperialist" rebelliousness freely invented for him by Zheng Yimei is added.[89] A short autobiographical note written by Wu Youru himself in 1893, has been overlooked:

> Generally, [the phrase by Su Dongpo written onto a colophon for a painting by the poet Wang Wei (699–759)] "in [his] *shi* poems there are paintings"[90] is a praise for Mojie's [= Wang Wei's] supernatural powers; and [the phrase in the *Shishuo xinyu* about Gu Kaizhi's painting of Pei Kai] "he added hairs to the chin [on a picture in order to bring out the spirit of Pei Kai]" is an encomium on the godlike [skills] of Zhangkang [Gu Kaizhi].[91] It is because in their excellence their method even surpassed the *samādhi*[-like refinement] that their fame rings through the ages.
>
> In my youth I have benefited from the largesse of my late father and fritted my time away playing without achieving anything. After I had reached my twentieth year, I came upon the Red Bandit [Taiping] troubles [in Suzhou], and, to get out of harm's way, I went to Shanghai where I took up the study of painting. Each time when I saw an original by a famous painter, my eyes, thoughts, and mind would be fixated to the point that sleep was gone and I could not eat. After delving into them for a long while it seems that I [myself, too,] arrived at some insight [regarding painting]. Only then I went out and made a name for myself, relying [on painting] for a living.[92]

Wu Youru thus was born in Suzhou and trained in Shanghai. He neither learned the brush-drawn New Years illustration style in the Shantang 山塘 shops in Suzhou nor the woodblock tradition in the Taohuawu 桃花塢 shops.[93] Elsewhere, Wu mentions his age, which gives a birth date somewhere between 1841 and 1845.[94] After the death of his father, who seems to have been a merchant,[95] and a leisurely adolescence, he fled the Taiping advance on Suzhou in

June 1860 by moving to the International Settlement in Shanghai, and took up painting. This was confirmed by a descendant.[96] According to a different oral source, Wu Youru took up painting in Mr. Zhang's Stationery and Fan Shop, 張臣記箋扇庄 situated in a small street west of the Yuyuan Gardens in the walled town of Shanghai. A branch shop set up in the International Settlement at the crossing of Nanjinglu and Henanlu was run by Zhang Jinfu 張錦甫, the maternal grandfather of the mother of Mr. Wu Zude, the source of this information.[97] One scholar pointed out that the Shanghai woodblock print tradition already depicted contemporary matters, mentioning such prints as the new Wusong Railway (上海新造鐵路火輪開往吳淞), the famous sites of the International Settlement (新出夷場十景), or the depiction of Nanjing lu (上海四馬路洋場勝景圖).[98] While it is unlikely that Wu Youru was involved in any of them and they are not clearly dated, they indicate a further realm of popular prints the *DSZHB* could tap into. These prints in turn show a similarity in taste with a literary genre that became popular in the International Settlement since the 1860s, the bamboo twig-ballads, *zhuzhi ci* 竹枝詞. Written in lively and simple doggerel form, these ballads relished in describing all that was new, shocking, and chic in Shanghai. Their regular publication in the *Shenbao* signaled their acceptability within a framework of aesthetic preferences that also defined the *DSZHB*.[99]

Little is known about Wu Youru's work before 1884.[100] In Wu's claiming grand masters such as Wang Wei and Gu Kaizhi as those whose work helped him gain some profound artistic insight, *huiwu* 會悟, one senses a certain defensiveness about the cultural status of his own art. No word is given about his ever having been a simple apprentice in a stationery and fan shop.

By the 1870s, the social status and life circumstances of professional painters, which had seen such fine days under the Qianlong emperor (reg. 1736–1796), had been reduced to the point that even the lady painter under whose paintings the empress dowager would sign her own name was so poorly financed that she had to sell to the outside market.[101] Because sponsorship by high officials within the context of their "secretary," *mufu*, entourage had also run its course, the booming Shanghai art market with its bent for innovation and the freedoms it promised held considerable attraction for artists. Many painters moved to the International Settlement.

The first dated Wu Youru work is a set of three hanging scrolls painted with ink and colors, dated 1878.[102] The theme, "A hundred boys playing in the garden," is a conventional topic in either *nianhua* print or ink painting. It shows Wu as an experienced artist with a lively brush and a capacity to engagingly present these boys at play. The scene might be set in the Yu Gardens in the walled city. The realistic detail with which the games are portrayed suggests that the painting might have served as a source of ideas for young boys and their educators. An undated woodblock print signed by Wu Youru, "Acrobatic Performance at Yu Gardens," shows features of Wu's later newspaintings such as perspective, focus on the action in the center, and a crowd of spectators signaling the high interest of the action.[103] While the line drawing is not common for woodblock prints, it has been used, for example, in the undated but certainly earlier prints about the Taiping and Nian wars from Suzhou.[104] Because the different acrobatic attractions are shown simultaneously, the print must be read as an advertisement for the spectacle of the group, done on order. With the resulting lack of focus, it certainly is not one of Wu's better works. I assume that it reflects Wu's style and life situation before he joined the *DSZHB*. In spring 1880, the Shanghai Daotai invited the Shanghai consular corps to a grand Western-style dinner in the Yu Gardens to celebrate the visit by the Prussian prince Heinrich. This was the first event of its kind and Wu Youru was commissioned to commemorate the occasion with a painting.[105] In the inscription, Wu is mentioned as a simple *huagong* 畫工, a painter/ illustrator who could be hired for such an occasion, but to get this assignment he must already have had some clout.

The *DSZHB* could thus bank on diverse traditions of newspainting. Wu Youru was more of a commercial painter than many of the "Shanghai-style" or *haipai* painters. A Ren Bonian might accept an assignment from Major to paint a New Year's painting with particular gods for reproduction, but normally would bank on the quality of his paintings to find buyers. All the allusions to Wang Wei and Gu Kaizhi notwithstanding, Wu Youru had an early affinity with the popular commercial print and the new urban fad of the actual, real, and sensational.

Major's choice of Wu Youru was a lucky one. Wu lived up to expectations and was instrumental in setting a style for the new paper, which was adapted by the other painters who joined if they were not selected for their affinity with it in the first place. Major had made his own aesthetic preferences clear in the statements quoted earlier. Only Li Gonglin's outline paintings got close to the Western style. It is no accident that Wu Youru used outline drawing in the *DSZHB*.

While there is no evidence that Wu Youru was "in charge" of the *DSZHB*, the pictorial evidence shows that he was Major's preferred illustrator. Much later, in November 1890, Wu even complained that he was not in charge of the *DSZHB*, but was just one of the painters there.

The [Chinese] illustrated paper is modeled after the West; it goes after the unusual and presents the newest so as to broaden what one has seen and heard, as well as to provide material for admonishment and warning. I liked them [the Western illustrated papers] at first sight, but each time when I set out to print something similar for public circulation I never got beyond the good intention. It so happened that the Dianshizhai was the first to publish [an illustrated paper], and they asked me to illustrate them. The connoisseurs all found that the illustrations I had done were not bad at all, but still in each issue only two or three out of ten [illustrations] were drawn by me. Shortly thereafter, I accepted the assignment by Zeng [Guoquan], the Guardian of the Heir Apparent, to paint pictures of the military successes of meritorious officials in suppressing the Cantonese rebels (= the Taipings). After their completion, the [pictures] were submitted to the imperial gaze [of Cixi] and happily enough met with august appreciation. After I had returned to Shanghai, the gentlemen from all over China were competing to line up in bringing white silk [for me to paint on] so that hardly a day was left for me to rest. So I set out to separately set up the *Feiyingge huabao* to satisfy [with reproduced paintings] these requests put to me.[106] Reality is so full of variety; newspaintings and explanations must strive to match it.[107]

Major himself signed the editorial explaining the purpose of the *DSZHB* and later editorial statements.[108] His interest in the reproduction of images is well attested and it is safe to assume that he personally was in charge of the *DSZHB* and of the Dianshizhai altogether. When Wu Youru entered the *DSZHB,* he was not a well-known painter. Neither does Major mention his name in his opening statement nor does he appear in the *DSZHB* advertisements. The first eighteen illustrations in the *DSZHB* are only signed with Wu Youru's seal, not with his name. We have to assume that the *DSZHB* made Wu Youru's name and fame. There is no source to substantiate the assumption that Wu Youru played a particular role in selecting the other painters or the topics for illustration.

When, in November 1884, the Shenbaoguan came out with its magisterial album of the great sights of Shanghai, the *Shenjiang shengjing tu* 申江勝景圖, with all illustrations commissioned by Major and supplied by Wu Youru, the preface made sure to muster Wu's newly gained fame by citing his name and adorning him with the title master painter *hua shi* 畫師;[109] only the eponym "famous," which was already used for quite a few Shanghai painters, was lacking. In line with the general practice of Major's management, however, there should have been little interference with the topics selected by the painters or their texts. As we will see, there were exceptions.

Wu Youru had seen and liked the Western illustrated papers on sale in Shanghai bookstores. He probably was familiar with the *Huanying huabao*. He had experience with the market-driven process of topic selection and product distribution, and even thought of setting up an illustrated paper himself. He certainly was ideally prepared to work for the *DSZHB*.

The painters were paid by the piece. Before the first *DSZHB* issue was out, Major had advertised in the *Shenbao* that he was looking for "hands famous for excellent paintings," *shanhua mingshou* 善畫名手, to submit drawings.[110] There was yet no offer of a monetary reward. Major might have thought that he could proceed as he did in the *Shenbao* or his journals; contributors did not have to pay to have their essays or poems published, but they certainly were not paid either. He was simply inviting a group of amateur painters interested in having their work published. Wu Youru was a commercial illustrator; he did not belong to this class. When this advertisement came out a week before the launching of the *DSZHB,* Major must already have secured from Wu Youru the drawings for the first several issues and paid for them. From the later issues, we know that the invitation to amateur illustrators was unsuccessful.

The first issue of the *DSZHB* was very quickly sold out, as was the second. People who had missed out on the first were clamoring for a reprint to have their set complete, and it was duly made. It seems that this very promising success of the new venture as well as the actual quality of the illustrations in the first issues prompted Major to shift tack and seriously woo professional painters of Wu Youru's kind, which had to include monetary rewards. Before the third issue was out, Major offered two foreign *yuan* 洋兩元 per drawing.[111] This is the first offer on record of publicly advertised payments for submissions of any kind to a newspaper in China. From then on, the names of the painters were marked on each painting, and the number of professional contributors quickly increased. None of the *DSZHB* painters was hired for a fixed salary; they were paid by the piece and continued to paint and draw for others. Wu's frustration that not more of his drawings were inserted into the *DSZHB* also involved income. But the construction of a deep disagreement between him and the Shenbaoguan, which eventually led him to set up his own *Feiyingge huabao,* is not convincing. The new paper was also distributed through the Shenbaoguan network.[112]

The *DSZHB* could bank on reader familiarity with the notion of newspainting. But, as opposed to the newssheets, it was a regular illustrated periodical not restricted to high-temperature moments. And while the popular prints had focused on great personalities in war, drama, heaven, or novel, the *DSZHB*'s most important breakthrough was to make the common man and woman worth an illustration.

THE *DIANSHIZHAI HUABAO* AND ITS ILLUSTRATORS

Studies of the *DSZHB* have hitherto been based on a reprint done first in 1897, which had been again reprinted down to our days. Thematic selections from them have been published in Chinese, German, English, and Japanese.[113] These reprints eliminate the cover page, the advertisements, the supplements, *fu* 附, and the oversized paintings glued in as inserts. To get an overall understanding of the *DSZHB* as a print product, one will have to go back to the originals. These are available in greater and smaller segments in different libraries, although even here the cover pages and, most important, the inserted lithographs are mostly missing.[114]

The *DSZHB* was in book format and came out three times a month in Shanghai from May 8, 1884, to August 16, 1898, in 528 issues with eight double pages of illustration plus text. It cost 5 *fen* per issue, with one hundred *fen* being one tael. Major enhanced the physical Chinese authenticity of his product in the same manner in which he had highlighted the foreignness of its predecessor. He used soft, high-quality, acid-free Chinese paper made from bamboo pulp printed on one side with the leaves folded. The notion of a "periodical" was still very new in China. In fact, most Western periodicals and even newspapers at the time came out as subsections of a book-to-be. The individual issues were eventually bound together. *DSZHB* readers were advised to collect the issues, and eventually have them bound as handy presents.[115] From the outset, the *DSZHB* had a well-developed complex numbering system. Each of the eventual six "collections" used a new numbering set, starting off with the ten heavenly and the twelve earthly stems, and ending with the four categories under which the hexagrams were subsumed. Each element in these categories would comprise ninety-six or ninety-seven double pages with illustrations plus an index. The covers with the title and date were of greenish or reddish thin paper of low quality. They were to be removed upon binding, and with them the date disappeared, which had tied the illustrations to a particular moment and event. From then on, the illustrations had to live by their timeless interest and attraction. The long life of the paper (1884–1898) and frequent reprints attest to fact that it was successful on both counts, actuality and timeless interest.

The *DSZHB* followed the Chinese calendar at a time when the Western calendar was spreading in Shanghai. The concept of the workweek and of Sunday as a day of rest and play had a most important impact on the lives of the city population. As a leisure paper, the *DSZHB* promised to fill exactly this newly fixed space. The demonstrative rejection of the Western calendar (after several shifts, the *Shenbao* printed both dates) points to a strategy of reaching a market beyond Shanghai where the new time construct was not now common. The title came in the archaic seal script much esteemed since the middle of the century in a calligraphy by Shen Yugui (1808–1898), a Shenbaoguan editor.[116]

Major himself wrote the programmatic preface for the first *DSZHB* issue. Because this is an exceedingly important document for the status change of the visual element in Chinese public communication, I will offer a full translation.

> Illustrated papers are much *en vogue* in the West. They generally select the most unusual items 事跡之穎異 from the various papers such as a device which has just come out, or something that has been seen for the first time ever, make a drawing of it, and add an an explanation. In this manner they have gained the confidence of their readers. In China, however, nothing has ever been heard of [such illustrated papers].
>
> In the beginning of the Tongzhi era (1862) a first Chinese-language newspaper came out in Shanghai.[117] Eventually the *Shenbao* continued in this line. In terms of all-encompassing reporting, selecting from a broad range of material, appreciating what is interesting and highlight what is curious 周諮博采, 賞奇析異 its form of presentation 體例 has gradually improved, and the facts it carries are invariably presented cleverly and in great detail. During the last decade or so, the *Shenbao* has become widely known within China

with ten thousand copies sold daily. This already left us no spare time, but the pictures alone continued to be missing. It turned out that the same was true for the Canton and Hong Kong papers. This shows that the Chinese rather enjoy seeing the world on the basis of written texts and definitely do not go by visual forms for its exploration.

I have endeavored to look into the causes for this. Generally spoken, Western drawing is different from Chinese. Those accomplished in the drawing of events in the Western method [with copper engravings] will make efforts to get a close likeness. Nearly all of them will furthermore use an acid for highlighting, and even in details as fine as finest hair and with a multitude of different layers [in the perspective], they still do not lack small empty spaces [between the lines]. With a magnifying glass one can fully appreciate their achievements in terms of space and depth. Their sophistication in laying on colors is such that the particulars of everything, shadows in the clouds, ripples in the water, the glow of a candle, the dark parts of the moon, clear weather and rain, morning and night will be clearly recognizable and visible. Therefore, if one just looks at [these illustrations], it is hard to make out all the details in the dense texture, but once one looks at them with an instrument [a magnifying glass] then it is as if one was personally entering into the scene there with the people in there acting as if they were all alive.

The Chinese painter [on the other hand] goes by established rules and has a set style. Before all else he already sets the basic arrangement, and then fills it out according to the circumstances, and it is in the density of the structure and the richness of the atmosphere that one will recognize the [painter's] level of scholarship and the breadth of his inspiration so that one can make up one's mind about his rank.

To sum up, the Western painter will put the premium on his capacity to imitate, while the Chinese painter most highly esteems his capacity to [paint] skillfully. Imitation presents the true [features] while [artistic] skill does not necessarily render the true [features]. But if [painting] is not altogether true to the [original], what is the use of supplementing the [written] report of an event by selecting a visual rendering?

However, from [Chinese] works such as the [Gujin] Tushu jicheng[118] and the Sancai tuhui[119] which do give [= illustrate] the mechanism for the use of instruments and present the variety of famous objects, the use of illustrations in books can be documented from olden and modern times with innumerable examples. As to the purpose [of this combination], if, faced with a confused mixture of things seen and heard and a confusion of names and designations [of places and objects], one exclusively relies on writing to convey [the information], one will be quite unable to convey it in all its intricacies, so that there are situations where it will be altogether impossible to spell out the news without using illustrations.

However, as with the changing times the [inherited] habits gradually open up, there are by now gentlemen from China who have some understanding of the form of Western writings, and as their familiarity grew with time, their preferences also shifted [in this direction].

Recently now, because the CHINESE court has decided to deploy its soldiers in the struggle between France and Vietnam, deep hatred for the enemy sweeps through the land. People who wish to do something good draw pictures about victories in this war, and they are bought and looked at in the market places, and quite easily become props for the conversation; from this we know that attitudes have not only come a long way with regard to news, we also can infer from this [acceptance of the illustrated newssheets] the same about the illustrated papers.

I have therefore asked people with a fine skill for drawing situations 精於 繪事者 to pick sensational 新奇 and entertaining 可喜 scenes and draw illustrations of them.

We will have three issues per month. As a rule they will have 8 leaves per issue so that those who enjoy news have something at hand to check out the situation. But when one opens it for easy enjoyment after drinking tea or wine, [this illustrated paper] will also contribute to the "pleasure of having one's mien dance and one's eyebrows fly."

As to the calculations by our company of the market [for our paper], how could I dare to talk about them as one would have to say that definitely once these drawings will be published, they will [sell so well as if they were] flying without having wings and rushing without having legs.

Guangxu 10th year in the last month of spring (May 1884) communicated by the Master of the "Appreciate News Studio 尊聞閣主人" (i.e., Ernest Major).

Seal 1 "Master of the Appreciate News Studio."

Seal 2 "Meicha 美查" (Major).[120]

Newspapers have already found acceptance in China, and the illustrated newssheets about the present war show that things are changing, too, in the visual realm. Illustrated papers in the West used the regular papers as a source of their stories. While Chinese painters traditionally did not go for realistic depiction, there is a tradition of using illustration to convey complex factual information. In a world with important and interesting events occurring worldwide, such illustrations become all the more important. With the *Shenbao* having prepared the ground, the new illustrated paper can count on quick acceptance, which also means that it will not be subsidized like missionary propaganda.

The text is a fine example of Major's "improvement" agenda. The benefits of illustration to convey complex reliable information and entertaining tidbits are clear and acceptance in China including commercial viability is now probable. While emphasizing the Western origin of the idea and painting style of an illustrated paper, Major inserts the DSZHB rhetorically and physically into the Chinese context, down to starting a new line whenever the Peking court is mentioned.

The care going into the production of the *DSZHB* signals the high cultural register into which it was inserted. The Shanghai Museum holds 4054 of the original drawings for the *DSZHB*. Their format is 28.4 x 47 cm. Because two of them belong to a single picture printed one half each on opposing pages, the total width was 56.8. Photographically reduced to 42 percent of the original size, the printed image has a width of 24 cm and a height of 20 cm.[121] (This reduction explains the small size of the characters in the texts.) The many glued-in corrections, which are not visible in the lithograph print, show how carefully the texts were proofread. The *DSZHB* took after the Shenbaoguan books, which have been praised for their editorial care.

From the outset, the *DSZHB* avoided the propaganda slant of the newssheets while offering illustrations of much higher quality. On its first illustration, Figure 2, the French attack on Bac Ninh, the French soldiers seem well enough organized and armed. However, not a human being is in sight among the dense of banners fluttering over the walls. The text explains the mystery.

In the battle for Bac Ninh the Chinese and the French alternately had victories and defeats. While [at this time] is cannot be said with assurance whether the town has been reconquered [by the Chinese], some military exploits can be recorded and the tactical alignment can be drawn up. At the [moment illustrated here,] the French were simultaneously advancing from three directions. Afraid of an ambush deep in the mountains or in the valleys, they formed a broad front to surround the town from all sides. Once the encirclement had been closed, they vigorously stormed the town from all sides. At once billowing smoke darkened the sky, the thunderous noise from all sides was beyond measure, the earth's very axis was shaking, and even the hundred streams were running astray—but the Chinese army had already withdrawn a day before to secure a strategic position.

The fox is good at being circumspect, but the rabbit is even craftier. It is just like a struggle between two excellent chess players, everyone tries to get the better of the other.

Seal: [Wu] You.

The illustration and the text strike a subtle balance between remaining true to the known facts and offering an intriguing scene where the French onslaught is elegantly evaded by the Black Flags. The historical echo with the "Ruse of the Empty City" is not made explicit, but optically present. Although without patriotic fervor, the illustration provided some comfort by showing that this time the rabbit was craftier. The text refuses to accept as confirmed reports that Liu Yongfu's Black Flags had in fact attacked the French on March 15 "when each Black Flag soldier proved himself equal to ten Frenchmen."[122]

With the shift from newspaper to illustrated news, the information was translated into a story with various comments and wisdoms attached. While not pervasive in Western illustrated papers, this was a standard feature of *DSZHB* reporting. The news is packaged into 'stories' in which strong opinions are expressed and the separation of news and comment is abandoned. The illustration is not comprehensible in itself. It offers a riddle that is solved only by the text. The texts are not taken verbatim from newspapers, and seem to have been drafted by the illustrators themselves.[123] The unified handwriting shows that they were calligraphed by other specialists.

The first issue already mapped the mental space the paper was to occupy. Military themes dominate the issue with more illustrations of the war, an American submarine and a military balloon, and a Jiangsu military official witnessing the explosion of an underwater mine. But then, the common folk come in. A bridge collapses in Shanghai under the weight of a crowd of spectators gathered to look at a fire; a judge has a corpse dug up for investigation in Suzhou; and the issue ends with a son cutting out a piece from his liver (which is on his left side here) for his sickly father to eat. The strong military and technical emphasis was not to stay. The next issue already is devoid of military and technical news altogether.

The journal's criteria for selection were actuality, sensational character, and entertainment value. Within this framework, news from Chinese and foreign courts had as much place as the murder on the next street, and the picture of an elephant would be as titillating as that of ambassador Zeng Jize, the deformed baby from Suzhou, or the dragon seen during a storm in Shanghai. The *DSZHB* continued the tradition of the *Huanying huabao* by reproducing pieces from foreign illustrated papers. While only a few imports have been actually traced back to the original, their order of magnitude is about 7 percent (145 of the 1920) of the regular illustrations in the first twenty collections. Wu Youru even copied the image of of Zeng Jize, the Chinese ambassador in London and Paris, from the *Illustrated London News* (Figures 3.5 and 3.6. Zeng's advocacy of a military strengthening of China in the face of the events in Vietnam prompted Wu to make a portrait "to give his admirers a portrait of him."[124] The picture marks the first step in the rise of a Chinese politician to stardom with high public image recognition. In other cases, illustrators took segments of foreign illustrations as props for quite different subjects (Figures 3.7 and 3.8).[125]

The Western illustrated papers in their turn soon discovered their new Chinese sister, and would occasionally copy its illustrations of some Chinese event (Figure 3.9). The *DSZHB* thus joined a worldwide family of illustrated papers who knew of each other, copied each other, and followed a similar agenda in their texts and images.[126]

The *DSZHB* could be ordered through the *Shenbao* distribution network, and bought in one of the many bookstores in different towns listed in its advertisements. While the *DSZHB* images reflected its privileged access to Jiangnan information and readers, it made great efforts to bring in information from elsewhere.[127]

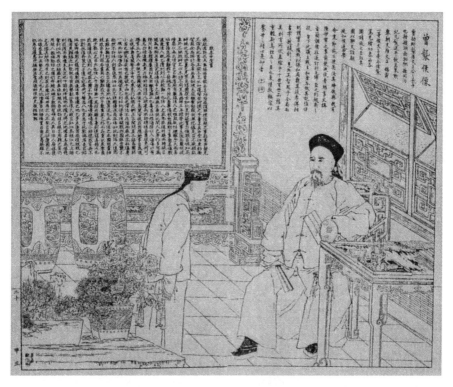

Figure 3.5. Wu Youru, "Portrait of Zeng Jize." Lithograph. *DSZHB*, Jia 20, May 27, 1984.

The *Shenbao* helped with an editorial review of the first issue from the "Look at the Visual Studio" 見所見齋.[128] The author with this programmatic emphasis on the image in his studio name bemoans the scarcity of illustrations in Chinese books; exceptions are only morality books with their illustrations of retributions, and the illustrations preceding the chapters in novels. Illustrated newssheets were sold by hawkers "who in the din of the streets and markets beat their gongs and call out with loud voices, a small flag fixed on their shoulder, in their hands a few sheets which they try to sell," much as in the Chunqiu period people would beat wooden clappers to make things publicly known. Often they simply made up the sensational news, fooling the populace in the process. Without newspapers, these illustrated sheets formerly had little to go by, and readers had no way of checking their truthfulness. With the linkage *Shenbao*/*DSZHB*, however, the author implies, a new age had begun. Apprehensions that the *DSZHB* might not catch on like the *Shenbao* had vanished. Before the second issue was out, the first already had to be reprinted. With the newspapers, news is now available quickly, and with the *DSZHB* illustrations, public warnings against evil are promptly spread. The paper also offers illustrations useful

THE MARQUIS TSENG,
CHINESE AMBASSADOR TO FRANCE AND ENGLAND.

Figure 3.6. "Portrait of Zeng Jize," *The Illustrated London News,* January 5, 1884.

Figure 3.7. "The Perfection of Touch and Tone." Advertisement for John Brinsmead & Sons, Pianos. *The Graphic*, November 17, 1888.

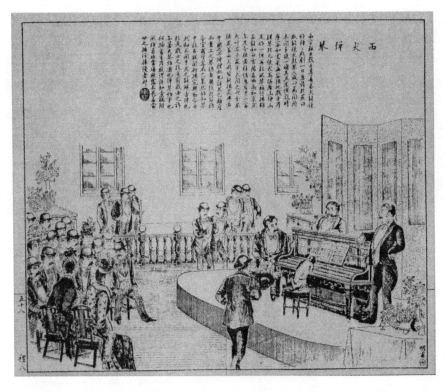

Figure 3.8. "Western Dog Plays the Piano." Lithograph. *DSZHB*, Li 8. 1895, second month. The dog replaces the lady in the previous illustration.

for the task of catching up with the Western techniques. Most important, the painters were now all Chinese. "The earlier reproductions [e.g., the *Huanying huabao*] were painted in the Western manner, while the illustrations now [in the *DSZHB*] do not overstep the bequests of China's classical painters."

Compared with Major's preface, this author focused on the "enlightenment" potential of the illustrated papers. His emphasis on the necessary link between the newspaper and the illustrated paper is well taken, and he sees the dangers of the claims to reliability of illustrated but invented stories.

Since the third issue, illustrators are offered payment and allowed to sign their names. After two issues by Wu Youru, Jin Chanxiang 金蟾香 or Jin Gui(sheng) 金桂 (生) joins in and both use different names to seemingly prop up the number of illustrators. The illustrator's seals after the text move next to their signature, and are replaced in their original place by seals with a terse comment on the story or a lesson to be drawn from it. These latter seals are often hard to read and might have had the character of an insider joke destined for the highly literate.

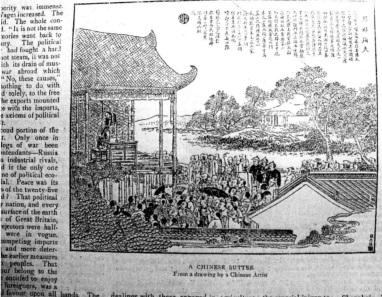

A CHINESE SUTTEE
From a drawing by a Chinese Artist

Figure 3.9. "A Chinese Suttee," *The Graphic*, November 23, 1890, taken from DSZHB, Yu 6, 1890, seventh month.

An illustrated periodical needed a stable group of illustrators and could not rely on amateur painters occasionally dashing off a drawing. Major's publicity and offer of payment per accepted illustration quickly attracted a stable set of Shanghai illustrators. For their freelance finances, the *DSZHB* was a boon. It offered a solid and regular source of income that would also allow them to paint and illustrate independently. In #5, Zhang Zhiying 張志瀛, Ma Ziming 麻子明, and Wu Zimei 吳子美 joined; in #6, Gu Yuezhou 顧月洲 and Jia Xingqing 賈醒卿; and the last to join for the first collection was Tian Zilin 天子琳 in #8. These eight contributors provided the bulk of illustrations for the first ten and many pieces for the later collections. They followed a common basic style, but retained a recognizable identity of topic and style. Only one other important illustrator, Zhou Muqiao 周慕喬 (1868–1922), joined later in this first year.[129]

Their share of illustrations was not equal, and changed over time. Wu Youru provided not 30 percent, as he later complained, but nearly 40 percent or 264 out of the first 680 illustrations, but would have liked to be the only illustrator. He temporarily left in May 1886 after #6 in the seventh collection.[130] He was followed by Jin Chanxiang (25 percent = 167), Tian Zilin (15 percent = 98), Zhou Muqiao (8 percent = 52), Zhang Zhiying (5 percent = 33). Illustrators such as Gu Yuezhou, Ma Ziming, Wu Ziming, and Jia Xingqing contributed smaller numbers, sometimes joining only for an issue or two and then dropping off for a while or permanently. In the first collection, five illustrators provided well over 90 percent of the illustrations. The paper had a stable set of contributors.

When Wu Youru left for other business between May 1886 and the end of July 1888,[131] other contributors simply increased their share. Tian Zilin contributed about a quarter of the remaining collection 己 (12 of 58), and other illustrators moved in such as Fu Jie 符節 (Liangxin 良心), who had only published two pieces in this collection before Wu left, and produced 11 after his departure. For the remaining three sets of this first collection, Fu Jie moved from 26 through 33 to 40 per set, eventually reaching about the original 40 percent share of Wu Youru (102 out of 324). He was followed by Jin Chanxiang (78), Tian Zilin (58), Ma Zilin (36) and Zhang Zhiying (20, only in the last two sets). Again five illustrators come up with over 90 percent of all the illustrations, with one of them providing the bulk. The journal maintained continuity and was able to quickly adjust to changes. Wu Youru's role was important in the first two years, but after a leave of two years, he only came back for another two from July 1888 until he set up his own paper in fall 1890. He was with the *DSZHB* four out of its fourteen-year lifespan. It was successful with him, and it was successful without him.

The painters kept their identifiable preferences and strengths. Wu Youru liked scenes of battles and similar commotions as well as portraits of important personalities; Fu Jie took on the misdoings of lower officials; Jin Chanxiang did many illustrations about Japan and Korea; Zhang Zhiying often painted scenes in temples and courtyards; and He Mingfu, who joined later, took on fake shamans, bonzes, and nuns. These individual preferences had an impact on topic selection. When Wu Youru left in May 1886 for Peking, the content tabulation offered by Nany Kim shows a drop in the topics he preferred and a steep increase in stories of the miraculous that he rather avoided. After his return, the proportion of stories of the miraculous dropped by nearly half, to steeply rise again when he finally left the *DSZHB*.[132] They had much freedom in the choice of their topical interest and no editor assigned them subjects to illustrate, but the editor probably could pick from a variety of submissions.

In terms of style, Wu Youru routinely used Western perspective. He drew in lively fine lines without the width variation familiar from brush painting. In his bold compositions with great outlines, he paid great attention to social types and their individuation. Jin Gui alone consistently hatched surfaces instead of just outlining the patterns. Zhang Zhiying and Tian Zilin developed similar types of outline drawing with strong affinity to some types of new year painting, and Fu Jie did all the technically right things but most of his drawings still lack character and movement. Wu Youru claimed that readers noticed which painter had done a drawing.

The *DSZHB* illustrators were active in many fields and on different levels. They produced New Year's paintings, made book illustrations of a much higher quality than the DSZHB illustrations, did paintings on commission and of their own choice, and some went for advertisement painting once this fashion had started. They occupied in the field of arts a similar diverse space as the new journalists studied by N. Vittinghoff and C. Yeh did in the field of writing. Both were early representatives of the new class of urban intellectuals.

What role did the *DSZHB* play in making them professional illustrators? The first two years may give an idea. If regular contributors were also paid two *yuan* per piece, Major spent about 680 *yuan* a year on the *DSZHB* illustrations. For his ten illustrations a month, a Wu Youru would make about 264 *yuan* a year. If we compare this income to the about 180 *yuan* of a full-time junior journalist of the *Shenbao* at the time, the *DSZHB* offered Wu a solid financial base, amply supplemented by income from the average three illustrations per month for *DSZHB* supplements, and by Shenbaoguan commissions for book illustrations, both of which were better paid. An example is Wu's entire set of sixty two illustrations for the splendid *Illustrated Famous Sights of Shanghai* (1884). While remaining freelance, Wu worked full-time and continuously for Major's company.

The *DSZHB* illustrations also helped some other illustrators to professionalize their work. With about 167 *yuan*/year, Jin Chanxiang had his livelihood secured, while DSZHB income was relevant for contributors such as Tian Zilin, Zhou Muqiao, and Zhang Zhiying, but not sufficient. They came up with a firm but modest number per set, but would increase their share according to circumstances or need. Commissions and painting sales were more important in their income than with Wu Youru and Jian Chanxiang.

The nine illustrations in the regular issue (seven full-page plus two half-page illustrations) would cost around sixteen *yuan*. As the paper cost 5 *fen* per issue, the illustration fees alone would take the total proceeds from 320 sold issues. Starting with a gross revenue of 150 to 200 *yuan* per issue for between 3000 and 4000 copies, the *DSZHB* reached about 350 *yuan* 1890 for 7000 issues.[133] While the fifty-five plus scribes and printers seen in the Dianshizhai studio were also doing other work besides the *DSZHB*, we see sizable machine investments as well as labor and materiel costs, not to mention distribution. To spend about 10 percent of the gross revenue of the paper on the drawings was no mean expense.

The *DSZHB* had a broad audience in mind. In his opening editorial for the *Shenbao*, Major had claimed news reporting would be done "in straight-forward but not vulgar style and this with a simple but clear narrative understandable for everyone from the scholar and grandee above to the farmers, craftsmen and tradesmen below."[134] His editorial for the *DSZHB* supplemented news reporting with the illustration. Because of the illustrations, the

DSZHB is often referred to as a "popular" magazine. The illustration texts, however, are written in a rich classical language full of classical and historical allusions and they do not make reading easier through interpunctuation or marking of personal and place names, techniques that even the *Shenbao* already had tried (and abandoned). The readership of the *Shenbao* consisted mostly of educated men; young men interested in new things might have found it particularly attractive.[135] We have to assume that the *Shenbao* and *DSZHB* largely reached the same readership.

While *DSZHB* like the *Shenbao* referred to Shanghai as "our place," it tried hard not to appear parochial. Still, its illustrations show an emphasis on areas best covered by newspapers, namely, Shanghai and the environs upriver until Nanjing, followed by Canton and Hong Kong, and Beijing.[136] The high number of Shanghai illustrations was not only of interest to Shanghai readers but to all wishing to get an idea of the modern urban world. Lu Xun lived still close enough in time to be trusted as a witness:

> "The influence of this illustrated newspaper at the time was very great, it was distributed throughout all provinces, it was in fact the ears and eyes for those who wanted to know about "current affairs"—which is what news was called at the time."[137]

The organization of the *DSZHB* issues for later binding, the high-quality print and paper, and the subscription price also point toward a relatively well-educated and affluent readership. Major already had slashed the *Huanying huabao* price by half, but with 5 *fen* the *DSZHB* was still over six times more expensive than the *Shenbao*. Just subscribing to both papers would have cost a junior *Shenbao* journalist as much as about 2 to 4 percent of his income. The *DSZHB* catered to people who could afford and did read a newspaper, and rather not to the "small urbanites," *xiaoshimin*, of Shanghai shop clerks, artisans, and house servants of Westerners.

The total amount of illustrations in the *DSZHB* is about 4500, excluding supplements and inserts. The remarks on them are based on a very incomplete perusal of the *DSZHB*, and barely a glance at Wu Youru's later illustrated paper, the *Feiyingge huabao*. The concept of newsworthy items changed little over time. In the early days, many of the *Shenbao* news items read like *chuanqi* stories. They took up the wondrous and bizarre, and infused it with a reassuring maxim. The illustrated papers basically adhered to this line of reporting, while the *Shenbao* professionalized its style.

Its origins notwithstanding, the difference between the *DSZHB* and the Western illustrated papers is quite striking. It presented a world where, as a matter of weekly routine, giant fish would land ashore, horses crash through the ceiling of houses, Irish women would beat up their husbands with their screwed-off lower leg, Koreans botched security regulations for their state examinations, and human reproduction is out of sync with a shocking amount of deformed births. Little of this would be found in the European and

American papers. The *DSZHB*, however, also carried quite a bit of unwitting social reporting about local riots being put down, refugee lovers coming to Shanghai, or nuns fooling the populace. Sometimes it became socially active. For the victims of the Henan flood in 1887, it produced illustrations and a map of the afflicted districts. It called for donations, and printed lists of donors, including the empress dowager. Even here the importance of the Shanghai base is visible. It writes: "In Shanghai donations will be collected in four district offices, in other cities this will be done in telegraph offices and the different relief institutions."[138] Still, it offered little of the detailed social reporting found especially in the *Illustrated London News*.

The *DSZHB* had a conservative outlook highly respectful of authority. The Peking court is only shown at its best, putting down rebellions and sending relief funds. The leading lights of the Yangwu current get positive portrait exposure. Criticisms of officials never go as high as a district magistrate, and their misdeeds are isolated. With its frequent portrayals of people hoodwinked by monks, nuns, and shamans, the *DSZHB* shares the *Shenbao* bias against religion.[139] The values expressed in the little introductions as well as in the mottoes are traditional. Very much like its Western counterparts, the *DSZHB* echoes the prevalent values among its readers and reinforces them with its images and stories. The figment of a stable world is maintained against all evidence where things could still be judged with confidence. At the same time, the content and the aesthetics as well as the hierarchy of the instruments of communication and the urban sensibility of the paper were in effect contributing to undermine the very stability they seemed to convey.

THE SUPPLEMENTS TO THE *DIANSHIZHAI HUABAO*

From early on, the paper had in addition to advertisements two kinds of free supplements: serialized illustrated books and lithographs to be taken out. They made the *DSZHB* into an illustrated, literary, and art journal combined. This feature was carried over from Western illustrated papers. Both the *Graphic* and *The Illustrated London News* carried black-and-white as well as colored supplements, and serialized novels, again with illustrations. These unstudied supplements are important for book and art historians. I will offer a survey.[140]

SERIALIZED BOOKS WITH IILLUSTRATIONS

While the regular pages of the *DSZHB* took up and transformed the realistic heritage of newssheets, military painting, and portraiture, the book supplements took after the book illustrations.[141]

It started off in 1884 with Wang Tao's (1828–1897) collection of jottings and anecdotes, *Idle Talk from a Shanghai Recluse,* with superior illustrations by Wu Youru and then Tian Zilin.[142] It was proudly announced as a "new *Liaozhai.*"[143] The instalments were numbered for separate binding.

The *Idle Talk* reportages required contemporary scenes, the specialty of the Dianshizhai illustrators. Such original high-register illustrated works helped upgrade the paper's cultural status, prompted readers to subscribe in order to get the full serialized work, and offered illustrators a platform for their higher skills.

Wang Tao had close links to the Shenbaoguan. He published there and helped with locating works for publication such as Shen Fu's *Six Chapters from a Floating Life*.[144] The original publication of *Idle Talk* in the *DSZHB* made him into one of the most appreciated *biji* writers of the time. Two more of his books followed in 1888 and 1889, the *Further Notes from a Shanghai Recluse*,[145] and the *Notes from a Leisurely Trip* to Europe,[146] with Tian Zilin starting the illustrations and Zhang Zhiying soon taking over and doing most of them.[147] From mid-1888, the *DSZHB* serialized *Fengzheng wu*, one of Li Yu's (1611–1680) most famous plays, with illustrations by Jin Chanxiang.[148]

For several months after Wu Youru's return from Peking, all supplements were taken from his new work. But since May 1890, the *Collection from the Ladies Quarters* was serialized with illustrations first by Wu Youru, and since October 1890 by Jin Chanxiang.[149] The Shenbaoguan had been very active in promoting writings by women. Shortly before the last instalment in February 1891, another new work, *Aiyuan's Riddles*, was started with an autobiographical preface by the author, probably the painter Xu Jiali 徐家禮.[150] I have not independently identified this text. It consists of quotations from texts ranging as far as the *Zuozhuan* and the *Liaozhai*.

This was followed in May 1891 by a series of twenty-five modern maps of the Chinese provinces with Chinese place names, the *Complete Maps of the Provinces Directly Administered by the [Qing] Court*.[151] It was based on a 1863 map that had been the beginning of modern map making in China.[152] An afterword by Major concluded the series.[153] It was in part a reprint of a 1879 book from the Dianshizhai, but with an important adjustment. The last map shows Zhenyou and Ili beyond the Jiagu pass because here the border with Russia had been changed consequent to Russia's occupation of Ili in 1871 and the Treaties of Livadia (1879) and St. Petersburg (1881). Xinjiang actually had been made into a directly administered Chinese province only in 1884 after the St. Petersburg Treaty had secured Chinese rights there.[154] In 1884, the Shenbaoguan had published the "Vertical Copper Engraving Map of the Directly Administered Provinces."[155] As far as I can see, the map serialized in the *DSZHB* is the first to delineate the borders with which the Chinese state entered the modern era, including territorial changes on the Sino-Russian border. The maps fit the Shenbaoguan policy of making information about China available to Chinese.

Before the map volume was concluded, a more entertaining item written 1890 and first staged in 1891 in Shanghai, the *chuanqi* play *The Tale of the Dragon Aflight*, was published here for the first time.[156] The author He

Guisheng (1841–1894) was a long-time *Shenbao* journalists and avid opera fan. The illustrations were by Jin Chanxiang.[157]

The last book serialized in the *DSZHB* was a large collection of Tang-dynasty *chuanqi* tales newly assembled under the title *Dianshizhai congchao*.It took three years, from 1892 through 1895, to serialize the three hundred tales with their anonymous illustrations.[158] The Shenbaoguan had been instrumental in pushing for a reevaluation of many genres that it deemed to be better fitting for a modern urban mentality, among them *chuanqi* tales, *chuanqi* plays, *biji*, and novels.

I have not been able to locate original *DSZHB* editions after #453 in the British Library, and therefore it may be that in the last seventy or so issues, more titles were serialized.

The regular inclusion of works of fiction made the *DSZHB* in effect into a literary journal as much as an illustrated paper. These works were either first editions, or they elevated and popularized a genre through high-quality publishing. The combination of these finely illustrated works and occasional other items, such as maps, upgraded the cultural status of the *DSZHB* while it continued to offer entertainment, information, and sensationalism.

The close links among the journalist, the author of new drama, the opera stars (and the courtesans), and the illustrators signal that these figures, all of whom newly rising stars of the modern public sphere with its center in Shanghai, might be shunned by some of the traditional elite, but had begun to form their own social world in which neither geographic origin counted much nor level of imperial examination achieved.

LITHOGRAPHY ART REPRODUCTIONS

The effort to give cultural cache to the *DSZHB* is in even sharper profile with the insertion of lithograph art reproductions. Major had close contacts with many "Shanghai-style" (*haipai*) painters. While some of them had also done book illustrations, they were in a different league from the *DSZHB* illustrators.

The new fold-in supplements started in mid-March 1885 with two oversized paintings by Ren Xun 任勳 (1835–1893). One was for the birthday of Śākyamuni Buddha, and dated first month 1885 (Figure 3.10). The other depicted the Venerable Kumârata. Both came with an inscription by the Shanghai painter Zhang Chong 張翀. The next issue came with a pair of fold-ins by Ren Bonian (1840–1896) and Sha Fu 沙馥 (1831–1906), again inscribed by Zhang Chong. As the Dianshizhai had also separately reproduced works by all three painters, they must have had a regular contractual relationship. The studio either bought only the right to reproduce the paintings or purchased the paintings and with that the right to reproduce them.

By New Year's 1886, when the first series of inserts ended, readers had received no less than twenty-nine paintings by Ren Xun, fourteen by Ren Bonian, eight by Guan Nianci 管念慈 (–1909) (Qu'an 劬安),[159] six by Sha

Figure 3.10. Ren Xun, "Śākyamuni Buddha." Lithograph.
Inserted into *DSZHB* #32, (丙8) mid-March 1885.

Fu, as well as two by Wu Youru, and one by Tian Zilin, the only "illustrators" allowed to join this august crowd. Many paintings were of the highest quality; some were linked, such as Ren Xun's series of Buddhist saints. Tian Zilin drew a large (66.5 x 36.3 cm) mother with child and some firecrackers popping, programmatically entitled "The entire world is one family!" 天地一家. This New Year's painting was hand colored.[160] Some planning was involved as the fold-in, by the illustrator Zhang Zhiying, only came on New Year's 1888.[161] The Shanghai school painters were not amateur literati, but professionals who painted for the market and lived off the proceeds. In the tradition of the Yangzhou painters of the late Ming, they favored a more "realistic" style that suited Major's aesthetic agenda.[162]

Wu Youru's Taiping Paintings

By July 1888, the *DSZHB* had a new sensation. Wu Youru was back from Peking. His invitation to the court had been a direct consequence of his work for the *DSZHB* and the Shenbaoguan. From the outset, he had specialized in military and official scenes for the *DSZHB*. Of his 138 illustrations published in the DSZHB until the signing of the Sino-French Treaty in July 1885, no less that 42 illustrated warfare (24) or were depictions of high officials and their ceremonies (18). There were only four such illustrations from other hands. Wu had shown quality and modernity as a military painter, and his texts had demonstrated his national commitment while generally remaining tied to the Shenbaoguan agenda of reliability. His portraits of leading Qing officials such as Zeng Jize, Li Hongzhang signing the Treaty, and Zeng Guoquan arriving in Shanghai (a fold-in) showed that he was able to handle this genre as well.[163] The Shenbaoguan in its turn had just published letters by Zeng Guofan and his diary, after having come out earlier with two chronologies of his life.[164] Because these materials must have come from the intimate family, it is reasonable to assume that Zeng Guoquan and Zeng Jize had good Shenbaoguan contacts.

Directly after the signing of the peace treaty with France, the Empress Dowager Cixi initiated a project to commemorate the Sino-French War in paintings. Probably to avoid criticism of elevating her own merits above those of the commanders in the Taiping, Nian, and Muslim Wars, the project was eventually expanded to include these. From the drafts of paintings submitted, some were to be selected and transferred to large silk canvasses by a group of artists under the Beijing field forces led by the banner man painter Qingkuan 慶寬 (1849–1927).[165] The canvasses would be displayed in the Purple Effulgence Pavilion within the imperial palace precinct. On March 22, 1886, Li Hongzhang was ordered to find a qualified painter for the purpose. He turned to Zeng Guoquan, at the time Liangjiang governor in Nanjing. Zeng turned to Wu Youru, who had become the most famous, and to him familiar, military painter at the time.[166] A century before, the Qing court had to order such battle drawings at huge cost in France from Jean Denis Attiret (1702–1768); now, a Chinese military painter was found who could do as well and for much less. Wu asked Zhou Muqiao, another *DSZHB* illustrator, to join him.[167] This imperial commission was the way to the top for Wu and created an upscale market for him without having to compete with the great painters about town.

Wu left in May 1886. He spent the next two years visiting the battlefields selected for depiction and reading the official Qing version of the defeat of the Taipings. The result was a series of sixteen paintings, which Zhang Hongxing has located in the History Museum in Beijing. They were submitted to imperial gaze and Wu Youru was to assert that they had found favor with Cixi herself:

I followed an order by Zeng Guoquan to paint the heroic feats of meritorious officials in the suppression of the Cantonese bandits. These were submitted to the Imperial gaze, and luckily found favorable appreciation. As a consequence, I gained some undeserved fame. When my business was done, I returned to Shanghai. People clamoring for a painting [from my hand] were lining up to the point that I had no spare time left at all. That is the reason why I set up the *Feiyingge huabao*.[168] 應曾忠襄共（曾國荃）之召命，續平定粵匪功臣戰績等圖. 進程禦覽，幸邀鑑賞. 余由是恭竊虛名，追事竣，旋滬. 索畫者坌集，幾於不暇給. 故設飛影閣畫報.

It is not quite clear what happened afterward. Zhang Hongxing has shown that the actual paintings executed by Qingkuan did not resemble Wu Youru's drafts. In my opinion, there can be no question that Wu Youru would not have made this public claim of imperial appreciation several times over if these paintings had been rejected. He had eulogized the empress dowager on various occasions, and was certainly anything but a dissident.

One Qing source claims that in 1892 Cixi went to the Xiyuan, and, upon finding that these paintings of meritorious ministers had become dilapidated, had Wu Youru called to repaint them. She also ordered having the old paintings photographed. Prints should be given to the meritorious ministers as presents so that posterity would again copy the pictures about the Restoration [after the Taipings]. But the court lost sight of the affair because of the war with Japan. When, in 1900, the allied armies entered Beijing, a Western general entered the Hall of Purple Efflorescence and saw the paintings still left there as well as several hundred photographs. Afterward the paintings were dispersed all over Europe. Someone once bought some in St. Petersburg. The Westerner [who sold them] said that these pictures had the same purpose as bronze statues [in the West], but did not last as long.[169]

This report has some credibility because a set of these photographs has survived in the library of Peking University, and because in fact quite a few of these paintings have been dispersed. There was some nervousness at court concerning paintings of the Taiping War heroes because there would unavoidably be "few Manchu and many Chinese."[170] Although he depicted in fact not a single Manchu, Wu Youru's efforts must have met with a positive response.

Once Wu was back in Shanghai, his entire set of paintings, battle scenes, and portraits of military leaders in the Taiping campaign was lithographed and folded into the *DSZHB* in the large format 25 x 27cm to be taken out, mounted, and hung onto the wall. They were published between late July and mid-October 1888.[171] At best, the copies Wu left in Beijing would have been transferred onto silk and hung in the Ziguangge, to which (to this day) hardly anyone has access. By accepting the Peking commission, Wu had not become a court painter. He sold the rights to reproduce his painting to the *DSZHB*. Their multiplication in the thousands, and their ending up as posters in the houses of *DSZHB* subscribers, made out of an official but secret court appreciation of these meritorious Han officials a public act beyond the control of the court. These officials are now available for public emulation, and the battles they won are enshrined in the public memory as glorious events, complete with texts explaining the details. The *DSZHB* subscriber would have, and see, paintings appreciated by the empress dowager herself.[172] Li Hongzhang and Zeng Guoquan did not object. The press by now had become a voice in national policy debates, and the public was clamoring for information about state affairs. The *DSZHB* now offered top Chinese officials the option to become public personalities, even public heroes. Their pictures would adorn the walls in homes where people lived who read papers, knew about their lives and actions, and appreciated their labors.

Through detailed studies of the battlefields and battle records, Wu tried to stay as realistic as he could manage. Although Wu's were in this sense historical newspaintings, the court commission greatly elevated the newspainting status altogether.[173] Given the impact the court still had on public taste, its appreciation of these paintings now added imperial glory to the allure of the budding metropolis Shanghai. While previously the DSZHB illustrators had at best been invited to do a fold-in New Year painting, the insertion of Wu Youru's Taiping series put a strongly Western-influenced genre of military painting on par with the great Shanghai school painters. Major harnessed them both to show the uses and attractions of the printed image.

Generally, we can infer the limits of the *DSZHB* illustrators' leeway only by contrasting their illustrations with newssheets by others on the same topic, and their texts with *Shenbao* reports. I have only located one item showing a direct conflict between Major and an illustrator, in this case Wu Yoru. The issue was patriotic propaganda. The depictions of the war with the French in the *DSZHB* clearly took a Chinese side; while not hiding the military might of the French, the *DSZHB* never depicted a Chinese defeat, even though they were reported in the *Shenbao,* but illustrated some Chinese victories, especially in battles in Taiwan, and denounced the execution by the French military in Tonkin of a French journalist for being in possession of military secrets.[174] At the same time, the *DSZHB* gave positive coverage to the Li/Fournier treaty of May 11, 1884, that was to end the hostilities; after the loss of most of the Chinese navy in Fuzhou in August 1884, Major had come out early in September with an editorial advocating an accommodation with France. China was ill equipped for this war, and reparation costs would block a further modernization.[175] Eventually, the *DSZHB* illustrated the peace treaty ceremony of June 9, 1885, and printed the entire text of the agreement. The illustration entitled "Signing the Peace Treaty" was done by Wu Youru (Figure 3.11). The accompanying text says that after the Chinese victory in Lang-son [which they had recaptured late in March 1885] "the French power deteriorated. Thereupon they submitted a proposal begging for peace 法勢頃衰，於是有乞和之議." After this had been graciously approved by the Chinese court, Li Hongzhang and the French ambassador concluded the ten-point treaty. In an official ceremony,

Figure 3.11. Wu Youru, "Signing the Peace Agreement," Heyi huaya 和議畫押. Lithograph. DSZHB #43 (丁5), mid-June 1885.

the treaty was signed in the presence of the diplomatic corps. Curiously, we have from this very period a lithograph print by Wu Youru from the Taohuawu in Suzhou entitled "The French Are Begging for Peace," *Faren qiuhe* 法人求和 (Figure 3.12).[176] It has been frequently reprinted in the PRC as an example of patriotic feelings among popular printmakers. Wang Bomin's *History of Chinese Prints* (1961) gives an interesting analysis. After listing different subjects of Taohuawu prints, he comes to the fourth:

> News about contemporary events. These are the most realistic depictions, and they have a definite political meaning. An example is the print "The French are begging for peace," that was sold by the Taohuawu. After the invading French armies had been beaten by the Black Flag army under Liu Yongfu in Vietnam, the capitulationist faction of Li Hongzhang proceeded, just to the contrary, to establish the Sino-French Treaty with the French, which was a Chinese sell-out. But the people did not accept the signing

Figure 3.12. Wu Youru, "The French Are Begging for Peace." *Faren qiuhe* 法人求和, Taohuawu lithograph print. Reproduced in Wang Bomin 王伯敏, *Zhongguo banhua shi* 中國版畫史, Shanghai 1961, p. 105, and Wang Shucun, ed., *Zhongguo minjian nianhua shi tulu*, Ill. 330.

of this treaty and even called it "The French are begging for peace." This print illustrates this idea. It evinces hot love for one's own fatherland and is imbued with patriotic thinking.

This short text highlights some of the tragedies of PRC scholarship. The author is fully aware that this scene is pure fiction in which the French admiral Courbet, a British ambassador Ba (who should be the French ambassador Patenôtre, but switched statehood here to show that all the Western powers are begging for peace), and the German customs advisor Detring were humbly begging Li Hongzhang and another Qing official (whose name I cannot decipher) for peace with the two of them having the backing of a mighty dragon about to blow the dark clouds away that roll in over the sea.[177] The Chinese military situation actually was anything but excellent.[178] The Taohuawu illustration is simple propaganda fantasy, coming with the claim of such illustrations to authentically depict events. Within the socialist–realist concept of "reality," however, it presents the "true essence" of the situation as opposed to its surface and shows things how they should have been instead of how they were. This progressive trait has earned the print a permanent place in PRC print histories.

With this drawing, Wu Youru left the Shenbaoguan agenda. The illustration is drawn in the style of the *DSZHB*, although its format proportions

(36 x 52 cm) do not fit. By this time, the Taohuawu had already started to use lithography, and this print seems to be done in this manner. The simultaneous existence of these two versions of the same event from the same hand suggests that Wu originally drew "The French Are Begging for Peace" for the *DSZHB*. This was rejected, I would presume by Major, as being incompatible with the realist agenda of the illustrations of his paper. Wu then drew another illustration of the event that appeared in the *DSZHB* with a text stating that the French were "begging for peace," but an image of the ceremony where the Chinese officials and the French are ritually on par as they were when the ceremony took place; his first version he had then publicized through the Taohuawu shops in Suzhou. The conflict—if I am right in my analysis—shows what fine line the *DSZHB* had to tread not just with its Chinese audiences, but also with its illustrators once issues of Chinese national concern were raised.

Wu's willingness to do two very different versions of the same event signals a modest professional self-assessment. He was an illustrator hired to do a job, and he would not risk destroying his excellent standing with the only illustrated newspaper in China over such a difference. The grand treatment of his Taiping paintings after his return as well as the resumption of his former prominent position in the regular pages of the *DSZHB* signal that there was no serious rift.

Since early November 1890, Wu Youru published his own illustrated journal, the *Feiyingge huabao*. While it was printed by another Shanghai lithograph printer, the Hongbaozhai 鴻寶齋, it was distributed through the Shenbaoguan channels even though it was a competitor for the *DSZHB*. Major had left the Shenbaoguan in 1889 and sold his shares. Wu Youru might have been prompted by Major's departure to set up his own shop.

MAJOR'S COLLECTION AND THE WOYOU SERIES

In mid-February 1889, just before the Taiping series had ended, a new series was started. It reproduced paintings through which one could "travel [with the eye] while reclining on one's seat," *woyou* 臥遊. The introduction offers a unique glance at Major's cultural interests and standing:

> Reading Paintings by a Window Looking out to the Mountain
>
> This is the first of the "Travel while Reclining" paintings. How did they come about? My friend, the Master of the Dianshizhai Studio (E. Major) was completely besotted with books and paintings and excelled in connoisseurship and discrimination 鑒別. He used to reproduce and circulate with lithography different kinds of picture copybooks, all of them finely done and impressive. As a consequence, Chinese collectors were all too happy to take out the authentic bequests of famous men from their travel trunks or convey them [to him] by way of pillar boxes, and they would discuss the six methods [of painting originally proposed by Xie He 謝赫] and the two schools

[as they showed up in these paintings]. The long scrolls and fat scrolls, the paper[-paintings] of a few square inches and the silk-[paintings] of a foot length [which he eventually got to see] were of a nearly unutterable beauty. What in the course of some ten years he managed to rejoice his eyes with were hardly less than a thousand and a few hundred paintings, and the number of painters represented there was well over a hundred from the Yuan and Ming on. Major was so overwhelmed with his appreciation that he could not bear the thought of letting these [paintings] out of his custody again. I have been copying [these] paintings as they came, and as throughout the years the numbers of these copies have become quite substantial, I put them together in a thick folder and called them, in emulation of the expression of [the painter] Song Shaowen 宗少文 [Bing 炳] (357–443) [who could not travel anymore because of sickness and then "traveled while reclining" through the paintings on his wall] *The Best of Travel while Reclining* 臥遊集勝 and now give it to the lithograph printers to print for common enjoyment.[179]

The author signs with the name Meiruo 美若. This is the *zi* of Xu Jiali 徐家禮, probably also the author of the *Aiyuan misheng* previously mentioned.[180] Major's publications of lithograph reproductions are described here as such a success that connoisseurs would bring their possessions to him for appreciation and joint discussion, and that a painter who calls him his "friend" will have the time to make copies of them that he then supplements with short poetic notes and has lithographed in the *DSZHB*. This close interaction between Chinese collectors and the manager of the Shenbaoguan enterprise to the point of his being able to view over a thousand original paintings by over a hundred painters signals a much stronger cultural interaction in concession Shanghai than scholarship hitherto has been willing to admit and able to document.

The *DSZHB* printed about one hundred and fifty Meiruo copies together with an index to make them into a collector's item, the *Woyou tu mingren* 臥遊圖名人.[181] Because Xu Jiali is giving the original painter for each item he copied, and often also provides information about the collection in which the painting was held, this might present a rather unique record of old paintings extant in the Shanghai region during the last decades of the nineteenth century. In quite a few cases, the originals may now be lost so that Xu's copies are all that is still available. It is to be hoped that historians of Chinese art will explore this treasure.

After this long series, the *DSZHB* continued to insert nearly sixty paintings, mostly fans, from Xu's own hand or copied from others, with several being large inserts.[182] These are mostly painted in the traditional styles. From then on, we find no more sensations. The policy of providing inserts was continued, but now the regulars from among the illustrators such as Jin Chanxiang, Zhang Zhiying, He Yuanning, and Fu Jie took over this field, with Jin Chanxiang continuing the tradition of Xu Jiali to offer copies of famous paintings.

SOME CONCLUSIONS

The Dianshizhai studio managed to develop a national market for the printed image, and had a strong impact on the aesthetic preferences dominating this market. It clearly contributed to the elevation of the cultural status of the realist and even the newspainters, and was the first clear articulation of the aesthetic preferences of the new urban classes, which developed in conjunction with similar preferences in Western and Japanese urban centers. Its literary contribution fits well into the program of the other publishing entities within the Shenbaoguan and did much to establish the *chuanqi* tale, the *zhiguai*, the *biji*, and the novel within the field of accepted and appreciated genres. Many of the big compilations of this literature in the 1920s such as the *Biji xiaoshuo daguan* used the Shenbaoguan compilations as their basic stock. The *DSZHB* managed to firmly establish the illustrated paper in the Chinese market, and for the next years and decades great numbers of illustrated papers would flourish all over the country.

The *DSZHB* linked up with the illustrated newspapers in the West and integrated China into a worldwide aesthetic agenda and a global exchange on the level of the image. The *DSZHJB* established a way of looking at the present world and its inmates as well as a way of perceiving things under the general motto of their being "interesting." The perception was national in that the paper took up items from all over the country, and it was international, as it did extensive reporting on the West, Japan, and the interaction of Chinese and Westerners in China. The paper cast social types as well as forms of social communication and conflict. These entered into the social perception and role-playing of later generations. The *DSZHB* stayed present in the market and in the mind through frequent reprints of the paper itself as well as of Wu Youru's collected paintings.

Little study has been done on the difficult question of the long-term effect of the *DSZHB*. The impact this journal might have had on how city reality was perceived, how social types were construed, how reality might have arranged itself into graphic scenes and rounded stories, and how, in turn, people might have emulated and imitated some of this in their own behavior, movement, and narration of reality is a subject that deserves closer investigation.

By way of suggesting such approaches, I will only shortly summarize the comments made by various observers on these questions without these observers' claiming in any manner to base themselves on more than anecdotal observation. Zheng Yimei claims that the modes of presentation, and from there of perception and action, were continued by the later illustrated periodicals, which were able to reproduce photographs.[183] Lu Xun suggests that they eventually fed into the inventory of social types and interesting scenes called on by the early Chinese schoolbook and filmmakers in Shanghai. The social type of the dandy, the *liumang* 流氓, appearing in the *DSZHB* with his glasses, slick smile, umbrella, and occasional cigarette became so much a fixture that Lu Xun complained in 1931 that even the heroes and "good" people presented in films of these years were looking like them and that the dandies in the drawings of his arch enemy Ye Lingfeng (1904–1975) (who had dared to draw a caricature of the great master) were not so much a copy of Beardsley's decadence than the offspring of Wu Youru's city slickers. The same was true for the young ladies in the films of the thirties who had come straight from the idealized courtesan types in the *DSZHB*.[184]

The *DSZHB* was a part of a social reporting with an emphasis on the visible and therefore "authentic." This had a strong market with regard to China where missionaries and diplomats of all descriptions vied with each other to give glimpses of Chinese life and customs, mostly accompanied by illustrations. Some Chinese joined in the enterprise such as Chen Jitong (Tcheng-ki-tong), the Chinese military attaché in Paris and easily the Chinese author best known in Europe in the latter part of the nineteenth century. Taking up the French frenzy of "physiologies," that is, physiological or sociological description of social types and customs, he wrote a book translated into many languages *Les Chinois Vues Par Eux-Memes* (The Chinese in their own eyes), which was replicated by the German diplomat von Brandt in 1911 with his commented reproductions from the *DSZHB* under the title *Der Chinese in der Öffentlichkeit und der Familie wie er sich selbst sieht und schildert* (The Chinese how he sees and depicts himself in public and at home).[185] The *DSZHB* thus forms an invaluable source for our understanding of the interior decoration of the minds of the most modern oriented Chinese of this period, quite apart from being the most important primary material for studying the emergence of the image at the core of Chinese public communication.

NOTES

1. Michael Twyman, *Breaking the Mould: The First Hundred Years of Lithography*, London: British Museum, 2001.

2. For a selection, see A. Bonfante-Warren, *Currier & Ives: Portrait of a Nation*, New York: Metro Books, 1998.

3. Mireille-Bénédicte Bouvet, *Le grand livre des images d'Épinal*, Paris: Editions Solar, 1996.

4. These papers would inform their readers about this community. The (*Leipziger*) *Illustrirte Zeitung* no. 2386, March 23, 1889, had a full page with the covers of their contemporaries, "Die Presse der Welt." The *Graphic* gave a detailed list of Western illustrated papers together with their circulation numbers on December 6, 1890, p. 647.

5. C. Baudelaire, *The Painter of Modern Life*, Jonathan Mayna, trans. and ed., London: Phaidon Press, 1964. Daumier, for one, did many of his scathing caricatures in lithograph, and eventually Toulouse-Lautrec discovered the potential of color lithography for his advertisement posters.

6. W. Benjamin, "Das Kunstwerk im Zeitalter seiner technischen Reproduzierbarkeit," in id., *Das Kunstwerk im Zeitalter seiner technischen Reproduzierbarkeit*, Frankfurt: Suhrkamp, 1963, pp. 7ff.

7. For some background on this fashion, see R. Wagner, "Oçerk, Physiologies, and the Limping Devil," in id., *Inside a Service Trade, Studies in Contemporary Chinese Prose*, Cambridge: Harvard University Press 1992, pp. 359–375.

8. For the one Chinese writer of "physiology," Chen Jitong, see Catherine Vance Yeh, "The Life-Style of Four Wenren in Late Qing Shanghai," *Harvard Journal of Asiatic Studies* 57(1997) 2: 419–470.

9. Xu Renhan 徐忍寒, *Shenbao qishiqinian shiliao* 申報七十七年史料, Liubuzhai wencun 六不齋文存1, Shanghai, 1962, mimeographed internal publication, copy in Zhongguo guojia tushuguan now publicly available, p. 8.

10. Xu Zaiping 徐載平, Xu Duanfang 徐端芳, *Qing mo sishinian* Shenbao *shiliao* 清末四十年申報史料, Peking: Xinhua 1988, p. 13.

11. David Hancock has traced this influence among Scottish and English merchants from modest backgrounds during the eighteenth century, *Citizens of the World: London Merchants and the Integration of the British Atlantic Community, 1735–1785*, Cambridge: Cambridge University Press, 1997, p. 386.

12. I am preparing a monograph on Ernest Major. For an example of his politics in China, see my "The Shenbao in Crisis: Guo Songtao vs. Ernest Major, " *Late Imperial China* 1999., and "The Role of the Foreign Community in the Chinese Public Sphere, " *China Quarterly* 142:423–443 (June 1995).

13. In the *Shanghai Desk Hong List* of 1869, he is not now mentioned. But Ann Gold has located a letter by Major, signed with his name and giving a Shanghai address, in the *North China Herald* on July 7, 1870. Cf. A. Gold, "Ernest Major and His Family," unpubl. paper.

14. The date given for the establishment of the Dianshizhai studio in modern Chinese scholarship wavers. Sun Yutang 孫毓棠, *Zhongguo jindai gongye shi ziliao* 中共近代工業史資料, Peking: Kexue, 1957, pp. 113–118, offers no source with a clear date. Gong Chanxing 龔產興, "Xinwen huajia Wu Youru—jiantan Wu Youru yanjiu zhong de jige wenti" 新聞畫家吳友如—兼談吳友如研究中的幾個問題, *Meishu shilun* 美術史論 10 (1990), p. 68, gives 1876. Shanghai shi gongshang xingzheng guanliju and Shanghai diyi diangongye jiqi gongye shiliao zu, eds., *Shanghai minzu jiqi gongye* 上海民族機器工業, Peking (1966) 1979, p. 187, even claims that the Dianshizhai studio was putting out illustrated papers, *huabao*, by 1876. Ch. Reed, whose paper "Steam Whistles and Fire-Wheels: Lithographic Printing and the origins of Shanghai's Printing Factory System, 1876–1898, " has been included, seemingly without attribution, as chapter 3 into Zhang Zhongli, ed., *Chengshi jinbu, qiye fazhan he Zhongguo xiandaihua*, Shanghai: Shanghai Shehuikexueyuan Press., 1994, p. 99, advances this date by one year to 1877 without providing evidence. Pan Yaochang 潘耀昌, "Cong Suzhou dao Shanghai, cong 'Dianshizhai' dao 'Feiyingge'—wan Qing huajia xintai guankui" 從蘇州到上海從點石齋到飛影

閣—晚清畫家心態管窺, *Xin meishu* 新美術, 2 (1994), p. 68, correctly but without source gives the date as 1878. The only reliable evidence, advertisements in the *Shenbao,* has not been used. On May 25, 1879, the Dianshizhai put its first advertisement into the *Shenbao:* "Our studio last year (1878) got from the West a set of new lithograph machines that can reproduce all books without difference to the original, and can reduce size. Photolithographic printing 照印 is a miracle; you don't have to strain your eyes for reading. It also can do pictures. Distribution through the Shenchang shuhuashi of the Shenbaoguan." From this date on we find regular advertisements of Dianshizhai publications. This squarely fixes the starting date. There is no earlier Dianshizhai publication.

15. *Shenjiang shengjing tu* 申江勝景圖, Shanghai: Shenbaoguan, 1884. The next to last illustration in the first volume is that of the Dianshizhai. The Shenbaoguan opens the second volume, Major's sumptuous house is the fourth from the end, and the Tushu jicheng ju, a part of the Shenbaoguan enterprise, is the next to last.

16. *Shenjiang shengjing tu,* vol. 1 text for second to last illustration.

17. See R. Wagner, "Commercializing Chinese Culture," unpubl.manuscript, and B. Mittler in this volume.

18. In the archaeological record, such a combination will be found in the Chu silk manuscript (fifth century B. C. E), a number of Qin bamboo texts, as well as the early Western Han Mawangdui silk manuscript. Liu Xiang's catalogue of the Han imperial library contained in the *Hanshu* lists a book with illustrations of the disciples of Confucius, *Hanshu,* Peking: Zhonghua shuju 1962, ch. 30, p. 1717, as well as two illustrated military treatises, the *Wu Sunzi bingfa* in 82 *pian* with 9 *juan* of illustrations, and the *Qi Sunzi* in 89 *pian* with 4 *juan* of illustrations. Chen Pingyuan 陳平原, "Yi tuxiang wei zhongxin—guanyu *Dianshizhai huabao*" 以圖象為中心—關于《點石齋畫報》, *Ershiyi shiji* 59 (June 2000) pp. 90–98, deals with the position of the *DSZHB* in the traditional text/image relationship. For Major's implicit reference to Zheng Qiao, see p. 116.

19. Zheng Qiao 鄭樵 (1104–1162), "Tupu lüe" 圖譜略, in his *Tongzhi ershi lüe* 通志二十略, Peking: Zhonghua, 1995, p. 1825. M. Lackner has written on the Song dynasty uses of diagrams to economically express thought. "Die Verplanung des Denkens am Beispiel der *tu*" in Helwig Schmidt-Glintzer, ed., *Lebenswelt und Weltanschauung im frühneuzeitlichen China,* Stuttgart: Franz Steiner, 1990, pp. 133–156; "Argumentation par diagrammes. Une architecture a base de mots. Le Ximing (Inscription Occidentale) depuis Zhang Zai jusqu'au *Yanjitu,*" *Extrême Orient-Extrême Occident* 14 (September 1992): 131–168.

20. *Shengyu xiangjie* 聖諭像解, compiled by Liang Yannian 梁延年, before 1681. I use a 1902 reprint.

21. *Tianlu licheng guanhua* 天路歷程官話 (The Pilgrim's Progress to Salvation Directed in Mandarin), translation by W. Burns, Xiamen, 1856, with illustrations by a Scotsman; technical illustrations in Wylie's journal *Liuhe congtan* 六合叢談 (1857–58) and the *Zhong Xi wenjian lu* 中西聞見錄, which came out in Beijing since 1872. The Jesuits published the "Child's Paper" *Xiaohai huabao* 小孩畫報 (1875 to 1915). Cf. Ge Boxi 葛伯熙, "'Xiaohai yuebao' kaozheng" 小孩月報考證, in *Xinwen yanjiu ziliao,* 31 (1985), pp. 168–175.

22. "Photo-lithographic Printing in Shanghai," *North China Herald,* May 25, 1889, p. 633.

23. R. Wagner, "Ernest Major's Shenbaoguan and the Formation of Late Qing Print Culture," in R. Wagner, *Ernest Major, The Life and Times of a Cultural Broker*, manuscript in preparation.

24. "Photo-lithographic printing in Shanghai," *North China Herald*, May 25, 1889, p. 633.

25. Advertisement *Shenbao*, May 26, 1876, p. 1. The *Shenbao* advertisements mention *Huanying huatu* 環瀛畫圖 in the title, within the advertisement itself speak of a *Huanying huabao* with Major signing as Huanying huabao zhuren, the manager of the *Huanying huabao*. *Shenbao*, May 12, 1877, p. 6. This advertisement was first spotted by Chen Gaowen 陳鎬汶, one of the authors of the *Shanghai xinwen shi* (1850–1949), p. 69. Mr. Chen was kind enough to inform me that he also failed to locate a copy.

26. It came with a note: "Because this painting is very large, we did not insert it into the paper. However, it may appropriately be mounted and hung onto the wall." The term used here, *bao* 報, "paper," signals that Major was thinking of this enterprise as a paper or journal. Quoted in Ma Guangren 馬光仁, ed., *Shanghai xinwen shi* 上海新聞史: (1850–1949), Shanghai: Fudan daxue chubanshe, 1996, p. 69. The consular interpreter Carles referred to this item as an issue of the Illustrated paper. FO 228/572 Shanghai 1876 Intelligence report for the Quarter May 1–July 31 by Mr. Carles, enclosed in Medhurst to Wade Desp. no. 130, 18 Aug 1876, p. 287b.

27. The *Tuhua ribao* 圖畫日報, 1 (1901), p. 1, still found it necessary to tell its readers what this strange wall was. It seems that Sun Yat-sen was the first to describe it as the preserver of the Chinese agriculturalist race against the marauding nomads. Cf. A. Waldron, *The Great Wall of China*, Cambridge: Cambridge University Press, 1990, pp. 194–215; the reference to Sun Yat-sen is on p. 215. Chinese early modern historians such as Zhang Xiangwen 張相文 (1867–1933) and Liang Qichao had by then already shown that the Ming wall had little in common with the edifice erected by Qin Shihuangdi. In Sun's description, the two are merged as in most Western descriptions at the time.

28. Advertisement *Shenbao*, June 7, 1876, p. 1; June 22, 1876, p. 1.

29. When the Qing court decided to close the railway down and buy the rails, some one hundred and fifty-one Shanghai merchants signed a petition asking the court to keep the railway in place. FO 228/593 from Shanghai July 9, 1877–end of year. Intelligence report from January 15, 1877 to June 30, 1877 by Donald Spence, forwarded to Peking by Davenport July 12, 1877; the petition is enclosed in Document No. 82, September 26, 1877, pp. 141ff.

30. The *Huibao* was published from June through August 1874. An example is the editorial in the *Huibao* on July 20, 1874, 'On the Wusung Railway' of which a translation is included in Enclosure 1 in Mr. Medhurst's Despatch no. 68, Shanghai 28 July 1874, in FO 228/540, p. 324. The Daotai's protest is in FO 228/571 (Beginning 1876 ff.), Inclosure No.12 in Medhurst No. 25 of February 26, 1876, p. 132: Despatch from the Taotai of Shanghai to Consul Medhurst, February 20, 1876.

31. Advertisement *Shenbao* September 9, 1876. The height was 4 chi 3 cun, the width 3 chi.

32. Although this map sold in many thousand copies, I have not been able to locate a single copy in either China or the West. When the copper plates were worn

out, the Dianshizhai studio came out with a lithograph reproduction in 1884, of which a hand-colored copy is in the Map Department of the Zhongguo Guojia Tushuguan in Beijing. This lithograph reprint seemingly is no match for the accuracy in detail the copper engravings had. I am exceedingly grateful to Prof. Li Xiaocong from the Geography Department of Peking University to have alerted me to this copy. The *Shenbao* continued to insert maps of specific areas of conflict into its pages, mostly, as in the beginning of the Sino-French War in 1884, on a single sheet that could be taken out.

33. Major was to publish the first professional map of Shanghai a few years later that carefully listed not just the Western Hongs but all the Chinese Hongs as well, and gave detailed plans of the *linong* blocks only summarily depicted in the Western Shanghai maps. *Shanghai shi quan ditu*, Shenbaoguan, 1882. On the importance and structure of this map, see Catherine V. Yeh, "Representing the City: Shanghai and its Maps" in David Faure, ed., *Town and Country in China: Identity and Perception*, Oxford: Palgrave, in association with St. Antony's College, pp. 166–202.

34. Advertisement *Shenbao* September 20, 1876. A month later extras were offered. Three yuan more bought it with a Chinese mounting, and for four it was glued on a firm matting in the Western style. For 3.5 *yuan*, one could get a box to store it in that was useful for its protection. Places in Ningpo, Hankow, Suzhou, Fuzhou, and Hong Kong were listed where one could buy the map. Most of these were foreign shops that must be seen in addition to the regular *Shenbao* outlets. Advertisement *Shenbao* 28 Oct., 1876.

35. There is some confusion about the title of this paper, which is often quoted as *Yinghuan huabao* 瀛寰畫報. The paper never had this name, but the early advertisements in the Shenbao carried this inverted title.

36. A Ying 阿英, *Zhongguo huabao fazhan de jingguo* 中國畫報發展的經過, appendix to his *Wan Qing xiaobao lu* 晚清小報錄 in his *Wanqing wenyi baokan shulüe*, Shanghai: Gudian wenxue Press, 1957, p. 90.

37. FO 228/593 from Shanghai July 9, 1877–end of year. Intelligence report from January 15, 1877 to June 30, 1877, by Donald Spence, forwarded to Peking by Davenport July 12, 1877, p. 24.

38. Ma Guangren, ed., *Shanghai xinwen shi*, p. 1101, wrongly assumes that the journal was done in lithograph technique. The statement in the same book, on p. 69, that it was printed from copper plates with the texts added in lithography is equally erroneous. The *Huanying tuhua* was printed from copper plates.

39. Zhang Hongxing, "Disappearing Print-Makers: Ernest Major's Illustrated Magazine in Shanghai in 1870s–1880s," unpubl. manuscript, London 1996, p. 5. I am grateful to Dr. Zhang for having made this manuscript available to me. According to him, the seventh print in the second volume shows the first Chinese ambassador to London, Guo Songtao, and his deputy, Liu Xihong. It is identical with the illustration in the *Illustrated London News* on February 24, 1877. The last illustration in the last volume (1879) reproduces a French oil painting and is based on the print in *The Graphic* on October 6, 1877. In his PhD dissertation, Dr. Zhang adduces a further example. The fourth issue, published on March 9, 1878, reproduces under the Chinese title "A Fort already Captured from the Russians by the Turkish Army" the "Attack on the Heights of St. Nicolas from the Shipka Side" in the war between Russia and the Ottoman Empire 1877 originally printed in *The Graphic* on September 29, 1877. Cf.

Zhang Hongxing, "Wu Youru's 'The Victory over the Taiping,' Painting and Censorship in 1886 China," unpublished PhD dissertation, University of London, 1999, pl. 90 and 91; and id., "Liusan zai haiwai de liang zu wan Qing gongting zhantu kaolüe" (A Study of Two Sets of Late Qing War Paintings from the Palace Now Dispersed Abroad), *Gugong bowuyuan yuankan*, 2 (2001) 2:1–13. Ge Boxi 葛伯熙, "Huanying huabao kao" 寰瀛畫報考, *Xinwen yanjiu ziliao* 41 (1988), p. 185, wrongly assumes that the paper was altogether edited in London. The copy seen by Dr. Zhang is now missing in the Shanghai Library.

40. FO 228/571 (beginning 1876), Intelligence report March quarter 1876 by Mr. Interpreter Allen, included into No. 20 Medhurst to Wade, February 16, 1876. Medhurst himself writes in his in cover letter, p. 81b: "In regard to the Shen Pao Newspaper, I may supplement Mr. Allen's information by stating that I have it on the proprietor's authority that circulation of this paper is at this moment only 5600 per day, owing to matters not having regained their equilibrium since the New Year, but that he quite looks forward to a circulation of 7000 before the end of the summer."

41. This journal had a Shanghai subscription price printed in each issue. The issues were welcomed by Chinese as gifts. "Everyone who has made a trip up-country, knows how popular with the people an *Illustrated London News* is. It is always an acceptable gift to a Chinaman, and if he had the pictures and readable matter in his own language accompanying them, he would be furnished with a perpetual source of entertainment and information." "Chinese Newspapers," *North China Herald*, August 28, 1875, p. 369.

42. Quoted in Ge Boxi, "*Huanying huabao* kao," p. 187. I have not seen the original and the Chinese text quoted here might contain errors.

43. Li Longmian (1049–1106) is known for his outline drawings on silk. The Musée Guimet has posted a series of anonymous paintings attributed to him, "Foreign peoples bringing tribute" sub Li Longmian under http://www.culture.gouv.fr/documentation/joconde/EXPOS/theme_guimetart.htm

44. *Shenbaoguan shumu*, Shanghai: Shenbaoguan 1877, pp. 2a–b.

45. The verbatim quotations from Zheng Qiao's *Tupu lüe* referred to above in note 19 show that Major was familiar with earlier Chinese discussions about the usefulness of illustrations.

46. Quoted in Ge Boxi, "*Huanying huabao* kao," pp. 187–188. I have not seen the original, and the Chinese text quoted here might contain errors. I assume the original read 奥窔 instead of 奥突 and 循名責實 instead of 循名質實. The *Shenbao* May 12, 1877 p. 6, carried an advertisement for the first issue of this journal, which was to come out in July of that year. The advertisement said that all matters of this journal were to be handled by the Shenbaoguan, but obviously it technically was not a Shenbaoguan product.

47. C. Yeh, *Shanghai Love: Courtesans, Intellectuals, and Entertainment Culture, 1850–1910*, Seattle: University of Washington Press, 2006, p. 184.

48. "Lun geguo xinbao zhi she" (On the establishment of newspapers in different nations), *Shenbao* July 18, 1873. "When originally the different Western states set up newspapers, they also deeply understood this insight of the [Chinese Sages] of old."

49. A copy of this single-page calendar, the *Shenbao yuefenpai* 申報月份牌, is preserved in the Shanghai tushuguan.

50. "Chinese Newspapers," *Celestial Empire*, June 9, 1877, pp. 565–56. The third issue did not contain fewer pictures, but more, namely, 12.

51. "An Illustrated Paper for China," *Celestial Empire*, September 21, 1878, p. 284.

52. An advertisement in the *Shenbao* on June 18–19, 79 announced the *Huanying huabao* no. 4, saying "this is a pictorial paper brought in from England, western paintings with Chinese explanations. The issue has twelve pictures, such as an illustration of the Chinese ambassador in England, pictures of the devastations in Shanxi, pictures of Indian local soldiers as well as those of other states. The pictures are detailed and the work is fine 圖精工細 and sophisticated 巧妙. A most impressive picture shows the negotiations between the Russians and the Turks with the Russians sitting proudly and the Turks all in tears."

53. The sequel to the Shenbaoguan shumu, the *Xu shumu* 續書目 (1879) does not contain an entry for the *Huanying huabao* anymore. This might signal a loss of interest.

54. Lithographed books were printed in Canton since at least 1850. An example is *Cantonese Dialogues: A Book of Chinese Phrases*. A handwritten note in the copy in SOAS says: "In Canton dialect, written by a learned Chinese in 1841, printed by lithography in 1850."

55. This date is extracted from an advertisement by the Dianshizhai, *Shenbao* May 25,1879, which said: "Our studio last year (78) got from the West a new lithograph machine that can reproduce all books without difference to the original and can reduce their size. Photolithography 照印 is a miracle, you do not have to strain your eyes for reading."

56. One of the problems with studying this important development is the failure of art or library collections to collect such reproductions. Available sources are advertisements.

57. Another painter, Que Lan 關嵐 (1758–1844), also went by this eponym, but since Li's accuracy in drawing was especially mentioned in the description of the *Huanying huabao* quoted earlier, I assume the Longmian shanren here refers to him.

58. *Dianzhizhai huabao* list of publications in issue no. 7 (甲7) Guangxu 10 (1884), sixth month.

59. *Shenbao*, February 21, 1879.

60. *Shenbao*, January 1, 1884.

61. *Shenbao*, June 20, 1879.

62. *Shenbao*, September 9, 1879.

63. *Dianzhizhai huabao* list of publications in issue no. 7 (甲7) Guangxu 10 (1884) sixth month.

64. *Shenbao*, May 24, 1879.

65. A fine copy of this work with sundry courtesan matters with a preface dated 1849 is in the Bibliothèque Nationale in Paris.

66. A review, in 1889, of "Photolithographic Printing in Shanghai," *North China Herald,* May 25, 1889, p. 633, talks of "hundred or two hundred" workers in a single lithographic print shop in Shanghai; the machines were already being driven by steam engine at that time.

67. Such an argument is indicated by Christopher Reed, "Steam Whistles and Fire-Wheels: Lithographic Printing and the Origins of Shanghai's Printing Factory System, 1876–1898," paper prepared for the Conference on Urban Progress, Business Development, amd Modernization in China, Shanghai, 1993.

68. L. Eastman, *Throne and Mandarins: China's Search for a Policy during the Sino-French Controversy 1880–1885*, Cambridge: Harvard University Press, 1967, pp. 101–102.

69. "The War in Tonquin," *The North China Herald*, February 20, 1884, pp. 200–201.

70. Cf. Wang Shucun 王樹村, ed., *Zhongguo minjian nianhua shi tulu* 中國民間年畫史圖錄, Shanghai: Shanghai renmin meishu 1991, vol. 1, Ill, p. 327, commentary.

71. Published in Wang Bomin, *Zhongguo banhua shi*, Shanghai: Shanghai renmin meishu chubanshe, 1961, pl. 106. See also Yao Qian, ed., *Taohuawu nianhua*, Beijing: Wenwu, 1985, ill. 113.

72. This might be the battle on February 4, 1884.

73. An example is the letter by Peng Yulin to the Shanghai Daotai summarized in the *Hubao* from which it is again summarized in the *North China Daily News* on February 13, 1884. It mentions a battle for Bac Ninh on January 10, 1884.

74. *North China Herald*, March 19, 1884. The article mistakes the depiction as referring to the battle on March 14. This is excluded by the dating given on the print.

75. Cf. Roswell Britton, *The Chinese Periodical Press 1800–1912*, Shanghai: Kelly and Walsh, 1933, pp. 5–7.

76. Shenjiang xinbaoju, "Picture of the great capture of complete victory by general Liu when the French attacked BacNinh," woodblock print, Public Record Office MPK 441/122. See the communication on the fall of Bac Ninh "through Chinese sources" obviously close to Liu Yongfu translated in the *North China Herald* on March 26, 1884. See also the public challenge to the French by Liu Yongfu, "Why Bac Ninh was given up," orig. in *Shenbao* and translated in the *North China Herald* March 26, 1884, p. 351. Liu claims to have left the city out of pity for the continuous loss of face by the French in previous battles.

77. Reports of an impending attack were frequent at the time. See *North China Daily News*, February 16, 1884. Reports about the reinforcements under way for the French contingent were also frequent. I have not located a report that combines the information in the way mentioned on the print.

78. Public Record Office MPK 441/122.

79. "Liu tidu kefu shuzhan desheng quantu 劉提督克復水戰得勝全圖, " published in Tianjin shi yishu bowuguan, ed., *Yangliuqing nianhua* 楊柳青年畫, Beijing: Wenwu, 1984, pl. 14.

80. See Zhang Hongxing, "Wu Youru's 'Victory over the Taiping,'" chapter 2.

81. See, for example, the nineteenth-century prints from Suzhou reproduced in Wang Shucun 王樹村, ed., *Zhongguo minjian nianhua shi tulu* 中國民間畫史圖錄, Shanghai: Shanghai renmin meishu, 1991, vol. 1, Ills. 303–305, 317–319, 325–329. These prints regularly mark the key persons with little name tags.

82. The history of this type of commemorative military painting is sketched in Zhang Hongxing, "Wu Youru's 'The Victory over the Taiping,'" ch. 2, "The Commemoration of War: An Official Tradition".

83. Advertisement *Shenbao,* February 6, 1884.

84. Advertisement *Shenbao* February 10, 1884: "Vietnam map. French-Vietnamese war, everyone wants to know the geography of the place. We used lithograph technique for making an extremely detailed map on [imported] white paper, it is not only easily readable, but also enables one to get very detailed information."

85. *Shenbao,* August 24, 1884. For the discussion about the war in the Shanghai papers see A. Janku, *Nur leere Reden: Politischer Diskurs und die Shanghaier Presse im China des späten 19. Jahrhunderts,* Wiesbaden: Harassowitz, 2003, pp. 111–141.

86. Yang Yi 楊逸, *Haishang molin* 海上墨林, Shanghai, 1920, j. 3, p. 25a. This entry is more or less taken up in Wu Yuan 武原, Sheng Shuqing 盛叔清, *Qingdai hua shi zeng bian* 清代畫史增編 (1927). Reprint Taipei: Guangwen shuju, 1970, p. 98. Cao Chongyuan 曹充源 et al., eds., *Wuxian zhi* 吳縣志 (1933). Reprint: Taipei: Wenhai, 1979, j. 75下, p. 21b. This entry also is the first to give Wu Youru's death date as 1893. All three misdate Wu Youru's painting of the suppression of the Taipings as being before the founding of the *DSZHB.*

87. Zheng Wei 鄭為, Dianshizhai huabao *shishi hua xuan* 點石齋畫報時事畫選, Peking: Zhongguo gudian yishu, 1958, introduction, p. 2. The claim is repeated in Yu Jianhua 俞劍華, ed., *Zhongguo meishujia renming cidian* 中國美術家人名辭典, Shanghai: Shanghai renmin meishu Pr., 1985, p. 307, entry Wu Jiayou 吳嘉猷; Zheng Jingwen 鄭經文, "Wu Youru," in Li Wenhai 李文海, Kong Xiangji 孔祥吉, eds., *Qingdai renwu zhuan* gao 清代人物傳稿, xiabian 下編 5j., Shenyang: Liaoning renmin, 1989, p. 367.

88. Zhang Tiexuan 張鐵弦, "Lüetan wan Qing shiqi de shiyin huabao" 略談晚清時期的石印畫報, *Wenwu* 1959.3, pp. 1–3.

89. Zheng Yimei 鄭逸梅, "Wu Youru he *Dianshizhai huabao*" 吳友如和點石齋畫報, in his *Qing yu manbi* 清娛漫筆, Shanghai: Shanghai shudian, 1982, pp. 38–40.

90. Cf. G. Debon, *Chou Yigui, Lob der Naturtreue. Das Xiaoshan huapu de Tsou I-kui,* Wiesbaden: Harrassowitz, 1969, p. 77, n. 100, for the references.

91. The expression 頰上添毫 is based on the expression 頰上三毛 in a story about Gu Kaizhi in the *Shishuo xinyu,* cf. Mather, *Shih-shuo hsin-yü,* Minneapolis: University of Minnesota Press, 1976, p. 367. After painting a portrait of the famous intellectual Pei Kai, Gu added three hairs to his chin. He explained that they would convey Gu's particular understanding of human abilities. Those looking at the painting indeed felt that his spirit was much better expressed than before the hairs had been applied. Cf. also *Jinshu* 92.35b.

92. Wu Youru, "*Feiyinge huace* xiaoqi" 飛影閣畫冊小啟, *Feiyingge huace* 1 p. 1, August 1893.

93. See Gong Chanxing, "Xinwen huajia Wu Youru," 73.

94. In a text accompanying a *DSZHB* drawing in September 1885, Wu Youru speaks of a storm in the Shanghai port where something like a dragon appeared. "In the forty years of my life I have never seen such a thing." 'Feilong zai tian' *DSZHB* no. 50 (=戎 2 no. 10) GX 11/7/xia (September 1885). This reference has been located by Ms. A Schlor in her MA thesis "'*Das Aussehen der Menschen in den fünf Himmel-srichtungen ist nicht gleich und man [muss] lernen, das jeweils Andere zu achten.'* Zur Wahrnehmung des Westens im späteren 19. Jahrhundert in China: Die Bildberichte

des Wu You-ru," Freiburg, n.d. (1987?), pp. 23f. The formula "In the forty years of my life" uses a rhetorical convention where decades are mentioned but not years. This would put his birth date around 1846 or a few years earlier. His birthplace Suzhou was taken by the Taipings in the fourth month of 1860. This would give a birthdate around 1841. Pan Huichang, "Cong Suhou dao Shanghai, cong 'Dianshizhai' dao 'Feiyingge'—wan Qing huajia xinti guangui, " *Xin meishu* 1994.2, p. 65, the most careful analysis published to date (although he failed to spot the reference provided by Ms. Schlor) assumes a birthdate shortly before 1840. There is no evidence for this early date.

95. Information from Wu's granddaughter, given to Gong Chanxing in 1958; cf. Gong Chanxing, "Xinwen huajia Wu Youru," p. 69.

96. Gong Chanxing has visited a granddaughter of Wu Youru's in Shanghai in 1958. She claimed to know from her grandfather that the family had been merchants in Suzhou, and that Wu Youru had taken up painting after coming to Shanghai. Gong Chanxing, "Xinwen huajia Wu Youru," 69. Zheng Yimei's claim that Wu tried to embellish his past seems ill founded. See Zheng Yimei 鄭逸梅, *Yilin sanye xupian* 藝林散葉續篇, Peking: Zhonghua, 1987, p. 63 no. 638. There is not a single known print by Wu from the 1850s or the 1860s.

97. Huang Ke 黃可, "Shishi fengsu huapai de fayuan" 時事風俗畫派的發源, *Wenhui bao* October 6, 1996. Mr. Huang graciously reacted to my inquiries by conducting this interview, the result of which he published in the *Wenhui bao*. I am indebted to him for sending this article to me.

98. Ibid.

99. Cf. Zhu Wenbing 朱文柄, ed., *Haishang zhuzhici* 海上竹枝詞, Shanghai: Jicheng tushu gongsi, 1908. Gu Bingquan, ed., *Shanghai yangchang zhuzhici* 上海洋場竹枝詞, Shanghai: Shanghai shudian Press, 1996.

100. The story that Zeng Guofan commissioned him in the early 1860s to paint his victory over the Taipings is based on the misreading of the autobiographical sketch already quoted. Yang Yi 楊逸 *Haishang molin* 海上墨林 (1920), repr. in the Shanghaitan yu Shanghairen congshu series, Shanghai: Shanghai guji, 1989, p. 78. Zheng Yimei 鄭逸梅, *Shubao jiuhua* 書報舊話, Shanghai: Xuelin, 1983, p. 86. For this commission see pp. 149–151.

101. Pan Yaochang. "Cong Suzhou dao Shanghai, cong 'Dianshizhai'dao'Feiyingge' —wan Qing huajia xintai guankui," p. 68.

102. Wu Youru, "A hundred boys playing in the garden," 1878. Set of three hanging scrolls, 10.5 x 20.5, Shanghai Museum.

103. Wu Youru, "Yuyuan baxi tu" 豫園把戲圖 (Acrobats in Yu Gardens), woodblock print, no date. In Zhang Hongxing, "Wu Youru's 'The Victory over the Taiping,'" ill. 82.

104. Wang Shucun, ed., *Zhongguo minjian nianhuashi tulu*, Ill, pp. 328, 329. See also the *Honglou meng* illustration, ill. 232.

105. Wu Youru, "Banquet at Yu Garden," 1880, hanging scroll, ink and colors, 64.7 x 64.5, Shanghai History Museum.

106. Wu Youru's work still is badly documented. The Shanghai Museum published a series of twelve paintings of young ladies in various pursuits by Wu Youru. They are

dated 1890, and provide some idea of the kind of things he was asked to paint. *Shanghai bowuguan cang haishang minghuajia jingpin ji* 上海博物館藏海上名畫家精品集, Hong Kong: Daye gongsi, 1991, Ill. 47.1–12. He also continued to illustrate books. The title of one of these books, *Wu Youru huitu diyi qingshu Tingyue lou* 吳友如畫圖第一情書 聽月 樓 (The Number One Book on Love, *Tingyue lou*, Illustrated by Wu Youru), of which I have seen a lithography print done in 1893 by the Liwenxian shuju 理文軒書局 in Shanghai, kept in the Zhongguo guojia tushuguan in Peking, indicates that by this time, Wu's fame was at its highest point.

107. Wu Youru, Preface, *Feiyingge huabao* no. 1.

108. For this editorial, see below. For later such texts, see the series on the Korean disturbances in *DSZHB* no. 31 (丙7, late March 1885), which seems to be in Major's handwriting. Major signs as Zunwenge zhuren and with his seal 'Meicha.' This text explains the value even of such a lowly thing as an illustrated paper for understanding contemporary events.

109. Preface by Huang Fengjia 黃逢甲 for the *Shenjiang shengjing tu*, p. 2.

110. Advertisement by the Manager of the Shenbaoguan, *Shenbao* May 8, 1884, p. 1.

111. *Shenbao* June 4, 1884, p. 1.

112. Zhang Hongxing has pointed out, however, one item of a criticism of Wu in the *DSZHB* after Wu had left. In an insert to *DSZHB* no. 247 (戌6, late December 1890), the *DSZHB* makes fun of its contemporary by pointing out that Wu Youru had copied his series of hundred animals from a book published in 1882 in Shanghai. Cf. Zhang Hongxing, Wu Youru's 'Victory over the Taiping,' p. 179, note 9.

113. The second page of the modern reprint still carries the date 丁酉九秋, fall 1897. This reprint was done by the Dianshizhai studio itself. It was a year before the *DSZHB* actually stopped publication. This reprint was reprinted in 1910 (a copy is in the possession of Columbia University Library), and again by the Guangdong renmin Press in 1983. A Chinese selection from this edition is *Dianshizhai huabao shishi hua xuan* 點石齋畫報時事畫選, Peking, 1958, while the small *DSZHB* selection in two vols. published in Hongkong, Guangjiaojing Press, 1983, is reprinted from original copies. Western selections include M.v. Brandt, *Der Chinese in der Öffentlichkeit und der Familie Chinese Wie Er Sich Selbst Sieht und Schildert,* Berlin: Dietrich Reimer, 1911; F. van Briessen, *Shanghai-Bildzeitung 1884–1898. Eine Illustrierte aus dem China des ausgehenden 19. Jahrhunderts,* Zurich: Atlantis, 1977; Don J. Cohn, ed., *Vignettes from the Chinese: Lithographs from Shanghai in the late Nineteenth Century,* Hongkong, 1987. Specialized selections from Wu Youru's lithographic work are *Wu Youru zhenji huaji* 吳友如真跡畫集, n.d., late Qing, one copy in the Beihai section of the Zhongguo guojia tushuguan, Peking, and Lin Chengxu 林承緒, ed., *Wu Youru huabao* 吳友如畫寶 (1909, repr. Shanghai: Shanghai guji 1984). A Japanese selection of *DSZHB* prints reflecting Shanghai social life is Masaya Takeda 武田雅哉, *Go Yûjo no jikenchô* 吳友如の事件 帖, Tokyo: Sakuhinsha, 1998. For studies, cf. Wang Ermin 王爾敏, "Zhongguo jindai zhishi pujihua chuanbo zhi tuhua xingshi—*Dianshizhai huabao* li" 中國近代知識普 及化傳播之圖說形式—點石齋畫報例, *Zhongyang yanjiuyuan jindaishi yanjiusuo jikan* (1980) 19, pp. 135–172; B. Jungmann, Traditionelle Muster und westliche Einflüsse in der Tien-shi-chai hua-pao untersucht am Beispiel der Darstellung von Europäerinnen und Amerikanerinnen, unpubl. MA dissertation, Heidelberg 1980; A. Schlor, „Das Aussehen der Menschen in den fünf Himmelsrichtungen ist nicht gleich"; Ye

Xiaoqing, *Popular Culture in Shanghai 1884–1898*, unpubl. PhD dissertation, Australian National University 1991, and *The Dianshizhai: Pictorial Shanghai Urban Life, 1884–1898*, Ann Arbor: University of Michigan Press, 2003. N. Kim, Die Dianshizhai huabao. Eine illustrierte Zeitung als literarisches Unterhaltungsmagazin, unpubl. MA dissertation, Heidelberg 1993; J. Henningsmeier, Von Schottenröcken, Prinzen, Anarchisten und weissen Elefanten. Die Verarbeitung englischen und amerikanischen Bildmaterials in der *DSZHB*, unpubl MA dissertation, Heidelberg 1993; Lisa Claypool, The Social Body. 'Beautiful Women' Imagery in Late Imperial China, unpubl. MA dissertation, University of Oregon, 1994. I assume that M. v. Brandt, *Der Chinese in der Öffentlichkeit und in der Familie,* and W. Mohr, *Die moderne chinesische Tagespresse: Ihre Entwicklung in Tafeln und Dokumenten,* three vols., Wiesbaden: Harassowitz, 1975, might have worked with originals in their possession. They also do not deal, however, with the supplements and inserts.

114. The largest holdings known to me are in the School of Oriental and African Studies in London, issues 1–467, with some pieces available in several copies. The cover leafs and inserts have been kept. The British Library has a nearly complete run from no. 289 (絲1 Guangxu 18/1中) to no. 467 (忠11 Guangxu 22/10下) along with cover leaves and inserts. The Cambridge University Library has the first *ji* 集 comprising the first ten chapters, all with their cover leaves containing the publication dates, but no inserts. The Bodleian Library has four loose copies with inserts and cover pages, *DSZHB* #16 乙4 (Guangxu 10, eighth month); #20 乙8 (Guangxu 10, ninth month); #34 丙10 (Guangxu 11, second month); and the issue Guangxu 23, eighth month, last decade. The Oriental Institute, Oxford University, has copies bound in Western style of vols. V–VI and VII–VIII, more not extant. Bound by Kue Hsing, bookbinder, stationer, and printer 16 Honan Rd, Shanghai. Bound with the cover leaves. Title in back spine "The Hua Pao 畫報." From Guangxu 11,7中 (no 49)= 戊 1–12 (= vol. V), 己 1–12 (= vol VI), last issue 己12 = Guangxu 12, 3上 (no. 72). The rare book room in the Harvard Yenching library has a few early copies with the inserts that originally were in the possession of Columbia University. The scattered Columbia University holdings have very few inserts. The Musée Guimet holds two batches, both from the Fonds Vissière. The first, issues 1–24 bound in two volumes, has the serialized supplements and the advertisements from these issues bound together at the end of each of the two volumes, but it does not contain any glue-ins. The second batch contains incomplete unbound items between nos. 1 and 160 (1884–1888). It has some Ren Bonian glue-ins with characters from the *Shiji* (in nos. 42 and 43), a large folded insert by Jin Gui depicting the Song emperor Renzong (no. 141, first month 1888), three of the Taiping paintings by Wu Youru (157, 158, and 160), seemingly glued into another issue than in the SOAS copy; and a portrait of Prince Gong (no. 159). The UC Berkeley has issues 463 to the last issue, no. 528. The Portheim Stiftung, Heidelberg, holds #277 (Guangxu 17, ninth month) through #290 (Guangxu 18, first month) as well as twenty-three issues from the series *li* 禮, *le* 樂, and *she* 射 (Guangxu 19, twelfth month through Guangxu 20, eighth month). There are many private collectors with larger or smaller holdings.

115. The explanation was given together with the cover page and the index to the first *ji*. It is contained in the modern reprint on the back of the first page. See my "China's First Literary Journals," paper prepared for a conference on early Chinese literary journals, Prague, 1998.

116. His signature and seal "Master of the Wenchun-studio" 問淳館主人 are only on the cover leaves. On Shen Yugui, see N. Gentz, "Useful Knowledge," in this volume. Shen provided calligraphy for the titles of many Shenbaoguan books.

117. The *Shanghai xinbao* 上海新報, published by the *North China Herald* between 1861 and 1872.

118. *Gujin tushu jicheng* 古今圖書集成, illustrated encyclopedia from the eighteenth century, which Major's Shenbaoguan was reprinting at the time.

119. Wang Qi 王圻 comp., *Sancai tuhui* 三才圖會, reprint of the 1603 edition, Taipei: Chengwen, 1970, illustrated encyclopedia. Reprinted by the Shenbaoguan.

120. *DSZHB*, preface, first issue. An interpunctuated version is included in A Ying 阿英, "Wan Qing xiaobao lu" 晚清小報錄, in A Ying, *Wan Qing wenyi baokan shulüe* 晚清文藝報刊 述略, Shanghai: Zhonghua, 1959, pp. 99–100.

121. Ms. Bao Lihua and Mr. Qian Zonghua from the Shanghai History Museum were kind enough to give me this information. The museum has in addition one thousand originals from the collection of Wu Youru's drawings published under the title *Wu Youru huabao* 吳友如畫寶.

122. The *North China Herald*, March 26, 1884, prints a special report "through Chinese sources" whose first half is very close to the report here. It continues with a description of the counterattack from which the quotation is taken.

123. Wu Youru, 'Feilong zai tian' *DSZHB* no. 50 (= 戎 2 no.10) GX 11/7/xia (September 1885); in the accompanying text, Wu refers to himself and his age, using the expression 'I,' *wu* 吾.

124. I am grateful to Dr. Zhang Hongxing for alerting me to this issue of *The Illustrated London News*.

125. Ms. J. Henningsmeier has written her MA dissertation in Heidelberg on the topic of these adaptations of Western illustrations in the *DSZHB*. She was able to locate quite a few of the original illustrations from which they had been adapted, as well as Western adaptations from the *DSZHB*. Cf. J. Henningsmeier, Von Schottenröcken, Prinzen, Anarchisten und weissen Elefanten. Die Verarbeitung englischen und amerikanischen Bildmaterials in der *DSZHB*, unpubl MA dissertation, Heidelberg 1993. For a summary of this study, see J. Henningsmeier, "The Foreign Sources of *Dianshizhai Huabao*, A Nineteenth Century Shanghai Illustrated Magazine" in: *Ming Qing Yanjiu* (1998), pp. 59–91.

126. The *Illustrirte Zeitung*, Leipzig, introduced the *DSZHB* to its readers, Jan. 4, 1890. See below, note 133.

127. Cf. the chapter by N. Kim in this volume.

128. "Yue huabao shuhou" 閱畫報書後, *Shenbao*, June 19, 1884.

129. Zhou Muqiao's first illustration appears in *DSZHB* #16 乙4, mid-September 1884.

130. The numbers of Wu's illustrations for the first collection are 甲 44, 乙 37, 丙 40, 丁 48, 戎 44, 己 27, 庚 23.

131. Wu Youru's last illustration in 1886 is 庚 48b in issue #79 (mid-June 1886). He reappears with 卯 3, which is the issue #158 (late July 1888).

132. See N. Kim, "New Wine in Old Bottles," in this volume. The full impact of his departure is seen in the *Zhu* series in 1892, when the stories of the miraculous more than doubled.

133. "China's einheimische Presse" (China's vernacular press), *Der Ostasiatische Lloyd* (Shanghai), September 2, 1889, p. 4. While this report contains many mistakes such as assuming that "the *DSZHB* is owned by Chinese," the writer might have had good information from his contact with the Portuguese Shenbaoguan manager Pereira. The *Leipziger Illustrierte Zeitung*, January 4, 1890, reused the information.

134. E. Major, editorial for the first issue of *Shenbao*. In 1876, Major had concluded that the texts were still too tough for the common folk. He opened another paper, *Minbao*, the *People's Paper*, to cater to this audience and groom it to a level where they could read the *Shenbao*. It foundered quickly.

135. See N. Kim, "Old Wine in New Bottles," p. 176.

136. Ibid. pp. 191f.

137. Lu Xun, "Shanghai wenyi zhi yipie" 上海文藝之一瞥, in *Lu Xun quanji*, Beijing: Renmin Press, 1981, vol. 4, pp. 292ff.

138. "Henan Zhengzhou suizai tu" 河南鄭州水災圖 *DSZHB* #130, 子10 (Guangxu 13 [1887], ninth month).

139. Cf. also Vincent Gossaert, "Anatomie d'un discours anti-clérical: Le Shenbao, 1872–1878," in id., ed. L'Anticléricalisme en Chine, *Extrême-Orient/Extrême-Occident: Cahiers de recherche comperative*, 24 (2002), pp. 133–152.

140. The paper did not attract many Chinese advertisers, and Western firms were not interested. The self-advertisements, however, contain valuable information.

141. The Dianshizhai studio reproduced old illustrated book editions, and it commissioned new ones such as the *Illustrated Flowers in the Mirror, Huitu Jinghua yuan* 繪圖鏡花緣 in 1888. A copy is in SOAS.

142. Wang Tao 王韜, *Songyin manlu* 淞隱漫錄, serialized in *DSZHB* from issue no. 6 (甲6, end of June 1884) to issue no. 122 (子2, mid-October, 1887). Reprint with illustrations by Wu Youru and, from #97 (壬1, mid-December 1886), by Tian Zilin, in *Biji wubian* 筆記五編, Taipei: Guangwen, 1976.

143. *Shenbao* advertisement, July 4, 1884.

144. Shen Fu 沈復, *Fusheng liuji* 浮生六記, in *Duwu an congchao* 獨悟庵叢抄, Shanghai: Shenbaoguan, 1878.

145. Wang Tao, *Songyin xulu* 淞隱續錄, serialized in the *DSZHB* from #126 (子6, late September 1887) to #174 (辰5. early January 1889).

146. Wang Tao, *Manyou suilu* 漫游隨錄, serialized in *DSZHB* no. 126 (子 6, late September 1887) to 173 (辰 4, end of December 1888).

147. Both were later published in book form by Dianzhishai.

148. Li Yu 李漁, *Fengzheng wu* 風箏物, serialized in the *DSZHB* from #153 (寅8, mid-June 1888) to #172 (辰3, mid-December 1888).

149. *Guiyuan conglu* 閨媛叢錄, serialized in *DSZHB* from #223 (申6, early May, 1890) to #260 (亥 7, late April, 1891.) Jin Chanxiang took over the illustrations from

#240 on. See also R. Wagner, "Women in Shenbaoguan Publishing, 1872–1890," paper prepared for the conference "Beyond Tradition and Modernity," Houston, 2005.

150. Aiyuan zhuren 藹園主人, *Aiyuan misheng* 藹園謎勝, serialized in *DSZHB* #253 (戎12, end of February 1891) to #279 (石3, early November 1891). This man might be identical with the man whose copies of many paintings had been later inserted into the *DSZHB*. A Xu Jiali 徐家禮 from Haining in Zhejiang had a *hao* called Aiyuan, and a *zi* Meiruo 美若. Cf. pp. 154f.

151. *Huangchao zhisheng diyu quantu* 皇朝直省地輿全圖. *DSZHB* from #262 (亥9, late May, 1891) through #286 (石10, January 1892) with cover page and table of contents added in #289 (絲1, mid-February 1892). The title inscription is dated the eighth month of 1889, and written by Zhu Yu 朱煜. In 1879, the Dianshizhai had published a map by this name. See entry 10.41 in Li Xiaocong 李孝聰, *A Descriptive Catalogue of pre-1900 Chinese Maps seen in Europe* 歐洲部分中文古地圖敘錄, Peking: Guoji wenhua Press 1996, pp. 212ff. It was based on a map put together in 1863 by Hu Linyi, Zou Shiyi, and Yan Shusen in the Hanzhen yutu ju 漢鎮輿圖局, an official publishing house in Hubei province, but the new treaty ports had been added.

152. See entry 10.36 in Li Xiaocong, *A Descriptive Catalogue*, pp. 203–204.

153. E. Major, 'Huangchao zhisheng diyu quantu hou' 皇朝直省地輿全圖書後, *DSZHB* #290 (絲2, end of February 1892). Major probably wrote the afterword at about the time when the volume had been finished in 1889.

154. Cf. I. Hsu, *The Ili Crisis: A Study in Sino-Russian Diplomacy, 1871–1881*, Oxford: Clarendon, 1965. The "Combined Map of Zhenyou and Yili beyond the Jiayu Pass" 嘉峪關外鎮迪伊犁合圖, a note said, had been originally produced by the (Guoxi) Hanzhen yutu ju in Hubei, but one section had to be changed to accommodate new developments. This changed version had been originally published by the Shanghai *Jinyuan bao* 晉源報 (?) with the inscriptions in Western characters; this paper had based itself on Russian military maps. The Dianshizhai Studio had reprinted this map in July 1880, but with Chinese characters. It shows the territories appropriated by Russia through a dotted line. Cf. advertisement in the *DSZHB* #130 (子10, tenth month 1887). Li Xiaocong has not noted this difference in his entry on this map, *A Descriptive Catalogue*, 10.44, pp. 215–216.

155. "Zhisheng tongban hengpi yutu" 直省銅版橫披輿圖, see advertisement in the *DSZHB* #7 (甲7, mid-June 1884).

156. He Guisheng 何桂笙 (Yong 墉), pen name Gaochang hanshi sheng 高昌寒食生, *Chenglong jiahua* 乘龍佳話, *DSZHB* from #280 (石4, mid-November 1891) through #297 (絲9, early May 1892). A synopsis by Liang Shu'an 梁淑安 in Ma Liangchun 馬良春 and Li Futian 李福田, eds., *Zhongguo wenxue dacidian* 中國文學大辭典, Tianjin: Tianjin renmin, 1991, p. 4864.

157. On He Guisheng, see N. Gentz, "Useful Knowledge and Appropriate Communication," in this volume.

158. *Dianshizhai congchao* 點石齋叢鈔, published in *DSZHB* #304 (竹4, mid-July 1892) through #413 (書5, mid-June, 1895).

159. A short biography is in *Zhongguo meishujia renming cidian*, p. 1259.

160. *DSZHB* #66, Guangxu 12, first month. Bodleian Library, Oxford.

161. *DSZHB* #102, New Year's issue Guangxu 13 (1887), 壬6. Size: 66.5 x 29.5.

162. Cf. Li Yu 李渝, *Ren Bonian—Qing mo de shimin huajia* 任伯年—清末的市民畫家, Taipei: Xiongshi tushi gongsi, 1978. Ren Bonian's Shenbaoguan link remains unstudied.

163. *DSZHB* #10 甲10 (end of July, 1884). In SOAS.

164. *Zeng Wenzheng gong jiashu* 曾文正公家書; *Zeng hou riji* 曾侯日記; *Zeng Wenzheng gong da shiji* 曾文正公大事記; *Zeng Wenzheng nianpu* 曾文正年譜, Shanghai: Shenbaoguan, 1875.

165. For Qingkuan's later life, see Zhao Zhenjing 趙振經, "Yiwei zhide zhongshi de gongting huajia" (A court painter deserving attention), *Guangming ribao* July 14, 1985.

166. For much of this information I rely on Zhang Hongxing, "Wu Youru's 'The Victory over the Taiping,'" pp. 11–13.

167. Zhou Muqiao also rose steeply after the return from Beijing. He joined Wu Youru in his *Feiyingge* enterprise, and later became one of the most important *yuefenpai* advertisement painters. For a short, if mistake-riddled, sketch of his life that shows his importance as a *yuefenpai* painter, see Chen Chaonan 陳超南 and Feng Yiyou 馮懿有, *Lao guanggao* 老廣告, Shanghai: Shanghai renmin meishu, 1998, pp. 12–14.

168. Wu Youru, "Feiyinge huace xiaoqi," 飛影閣畫冊小啟 *Feiyingge huace* 1 p. 1, August 1893. See also Wu Youru, *Feiyingge huabao* 1 (1890), p. 1, preface.

169. *Zhen Ya suimo xuji* 枕亞碎墨續集1, Qing shi shiyi 清史拾遺, section Ziguangge gongchen xiang 紫光閣功臣像, pp. 31–32.

170. Ibid., p. 30.

171. *DSZHB* #158 (卯1) through #201 (午8). Full or partial sets in SOAS and Musée Guimet.

172. In 1894, the journal would celebrate Cixi's birthday. *DSZHB* #28 (丙4), twelfth month, Guangxu 10.

173. Another DSZHB illustrator, Guan Nianci, also once held a court appointment as a painter. But court outlays for such purposes had become rather miserable, and he eventually went to Shanghai.

174. *DSZHB* #31 (丙7), first month Guangxu 11.

175. Cf. A. Janku, *Nur leere Reden,* 112 f.

176. Wang Bomin 王伯敏, *Zhongguo banhua shi* 中國版畫史, Shanghai, 1961, p. 105. See also Wang Shucun ed., *Zhongguo minjian nianhua shi tulu,* Ill. 330.

177. Wang Bomin, *Zhongguo banhua shi,* p. 174.

178. L. Eastman, *Throne and Mandarins: China's Search for a Policy during the Sino-French Controversy 1880–1885,* Cambridge: Harvard University Press, 1967, pp. 188 ff. Kwang-ching Liu, "The Military Challenge: The North-West and the Coast," in John K. Fairbank and Kwang-ching Liu, eds., *The Cambridge History of China vol. 11, Late Ch'ing,* pt. 2, Cambridge: Cambridge University Press, 1980, p. 251.

179. Text on illustration inserted into *DSZHB* #178 (辰9, mid-February 1989).

180. I have not been able to find much information about Xu Jiali beyond a short entry in the *Zhongguo meishujia renming cidian.*

181. The inserts run from *DSZHB* #178 (辰9, mid-February 1889) to #289 (絲1, mid-February 1892).

182. The last painting by Xu Jiali (Meiruo) is in *DSZHB* #339 (革3, early July 1893).

183. Cf. Zheng Yimei, "Shanghai de huabao chao" 上海的畫報潮, in his *Shubao hua-jiu* 書報話舊, Shanghai: Xuelin Press, 1983, pp. 244ff.

184. Cf. Lu Xun, "Lüe lun Zhongguo ren de lian" 略論中國人的臉, *Lu Xun quanji*, Beijing: Jenmin Press, 1957, vol. 12, p. 311; id., "Shanghai wenyi zhi yipie" 上海文藝之一瞥, in *Lu Xun quanji*, Beijing: Renmin chubanshe, 1981, vol. 4, pp. 292ff.

185. M. v. Brandt, *Der Chinese in der Öffentlichkeit.*

CHAPTER 4

New Wine in Old Bottles?

Making and Reading an Illustrated Magazine

from Late Nineteenth-Century Shanghai

Nanny Kim

The *Illustrated News from the Dianshizhai, Dianshizhai huabao* (*DSZHB*)[1] (1884–1898) has been called the founding father of the Chinese illustrated magazine,[2] although, strictly speaking it was not the first of its kind;[3] and has been regarded as authentically Chinese,[4] even though the founder was British and its model Western.

A major factor contributing to Shanghai's stature as a place representing and radiating "modernity" since the 1870s was its modern publishing sector. The *DSZHB,* together with the lithograph reproductions of art, illustrations, and books, were among the range of these new print products.[5] The *DSZHB* was eager to find and even create a market for its products. Since Shanghai culture was made by the people who participated in it—whether actively or passively—I will look at the interests and conceptions of producers and readers of the *DSZHB* in order to study this process.

The *DSZHB* has been used as a source of social history,[6] and studied in the context of "China's encounter with the West."[7] This chapter will focus on a hitherto unstudied part of the magazine's content that fits neither slot: miracles, monsters, and other strange or curious things. These seemed lacking in modernity and therefore have been relegated to "trivia" by social historians such as Wang Ermin, who writes:

> Apart from reports on current affairs, on personalities, inventions, curious
> foreign things, important national news, popular customs and festivals, we
> also find all sorts of trivia in the magazine, such as gods, ghosts, monsters

and strange things, calamities caused by fire and water, robbery and murder, shameless Buddhist and Daoist monks, thugs and cheats. These take up considerable space, but will not be further treated here. Ridiculous absurdities and gossip picked up at the roadside, they often have neither head nor tail, have no grasp of what news is, and are worthless as sources of history.[8]

From a sample of roughly one-ninth of all picture-reports published in the magazine it emerges that these "trivial" topics constituted in fact the bulk of picture-reports in the *DSZHB;* some issues contained nothing else. Readers at the time could not have skipped over them. Because these must have been topics they expected and intended to read, they may tell us a great deal about readers' interests.

Ge Gongzhen succinctly and sourly characterized the *DSZHB* stories in his influential *History of Chinese Journalism* (1926) as being factually unreliable "in the style of the *Liaozhai zhiyi,*" Pu Songling's famous collection of stories of the supernatural.[9] Whatever his evaluation, the link with the literary genre of *chuanqi* or *zhiguai* studies about the supernatural is insightful.[10] It opens up the possibility of considering the magazine less in terms of news information than in terms of literary production. It is intriguing to see that at a time when journalistic writing was still weighed down with the effort to emulate the style of the examination essay, the *DSZHB* would adopt the playful and versatile literary style of the *zhiguai/chuanqi.*[11] This chapter will show that this style extends to themes beyond miracles and monsters, and even to the mode of pictorial representation.

A READERSHIP ORIENTED TOWARD SHANGHAI

Most obligingly, the magazine provides us with a depiction of its ideal reader: a young man, in well-to-do circumstances as his fashionable outfit and the elaborate chair imply, with both the education and the leisure to enjoy the magazine (Figure 4.1). But how typical was he? Might not this young gentleman be merely a flattering depiction of the sort of shop assistant who notoriously read novels instead of looking after his master's business? (Figure 4.2) Real-life readers more or less resembling these two could be found in Shanghai, particularly in the Foreign Concessions, but also in cities, where the magazine was available through the Shenbaoguan distribution network.

Circulation numbers of Shanghai's largest newspapers at the time were counted only in thousands, which hardly qualified as a mass market,[12] but the new *DSZHB* offered an entirely novel theme: urban life in treaty port Shanghai. Its readers came most likely from a subgroup of educated townspeople who had become interested in Shanghai and new knowledge, while at the same time continuing their traditional careers and sharing established tastes. This is suggested by the magazine's layout, form of publication, tone and place of advertisements, and its channels of distribution.

Figure 4.1. Drawing of the ideal reader, by Fu Jie, *DSZHB, Yi* 7b.

Although the public had to be familiarized with the form of a serial appearing three times a month, *DSZHB* looked familiar in its narrow book format with a thin dustcover usually containing nine picture-reports and some supplements, all on folded Chinese paper that was printed only on one side.[13] The issues formed series, which were supposed to be bound together with the index

Figure 4.2. A possible reader. Detail from drawing by Zhang Qi, *DSZHB*, *Ji* 6.

included in the last issue moved to the front. The serialized supplements were to be bound separately. Each picture-report was an integrated unit, consisting of an ink drawing, complete with signature and seal of the painter, and a report made up of the title, the text, and a seal containing a summarizing motto, all inscribed in the free space in the upper part of the drawing. Thus, the picture-report presented itself as a genre painting in the album-leaf format.

The price in "5 fen foreign minted currency" was in the trading currency of the Lower Yangtse or Jiangnan region, where is was expected that most copies would be sold. The magazine was a collector's item for readers of regular habits, who appreciated new issues at regular intervals, frequented bookshops, and liked to store things and look at them again. This reader was not only literate, but had the leisure and fine taste to appreciate black-and-white prints full of details and seal-script, as well as housing conditions permitting the storage of books. This put the *DSZHB* beyond the purview of the laboring classes. Literacy rates and distribution support this reader profile.[14]

New *DSZHB* issues were regularly announced on the first page of the *Shenbao*. One source suggests a division of reading matter within the family. The journalist and novelist Bao Tianxiao (1875–1973) reminisced that as a teenager in the 1890s he had been an avid reader of the *DSZHB*, while his uncle read the *Shenbao*.[15]

In his foreword to the first issue, Major presented the new picture-paper as a Western media that complemented newspapers. He praised illustrations for their ability to provide information where verbal description failed, for example, in depictions of the mechanisms of machines. He also stressed the entertainment value of the new medium, which could be "leafed through after tea or wine."[16] He addressed himself to a readership with enough of an open and positive interest in current and interesting—including Western—affairs, that light elements of it could even enter their leisure time.

Because we have no independent sources to get beyond this vague portrait, I suggest inversing the process and reading the *DSZHB* as a source for the preferences of the reader. Different from subsidized missionary or political publications, it had to survive on the market. While the implied reader and the real reader are not necessarily related, the need to sell on the market brought the two together and legitimizes this procedure.

EDITORIAL ORGANIZATION

Little is known about the organization and production of the *DSZHB* beyond scattered information on Ernest Major, on the twenty-two painters who had signed the illustrations, and the name of a *Shenbao* editor who provided the calligraphy of the title.[17]

However, the relative homogeneity of style and the continuous publication over a period of fourteen years suggest some form of editorial organization. Major, with his active interest in illustration, must have been responsible for fundamentals, such as hiring staff, frequency of publication, broadness of content, and direction of editorial policy.[18]

Cooperation between *Shenbao* and the *DSZHB* was close and is repeatedly referred to,[19] but we do not know by whom and according to what criteria news items for the magazine were chosen, and who composed the reports. Due to the marked differences between the reports in *Shenbao* and *DSZHB*, the painters seem the most likely candidates for the job of editing the texts accompanying the illustrations.[20] This division of labor suggests an organizational framework set along Western lines, which was filled by Chinese employees. In order to see what in the daily routine was made of this framework, I will look more closely at the painters and their painting.

THE PAINTERS

The painters for the magazine all employ a common style, with the exception of one occasional contributor.[21] Five of the seven painters of the core group can be tracked down to the Suzhou New Year print business, which must have had the strongest influence.[22] A few also did book illustrations for the *Dianshizhai* and other publishers[23] (Figure 4.3). Only Wu Youru has been accepted into the "high tradition" of literati painting.[24] In short, the painters of the *DSZHB* used the new possibilities available in Shanghai and entertained new ways—without, however, being outspoken or assertive about it.

PICTORIAL STYLES AND ELEMENTS

"*Taohuawu* New Year painting" is the somewhat misleading designation for professional painting done for the printing trade. The street *Taohuawu* in Suzhou was lined with workshops that produced high-quality woodcuts. New Year painting and printing was a large and specialized trade with a high degree of division of labor and a wide range of topics. Wu Youru and some of the other *DSZHB* painters would have also been familiar with these prints from illustrated broadsheets, illustrations for novels and drama, and perhaps portraits.

They offered models of painting for printing with a variety of drawing techniques. These included working with a large set of pictorial elements for landscapes, architecture, animals, or human figures; the depiction of detailed scenes from contemporary daily urban life; the use of "Western drawing techniques," that is, shading and hatching, and some kind of composite or occasionally central perspective; views of Suzhou and famous sites; or illustrations of novels and operas set before realistic backgrounds of the time.[25]

Some of these techniques are readily discernible in the *DSZHB*. The opera scenes become dramatic news events in actual settings; depictions of the city of Suzhou and of city life are enriched by new views, activities, and social types to be found in Shanghai. Western people and things are copied and become part of the standard repertoire, for example, streetlamps—which in the *DSZHB* are always drawn in Western style, irrespective of their surroundings. Illustrated broadsheets were produced as a sideline by many printing shops. They belonged to the category of semilegal or illegal small-scale publications (*xiaobao,*

女魁星

Figure 4.3. An illustration by Wu Youru for the novel by Li Ruzhen, *Huitu jingmeng lu* [The record of mirrors and flowers, with illustrations]. Original 1888, repr. Beijing: Zhongguo shudian, 1985, vol. 1, illustrations p. 1.

xinwen).[26] The *DSZHB* reports on wars employ a limited set of wildly martial human types grouped into rhythmic masses, and military utensils such as tents, cannons, and flags.[27] The texts differ from reports on other matters through their polemical, unadorned relating of events. Rather than following the precedent of the *Shenbao*, they imitated the pattern of the broadsheet in this area.

Xiuxianghua, full-body portraits of the main protagonists of a novel, may have served as a pattern for portraits in the magazine. But, here again, the portraits in the *DSZHB* depict contemporary personalities and are sometimes based on photographs.[28] The pictures with their rich detail, fine execution, and dramatic scene take up most of the space. They require "reading" and an understanding of the pictorial elements used. However, the *DSZHB* was not a serialized reproduction of genre paintings. In most cases, the scene could only be understood with the help of the texts, whereas the reports, if separated from the pictures, were still complete miniature narratives.

The pictures are not "drawings from life," but compositions made up of distinct pictorial modules. As a rule, they were drawn according to the information provided by a written source. Thus, the pictures are substantially illustrations of the texts, and the texts are certainly not subordinate to the pictures. With a handful of exceptions, such as depictions of famous buildings in Shanghai and Beijing, maps, and some portraits drawn after photos, the drawings did not reproduce the visual form of a unique event or phenomenon, but offered a typified representation instead. Depending on the painter's ability and experience, the pictures could be highly detailed while still remaining accurate to the type. (Figures 4.4 and 4.5)

LITERARY REPORTS

The editors of the reports are unknown. The reports were not simply copied from whichever source they came, but rewritten into little narratives.[29] The language is a simple *wenyan* interspersed with vernacular for direct speech. No Suzhou or Shanghai dialect appears. A range of literary phrases and classical quotations is frequently used; on some occasions we come across half-colloquial proverbs. The literariness and style of language vary among different reports and according to the different topics. Wang Ermin considers the *DSZHB* to "have been very easily understandable to people at the time" who had received some basic classical education in their childhood.[30]

The writing loosely follows a tripartite structure of generalizing introduction, narrative, and a conclusion giving a comment or, more often, drawing a moral lesson. This framed structure seems to have been necessary in narrative, "middle-brow" writing to make a story "complete," and was still observed by authors of popular short novels in Republican times. The introductions often present the theme by means of a quotation or a precedent. The event narrated begins with a formula introducing the setting—that is, the time and the place of the event and the persons involved. The event is related in some detail, often down to measurements. The conclusion is marked by an interjection or a formula introducing an evaluation, for example, "*shuozhe wei*" (the narrator is of the opinion that). By drawing a moral lesson or qualifying

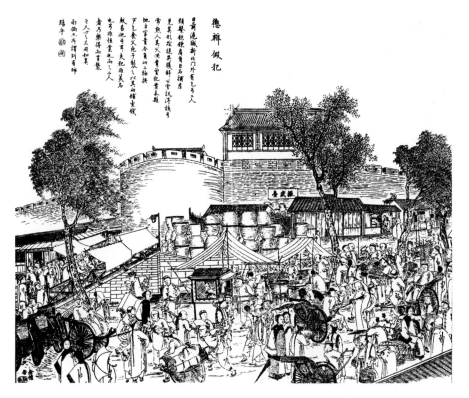

Figure 4.4. The new North Gate of the walled city of Shanghai in the *DSZHB*. Drawing by Jin Gui; from *DSZHB, Jia* 41.

the event as "shocking," "curious," or otherwise, the conclusion also justifies the inclusion of the particular news (this is sometimes made explicit by the phrase "and therefore we recorded it"). These remarks on language and structure confirm Ge Gongzhen's general characterization of *DSZHB* reporting as being "in the style of *Liaozhai zhiyi*." According to the topic treated, the reports also fall back on literary genres such as biographical notes and *biji*, in which local customs, culturally or otherwise interesting events, famous places, and so on are described. The various types of novels are drawn on in reports with corresponding protagonists or settings, for example, the *Rulin waishi* (The Scholars) for social criticism, detective stories (*gong'an xiaoshuo*) for criminal cases, the *Shuihu zhuan* (Water Margin) for news of bandit activities, and knight-errant stories for people with exceptional martial abilities. *Caizi* (talented scholars) and *jiaren* (beauties) vocabulary appears in reports of liasons of young scholars with girls from the neighborhood. Traces of military novels and the *Sanguo yanyi* (Three Kingdoms) can be found in news reports on military conflict.

Figure 4.5. A photograph of the same gate. From Shanghai lishi bowuguan ed., *Shanghai bainian lueying* 1840s–1940s [Survey of Shanghai 1840s–1940s], Shanghai: Shanghai renmin yishu chubanshe, 1994, p. 14.

By adhering to these basic characteristics of literary writing, the picture-reports seem at times to oscillate between being news and historical report, and to assume much of the nature of illustrated literature.

READERS WITH LITERATI ASPIRATIONS

From the pictures and reports we can extract the following concerning the interests and tastes of the magazine's readers: while attracted to new, "overseas" things, readers felt no need to break with traditional ways. On the contrary, the new medium was adjusted to suit established tastes. The traditional forms of writing and illustration already required some understanding of literature and art. These forms were modified and combined with new elements suitable to the new medium. Particular aspects of modern life were shown before a background of the familiar, and thus became highly visible, whereas the underlying pattern of perception—if it changed at all—did so almost imperceptibly.[31]

Both the trendy young gentleman and the distracted shop assistant are conceivable as readers for whom the magazine was intended. If we imagine a social scale marked by these two at its upper and lower end, most intended readers would be found within it. A serious man of letters would consider the magazine too lowly, while "laborers, women, and children," to whom the magazine was also directed,[32] nevertheless probably lacked the means and the interest for such a half-literary–half-artistic publication. This naturally does not imply that people from other backgrounds or with other interests never read the *DSZHB*. Numerous wives, children, and perhaps even workers read the magazine as it was handed on and passed down in the social scale.

PICTURE-REPORTS ON EVERYTHING

We turn to the magazine's content. While previous researchers have selected picture-reports according to their particular interest or conception of the magazine, we will take all picture-reports in a representative sample as the basis of our analysis. The sample is made up of 10 out the total of 45 series of the magazine, published in approximately equal intervals.[33] From the 12 issues in each series, all the issues with uneven numbers were selected. The sample thus consists of 60 out of a total of 540 issues, and 534 out of over 4500 picture-reports.

The range and frequency of occurrence of topics will be indicated by the following histogram. The *DSZHB* does not itself offer categories, but several of the categories into which Yu Yueting and Wang Ermin had grouped the news reports were of help.[34] The ten groups of topics in the histogram have been gradually developed from summaries of the actual reports, using the

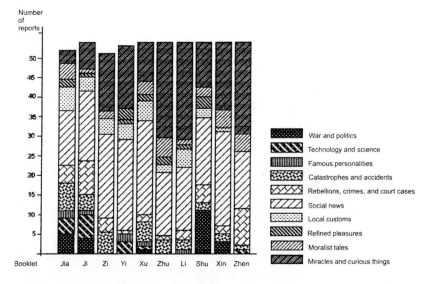

The distribution of topics in the *DSZHB*.

pictures as indicators of the central point of the event reported. Some reports have been attributed to two groups.

With the ten groups arranged according to modern notions of news value, the distribution is shown in the histogram. The first five groups of topics would in principle be acceptable as news reports on the main pages of a newspaper. In the first two issues analyzed, these topics take up about half of the magazine, but then suddenly shrink to a fifth of the total, and remain at a low level afterward. A clear shift in the distribution of topics took place sometime between the series *Ji* (ending 1886.4) and *Zi* (beginning 1887.7), marked by a sharp rise in the numbers of reports on miraculous and curious events at the expense of the first two groups. This corresponds to the time period when Wu Youru left for the Peking court to paint a series of tableaus of the Taiping War.[35] Not visible from the histogram is the tendency of fantastic or marvelous elements not only to be reported on in more detail, but also to seep into the categories of what might be regarded as more serious information.[36]

The distribution of topics in the *DSZHB*

Here is a summary of the ten groups:

1. Reports on war and important political issues surge when China is at war with foreign powers, such as the 1884 Chinese-French conflict and the Chinese-Japanese War of 1894/1895. The two series of war reports are markedly different in focus. While the reports in *Jia* and *Ji* describe battles and the political consequences of the conflict, the majority of reports in *Shu* are purely anecdotal.

2. Reports on science and technology almost exclusively present Western inventions; only one deals with newly introduced weapons tested for the Chinese army. The sizable coverage of these topics in the first two series suggests that it was part of the original setup of the magazine. Afterward, such reports became rare, and they increasingly lean toward the fantastic or entertaining[37] (Figure 4.6).

3. Portraits similarly become both more rare and less informative from the third series onward. However, in addition to the few

Figure 4.6. A Krupp canon. Drawing by Wu Youru, *DSZHB*, Yi 26.

portraits included in the main part of the magazine, numerous portraits were found among the foldouts and supplement pages, which are not included in the reprint.

4–5. Reports on catastrophes, accidents, and criminal cases brought to court show a comparable decline in numbers.

Picture-reports from the remaining five topical groups would only appear among miscellanea in a modern newspaper, if at all.

6. Incidents of human interest, termed "social news" in the early twentieth century, comprise all those interesting but inconsequential news items we like to read about in the papers, such as the runaway crocodile or the boy who, inspired by a children's novel, jumped of a balcony on the third floor but miraculously landed unharmed, and so on. Both Chinese and Western newspapers of the time extensively reported on matters like these and in the *DSZHB* they form a large group throughout. Here we usually find stories about social types acting out their roles or behaving contrary to expectation. The types most frequently appearing as protagonists are monks and nuns, mostly despicable (17), courtesans, usually virtuous, and their morally dubious clients and servants (17), cunning thieves (13), and fearless bandits taking after those of the *Water Margin* (10).[38] New social types from Shanghai also appear, such as ruthless rowdies (3), dandies neglecting propriety (2), and an abominable comprador (1). These new types seem to have been most vivid in Lu Xun's mind when he remembered the magazine in Republican times.[39] However, the majority of protagonists of this group are types well known from literature of the period and handled in a conventional way (Figure 4.7).

7–8. In these two groups, the texts are mainly descriptive and seem related to *biji*. Reports on customs and festivals fade toward the end of publication. The majority of them condemn or ridicule Buddhist popular beliefs or rain ceremonies,[40] positive evaluations are expressed, however, on festivals in Shanghai, such as the 50th anniversary of the British settlement,[41] and some elegant customs.[42] Refined enjoyments, notes on scenic sites, flowers, art, and the like, may seem rather similar to the previous group, but they do not require a comment or a morale.

9. Moralist tales present recent cases of either exemplary virtue or vice. Most expound Confucian ethics. Filial piety is the dominant theme, but there are also cases of religious virtue and a few social virtues, which border on the group identified as concerned with social news, such as supporting the poor or faithfully returning lost goods.

Figure 4.7. Shanghai types: dandy and rickshaw coolie. Drawing by Wu Youru, from *DSZHB* Jia 82a.

10. Picture-reports on the curious and the strange are rare in the beginning, but soon form the largest group, making up 29 percent of the sample. The following subgroups were combined under this category:

- Outright miracles, such as manifestations of heavenly beings or powers (14 reports: on dragons and related deities of the waters and other beings); religious miracles (7: with either tragic, positive, or neutral results).

- Ghosts (22) and visits from or to the nether world (2).

- Monstrous and strange creatures such as fox-ghosts (5), miraculous, monstrous, or merely strange animals (34: some are instruments of retribution); animals displaying human feelings (6).

- Curious humans, such as human anomalies (11: dwarfs or giants, cripples) and humans with extraordinary abilities (20: Daoist or Buddhist eccentrics, masters of martial arts, and abnormally strong women).
- Monstrous births of humans (4) and of animals (4). Finally, sudden riches (8: one is a heavenly retribution), and other marvelous or strange occurrences (9) (Figure 4.8).

Not surprisingly, there is a marked affinity between the category of moralistic tales and that of the curious and strange since moralistic tales often use miracles and supernatural elements to make their message more salient, while the reports on the strange tend to include a moralistic comment to enhance their stature. Sometimes the distinction is hard to draw. A picture-report tells of a good landlord who is rewarded with a fish in whose intestines a miraculous pearl is found, and another one shows a chaste widow who suddenly grows a beard when pressed to remarry[43] (Figure 4.9).

The wide range of the topics treated indicates an attempt to be comprehensive or even all-encompassing in order to reach the widest possible audience. Quite contrary to seeing the magazine as only addressing a particular group, it must be recognized as a pioneer in striving to create a broad readership for the new medium.

The variety of picture-reports gains consistency and justification through the artistic illustration and the moralistic overtone. A wheelbarrow accident should be a warning for unwary wheelbarrow-pushers and women traveling without necessity,[44] a curious observation is explained as an omen of retribution—everything comes with a raison d'être. It is impossible for me to judge

Figure 4.8.1. Drawing of a ghost, by He Yuanjun, detail from *Zhen* 25a.
Figure 4.8.2. Drawing of a six-legged pig, by Zhang Qi, detail from *Zhu* 86.
Figure 4.8.3. Drawing of a monstrous newborn, by Wu Youru; detail from *Ji* 86.

Figure 4.9. Drawing of a chaste widow growing a
beard, by He Yuanjun, detail from *Zhen* 35.

whether these lessons were meant to be taken seriously, or whether they were
sometimes excuses rather than motivations.

Picture-reports repeat stereotypes, most markedly in items of social news.
The magazine makes an effort to hold up literati standards of social judgment
and prejudice, albeit not wholly consistently. Buddhist monks and nuns, for

example, are mostly greedy and licentious; statues in the temples are there to impress the populace, but do not really possess divine powers. There are, however, exceptions to this; good monks or nuns are rare, but religious miracles and manifestations are not uncommon. A local shrine may even help a candidate in the highest state examinations.[45]

The change in the distribution of topics, which occurred between summer 1886 and 1887, marks a shift in emphasis from education and progress to entertainment and morals. The "quality" fell; *zhiguai* topics spread at the expense of serious news, while the drawings also became less detailed. Major's standards of immediate, accurate information, if followed at all, did not last long. However, the entertainment value of the magazine was preserved. It may be added that some of the stock topics of the Western illustrated magazine were either impossible in China or qualitatively changed when presented to a Chinese readership. The same report about some technological achievement would have a qualitatively different meaning for Western and Chinese readers. Even for the most technically ignorant Westerner, it was another proud symbol of progress. To his Chinese contemporary it was another symbol of foreign material superiority, perhaps admirable, but deeply threatening. In contrast, the strange and miraculous provided an opportunity for a display of professional art, while summoning up a copy world of inconsequential mild horror. Thus, the monsters and miracles could create cohesion in the *DSZHB* world.

REPORTS FROM EVERYWHERE

News reports and *zhiguai* genre require some information on location and time of the events, persons involved, and sources of information. Picture-reports of the *DSZHB* were somewhat lax in providing these. Locations of the events reported on were usually given, time and persons frequently, but sources were rarely specified. The location of the event or phenomenon reported on is omitted in less than 9 percent of the reports (35 of 534). The distribution of places reported from is relatively stable. If arranged in concentric zones corresponding to increasing distance from Shanghai, we find for the whole sample that reports from Shanghai and its immediate hinterland account for 16.4 percent (65 + 24) of the total, the Jiangnan area exclusive of Shanghai for 29 percent (154), major centers along the main traffic routes on the coast, the Changjiang above Nanjing and the Great Canal for 17 percent, Beijing for 6.5 percent other inland centers for 1 percent, inland China for 10 percent, and foreign countries for 2 percent. Some major cities other than Shanghai and the capital receive comparatively intensive coverage. Among these are the old centers of the Jiangnan region Suzhou (7 percent), Hangzhou (4 percent), Nanjing (5 percent), Ningbo (5 percent) and Yangzhou (2 percent), and the leading coastal cities Guangzhou (5 percent) and Tianjin (1.5 percent). Shanghai clearly is the city most reported on, followed by Suzhou and Beijing, which retains its stature as the capital. Interestingly,

Shanghai is not the main focus of the magazine. Rather, reports on many places within China and abroad are included. The distribution of location generally follows the connections of trade. Places beyond the trade networks appear only sporadically.

This distribution of places reported from can be explained through the fact that news travels along the same routes as trade and people. There is, however, another possible explanation extending the first. Similar to the wide range of topics, the geographic comprehensiveness could indicate a conscious attempt to address the most general readership possible. This would not only be reflected in the inclusion of readers living outside Shanghai. Most Shanghai readers had recently moved there from one or the other of the places that appeared in the *DSZHB*. The geographical distribution of reported items in fact roughly reflects the composition of the Shanghai population. We can conclude that readers both in and outside Shanghai could find picture-reports on their native places. They could enter the Shanghai network, which connected China to the world at large and new to traditional ways of life.

Miraculous and marvelous events are not relegated to far-off places, but can happen everywhere. Some kinds of marvels are virtually world-encompassing. For instance, among major monstrous or supernatural phenomena from the waters we can find: a tasty giant fish washed ashore near Yancheng in Subei (*Zi* 36); fish with legs in the Guilin River (*Zi* 81b); a giant clam in the Yangtse near Yangzhou (*Zhu* 17b); an island that really is a giant fish (*Zhu* 82);[46] an old man turning into a dragon on the Yangtse near Zhenjiang (*Li* 38); half-human clam-beings at the icy shore of the polar sea (*Li* 83); a crocodile killing a child in South-East Asia (*Li* 85); a giant fish saving a fisher who once released a strange fish off the coast of Fujian (*Xin* 71); a monster warning a Western technician against dynamiting the rapids in the Yangtse near Yichang (*Zhen* 5); a giant clam carrying a pearl and a dragon near Baoshan (*Zhen* 39); a strange creature washed ashore near Haiyan (*Zhen* 41a); or an oxen changing into a dragon near Haizhou (*Zhen* 72).

Among the abnormally tall or short people in the sample, we find a Korean dwarf (*Ji* 41a); dwarflike pygmies discovered by a Westerner in Africa (*Zi* 67); a giant girl in England (*Zi* 7); and a giant old peasant in Shandong (*Zhu* 22). One of the four women giving birth to monstrous babies is an Italian female convict in prison who gives birth to a monstrous baby without a head (*Ji* 68). Among strange humans and half-humans we find a Mexican woman with extremely long hair (*Zhu* 65b) and hairy little half-humans exhibited in the Berlin Zoo (*Xin* 66).

Other marvels, such as fox-ghosts, occur only in East Asia. A Chinese traveler narrowly escapes a Japanese fox-woman (*Zi* 56), and a Westerner observed a fox-ghost's self-cremation near Seoul (*Ji* 52).[47]

Chinese experience adventures with devoted animals saving their masters or showing human feeling toward them in China and abroad. Such cases of dogs and monkeys are reported from a place near Yangzhou (*Jia* 21), from

Beijing (*Zi* 17b), Sumatra (*Zhu* 70), and Guangzhou (*Zhen* 65b). There is also a drunk Westerner who is defended against the police by his two dogs in New York (*Xin* 69).

Even more bewildering than these occurrences may be the activity of the forces of heaven to punish those guilty of moral crimes. Of ten reports on lightning, seven are direct punishments of unfilial behaviour, murder or intended murder (*Jia* 85 in Chuzhou in Zhejiang, *Yi* 21 near Suzhou, *Zi* 39 in Wudu in Fujian, *Zhu* 37 and *Shu* 40 near Nanjing, *Zhen* 21 near Shanghai, *Zhen* 38 in Xinjian in Jiangxi). In one case, an immoral wife succeeds in bribing the god of lightning with the promise of a generous donation (*Zhu* 53). The two remaining picture-reports involve no moral crime. One is about a baby left for dead after birth and revived by lightning; the other concerns a Western missionary who "does not believe in lightning" until his servant gets killed by lightning on a boat journey in Shandong (*Jia* 34b).

NOT EXACTLY HARD NEWS

Knowing the time of an event was less important for authenticity than knowing the place. Only 39 percent of the picture-reports in the sample indicate the time, either in a vague way, such as "recently" (23 percent), or with a date (16 percent). The reports about strange occurrences give the time even less often; 27 percent contain some specification, 19 percent in a vague, 8 percent in precise way. Usually it is implied that the event reported happened "recently." There are, however, exceptions, such as one report about an event from the Ming dynasty! Reports on hearsay about strange events seem to get by with less stringent rules: 58 percent of the reports analyzed relate an event experienced or observed by one or several human protagonists. These protagonists are in every case presented to the reader and can be identified by full name or family name, occupation, title, or by the place where they live or originally came from. In the mostly narrative group of miracles and marvels a high percentage of 87 percent are centered on human protagonists.

The sources of the reports are rarely given. For only 9 percent of the picture-reports a source is named, either a newspaper (19 reports), somebody passing through Shanghai (21 reports), or even the personal experiences of one of the painters or journalists (3).[48] In 11 percent of the reports on miracles, sources are given; five of them are based on newspapers, the remaining twelve on traveler's tales and other sources.

CONCLUSIONS

What role did all these curious matters play in *DSZHB?* Ye Xiaoqing sees them as filling material.[49] This they were, to some extent. They often occupy the first and last pages, which came as single and not as double-page illustrations and were often filled with less important items.[50] However, they are far too numerous to be no more than that. Several explanations offer themselves. The topic was particularly well suited for illustration, more so than, for example, social occurrences. From the New Year paintings and book illustrators, the *DSZHB* painters knew the whole repertoire of monsters, deities, ghosts, strange humans, and animals. These topics offered the possibility for skillful illustrations, often on the border between the amusing and the frightening. As a traditional kind of light reading matter, the *zhiguai* topics made the magazine more colorful. They added to its entertainment value, while toning down the horror of reports on man-made and natural disasters. In this topical group, the *DSZHB* used a mixture of horror, curiosity, and amusement that was certain to appeal to almost any reader. However, this "tabloid" content was processed and elevated with the help of genre painting and literary writing. As a result, the texts as well as the pictures could be enjoyed as entertaining art, while their factual reliability became of secondary importance.

Turning to the visual aspect of the picture-reports, their open perspective from an elevated point of view makes no attempt to captivate the reader or enforce a particular, fixed perspective. Similarly, the texts share their safe, omniscient perspective with their reader. The pictures allow one to choose where to direct one's interest, and the reports are to be enjoyed for the detailed depictions and funny, weird, or hair-rising stories. Readers would not need to believe everything, but could feel safe and superior. However, they were equally free to consider miraculous phenomena as historical matter.[51]

By demonstrating that weird things could happen anywhere, and that all humans were ultimately subjected to the same natural or heavenly powers, the picture-reports on strange matters introduced an element of stability into the rapidly changing city of Shanghai and the life of its inhabitants, creating a continuity for the new periodical as well as for the community newcomers. Nearly every third picture-report in the magazine told its readers that the world was as strange and impossible to fathom as it had always been. Besides, the magazine would appeal to a frame of mind that found satisfaction in seeing that even Western technicians had to give up in the face of a river monster.[52]

The *DSZHB* seemed to confirm the existing order of things. Piety toward elders remained the highest virtue and those offending against these morals might still be struck by lightning or otherwise drastically punished, even in the vicinity of Shanghai.[53] In a predominantly male society of sojourners, however, this might have been no more than the striking of a familiar ring or merely a gesture of cultural cohesion.

At the same time, the magazine also offered possibilities to test new or extraordinary things in a noncommittal way. During the life of the *DSZHB*, "*woyou*" was becoming the term for "armchair traveling,"[54] that is, a very gradual form of getting used to the foreign world breaking into China. For such armchair-travelers, the *DSZHB* provided information about the trends and fashions of Shanghai, customs in other regions and countries, and adventures and interesting things all over the world. It recycled existing images and stereotypes and in the process created new ones for the Shanghai modernity.

Potential readers of the *DSZHB* in Shanghai were a special brand of people. Most were young male newcomers who had come to make a living, often leaving their families behind. They might ruin themselves in courtesan houses, make a fortune, squander their families' fortune, or become employees. They mingled freely at a safe distance from clan elders, and had the possibility of comparing their own habits with different local and "overseas" ones. They had to create new social groupings, stratifications, and lifestyles. Socializing and entertainment shifted from the residences of the "big families" and the religious realm of temples into public places such as teahouses, restaurants, courtesan houses, parks, and semireligious places such as guildhalls. In the form of books and periodicals, it also began moving into the private sphere.

Contributing to this trend, the *DSZHB* provided entertainment to be consumed in private in the small household or with a few friends. Furthermore, in a city of strangers where contacts needed to be established and maintained outside a stable net of relatives and acquaintances, the magazine offered anecdotes for conversation and pictures to show around. While answering a particular need of Shanghai sojourners the *DSZHB* also offered the possibility of partaking a little in this new world to people oriented toward Shanghai but not living there.

The *DSZHB* reports were never totally without factual basis, but they generally put little emphasis on the accuracy of the information given. Specification of place, time, and person constituted the introduction to a story in the tradition of historical literary writing. However, sources are very rarely named, the pictures are compositions of pictorial elements, and the story is embellished with evaluations and free associations. The sample contains seven picture-reports on dreams and one of a Ming dynasty event.[55] Nevertheless, the people who made the magazine were not unaware of the question of factuality. In one example, the text voices doubts about likeliness of the particular news item illustrated.[56] The fact that this story about peasant women defeating government troops was included all the same indicates that the decisive element of a report "in the style of *Liaozhai zhiyi*" was the good story irrespective of its factual basis.

The mixture of topics and the indifference toward the factual and the factitious may indicate a groping for understanding in a confusing world. Perhaps the tastes of the *DSZHB*'s readership are best characterized by a set of adjectives often used for describing Shanghai's new cultural scene: *xin* (new), *qi* (curious or marvelous), *yi* (strange or astounding), *guai* (weird or monstrous), completed by the *kejing* (shocking), *kexi* (pleasant)—that is, the news. Such tastes would imply an attitude not unlike exoticism: a safe and entertaining way to confront the strange or the other.

Rather than "new wine in old bottles," the magazine could be described as offering its readers wine that pretended to be new in bottles that pretended to be old. These pretensions, together with the irreverent combination of widely divergent elements they motivate, perhaps are the factors making the magazine Shanghainese. It lightly combined the incompatible, and smoothly popularized something essentially new: reading periodicals for entertainment.

NOTES

1. I would like to thank Rudolf G. Wagner and Catherine V. Yeh for their encouragement and many insightful suggestions.

2. Sa Kongliao, "Wushi nian lai Zhongguo huabao zhi sige shiqi" [The four stages of the Chinese illustrated magazine during the last fifty years] (1931), in Zhang Jinglu, ed., *Zhongguo xiandai chuban shiliao*, Shanghai: Zhonghua shuju, 1955, vol. 2, p. 508. Taken up by Yu Yueting, "Woguo huabao de shizu—*Dianshizhai huabao* chutan" [The founding father of the illustrated magazine in China: Preliminary investigations into the *Dianshizhai Huabao*], *Xinwen yanjiu ziliao 10* (May 1981), pp. 149–181.

3. See R. Wagner, "Joining the Global Imaginaire" in this volume.

4. Chinese and Western publications frequently used pictures from the *DSZHB* to illustrate Chinese views. An 1889 German article claimed "the owners [of the DSZHB] are Chinese," quoted in Wagner, "Joining the Global Imaginaire," note 133. A 1928 Chinese article extolling the English illustrated magazines also presents the *DSZHB* without reference to its foreign ownership and model. See Wu Yue, "Huabao jinbu tan" [On the progress of the illustrated magazine], *Beiyang huabao*, December 1, 1928, p. 7.

5. For the illustrated literature, see A Ying, *Xiaoshuo xianhua si zhong, Santan* [Rambling talks about novels in four parts, part three], Shanghai: Shanghai guji chubanshe, 1985, pp. 226–241; and Lu Gong, *Fanshu jianwenlu* [Lavish books seen or heard about], Shanghai: Shanghai guji chubanshe, 1985. In 1884, the Shenbaoguan published a richly illustrated guide to Shanghai, the *Shenjiang shengjingtu.*

6. Ye Xiaoqing, "*Dianshizhai Huabao* zhong de Shanghai pingmin wenhua" [Shanghai popular culture in the *Dianshizhai huabao*], *Ershi shiji 1* (January 1990), p. 36–47, and *The Dianshizhai Pictorial : Shanghai Urban Life, 1884–1898*, Ann Arbor: University of Michigan Press, 2003. Also Erik Zürcher, "Middle-class Ambivalence. Religious Attitudes in the *Dianshizhai huabao*," *Études chinoises* 13–1/2 (spring 1994), pp. 109–141. Chen Pingyuan, Xia Xiaohong eds., *Tuxiang wan Qing:* Dianshizhai huabao, Tianjin: Baihua wenyi chubanshe, 2001.

7. The *DSZHB* has been variously characterized: as a Chinese "physiognomy" (= typical social scenes), by Max August Scipio von Brandt, *Der Chinese in der Öffentlichkeit und der Familie wie er sich selbst sieht und schildert, Mit 82 Zeichnungen nach chinesischen Originalen*, Berlin: Reimer, 1911; as the repository of modern Shanghai imagery, by Lu Xun, *Shanghai wenyi zhi yipie* [A glance on Shanghai literature and art], (first publ. 1931), *Lu Xun quanji*, Beijing: Renmin wenxue chubanshe, 1989, vol.

IV, pp. 229–230; postscript to *Chaohua xishi* [Morning flowers picked in the evening], (first publ. 1927), *Lu Xun quanji*, vol. II, pp. 289–295; *Lue lun Zhongguoren de lian* [Some remarks on Chinese faces], (first publ. 1927), *Lu Xun quanji*, vol. III, p. 311; see also two letters to Wei Mengke (1934) in *Lu Xun quanji*, vol. XII, pp. 371–372, 380–382; as a transitional form between traditional printed illustrations and the modern illustrated magazine, by Bodo Wiethoff, "Berichte über Europa und Europäer in einem frühen chinesischen Bildermagazin," *Nachrichten der Gesellschaft für Natur- und Völkerkunde Ostasiens 95/96* (December 1964), pp. 113–125; as a progressive but still intermediate form that introduced the illustrated magazine to China, by Yu Yueting, "Woguo huabao de shizu"; as a vehicle for enlightenment, by Wang Ermin, "Zhongguo jindai zhishi pujihua chuanbo zhi tushuo xingshi—*Dianshizhai huabao*" [An illustrated means for the popularization of knowledge in modern China: The *Dianshizhai huabao*], *Zhongyang yanjiuyuan jindaishi yanjiusuo jikan 19* (1990), pp. 135–172; as one of the links connecting Shanghai to world culture by Rudolf Wagner, "Joining the Global Imaginaire," in the present volume.

8. Wang Ermin, "Zhongguo jindai zhishi pujihua," p. 166.

9. Ge Gongzhen, *Zhongguo baoxueshi* [A history of Chinese journalism] (1926), Reprint: Taibei: Xuesheng shuju, 1982, p. 333.

10. Many of the stories carried by the *DSZHB* were not meant to be reliable news.

11. The *zhiguai* was a branch-off from historical writing, originating during the Jin dynasty (fourth–fifth century) while the *chuanqi* took shape as narrative form during the Tang. By the Qing-dynasty, the two were no longer clearly distinguishable. Pu Songling's *Liaozhai zhiyi* combined characteristics of both, revitalized the genre, and raised its literary standing. As a consequence, it became immensely popular in the second half of the Qing. Fanciful, and specialized on the curious and strange, the *zhiguai* nevertheless has preserved characteristics of the historic record in its narrative style, in its need for a source, a date, and a place, and in reporting on recent events. See Kenneth J. Dewoskin, "The *Sou-shen-chi* and the *chih-kuai* tradition: A Bibliographic and Generic Study," PhD dissertation, Columbia University, 1974, pp. 308ff., and Chen Bohai and Yuan Jin, *Shanghai jindai wenxue shi* [A History of modern Shanghai literature], Shanghai: Shanghai renmin chubanshe, 1993, p. 231. It should be noted that the *Shenbao* also carried such *zhiguai* items, and was taken to task for them by its Western contemporaries. See B. Mittler, "Domesticating an Alien Medium: Incorporating the Western-style Newspaper into the Chinese Public Sphere," in this volume.

12. It is estimated that the circulation numbers of the *Shenbao* averaged around 10,000–12,000 in the period under consideration, although Wolfgang Mohr, *Die moderne chinesische Tagespresse*, vol. 1, pp. 104–105, vol. 2, 160, claims that only by 1912 was the 10,000 mark crossed. The *Penny Magazine*, the first mass-market magazine, reached a circulation between 100,000 and 200,000 in 1832–1835, among a much smaller population. Bennett Scott, "Revolutions in Thought: Serial Publication and the Mass Market for Teaching," in Joanne Shattock and Michael Wolff, eds., *The Victorian Periodical Press: Samplings and Soundings*, Leicester: Leicester University Press, 1982, p. 237.

13. The reprint (Guangzhou 1984), on which the present study is based, does not contain the supplements, inserts, and advertisements. For a study of the supplements and inserts see Wagner, "Joining the Global Imaginaire," in this volume.

14. Chen/Yuan, *Shanghai jindai wenxue shi,* Shanghai: Shanghai renmin chubanshe, 1993, p. 40.

15. Bao Tianxiao, *Chuanyinglou huiyi lu,* Taibei: Longwen chubanshe, 1971, p. 134.

16. *Jia* 1–2. A translation of this foreword will be found in Wagner, "Joining the Global Imaginaire" in this volume.

17. The *Shenbao* editor Shen Jinhuan provided the calligraphy of the magazine's title; see the inner title page *Jia* 1, and of the title of one thematic issue, see Bing 41b. Shen's calligraphy prompted Wang Ermin to propose Shen as the head of an assumed editorial board of the *DSZHB;* see Wang Ermin, "Zhongguo jindai zhishi pujihua," pp. 144 and 165. Since calligraphed titles are generally signed, this seems too thin a basis for the assumption that Shen played a role in the editing of the magazine.

18. Major wrote the foreword to the first issue, *Jia* 1–2, and a postscript to another early issue, *Bing* 7–48a. Regular announcements of each new issue in the *Shenbao* were made in Major´s name. This indicates that this was done on his initiative. Major is credited with speaking and writing Chinese and giving the *Shenbao* editors a free hand; see Ge Gongzhen, *Zhongguo baoxueshi,* p. 106.

19. E. g., an article about illustrated magazines in the *Shenbao* of June 19, 1884, and a notice in the *Shenbao* (repeatedly June 4, from 1884) asking for contributions to the *DSZHB* by painters living outside Shanghai both state that the *DSZHB* illustrated what previously had been reported in the *Shenbao.*

20. The difference in reports on wars between China and foreign powers is remarkable. While the *Shenbao* was highly regarded for well-informed and accurate news, the *DSZHB* invariably reported Chinese victories, sometimes achieved by romanesque means. Some reports, such as one on an English industrial plant producing salt and fertilizer from dead bodies (*Mao* 29) or one on a chemical process developed by an American doctor to shrink dead bodies (*Mao* 32a) would hardly have slipped by under the supervision of Major or a *Shenbao* editor.

21. Even the two contributors, who, according to their signatures, lived in Beijing, painted in the same style; see *Jia* 68 and 69 for Gu Yuezhou and *Ren* 32 for Jin Ding. The only contributor with a different style was Ge Longzhi, a native from Haining in Zhejiang who lived in Shanghai. He was deaf and a recognized painter in the high tradition; see Yu Jianhua, ed., *Zhongguo meishujia renming cidian* [Biographical dictionary of Chinese artists], Shanghai: Shanghai renmin yishu chubanshe, 1980, p. 1213c.

22. They are Wu Youru, Jin Gui, Zhou Quan, He Yuanjun, and Fu Jie. See Duan Benluo and Zhang Xifu, eds., *Suzhou shougongye shi* [A history of Suzhou crafts], Suzhou: Jiangsu guji chubanshe, 1986, pp. 92, 185, and Bao Songnian, *Zhongguo nianhua shi* [A history of Chinese New Year prints], Shenyang: Liaoning meishu chubanshe, 1986, p. 168. See also Wang Ermin, "Zhongguo jindai zhishi pujihua" (1990), p. 144. However, Wang overlooked the involvement of the *DSZHB* painters in the New Year painting, and therefore perhaps sees them too directly linked to literati painting. Wagner, "Joining the Global Imaginaire," disputes Wu Youru's involvement with Suzhou New Year's prints.

23. Four such painters are mentioned in A Ying, *Xiaoshuo sizhong,* pp. 226–241.

24. On Wu Youru, see Wagner, "Joining the Global Imaginaire." Wu is mentioned in painter dictionaries or collected biographies. See, e. g., Cao Xuyuan, ed., *Wuxian zhi*

[Gazetteer of the district Wu], 4 vols. (1933) Reprint: *Zhongguo fangzhi congshu: Hua-zhong difang 18*, Taibei: Chengwen chubanshe, 1979, *Juan* 21: "Biographies of Suzhou painters," p. 75; Yang Yi, *Haishang Molin* [The ink forest of Shanghai], (orig. 1920) Reprinted in *Shanghaitan yu Shanghairen congshu*, Shanghai: Shanghai guji chubanshe, 1989, p. 78; Yu Jianhua, *Zhongguo meishujia renming cidian*, p. 1213c. Eighteen of his colleagues are only mentioned an attachment to his entry in Yang Yi´s biographical notes on Shanghai painters, *Haishang molin*, p. 78.

25. For New Year prints from Suzhou, see Wang Shucun, ed., *Zhongguo min-jian nianhuashi tulu* [A catalogue of the history of popular Chinese New Year prints], Shanghai: Shanghai renmin yishu chubanshe, 1991; Bao Songnian *Zhongguo nianhua shi*, pp. 34ff. and 72; Yao Qian, ed., *Taohuawu nianhua*, Beijing: Wenwu chubanshe, 1985. For the close connection and reciprocal influence of Suzhou and Shanghai New Year printing trade, see Wu Guifang, "Jindai Shanghai chubanshi xiaobian" [A brief history of the publishing industry of Shanghai], *Chuban shiliao 17/18* (November 1989), pp. 71–72.

26. Fan Xianmo, "Qingchu de yulun yu chaobao—jindai Zhongguo baoshi chu-bian (xu)" [Public opinion in the early Qing and the Court News: draft edition of a history of newspapers in modern China (sequel)], *Xinwen yanjiu ziliao 8* (November 1981), pp. 245–262; Mohr, *Die moderne chinesische Tagespresse*, vol. 1, p. 18. See also undated reproductions in Zhongguo lishi bowuguan, ed., *Zhongguo jindaishi cankao tulu* [Pictorial sources on modern Chinese history], Shanghai: Zhongguo lishi bowu-guan, 1986.

27. See Figure 3.3 in Wagner, "Joining the Global Imaginaire."

28. For an example, see Figure 3.5 in ibid. Another example is the portrait of Feng Zicai by Jin Gui, *DSZHB Yi* 81b, which is based on a photograph, dated 1885, in Zhongguo lishi bowuguan ed., *Zhongguo jindaishi cankao tulu*, p. 224.

29. Wagner, "Joining the Global Imaginaire," p. 136.

30. Wang Ermin, "Zhongguo jindai zhishi pujihua," p. 166.

31. For examples, see Catherine V. Yeh, *Shanghai Love: Courtesans, Intellectuals and Entertainment Culture, 1850–1810*, Seattle: University of Washington Press, 2006, chapter 1.

32. Quoted in Ye Xiaoqing, *Popular Culture in Shanghai*, p. 1, from an article from May 8, 1884. I see this claim as a rhetorical formula employed regularly by the new press.

33. The ten series are: *Jia* (summer 1884), *Ji* (winter/spring 1886), *Zi* (summer/autumn 1887), *Yi* (spring 1889), *Xu* (autumn/winter 1890/91), Zhu (summer 1892), *Li* (winter/spring 1894), *Shu* (summer 1895), *Xin* (winter/spring 1896/97), and *Zhen* (spring/summer 1898).

34. Yu Yueting "Woguo huabao de shizu," pp. 157–159; Wang Ermin, "Zhongguo jindai zhishi pujihua."

35. See R. Wagner, "Joining the Global Imaginaire," pp. 149–151.

36. The change also extends to the treatment of items reported. Only in the first two booklets do we find examples of a critical attitude toward the validity of events reported, as in *Ji* 87 or in the rectification of *Yi* 7 (which is not in the sample). This

attitude is also visible in the evaluation of the events. E.g., the first of four reports on filial children trying to cure sick parents with their own flesh appears in *Jia* 10a. This son takes the drastic step of cutting out his own liver to cure his father. He is criticized for committing an absurdity that is more likely to kill him than to cure his father. All later cases of children cutting out bits of their own flesh are, however, highly praised as models of virtue, with the treatment presented as being effective, as in *Yi* 16b, *Zi* 6, or *Xin* 49b.

37. The reports in *Jia* and *Ji* closely follow their Western source. After *Yi*, the reports on technology become either entertaining: e.g., a faithful copy from Western drawings of various fun fair machines (*Yi* 56) or a specially constructed pavilion (*Yi* 53); or fantastic: e.g., a flying sailship (*Xu* 57a) or an underwater train (*Xin* 39).

38. In one case, this is stated explicitly (*Zi* 64).

39. Lu Xun, "Shanghai wenyi zhi yipie" in *Lu Xun quanji*, vol. 4, pp. 292–293 and "Lue lun Zhongguoren de lian," pp. 414–415.

40. E.g., *Jia* 86, *Zi* 66.

41. *Jia* 53 and 54.

42. E.g., *Li* 25a.

43. *Zhen* 34, 35. I assigned this kind of report to both groups.

44. *Xu* 25a.

45. *Zhen* 18.

46. This traveling tale of the island fish is presented as the personal experience of an old Chinese sailor.

47. There also three cases of experiences with fox-ghosts in China, in *Li* 68, 87, 88.

48. *Yi* 82, 83, *Xu* 84.

49. Ye Xiaoqing, *Popular Culture in Shanghai*, p. 49.

50. 29 percent of all picture-reports from the sample are miracles and marvels, but they occupy 38 percent of all first and last pages. Important events tend to appear on the first double page. The only exceptions are portraits, which were well suited for a narrow format.

51. At the time, miracles and monsters were not dismissed as products of primitive superstition; even local gazetteers duly recorded supernatural phenomena.

52. *Zhen* 5.

53. *Zhen* 21.

54. E.g., preface by Huang Lianjia to *Shenjiang shengjing tu*. See also the comments in Wagner, "Joining the Global Imaginaire," pp. 154–155.

55. Dreams are reported on in *Ji* 22, *Zi* 81, *Li* 6 u. 18, *Shu* 5, *Xin* 65b, *Zhen* 52.

56. *DSZHB Ji* 87.

CHAPTER 5

Shanghai Leisure, Print Entertainment, and the Tabloids, *xiaobao* 小報

Catherine Vance Yeh

THE INVENTION OF LEISURE

Shanghai's ascendance to China's premier center of trade and commerce was both conditioned and accompanied by its ascendance to the Chinese capital of entertainment. By the 1860s and 1870s, entertainment had become one of the city's main attractions for wealthy retirees and active businessmen. It was a major source of revenue. The process resembles that of Paris as its attractions made it into the country's financial "milk cow."[1] The Shanghai Foreign Settlements were run by a city council made up of Western land-holders. This council was primarily engaged in securing urban comfort and order as the optimal environment for business pursuits. It was imposing "decent" urban behavior, but was not policing morals in the manner Chinese officialdom did. As the Shanghai Foreign Settlements quickly became an entity in their own right, neither the Qing government restrictions nor the social and moral constraints prevailing elsewhere in China could thwart the growth of Shanghai entertainment business into a full-scale industry. The rise of newspapers, and entertainment newspapers in particular, is intricately linked to this development.

Shanghai entertainment incorporated elements from different Chinese regions such as the Lower Yangtze Valley and Canton, as well as from such foreign centers as Yokohama, Edo, London, and Paris, and merged them into a particular and very distinct form.[2] In the formation and development of this entertainment culture, the city's new literati, *wenren* 文人, sometimes referred to as the "Foreign Settlement talents," *yangchang caizi* 洋場才子, played a

201

crucial role. Attracted by the thrill and the new career opportunities offered by the city, growing numbers of traditionally educated Chinese men of letters moved to the Settlements. The relationship of this new class with the Shanghai entertainment industry was that of a patron turned broker. In their search for a role in the economic and cultural life of the city, they became the cultural middlemen. Having neither the financial capital of the compradors and merchants nor the entertainment skills of courtesans, they banked on the cultural capital and their literary skills, which many of them put to the service of the growing entertainment industry.

The infrastructure necessary for the development of entertainment into an industry was created by the city council. In its eagerness to put Shanghai into the forefront of international urban development and to offer an attractive quality of life, it developed the urban amenities such as clean drinking water, paved and clean roads with regulated traffic, and gas and then electric light (in 1865 and 1882, respectively) for the streets. This opened public spaces and extended the day deep into the night for entertainment and reading.

By introducing the concept of leisure into the daily lives of the new urbanites, the *xiao shimin* 小市民, entertainment publishing eventually created a mass market and helped shape popular cultural habits to a significant degree. The notion of leisure, which formerly had belonged to a leisure class without a particular time slot allotted to its exercise, was now set off against work time and filled with characteristic content.[3] Restaurants and theaters as well as tea and courtesan houses eagerly and successfully explored this time/space. The city offered many "sites of pleasure": one might have a meal at the fancy Western-style restaurant Yipinxiang 一品香; go for a brougham ride through the financial and commercial districts such as Nanjing Road and the Bund with their fabulously wealthy Hongs and grand buildings; drink tea at the sumptuously decorated five-story teahouse Wuceng lou 五層樓; play a game of billiards in the Zhang Gardens 張園; listen to the "maoerxi" 貓 (貌) 兒戲 opera in the Yu Gardens 愚園 with their unique all-female cast; go to the semiannual horse races; spend an evening watching the American or the Italian circus perform, and so on.

The city's print industry, which had been rapidly expanding since the 1870s, spotted the market opportunity for print entertainment. Since the founding of the Shenbao guan 申報館 publishing house in 1872 and down to the Commercial Press 商務印書館 two and a half decades later, the publication of leisurely reading matter had come to constitute a sizable part of publishing activity. A natural focus of the books, illustrated volumes, and serials forming this print entertainment were the increasingly famous Shanghai entertainment establishments and their performers, above all the courtesans and opera actors. Many Settlement intellectuals became habitués and connoisseurs of this domain, and went public with their knowledge as a means of making a living. In this way they made themselves an indispensable part in the life of this only metropolitan city in China.

Print entertainment was one of the most open yet innocuous ways in which notions of "the world" (*shijie* 世界) and of Western civilization were introduced into the daily lives of the general public. The world and the West in general, and China's position with regard to it, certainly were major topics for discussion among the leading lights of the time. But they often found their way into the daily lives of people not through grand proclamations on China's need to modernize, but more through innocuous and trivial matter such as foreign loan words, images, advertisement, matches, buttons, or new printing technologies, among them metal font type and lithography. The textual and pictorial genres of Shanghai print entertainment were cultural hybrids in form, content, and technology. They played an important if little observed role in the insertion of Western-derived notions, goods, and attitudes into the normality of urban life.

MARKETING THE NOTION OF "PLAY"

From the outset, Shanghai entertainment was strongly commercialized. And like its development into a trade and financial metropolis, Shanghai's emergence as the "big playground," *youxichang,* was accompanied and promoted by print products, especially newspapers. In the early days, there was no specialization. The big dailies such as the *Shenbao* carried news, commentary, and literary pieces on entertainment next to political and business news. By the mid-1890s, the time was ripe for the first specialized entertainment papers to appear. They mark the beginning of an entire branch of the Chinese newspaper industry of the Republican period known under the collective name of "small papers," *xiaobao*. Considering their importance, the focus of newspaper studies on the political, and as a far distant second the commercial papers, has left out the entertainment papers altogether. A Ying again is the only early scholar to save this genre from oblivion, and, after 1949, only one author offered an overview.[4] Foreign examples had shown to the pioneer of this genre, Li Boyuan 李伯元 (1897–1906), that amusement could be a marketable literary endeavor in and of itself.[5] The Shanghai entertainment market had reached a dimension in the city and fame throughout the country that it was able to sustain regular serialized and specialized publications. The entertainment tabloids made their appearance, on which this chapter will focus.

These papers very consciously inserted themselves into the new time division between work and leisure. One of the first, appropriately called *Leisure, Xiaoxian bao,* founded in November 1897, neatly explained this new concept in an article entitled "What is the meaning of giving the name *Leisure* to this paper," Shi *Xiaoxian bao* mingming zhiyi 釋<消閑報> 命名之意:

> Leisure is the opposite of work. [The officials] are working so hard at the emperor's affairs, [the businessmen] are so busy with their account books that if there was no set time for recuperation this would seem to go against the

principle of taking care of one's spirit. Thus people from the past had the saying "every hundred days [one should take a] rest."

But now, the Westerner's way of counting time for rest is the [Sunday in the] seven-day cycle; moreover, they also have an appointed time within a day for rest. If there is to be rest, then there is leisure; if there is leisure, then there should be ways of diverting oneself. A laughter bursting forth once the eye is caught by a page [in our paper] might not be the [orthodox] method of recuperating one's mental vigor; but at least it can help drive away boredom and dissipate worries.[6]

閑者, 勞之對也. 王事賢勞, 簿書鞅 掌, 使無養息以節之, 似背于愛惜 精神之理, 故古人有'十旬休暇'之 說. 今之西人, 休息之期, 則以七 日一來復, 而晨昏歇息之時, 亦有定 候. 既歇息, 則閑矣, 既閑, 則當有 消閑之法矣. 一篇入目, 笑口既開, 雖非調攝精力之方, 要亦可為遣悶 排愁之助也.

These papers helped present and establish leisure or "play" as occupying a specific urban cultural time/space distinct from work, and spelled out time and again the particular way in which cultural/commercial products were to enhance its enjoyment. They presented Shanghai as the fantasy world of play, defining it as "China's biggest big playground," Zhongguo jueda youxi zhi chang 中國絕大游戲之場.[7]

With their daily reports on the life and business of the city's top-ranking entertainers, the courtesan stars, mingji 名妓, and the male opera stars, mingyou 名優, these papers transformed their readers into urban voyeurs. Most of them were getting their entertainment and fun not so much from participating in the gaudy lives of these stars but from their daily peep-show of articles featuring the city's entertainment life and its celebrities. For seven cents a day, the standard cost for the xiaobao during the late Qing, the reader could participate in this new form of entertainment of looking in onto these glamorous lives. This required neither action nor money. Like a traveler making a journey by reading a travelogue "with his mind," xinyou 心遊, or "while reclining [on his couch]," woyou 臥遊, the reader could enjoy a free look at the Shanghai entertainment landscape and was able to "look in" on the scene without being seen, risking his reputation, or spending big money. In the process, the paper enabled whose who could not afford these entertainments to take part, and remade those who were able to participate as entertainers or customers into personalities and stars.

The assignment of different reading matter for different times of the day and week is nicely captured decades later when the literary illustrated journal Libailiu 禮拜六 (Saturday) explained its own name in its first issue in 1914: "Monday, Tuesday, Wednesday, Thursday, and Friday—these are the days when people are engaged in their professions, only Saturday and Sunday can they rest and read novels." Reflecting the new lifestyle of the urban family, it went on to suggest that the best and most inexpensive way of entertainment for the male readers was to read this magazine "side by side with their wives."[8]

In a radical shift away from the Chinese newspaper tradition, the entertainment papers reinvented a new type of implied reader. The big early dailies such as the *Shenbao* in Shanghai and the *Xunhuan ribao* in Hong Kong had inserted themselves into the traditional slot of reports on the customs and mutterings of the people below, the loyal remonstrance to the mighty from a censor, and the advice to the emperor on matters of national concern.[9] Nothing of this characterized the entertainment papers. They came in with a new editorial persona, a new mixture of content, a wider concept of the public sphere in which fun had a legitimate place, and, finally, the urban reader as the ultimate addressee.

LI BOYUAN'S *ENTERTAINMENT*

The most important early paper of this kind, appropriately called *Entertainment, Youxi bao* 游戲報, was founded in 1897 by Li Boyuan, a man mostly known today as the author of novels of social and political criticism written around the turn of the century.[10] The "play," *youxi* 游戲, in the title of the *Entertainment* suggests both the focus of the paper and the playful way in which it addressed the reader.

Li Boyuan was already twenty-nine years old, had failed the higher degrees in the imperial examination, and was perfectly unknown when he came to Shanghai in spring 1896.[11] Within months, however, he became the most successful journalist in a new line of Chinese-language papers that focused on entertainment. In June 1896, he had a first try with *The Guide* (*Zhinan bao* 指南報). It quickly faltered, but with its title announcing it as a daily guide to the Shanghai courtesan world it already contained the core ingredients of the *Entertainment,* namely, courtesan news and literature.[12]

Li Boyuan did not invent the genre. Entertainment papers had accompanied the rise of entertainment centers such as Paris or Edo Japan.[13] Li Boyuan openly and proudly announced the Western origin of his idea and even of the title *Youxi bao.*[14] In the West, he wrote, such papers were extremely popular, enjoyed a nationwide distribution, and had a daily circulation between 700 and 2000 copies.[15]

The *Entertainment* fixed the format for the genre, which was small in comparison to the regular dailies with the Shanghai *Shenbao* as their standard. During the late Qing, the *xiaobao* standard size measured 29 x 55 cm. They were folded into two pages in a square shape. This gave them the alternative name of "square paper," *fangxing bao* 方型報. They were printed in #4 font with separators between the lines, for easy reading. (Figure 5.1)

The *Entertainment* was a daily and entertaining guide to the city's best-known attraction—courtesan entertainment. From early on, Li Boyuan followed in the tracks of his contemporary, the "big" paper *Shenbao,* and made strenuous efforts to secure a distribution of his paper beyond Shanghai in the major agglomerations. Readers' letters and some other evidence suggest that

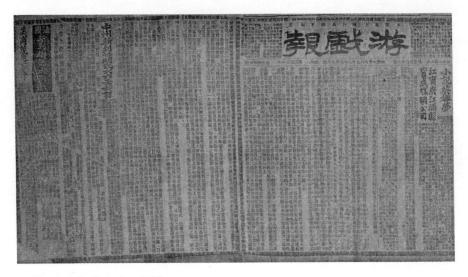

Figure 5.1. *Youxi bao*, 1897.

the fame and notoriety of the Shanghai courtesans had been rumored about and had made an impression deep enough on quite a few visitors to the town that a paper reporting on their daily moves and antics did have a market. During peak times, his print run would soon exceed the ten thousand mark, and it seems that this number became the basic reference after 1900. Three months after the founding of the *Entertainment,* the paper already sold so well that Li Boyuan could afford to move his office into the city's most glamorous commercial and entertainment hub, Si malu 四馬路, today's Fuzhou Road.[16]

The *Entertainment* was roughly divided into three segments: advertisements on the front page as well as at the end of the paper; editorials on the front page; and daily news about the city's entertainment on the second and part of the third page. Over time, it grew to four and finally six pages. It had a series of fixed columns such as short editorials, daily reports on courtesans, jokes, anecdotes, announcements of stage performances, and, most important, advertisements. These offered a wide range of luxury goods one might purchase, services one might want, and more fun to be had in Shanghai. The tone was mostly lighthearted, playful, and boastful of insider knowledge. At times though, it could be quite serious, addressing such issues as prices, bad service attitudes, failure of clients to pay their bills, or mistreatment of courtesans by their foster mothers.

The paper's tone is not intimate, but assumes a familiar reader sharing its values. The editorials as well as articles contributed by readers and published in the editorial section state their opinions strongly and often in a definite tone. In conjunction with the gossipy and quite uncritical news about the lives and loves of the courtesans, the strong editorial voice, which often has a critical and even ironical distance, marked the paper's efforts at securing for itself some independent and even moral stature.

The *Entertainment* reflects city life on many different levels. It is a unique source, providing us with a rich and diverse record of Shanghai and its sojourners at the turn of the century, particularly the formation of the tastes and fashions of the city. In the process, it reveals the complex ways in which the writers of the paper, most of them brought up as traditional men of letters, managed to create and reinforce an image of themselves that, while reflecting the city's dazzling mix of foreign institutions, industrial advancement, commercial power, and modernity in physical appearances and city management, also set them off from the common crowd with a critical authority of their own, even with articles focusing on entertainment. Shanghai is wonderful, it is wonderland in China, Li Boyuan shows, but at the same time it has its grotesque sides, and is nothing but a grand illusion.[17]

A GAME OF AMBIGUITY: WRITER–READER, COURTESAN–CLIENT, AND THE CITY

THE WRITER

Li Boyuan was very much involved in the day-by-day writing and management of the paper. He collected much of the news, wrote most of the articles, and was constantly coming up with new projects and forays. He went so far as to announce in his paper that he would be available for visitors only during a single fixed hour every day.[18] While this looks like the busy and exciting city life of a journalist/editor single-handedly running a paper, a certain ambiguity and unease remain visible in the way in which he saw his paper and his role in it.

He would refer to himself proudly and quite traditionally as "the manager of the kingdom of flowers" [= courtesans] (Huaguo zhushiren 花國主事人) as if he was on top of the courtesan world and had some discretionary power; at the same time, he would strike the self-ironical pose of the disillusioned man of letters by assuming the pen name "master of entertainment" 游戲主人 for his persona in the paper.

An editorial "On the basic purpose of the *Entertainment*" and the announcement of the move of his office highlight this ambiguity. The moving announcement, while not sparing with excitement about the transfer, also seemed defensive: was he just into having fun and success with his paper and daring to neglect the pressing issues of the nation?

> Once someone asked the Master [of Entertainment] (Li Boyuan's studio name): "True, the *Entertainment* has recently been the rage in Shanghai and elsewhere. Yet, it writes nothing on the court, on politics, or on the nation, and consists of nothing but courtesan banter and amusing anecdotes; what might be the reason for people to appreciate it so much?"

The Master answered: "My dear sir, you might understand one half of it, but you don't understand the other half. My company actually did not set up this paper to exclusively focus on entertainment; in reality it is our intention to make the great visible through the small 以小觀大, and make use of events for indirect statements—and all this for no other purpose than to rouse the ignorant and foolish to open their eyes!"[19]

Li Boyuan seems so uneasy about the gap between the professed higher purpose of his paper and its surface appearance as light entertainment that he articulates this misreading in order to refute it. In the editorial "On the basic purpose of the *Entertainment*," he had already claimed that "the basic purpose" of his paper was "to use its light style with a humorous pen . . . in order to exhort and warn, and as a way to enlighten the world."[20] The paper, he assures the readers, actually owes its success to this deeper purpose. Only a shallow reader would fail to grasp the sophisticated interplay between surface text and hidden message, and wonder how such light fare could make it in times as these after the defeat in the war with Japan and in the midst of a flurry of reform proposals (and their coming defeat).

Seemingly, the paper was catering enough to the tastes of a broader reading public to make this shallow reading a viable option. It secured commercial success to him as a freshman editor and journalist. His proclamations of a deeper and ultimately patriotic purpose of the paper are there to secure his status of a bona-fide man of letters with a mandatory concern for the state, and even to let his readers share a sense of greater sophistication. This ambiguous juxtaposition of commercial drive and higher purpose signals some of the quandaries these new urban intellectuals had with their own role, and even with the city.

Li Boyuan himself did not escape this dilemma. The importance the paper attributed to itself flowed from its self-assigned function of being, as a business newspaper for the courtesan entertainment, in charge of setting standards for behavior in this business. This helped to spare writer and reader the awkwardness of realizing that they were writing and reading a seriously lowbrow paper. But the deeper reason for the overbearing stance of the *Entertainment* is the frustration of a man with the status expectations of a man of letters who is living and making a living in Settlement Shanghai. The city provided nothing of the required social environment or status for him to reassume a role of moral authority here. The impulse, however, remained.

The new social position of these men as media professionals in Settlement Shanghai prompted a behavior full of contradictions. This might be atypical for a traditional man of letters in a familiar setting, but it is typical for the Shanghai intellectuals of this time. The confusion is lived out in the paper's daily dilemma concerning the standards on which to base judgments. How should one behave in this place that simultaneously was Chinese and everything but Chinese, Western and everything but Western?

An 1899 editorial entitled "The Shanghai courtesans are overdoing it" may serve as an example. It builds its case by first describing the grand courtesan entertainment centers of the past and their cultural achievements. What had made a famous courtesan, *mingji* 名妓, in these centers was her capacity for a profound relationship with cultured men of letters (*yaren* 雅人) of her time. Although this tradition of "cultivated relationship," *fengya* 風雅, could still be seen in some of the late Ming courtesans, the Qing only had flourishing centers of courtesan entertainment such as Yangzhou and Wuxi, but no more grand courtesans. Now the Shanghai Settlements had become the leading commercial hub and flourishing center of courtesan entertainment. But although the entertainment business here is singularly developed, the courtesans have no other arts left to recommend them besides singing and social entertainment. Worse, even these skills are fading, and the top courtesans have become conceited, pompous, and unprofessional.

> Since the opening [of the treaty port of Shanghai] until today, the situation has gone from bad to worse. Those courtesans who have become presumptuous on account of their being *en vogue* not only neglect [even] the practice of playing [the pipa] and singing, and provide no entertaining talk, their imperious and arrogant ways are just beyond belief. And there are finally those for whom even rich meats and fine rice are not good enough for food, even an elegantly embroidered quilt will not do for a coverlet, and even the sons of the rich and powerful are not worthy of a single glance while they will make opera singers their lovers, snatch away [other courtesan's] clients, drive around in [open] carriages and publicly display licentiousness, in short there is no vulgar thing they do not go after. . . . And not only this. For the smallest trifle or a single unfriendly glance, they will hurl abuses and even engage in fistfights [with each other]. Even for those [like our paper] who regard them with the warmest concern they don't care, and it comes to the point that they are not afraid of the anger of all others, and have no feeling for their words. Alas! What a scene the flowers of the fragrant kingdom have become![21]

Laments about the decline in the arts of courtesan entertainment are a common literary trope throughout the dynasties. The emblematized grand poetess courtesan of Tang-dynasty Changan, and the scholar-artist courtesans of the late Ming had no equal. While the previous lines belong to this trope, it has a new context here. The legal and social structure of the Shanghai Settlements has given the courtesan the freedom to carry on as she pleases. As long as her business was successful, she seemed neither to need nor to heed public opinion or the professional standards advocated by the likes of the *Entertainment*.

In this singular place, the courtesan enjoyed the same rights as any other class of people, including that of the men of letters themselves. The moral authority of the literati had no real pull here. Li Boyuan's "alas" is a collective sigh about his and his peers' fading influence and loss of social stature. It can be recuperated only by his claim to speak for a general public.

Once, the men of letters had been able to inspire the courtesans with grand emotions, but now they were reduced to playing the "master of entertainment" for these brazen women.   In this double and broken identity of a guest anchored in some other real world, and a host on most intimate terms with the city, the ironical mind-set of modern urban sophistication develops.[22]

At the same time, Li Boyuan buttressed his own standing not as a man of letters but as a professional by publicly speaking out for the public. In this way, he tried to set standards for the entertainment business. In one editorial he would reprimand the courtesan establishments for the poor quality of their arts of entertainment and remind them that, without this part, their whole business would come to naught. He would hold up the courtesan star Lu Lan-fen as an example of a true professional.[23] In others, he would offer suggestions for new attractive features or ventures.

The Reader and Client

In this entertainment paper enterprise, the reader was an active participant entitled to his own opinion. Those opinions were heard and printed, more often than not disagreeing with something the editor wrote. The paper offered a very modern platform for the exercise of public opinion in a politically rather innocent field. The manifestly playful character of the enterprise allowed for a level of innovative openness not found elsewhere at the time.

In the lively and well-defined scenes of the courtesan world reported in the daily news, an important figure is constantly present but rarely the focus of attention—the "client" or "guest." This usually anonymous character is the paper's implied reader. There are two aspects to the figure of the "guest" projected by the *Entertainment*. He is the courtesan's client looking for entertainment, and, because in many cases he will be a visitor to town, the paper will inform him how to behave, where to go, and what to expect. But he is also the "guest" in the broader sense of "the traveler" or "the sojourner" in this city, whose existential transitoriness the paper tries to capture, and to whom it offers a vague sense of belonging and coherence. The continuous references of the *Entertainment* to its readers as "guests from other lands" and its self-assigned duty to comfort these "forlorn sojourners," *piaoling zhi ke* 飄零之客,[24] is indicative of the troubled state of these men in dealing with their existence in Shanghai. The courtesan world in the *Entertainment* becomes the window through which they look out onto the city; it is at the same time the lure drawing them into it. With the mediation of the paper and its ironical distance, the "guest" thus becomes an inmate and insider of the city's heart, but at the same time retains a distance that allows him to go on with his normal life.

Being a "guest" and sojourner was in fact the basic condition of everyone in this new settlement, which actually did not have any "original" inhabitants. Even a man such as Ge Yuanxu 葛元煦, who by the time he wrote the first Chinese-language Shanghai city guide in 1877 had lived in Shanghai for fifteen years, continued to call himself a "guest" in this city; in his writing he assumed the persona of a temporary sojourner.[25] He was no exception. Many of these men remained deeply ambivalent about the city, which had lured them here, and about the professions they had assumed in it. They kept their mental distance from the city and from the responsibility for themselves by persisting in the temporary role of the "guest."

Li Boyuan's paper created a unique opportunity for the Shanghai sojourners to participate in a private as well as a public manner in the life of the city. The paper was a forum for a public discussion of all that had to do with courtesan entertainment. The reader participated daily in this ongoing story. He might be at the same time a client of a courtesan, and one of the many readers following her (and his own) tracks in the paper. The paper transformed what once had been an exclusive or even private experience into a public, collective, and shared enterprise.

This transformation of the traditional courtesan and client relationship was brought about by the way in which the city exerted its demands on its sojourners. Shanghai was not a traditional Chinese capital or town, it was a new place governed by foreigners with a set of unfamiliar civic and cultural codes. In political and social terms, the city forged new relationships with and among its citizens. The old social networks and moral standards still formed a part of the city's moral and social structure, but their hegemony did not extend to Shanghai. For those "guests" who came here to spend a few weeks as well as those who would spend the rest of their life in the city, the courtesans and the courtesan houses as portrayed in Li Boyuan's papers were there to bridge their sense of alienated distance. They offered to simulate the soothing "old order," but under the conditions of the new.

In this scenario, the Shanghai courtesans and the courtesan houses provided a "traditional" environment to the "guests," but this tradition was now staged under a set of new rules, which took into account the stature and independence of action the top courtesans had gained in the Settlements. The newcomer might not be familiar with them; the *Entertainment* offers an introduction. With this staging of a soothing past, the Shanghai courtesan establishments became a thoroughly Shanghai phenomenon, reacting with fine business acumen to a perceived need and demand among their clientele.

These needs and demands were not only in the realms of companionship and entertainment. From the *Entertainment*, we gather that one of the main functions (as well as a main source of revenue) of these houses was to provide guests with luxurious settings for banquets and dinner parties. In this capacity, the courtesan houses became an important gathering place for men of letters and government officials living in the city or passing through.

Since most of the men of letters who had come to Shanghai and remained there had given up—if reluctantly—on reaching officialdom and thus on gaining an official voice through the examination system, the courtesan houses and the entertainment papers became for them a public stage. Much that went on in the courtesan houses ended up as reports or poems published the next day. Here, in the beautifully decorated and brightly lit halls, the "guests" gave and attended banquets, discussing the social and political issues facing the nation. During the period when the *Entertainment* appeared (1897–1910), much of late Qing political reform, revolution, and restoration was discussed in these quarters. The novels serialized in the later entertainment papers are full of these discussions.

The participation of the reading public in the paper and the public discussion of the Shanghai courtesans marks a realignment of borders; the once private or semiprivate realm of social intercourse evoked in poetry has been made into a public concern. The public display and debate of this realm become themselves an entertainment business, with the readers paying seven cents each day for the privilege of participation and enjoyment.

By presenting the Shanghai courtesan houses as semiprivate spaces made public, the *Entertainment* created for itself the new role of the manager of public opinion through editorials and news reporting. The paper supplemented the abstract and issue-oriented reporting of the other commercial papers with its highly personalized approach and its elevation of the gossip among the chic and trendy to the level of newsworthy information. In this way, it enlarged the options open to the Shanghai men of letters beyond straight journalism as practiced in papers such as the *Shenbao, Shibao,* or *Xinwen bao.* To edit a Shanghai entertainment business paper and to write for it offered a way of making a living in town while not requiring a full-scale change in lifestyle. In the daily news reporting about the Shanghai courtesans, a new public persona of the Shanghai *wenren* took shape: in the traditional garb of the "protector of flowers," *huhua ren* 護花人, he helped in establishing and maintaining standards, and in criticizing abuses in what was a very professional and innovative entertainment business. The paper would take on issues such as mistreatment of courtesans by their madams; publicize cases brought by courtesans against clients who failed to pay their bills; write in support of courtesans' efforts to raise money for a cemetery for courtesans who had died in poverty; or take on the top courtesans for their pompous airs.

The paper's appeal for the readers was its ability to navigate the borders between the private and the public in terms of both its news and its social relations with the readers. The readers' letters show that they associated the paper personally with the owner Li Boyuan, and they proceeded to have a personal exchange of ideas with him on the public forum provided by the paper. A letter to the "Master of Entertainment" from a traveler passing through town on his way north, published on the front page of the *Entertainment,* may serve as an example. It first praises Li Boyuan for organizing a competition among the Shanghai courtesans in such gallant and fair spirit. Since the traveler had to leave Shanghai before the final result was published, he bought the paper daily after he arrived in Peking to keep up with developments; he noted in an aside that the paper was extremely popular in the offices of the capital, where it was read and passed around. The main point of the letter was a defense of the famous Lin Daiyu 林黛玉. The writer details to Li Boyuan (and the public) his private concerns and his relationship with the courtesan, and argues against the slanders leveled at her:

> The *xiaoshu* 校書 (top-ranking courtesan) Lin Daiyu hails from Songjiang. When I met her years ago in Tianjin, her bright eyes and skill in the art of love had already established her as a top courtesan with incomparable fame. Shortly afterwards she established herself in Shanghai, and her fame soared to new heights. During the past ten years, everyone who happened to come to Shanghai from high-ranking official to noble lord, from poet to scholar considered her the number one. While well-versed in the literary arts, and skilled in poetry composition and singing, this *xiaoshu* is particularly skilled in social intercourse and knows the art of pleasing. Those critics who sneer at her, reproach and slander her do so not on the basis of having observed her behavior, but on the basis of rumors. In truth, nothing in her behavior needs to be concealed. But [the harm is done by] those who discuss [her case] without being able to make the distinction between black and white [truth and falsehood]. As a result they have eclipsed her virtue instead of making it known. This is what I find so lamentable.
>
> Your intention has always been to deal with particular events in a straight-forward manner with the purpose of punishing wickedness and encouraging virtue. In this you have demonstrated your deep commitment to public well being. But is it also the purpose of your paper to be fair in the judgment between the good and the bad? I have known this courtesan for fifteen years; can I, being [myself] so far away, be so presumptuous as to relay the case to you as the one who is able to understand me, and to beg for [your] judgment and the dispersal of these slanders?[26]

The letter shows the tenuous line between the "public" and the "private." The patron's sense of personal responsibility toward the courtesan and his wish to publicly defend her reputation find an outlet in the newspaper. Using his private relationship with her as the basis of his judgment, he addresses Li Boyuan personally with the request that he should intervene to put the unfounded rumors to rest. In the persona of the "protector of the flowers," this writer-cum-reader of the newspaper makes use of the public forum of the paper to voice his opinion and to appeal for justice. In this manner, the *Entertainment* succeeded in making the business of the Shanghai courtesan and her clients a public subject.

In a supreme exercise of serious display of taste, political mockery, and self-irony, the paper involved the clients/readers to join as democratic judges in public courtesan contests. Such contests have a long history, and it was also customary to use terms such as *zhuangyuan* for the winning courtesan; in another world of competition these were used for the successful candidates on the highest level of the imperial examinations. This was not uncontroversial because early during the Qing one sponsor of such a courtesan contest was put to death for daring to make use of this august nomenclature.[27]

In the heady years of 1897 and 1898, straight into the Hundred Days Reform in June 1898 and its collapse three months later, Li Boyuan organized his courtesan competitions. The ironical relation of these competitions with the events in Peking could not be missed, and Li Boyuan obliged by making it quite explicit.

The democratic principle underlying this procedure was quite sensational and unfamiliar at this early time in China. Li Boyuan explained: "The completion held at this time will be modeled on the example of the Western democratic voting [system]. The results are decided by the relative number of write-ins [for a particular courtesan]."[28] The criteria for this first competition were both, beauty, *se* 色, and artistic achievement, *yi* 藝.[29] A few months later, a second competition was held, this time based solely on the performing arts. The counterpart was the traditional military examination, which was held apart from the civil examinations. As might be expected, this flower competition was to result in a "Publicly displayed list of [successful] military candidates," *wubang* 武榜.[30]

There was some question as to the moral standards to be applied when judging flowers. But who would downgrade a courtesan because she had changed clients, given the fact that the highest officials of the realm had themselves handsomely bribed by the Japanese in the midst of Japan's war with China? Autocracy takes over again in Peking with the emperor himself put under house arrest and Kang Youwei, who had been successful in the imperial examination a few years ago, running for his life. The impact of men of letters on the government clearly was at its lowest, and so was the trust in the impartiality of the examiners. But here in Shanghai the "Master of Entertainment" calls on the men of taste and judgment to join in a democratic, open, and informed selection that even had the name of the imperial examinations, to balance the relative weight of musical and literary skills, entertaining liveliness, and beauty in the top courtesans, and come to a democratically counted vote.

THE COURTESAN

It is time to talk about the main protagonist of the *Entertainment*, the courtesans. In a symbiotic relationship, the courtesans needed and used the papers for their self-promotion, and the paper created them as stars to sharpen their profile and create selling points.

Immediately after setting up the *Entertainment*, Li Boyuan organized the first courtesan competition. It was successful enough to be made into a regular event. The practice of ranking women with terms taken from the rankings in the imperial examinations already had a long tradition and was regularly used,[31] for example, in the early nineteenth-century novel *Flowers in the Mirror* (Jinghua yuan 鏡花緣).[32] Although Li Boyuan kept to the old terminology, his introduction of the public contest, the newspaper as the forum, the photograph of the winner as well as the general attention showered on every detail of the courtesans' personae as well as their private and public life set the most prominent among them on the way to become public figures and even the first public stars in China. In the *Youxi bao*'s flower contest we see the beginnings of a modern star culture, which would eventually develop into the frenzy surrounding the movie stars of the 1920s and 1930s.

The "star" is a marketable image. Like a brand name, the star must represent not only him- or herself individually but emblemize the lure of the entire industry. The success of Li Boyuan's courtesan paper is based on a skillful combination of generating a star culture and highlighting the attractions of the entertainment industry as a whole, an industry that would also be his main advertising clients. The paper indeed promoted the entire industry by creating such stars.

As a result of these competitions, the top courtesans gained instantaneous fame, their business thrived, each of their moves was reported in the *Entertainment*, and offers of marriage were made to many of them soon after the competition.[33] The most famous stars emerging from the early *Entertainment* were the "Four Great Diamond Cutters of Shanghai," Shanghai si da jin' gang 上海四大金剛, a term taken from the name of the mighty door guardian sculptures of Buddhist temples. These women were Lin Daiyu 林黛玉, Lu Lanfen 陸蘭芬, Jin Xiaobao 金小寶, and Zhang Shuyu 張書玉.[34] Through this term with its slightly ironic associations, Li Boyuan, who had coined the term, made the four courtesans memorable,[35] and by a continuous stream of daily reports about them he created a public awareness and expectation that the four women were not slow in living up to. With titles such as "Lin Daiyu chooses an auspicious day to open business,"[36] "A congratulatory poem dedicated to Jin Xiaobao on the occasion of her moving [to more elegant quarters],"[37] "A short history of Zhang Shuyu,"[38] "The biography of Jin Xiaobao,"[39] "Lu Lanfen goes to the park taking with her two handsome youths,"[40] "The [Four Shanghai] Great Diamond Cutters choose a day when to put on their [new] hats,"[41] and "Lin Daiyu's dress most extravagant,"[42] the reader followed what was presented as the sensational and sometimes provocative life of these women, a glimpse of whose real-life persona he might catch here and there in the fancy places of town.

These stars became separated from the crowd; they were individualized figures of focus, attention, admiration, and censure in the readers' minds. They were to set the trends and the pace of the courtesan world and were eagerly imitated by the wives and concubines of the well-to-do.[43] In them, and with their willing cooperation, Li Boyuan created Shanghai's new cultural icon. Like the movie stars later to come, the courtesan star opened up the once private and exclusive "man and women"—client and courtesan—relationship to the marketplace, to a public performance of status and attention for public consumption. With the imitations of these stars among the lower orders of the entertainment world and society at large, they had a strong impact on urban lifestyle and the broader entertainment culture in the city.

As much as the flower competitions enhanced the fame of some courtesans, the paper also reported a doubling of its sales from 4000 to 8000. This firmly established Li Boyuan and his *Entertainment* as the leading voice in the world of entertainment.[44] The competition also generated a lively public debate about the process of selection. Li Boyuan defended the result by explaining the principle behind democratic voting: the taste of one man should not have more sway than another's. After the competition, the paper had published many readers' letters, encouraging the process of the public airing of differences in taste and opinion.

The revival and restructuring of a traditional cultural forum became Li Boyuan's strategy with regard to the commercial culture of the Shanghai Settlements. To compete through constant innovation was the basic mode of operation here, and more so in the entertainment sector than elsewhere. In this process, Li Boyuan managed to put to use a traditional cultural skill and preference of the *wenren* in this modern environment, and helped to construct successful life projects for both *wenren* and courtesans that were adapted to the new environment while not being utterly alienated from the past.

The courtesans quickly spotted the advantages of such extensive newspaper coverage, and made good and increasingly self-confident use of it. They would advertise their change of residence, or make themselves newsworthy through extravagant clothes, jewelry, carriages, pastimes, or not-so-secret love affairs with opera stars or other pretty boys. They also made headline news through well-orchestrated public appearances. The public not only knew the top Shanghai courtesans by name but now they were also recognized by sight. They were seen at the Ankaidi 安塏第 teahouse in the Chang gardens; at the famous Yipinxiang 一品香 restaurant, which served Western cuisine; or simply riding in an open carriage with their client through the city's chicest commercial districts. The heightened attention during the competitions became one of the prime occasions during which they propelled themselves, and were propelled, into the limelight on their way up.[45] The newspaper was their public stage.

Public charity projects were one more way in which these star courtesans created and cultivated their new social stature and public persona. Again, the *Entertainment* played a crucial role as public platform for debate, fundraising, and critical evaluation of the effort. The most publicized case was the project to create a charity public graveyard for Shanghai courtesans who had died in poverty. The "Flower Cemetery," Huazhong 花塚, project was promoted by Lin Daiyu, one of the Four Great Diamond Cutters, in an open letter published in the *Entertainment;* and later the four together headed the fundraising drive.[46] The publicity created by the paper's reporting gave personality and status to these top courtesans. It also fixed their expected behavior and set the tone for reports about it. These were later followed in the main by the movie stars down to their celebrity support for worthy causes, and by the tabloids in their reporting.

IMAGE AND PHOTOGRAPH

On September 30, 1898, the *Entertainment* featured something brand-new: it glued the photograph of the courtesan who had won the flower competition onto the front page of each issue of the paper, with her name, age, address, and "ranking" (among the flowers) added underneath. The photograph was accompanied by the traditional dedication poem written to the courtesan by an admirer (Figure 5.2). In the paper's announcement, "On attaching the image of the famous flower to the paper," the editor explains:

> In ancient times there were paintings but no photographs. However, skills in painting not being equal, it is already difficult with a whole day's exertion to get a single leaf done with some similarity to the shape [of the object depicted]. How much more is this the case for similarity to the spirit! And

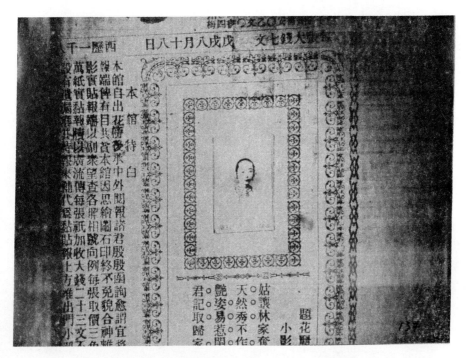

Figure 5.2. Hua Lijuan, Shanghai courtesan. Photographed by Yaohua studio, Shanghai, 1898. Hua Lijuan had taken second place in the *Entertainment* "flower competition" of fall 1898. To publicize the event, the paper offered the photographs of the top three winners as glue-ins in the newspaper (*Youxi bao*, October 3, 1898, p.1).

how many are there who [have the supreme skill to] manage what is called "painting some hairs onto the chin [as done by the famous painter Gu Kaizhi to bring out the character of the scholar Pei Kai]?" Since the photography procedure from the West has become available one barely needs a moment and one already has managed to execute [a picture] according to one's wishes with none that is not pleasing in mien and utterly lifelike; one can't deny that this is a divine invention.[47]

The idea of including the photograph of the courtesan into the paper arose from popular demand. After the courtesan contest, readers of the paper wrote and suggested that the winners should have their portrait attached to the paper. The choice was between a Chinese-style portrait drawing rendered in lithograph and a Western style photograph. Li Boyuan went for the photograph because of its novelty; his editorial on the matter claims that its higher quality of likeness and the speed with which it could be produced supported his decision. Of course, the customer had to pay more for these issues. The Yaohua photography studio, which had made courtesan photographs their specialty, was the natural partner for the enterprise.[48]

To have a photo taken and give it to a client had become a fashion among courtesans decades before the *Entertainment*'s extravaganza. As the technique of making many and enlarged copies from a single negative was already available, courtesan photos were sold in the photography studios.[49] The newspaper insert of the photograph, however, was a first and big step at mass production of the courtesan image. It presupposed a close cooperation between the courtesans, the photography studio, and the paper.

The Shanghai courtesans themselves had gone a step further by becoming very public persons, parading themselves and their clients through town in their high open carriages and showing up at the teahouses in their most fancy dresses. But it was Li Boyuan who made the image of the courtesan a collective and public enterprise. The photograph had the purpose of enhancing the prestige and circulation of the paper, and in this it succeeded beyond expectation.

These special issues were so well received that the streets outside the *Youxi bao* office were clogged; after printing 10,000 copies for that day, the paper had to reprint thousands more copies for the next two days to meet popular demand.[50] At the same time this was good advertisement for the courtesan business. Although this sensational supplement was a one-time affair—according to Li Boyuan, this was an extremely costly extravaganza, which he decided to do for the fun of it[51]—the impact of the photograph was revolutionary. It marked the end of an era in which the wood engraving and the—already very innovative—lithograph, both done with little effort to bring out individual features, dominated the image of the courtesan. The introduction of photography transformed this image as well as her relationship to the traditional set of cultural associations and the social rituals linked to her. Already in many of the lithographs coming out of the Dianshizhai studio since the late 1870s her image had been associated with the allure of modern technology,[52] and the photograph enhanced this notion with additional luster. It now presented her not anymore as the generic courtesan, but as a very distinct individual.

With this shift, beauty, a feature much lower on the scale of courtesan connoisseurs who mostly emphasized entertainment skills, greatly gained in importance. But in the same process, this beautiful individual was, as this beautiful individual, transformed by the *Entertainment* into a cultural commodity, a "specialité," in the luxury industry. In the act of publishing her image, Li Boyuan realized its potential commercial value. The elusive and exclusive attraction of the courtesan here becomes the pull of her market value, which was soon discovered not just to drive up the sales of entertainment papers, but for advertisement as well.

The individuality of the courtesan up to that time had greatly depended on what the men of letters wrote about her. Earlier courtesan handbooks featuring images of courtesans in block print or lithographs always accompanied these images with personal reminiscences of her clients. In these elaborations, she always transcended the limitations of reality, and the literary devices used to convey an impression of her person tended to evoke a certain otherworldliness.

A fine example is the *Jingying xiaosheng* 鏡影簫聲, a set of illustrated biographies of Shanghai courtesans published in 1885.[53] The volume, which is illustrated with copper engravings and was printed in Tokyo, offers Chinese portraits of courtesans surrounded by traditional emblems such as bamboo, stone, flower, and tree (Figure 5.3). In its composition, the portrait emphasizes sensuality in a traditional setting. The particular lifestyle of the Shanghai courtesan in the Shanghai Settlements is not part of this portrait. The image is not intended to be realistic. It is coded. In her collective non-individualized image and surroundings, the courtesan evokes in the viewer's mind fantasies of life in a dreamland enriched by many layers of poems and reminiscences left behind by famous scholars, statesmen, and poets of the past. Good looks and beauty were not high priorities to qualify for a great courtesan. Instead, the art of entertaining, literary achievements, skills in music, and liveliness in speech and manner have traditionally been much more appreciated.[54]

Against this background, the introduction of the photographic image was culturally a complicated and very bold act. While certainly motivated by economic concerns and business tactics, the publication of the courtesan photograph still had a "democratic" and very modern urban element to it. It removed the exclusiveness of the client's claim on the courtesan. Every reader of the *Youxi bao* could now enjoy a look at the favorite courtesan of the wealthiest businessman, at a cost of a few pennies. The image of the individual courtesan, which once was inaccessible except for the few who could afford direct contact with her, was now reproduced in unlimited quantity. Under the influence of the expanding newspaper business and its increasingly innovative advertisement, and very much in tune with the new business strategies of the Shanghai courtesans themselves, the new marketable high-profile

Figure 5.3. Courtesan. *Jingying xiaosheng chuji* 鏡影蕭聲初集 (Mirror reflections and flute sounds, first collection). Copperplate engraving. Tokyo, 1887.

individual, the forerunner of the modern star, replaced the collective cultural image of the courtesan. The real image replaces the literary image. The break was sensational, but not brutal. The men of letters easily transferred the practice of writing appreciative poems about the courtesan in the "protector of flowers" stance to the new image, the photograph, and the new medium, the newspaper. The interaction between man of letters and courtesan survived in a new cultural packaging.

By moving the image of the courtesan from the exclusive high culture domain into the market of the mass media, the *Entertainment* helped to put this image onto the larger map of Shanghai's commercial culture, which by the 1890s was already quite established. With its orientation toward individualized choice in the popular consumption of semblances of traditional culture, its combination of business considerations, marketing of goods, and the glamour of the commodity, this new image signaled the development of a new urban sensibility. The courtesan in pursuit of stardom, with the publicity and promotion given to her by Li Boyuan's papers, became the city's avant-garde in setting new fashions and trends. Her photographs spread to other media; as late as the 1910s, literary journals such as *Fiction Monthly* or *Fiction Prospect* would reproduce these images as emblems of the exotic and glamorous.[55]

The direction of things can be seen in the 1918 competition among the flowers. When the entertainment paper *New World* (*Xin shijie bao* 新世界報) held its Shanghai courtesan competition in that year, it was no longer referred to as "Public Listing of Flowers," *huabang* 花榜, a term again modeled on the publicly displayed lists of ranked successful candidates in the imperial examinations, but as "Election of Flowers," *huaxuan* 花選, in proper democratic spirit, with the winner no longer called "Winner of the Imperial Examinations," *zhuangyuan* 狀元, but in true Republican spirit "President of the Kingdom of Flowers," Huaguo da zongtong 花國大總統.[56] The photograph of the president of the kingdom of flowers, a courtesan called Judi 菊第, is a composite between her picture and the blossoming lotus. The symbol is traditional and signals that, although she grows like the lotus out of the mud, she is intrinsically pure. The composition of the photograph turns toward tradition while inserting the new image of the courtesan in this "age of mechanical reproduction" into the modern city. The "democratic victory" of the president gives it a distinctly modern and fantastic air against the background of warlord China.

THE CITY

In the relationship between entertainment paper and courtesan, writer and reader, a third figure retains a distinct presence, the city itself. Functioning as the backdrop of all activities, it looms behind the seemingly traditional scenes with their courtesans and clients. From this contrast and interaction, these scenes are oddly energized and provided with an urban ambiance of theatrical staging and role-playing.

At the same time, the city imposed itself on all its denizens. The *Entertainment* and its contemporaries were strictly urban phenomena as was the world they were writing about. The authors, the reader, the client, the courtesan—all were engaged in an exercise of urban modernity that came with the enormous attraction of not sharing the heaviness and darkness of the national discourse. In the process, the city itself shifted from being the admired dreamscape of modern comfort to being the fermentation tub for urban modernity with its glories and crassness, its money obsession and cultural flourishing, its corruption and the muckraking novel to unmask it. Like the Shanghai courtesan, the entertainment paper was a Shanghai specialité. Both were seen as part of this city's self-staging.

THE GENRE ESTABLISHED:
THE *XIAOBAO* AS A LITERARY JOURNAL

Li Boyuan's success with the *Entertainment* prompted others to follow suit. To name but a few: *Leisure* (Xiaoxian bao 消閑報, November 1897), *Variety* (*Caifeng bao* 采風報, May 1898), *Amusement* (*Qu bao* 趣報, 1898), *Flowery Moon over the Spring River* (*Chunjiang huayue bao* 春江花月報, 1901), and *Fun for all Seasons* (*Jishi xingle* 及時行樂, 1901). In the midst of this flurry, Li Boyuan decided to start a second entertainment paper to be run simultaneously with the *Entertainment*, the *World Vanity Fair* (*Shijie fanhua bao* 世界繁華報). It added another rising star, the Peking opera performer. Needless to say, this second venture did not stop the flow; others sprang up such as *A Sky Full with Flowers* (*Huatian ribao* 花天日報, 1902), or *Amusement Daily* (*Yule ribao* 娛樂日報, 1905).[57] These titles all play on the notion of leisure and fun and suggest a new urban sensibility for leisure.

In *World Vanity Fair*, Li Boyuan's most important innovation, however, was to establish literature, especially fiction, among the core ingredients of the *xiaobao*. The stand taken by Li Boyuan in his response to the question why such light reading matter as the *Entertainment* could be successful might have sounded defensive at the time, but it certainly was borne out by the literary works later published in his papers. These political satires did not even have to leave the courtesan house far behind because a fair part of the scenes are set right there, where real life would have had them.

Literature came in a variety of genres, both big and small. The smaller genres included "stories," *chuanqi* 傳奇, "allegories," *yuyan* 寓言, "prefaces and postscripts," *xuba* 序跋, and "biographies" *chuanji* 傳記. And Li Boyuan expanded the literary items in *World Vanity Fair* to the point that they dominated the different columns. The main categories were "satirical poetry," *fenglin* 諷林, "editorials," *lunshuo* 論說, most recent telegraphic dispatches, *zuixin dianbao* 最新電報, "satires on contemporary affairs," *shishi xitan* 時事喜談, "essentials from the opera world," *juebu yaolu* 菊部要錄, "daily record of Shanghai flowers," *Haishang kanhua riji* 海上看花日記, "readers' letters," *laihan zhaodeng* 來函照登, "new operas on contemporary events," *xinbian shishi* xinxi 新編時事新戲, "literary small talk," *tancong* 談叢, "new publications in literature and the arts," *yiwenzhi* 藝文志, "unofficial history," *yeshi* 野史, "travelogues," *youji* 游記, "local customs," *fengsu zhi* 風俗志, and "records of courtesan life," *beili zhi* 北里志. Quickly, old categories were replaced and new ones were added, such as "reports on opera singers" *guchui lu* 鼓吹錄, and the satirical "chronicle of Shanghai things unmatched elsewhere," *Shanghai wushuangpu* 上海無雙譜. The more strictly literary columns included "stories," *shehu lu* 射虎錄, "new sayings the world is talking about," *shishuo xinyu* 世說新語, "jokes," *huaji hun* 滑稽魂, and "scattered notes on the glamour [of the Shanghai courtesan and opera stars]," *fanhua zazhi* 繁華雜志.

Compared to the short literary genres, the longer forms had a modest beginning. The manuscript of an unpublished romantic libretto came into Li's hands in 1897, and he serialized it.[58] One of his earliest contemporaries, the *Variety* (*Caifeng bao* 采風報, May 1898), which was edited by Sun Yusheng 孫玉聲 (Sun Jiazheng 孫家振, often using the penname Haishang shushi sheng 海上漱石生), was the first to insert a new novel in separate installments. It dealt with contemporary and urban (courtesan) affairs from his hand, the *Haishang fanhua meng* (海上繁華夢, *Dreams of Shanghai's Glamour*). Once Li Boyuan had set up the *Shijie fanhua bao* in 1901, he began serializing his first major work of political and social criticism, the *Tanci on the national crisis of 1900* (*Gengzi guobian tanci* 庚子國變彈詞) as part of the paper itself; this was followed between 1903 and 1905 by his scathing satire of Qing officialdom *Bureaucracy Exposed* (*Guanchang xianxing ji* 官場現形記), and then by his friend Wu Jianren's *Confused World* (*Hutu shijie* 糊塗世界).[59] Since 1906, "short stories," *duanpian xiaoshuo* 短篇小說, and "vernacular talk," *baihua* 白話, were added.

By constantly creating and inventing new columns and literary categories, Li Boyuan presented his readers and the entire newspaper industry with a startling new horizon of literary "play" that made literary innovation an art in its own right. The mosaic display of "literary fun" became the trademark of the *xiaobao*. The layout of *Entertainment* and *World Vanity Fair* constantly surprised with new things. This included the setup of the different columns, the length of the paper, the position of the advertisements, and so on. To dazzle the reader with new inventions and to be unique was Li Boyuan's personal interest and his business strategy.[60]

With his two papers, Li Boyuan sketched the new way in which literature was to function in the entertainment newspaper, and established the novel firmly within the popular entertainment press. With their combination of entertainment and literature, the two papers also helped to articulate and popularize a particular kind of ironical urban stance. While this stance certainly fed on the rancor of these men with themselves and with late Qing society and politics, it became a hallmark of Shanghai entertainment culture, and a constant irritant to the high pontificators with their tragic pose and grand words.

LATER DEVELOPMENTS

The *xiaobao* quickly became a popular reading matter with a substantial circulation in the 10,000 range.[61] While throughout the subsequent decades into the 1920s and 1930s, they constantly found new sources of inspiration, spread to new urban centers, and developed new ways to keep their readers' interest, they invariably stuck with the main features of the genre as they had been established by Li Boyuan's pioneering enterprises—until, of course, 1949 when all *xiaobao* were closed. This remarkable resilience and stability of the *xiaobao* as a genre attests to the powers of Li Boyuan's precedent. It also shows to what degree the Shanghai Settlements shaped the cultural habits and preferences of later generations across the land.

In the development of the entertainment papers, the amusement park papers took the *xiaobao* into a new direction. The *Da shijie* 大世界 (The Great World), was one of the first entertainment newspapers directly linked to an entertainment center.[62] It was founded in 1917 as part of the Great World enterprise. The owner of the Great World, Huang Chujiu 黃楚久, was an old friend of Sun Yusheng, then one of Shanghai's most famous writers and newspapermen. Huang elicited Sun's help in creating a special daily newspaper for the Great World amusement center, which marks the first time that a *xiaobao* and an entertainment business were run by the same company.

The paper had a 39 x 55 cm format, and came in two sheets that folded in the middle, making it into four pages (Figure 5.4). The cover page and the last page were devoted to the listing of theatrical programs offered by the Great World and the results of its lottery; pages 3 and 4 contained different literary columns, including one on theater, the *youmeng shijie* 優孟世界, one on novels, the *yuyan shijie* 寓言世界, commentary on flowers, *meihua shijie* 玫花世界, one

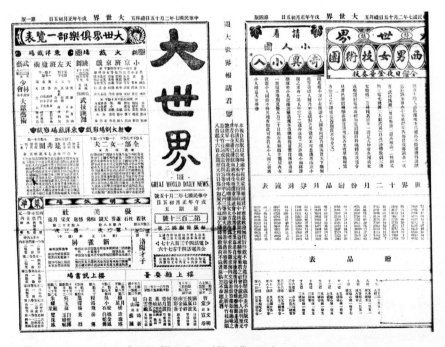

Figure 5.4. *Da shijie* 大世界 (The Great World), 1918, p. 1.

with historical anecdotes, *hongxue shijie* 鴻雪世界, one with correspondences with readers, *yingqiu shijie* 嚶求世界, one on Western science, *shizhou shijie* 十洲世界, one on literary games, *youyi shijie* 游藝世界, and one with humor, *huaji shijie* 滑稽世界, with each of them presenting another segment of the Great World.

The impact of Li Boyuan's paper *World Vanity Fair* can again be seen in all aspects of this paper. Together with the further development of the concept of the "big playground," the connection between the business of entertainment and the *xiaobao* pioneered by Li Boyuan is now fully realized. The titles of the various columns recall those used by Li Boyuan; they show the same propensity to create strange and new terms for the different literary columns so as to enhance the sense of literary playfulness. Most notable is the central position of the novel in this paper. In serialized form, the *Da Shijie* often carried segments from two or three novels in the same issue.

The wider Shanghai business community soon understood the cultural importance of xiaobao when it began to integrate entertainment with the sale of consumer goods. When Shanghai's first modern department store, the Xianshi gongsi 先施公司, was founded in 1917, an amusement center was added on the top floor of this four-story building; with it came another entertainment newspaper, the *Xianshi leyuan ribao* 先施樂園日報 with the suggestive English title *The Eden*, edited by the famous novelist and writer Zhou Shoujuan 周瘦鵑.[63] Following the format of the *Da shijie*, the *Xianshi Leyuan* exemplified Li Boyuan's concept of Shanghai as the "world's greatest playground" with its paradise/Eden language. By now, the ironic stance, which originally justified the *wenren*'s participation in such lowly endeavors, had quietly disappeared; the ironic references to the "big playground" are transformed and reduced to advertising Eden's remorseless pleasures.

The *Jing bao* 晶報, or *Crystal*, was founded in Shanghai in 1919, first appearing every three days as the supplement to the *Shenzhou ribao*.[64] Since it was doing better than its mother paper, it became an independent *xiaobao*. Together with the exotically named *Fuermosi* 福爾摩斯 (Sherlock Holmes), *Loubinhan* 羅賓漢 (Robin Hood), and *Jingang zuan* 金剛鑽 (Diamond Cutter), it dominated the scene of the *xiaobao* in the early 1920s.

Like Li Boyuan's two papers, the *Crystal* focused on Shanghai courtesans and opera stars. Through literary and pictorial renderings to Shanghai life, it further developed Li Boyuan's concept of a Shanghai urban identity largely based on Shanghai entertainment. The paper included photographs of courtesans and actors, news and comments on the theater, novels, and social commentary. Many well-known novelists of the time such as Bao Tianxiao 包天笑, Zhou Shoujuan 周瘦鵑, and Li Hanqiu 李函秋 serialized their work in this paper. It also featured the works of some of the commercially most successful cartoonists, such as Ding Song 丁悚, Shen Bochen 沈伯塵 and Huang Wennong 黃文農. As an independent paper that was not directly linked to any particular business interest or company, however, the *Crystal* remained much closer to Li Boyuan's critical intellectual approach.

From these samples of *xiaobao* in the late 1910s and early 1920s the striking presence of late Qing entertainment newspapers becomes apparent. In form, these *xiaobao* maintained the small format as compared to the big dailies to signal their identity. In content, the *xiaobao* maintained the close association with the Shanghai entertainment world in general and with the courtesan and opera stars in particular. They maintained and further developed the central position of the novel in these papers with their critical approach to entertainment and social issues.

There were changes as well. The organization and publication of the *xiaobao* changed during the Republican era. They were no longer a one-man show. Even Li Boyuan later hired Ouyang Juyuan 歐陽鉅源 to help him.[65] Li Boyuan had a personal commitment to the paper.[66] The later *xiaobao* were run by writers who would ask their writer friends to contribute, or, as in the case of the *Crystal,* they were run by a manager who himself was not a writer but had many social connections.[67] But the most marked change was in the mood and values expressed in these later papers. When the new generation of Shanghai urban intellectual writers began contributing to these papers, there was little left of the bitterness and sarcasm so acutely expressed by Li Boyuan. The papers, as much as the novels of this period, were of a calm and amusing kind. The dominating literary value is that of *wenya* 文雅 or cultivation.

The *xiaobao* later developed into many different directions, for a time even becoming a medium for battles among political factions in the late 1920s.[68] Other *xiaobao* were exclusively devoted to fiction. But, in the main, the *xiaobao* remained a part of the Shanghai urban cultural landscape, focusing on the different kinds of performing arts such as the theater, the cinema, the opera, and their stars. As a newspaper genre, they were among the liveliest sprouts of an urban culture that defied the hard separations between high and low. The genre's vitality and flexibility attest to the close fit with which Li Boyuan had inserted its founding stones into the framework of the developing Shanghai urban culture.

THEME PARK SHANGHAI

The link between entertainment business and the *xiaobao* opened up a mutually advantageous alliance in which *xiaobao* reporting became an indispensable part of promoting entertainment establishments. At the same time, public reporting increased the pressure in the establishments to conform to standards of professionalism in their business. The *xiaobao* also helped to promote and reinforce what was to become one of the most important conceptual frameworks for Shanghai entertainment business: the "theme park" idea where "fun" could be had as a single experience with multiple dimensions. Li Boyuan's two papers showed entertainment to be a "field of play" where different kinds of pleasures could be integrated.

In the 1890s, the theme park idea was still new. When the Zhangyuan had opened to the public in 1885, it already included a Western-style building with rooms for performances and meetings, the "Arcadia," Ankaidi 安塏第. The park offered more amusements; there was a billiard parlor, a photography studio, a tennis curt, a teahouse, a meeting hall, a theater for female opera performances, a storytelling hall, a hall for camera obscura shows, different types of restaurants, and a guesthouse.[69] In promoting the idea of the theme park with its ever-changing attractions in different fields of entertainment, the *xiaobao* became and came to be seen as an indispensable part of this universe of fun. As we have seen with the "Great World," the newspaper that was created was devoted entirely to the establishment carrying its name. The virtual universe of entertainment in the paper had found its real-life counterpart.

CONCLUSION

The entertainment newspaper from the turn of the twentieth century marks an important step in the development and diversification of China's public sphere. Entertainment had a place in newspapers such as the *Shenbao*, but had no clearly identified slot or column. The arrival of papers specializing in entertainment (including political satire) signals the size, maturity, and legitimacy of the entertainment sector in Shanghai, but also a new role for literati such as Li Boyuan. They became brokers between the market and culture, between entertainment businesses and the newspaper. In the process, their papers extricated themselves from the vertical top–down/bottom–up communication model. Their communication was strictly horizontal, addressed as it was to an urban audience of connoisseurs and *xiao shimin*. In this manner, they reflected and promoted a change in the structure of the public sphere that reacted to the vitality and power of the new urban lifestyle in Shanghai.

The entertainment newspapers were part of the growing Shanghai-based print entertainment, where they joined illustrated magazines, literary journals, and novels. They lived on, and reinforced, the new work/leisure division of time. This strange Western separation, which still seemed outlandish to visitors, quickly spread through the Shangai public arena, and gradually made its way from there into the modernizing sectors of other urban centers. (It should be kept in mind, however, that the unification of time reckoning and of the association of time and social rituals in cities with large-scale provincial immigration such as Paris or London was achieved only gradually by the end of the century.) The entertainment papers offered ideas and contributed to develop standards for socially acceptable entertainment.

Given the dependence of the entertainment business on publicity and public attraction, the Shanghai courtesans—as the first generation of modern businesswomen in this city—astutely used the extraordinary new options offered by the papers to promote themselves, while these papers were only too eager to see their market flourish. In this manner the old and closely interwoven relationship between courtesan and *wenren* was continued in the interaction between the modern woman entertainer and the journalist, albeit with a different power dynamics.

As the men of letters gradually came to grips with their new station, the mood of their courtesan writing changed from nostalgia to urban irony. Their misty language of the Shanghai dreamland with its courtesans shifted, by the end of the century, to a market-savvy journalistic attitude that was both aware of the paper's dependence on the courtesans and of the fact that only through a modicum of critical distance to them could they keep their readership interested.

With the *Entertainment* setting the example, the *xiaobao* that followed in the next years all took the Shanghai courtesan as their main focus; with Li Boyu-an's *World Vanity Fair,* actors entered as a second main focus. The promotion of entertainers as public figures was revolutionary in itself. Under the light cloak of commerce and amusement, the early *xiaobao* brought about a conceptual shift in the qualifying standards for protagonists on the public stage. In marketing the lives of the Shanghai courtesan and the opera singer for mass consumption, and in transforming them into identifiable individuals, these papers articulated the ingredients of a media-based star culture that stole the show from many a political strongman. The promotion of star photography by these papers is at the root of the blossoming Chinese star culture of the 1920s and 1930s.

The entertainment paper also articulated a new sense of urban identity with regard to the city. In their presentation of Shanghai as amusement park, these papers helped shape an urban sensibility for this unique environment. As much as they might ridicule the city's gregarious extravagance and appetite for conspicuous consumption, they also subvert their own critical stance through the unabashed pride and self-confidence with which they advertise the pleasures of the city to their readers. In their later critiques of the city, the sense of Shanghai identity and self-confidence forged in the years of the 1880s and 90s remains visible.

The entertainment papers spread to other Chinese cities after the 1911 revolution. But as in the same way Shanghai continued to be the capital of China's print industry until 1949, it remained the place where the bulk of the entertainment papers came out.

NOTES

1. L. S. Mercier, *Nouveau Paris,* Paris, 1799, vol. 3, p. 56.

2. C. Yeh, *Shanghai Love, Courtesans, Intellectuals, and Entertainment Culture, 1850–1910.* Seattle: University of Washington Press, 2006.

3. For this juxtaposition, see also R. Wagner, "The Concept of Work/Labor/Arbeit in the Chinese World. First Explorations," in W. Bierwisch, ed., *Die Rolle der Arbeit in verschiedenen Epochen und Kulturen*, Akademie-Verlag Berlin, 2003, pp.103–127.

4. A Ying 阿英, *Wan Qing wenyi baokan shulüe* 晚清文藝報刊述略 (Introduction to late Qing literary journals), Beijing: Zhonghua shuju, 1959. Zhu Junzhou 祝均宙, "Shanghai xiaobao de lishi yange" 上海小報的歷史沿革 (The historical development of Shanghai tabloids), in *Xinwen yanjiu ziliao*, 42:163–179 (1988); 43:137–153 (1988); 44:211–220 (1988). The library of the Institute of Chinese Studies, University of Heidelberg, has substantial microfilmed holdings of these tabloids. It should be noted that the generic term *xiaobao* was only coined much later.

5. "Benbao tianyin fuzhangxiang qi" 本報添印附張像起 (On the occasion of our paper's printing a supplement), *Youxi bao*, June 9, 1899.

6. Quoted from A Ying 阿英, *Wanqing wenyi baokan shulüe* 晚清文藝報刊述略, Shanghai: Gudian wenxue Press, 1958, p. 66.

7. "Benguan qianju Si malu shuo" 本館遷居四馬路說 (On the removal of our company to Si malu), *Youxi bao*, October 2, 1897.

8. *Libailiu* 禮拜六 (*Saturday*), 1:1 (1914); Reprint Nanjing: Jiangxi Guangling guji keyingshe, 1987. For a study on time in the everyday life urban professionals, see Wen-Hsin Yeh, "Corporate Space, Communal Time: Everyday Life in Shanghai's Bank of China," *The American Historical Review*, Vol. 100, No. 1 (February 1995), pp. 97–122.

9. See Wang Tao's explanation of the purpose of his paper in N. Vittinghoff, "Useful Knowledge and Appropriate Communication," in this volume.

10. The best-known novels written by Li Boyuan are *Guanchang xianxing ji* 官場現形記, first serialized in *Shijie fanhua bao*, 1903, *Wenming xiaoshi* 文明小史 (1903), *Huo diyu* 活地獄 (1906), and *Zhongguo xianzai ji* 中國現在記 (1906).

11. After the death of his uncle, who had been his provider, he was penniless. Like many others in similar circumstances, he had only his literary skills to offer. The success of his two entertainment papers gave him him some financial security. For details on his life, see Wei Shaochang, ed., *Li Boyuan yanjiu ziliao* 李伯元研究資料 (Research materials on Li Boyuan), Shanghai: Shanghai guji chubanshe, 1980; Catherine Yeh, "The Intellectual as the Courtesan: A Trope in Twentieth Century Chinese Literature," conference paper presented at Harvard University, 1990; id., "The Life of Four Late Qing Wenren in Shanghai," *Horvard Journal of Asiatic Studies* 57.2 (December 1997).

12. Nothing seems to survive of the *Guide*. The only note dealing with this paper is Zhu Junzhou, "Li Boyuan yu *Zhinan bao*" 李伯元與指南報, *Xinwen daxue* 新聞大學, Winter issue, (1990), pp. 48–50.

13. For a fine introduction of the Paris tabloids and other entertainment media of the Second Empire, see Laurent Fraison, "Offenbach: Une Iconographie Monumentale," in Jean-Claude Yon, *Offenbach*, Catalogue of an exhibition in the Musée d'Orsay March 26–June 23, 1996, Paris: Les Dossiers du Musée d'Orsay, 1996, pp. 79–136.

14. "*Youxi bao* zhi benyi" 游戲報之本意 (On the purpose of the *Youxi bao*), *Youxi bao*, August 28, 1897; "Benbao tianyin fuzhangxiang qi" 本報添印附張像起 (On the occasion of our paper's printing a supplement) *Youxi bao*, June 9, 1899; "Ji benbao kaichuang yilai qingxing" 記本報開創以來情形 (On the situation of our newspaper since the time of its creation), *Youxi bao*, January 16, 1898.

15. *Youxi bao,* October 1, 1898.

16. "Benguan qianju Si malu shuo" 本館遷居四 馬路說 (On the removal of our company to Si malu), *Youxi bao,* October 2, 1897.

17. *Youxi bao,* October 2, 1897.

18. Li Boyuan, "Youxi zhuren gaobai" (Announcement from the Master of Entertainment), *Youxi bao,* March 19, 1899, p. 1.

19. "Benguan qianju Si malu shuo" 本館遷居四馬 路說 (On the removal of our company to Si malu), *Youxi bao,* October 2, 1897.

20. "Lun *Youxi bao* zhi benyi" 論 <游戲報> 之本意 (On the basic purpose of the *Youxi bao*), *Youxi bao,* August 25, 1897.

21. "Lun Huji jixi tai shen" 論滬妓積習太甚 (The Shanghai courtesans are overdoing it), *Youxi bao,* July 20, 1899, p. 1.

22. Cf. my "The Life of Four Late Qing *Wenren* in Shanghai," *HJAS* 57.2 (December 1997).

23. "Lun Hu bin shuyu yingchou dangyi Lu Lanfen wei diyi" 論滬濱書寓應酬當 以陸蘭芬為第一 (Why Lu Lanfen should be considered Shanghai's number one in the arts of courtesan entertainment), *Youxi bao* September 18, 1897.

24. Wang Tao 王韜 (1828–1897), "Zixu" (preface by author) in *Haizou yeyou lu* 海 陬冶游錄 (Record of visits to the courtesan houses in a distant corner of the sea), preface, 1860. Reprint in Zhang Tinghua, ed., *Xiangyan congshu,* Beijing: Renmin wenxue chubanshe, 1992, vol. 5, p. 5637.

25. Ge Yuanxu writes in the introduction to his guide: "I have been playing in Shanghai for fifteen years now, and have sojourned in the Foreign Concessions living in my thatched hut. From what reached my ears and eyes, anecdotes gradually piled up" (余游上 海十五年矣. 寓廬屬在洋場, 耳目所及, 見聞逐夥), in Ge Yuanxu 葛元煦, *Huyou zaji* 滬游雜 記 (Shanghai Miscellany) (1877). Reprint: Shanghai: Shanghai guji chubanshe, 1989, p.7.

26. "A letter on [the courtesan] Lin Daiyu to the 'Master of Entertainment'" (Zhi Youxi zhuren lun Lin Daiyu shu 致游戲主人論林黛玉書), *Youxi bao,* November 2, 1897.

27. Wang Shunu 王書奴, *Zhongguo changji shi* 中國娼妓史 (The history of prostitution in China) (1933). Reprint: Shanghai: Sanlian shudian, 1988, p. 311.

28. Zhou Shoujuan, *Lao Shanghai sanshinian,* Shanghai: Dadong shuju, 1928, p.27.

29. *Youxi bao,* August 5, 1897.

30. For details, see Zhou Shoujuan, *Lao Shanghai sanshinian,* p. 33.

31. The first recorded flower competition was during the Song; for details, see Wang Liaoweng 汪了翁, *Shanghai lushinian huajie shi* 上海六 十年花界史 (A sixty-year history of the Shanghai flower world), Shanghai: Shixin shuju, 1922, pp. 77–96.

32. Li Ruzhen 李汝珍 (1763–1830), *Jinghua yuan* 鏡花緣, first published in 1828; for a modern edition, see Peking: Renmin chubanshe, 1986, 2 vols.

33. During the period after the competition, the *Youxi bao* made headline news out of the winners from the competition finding husbands.

34. Li Boyuan gave this name to the four top courtesans when he met them at the tea house in Zhang Gardens, where each day they would be sitting at the same table by the door; for details see Chen Wuwo 陳無我, *Lao Shanghai sanshinian jianwenlu* 老

LEISURE, PRINT ENTERTAINMENT, TABLOIDS

EISURE, PRINT ENTERTAINMENT, TABLOIDS 231

上海 三十年見聞錄 (A record of things seen and heard by an old Shanghai hand in the last thirty years), Shanghai: Dadong shuju, 1928, vol.1, p. 34; for a study, see Gail Hershatter, *Dangerous Pleasures. Prostitution and Modernity in Twentieth-Century Shanghai*, Berkeley: University of California Press, 1997, pp.169–171.

35. "You Zhangyuan 'Sida jingang'" (The Four Great Golden Diamonds Cutters visit the Zhang Gardens), *Youxi bao*, October 12, 1897, p. 2.

36. "Lin Daiyu zeqi kaishi" 林黛玉擇期開市 (Lin Daiyu chooses an auspicious day to open business), *Youxi bao*, October 5, 1897.

37. "Wen Jin Xiaobao qiaoqian shi yi he zhi" 聞金小寶喬遷詩以賀之 (A congratulatory poem dedicated to Jin Xiaobao on the occasion of her moving [to more elegant quarters]), *Youxi bao*, September 21, 1897

38. "Zhang Shuyu lüli" 張書玉履歷 (A short history of Zhang Shuyu), *Youxi bao*, November 11, 1897.

39. "Jin Xiaobao zhuan" 金小寶傳 (A biography of Jin Xiaobao), *Youxi bao*, November 18, 1897.

40. "Lu Xiaoshu youyuan xie er mei" 陸校書游 園偕二美 (Lu Lanfen goes to the park taking with her two handsome youths), *Youxi bao*, 2 November, 1897.

41. "Da Jinggang zeqi daimao" 大金剛擇期戴帽 (The Great Diamond Cutters choose a date when to put on their [new] hats), *Youxi bao*, October 18, 1897

42. "Lin Daiyu yishang chuse" 林黛玉衣裳出色 (Lin Daiyu's dress most extravagant), *Youxi bao*, October 11, 1897.

43. See C. Yeh, *Shanghai Love*, ch. 1.

44. *Youxi bao*, October 4, 1897.

45. The *Entertainment*, furthermore, put out an advertisement for the compilation of "The history of Shanghai flowers," *Chunjiang huashi* 春江花史, which was to be based on the competition, but might also include those courtesans who had been overlooked. It was to have the biographies of the winners of all three levels of the competition, altogether one hundred and forty courtesans with three in the top, thirty in the second, and one hundred and seven in the third rank. *Youxi bao*, August 26, 1897.

46. "Dai Xiaoshu Lin Daiyu deng ni mujuan gouzhi huazhong xiaoqi" 代校書林黛玉等擬募捐購置花塚小啟 (Announcement of a draft fundraising proposal for establishing a public graveyard for courtesans, written on behalf of the *xiaoshu* Lin Daiyu and others), *Youxi bao*, October 9, 1897; for details see Zhou Shoujuan, *Lao Shanghai sanshinian*, pp. 122–130.

47. "Ji jinri benguan fuchu minghua xiaoying" 紀今日本館附出名花小影 (In commemoration of the insertion of a photograph of the famous flower into today's paper), *Youxi bao*, September 30, 1898, p. 1.

48. For more detail on Yaohua photography studio, see Catherine Yeh, *Shanghai Love*, p. 88.

49. Ge Yuanxu's 葛元旭 *Huyou zaji* 滬游雜記 (Shanghai miscellaneous), p. 57, records under the heading "The photography shop" how courtesans were having themselves photographed, and later passed these prints on to potential clients. Wang Tao's early account of the Shanghai courtesan also mentions the fashion among some courtesans to have their photograph taken; see Wang Tao 王韜, *Haizou yeyou fulu* 海陬冶

游附錄 (Sequel to the record of Shanghai courtesan entertainment) (1879). Reprint: Chong Tianzi, ed., *Xiangyan congshu* 香艷叢書, Beijing: Renmin wenxue chubanshe, 1992, p. 5720. For studies, see Regine Thiriez, "Photography and portraiture in nineteenth-century China," *East Asian History* 17/18:77–102 (June/December 1999).

50. *Youxi bao,* October 1, 1898.

51. *Youxi bao,* September 30, 1898, p. 1.

52. See C. Yeh, *Shanghai Love,* ch. 1.

53. *Jingying xiaosheng chuji* 鏡影蕭聲初集 (Mirror reflections and flute sounds, first collection), copperplate engraving, Tokyo, 1887.

54. See, for example, Cui Lingqin 崔令欽 (Tang period), *Jiaofang ji* 教坊記 (Record of the court entertainment bureau) (714). Reprint: Sun Jialuo, ed., *Zhongguo xueshu mingzhu.* vol. 1 (3) pp.1–19; Sun Qi 孫棨 (Tang period), *Beili zhi* 北里志 (Record of the northern section), reprt. Sun Jialuo, ed., *Zhongguo xueshu mingzhu,* vol. 1 (3) pp. 21–42; Yu Huai 余懷, *Banqiao zaji,* 板橋雜記 (Random notes of the wooden bridge), 1654, reprt. Chong Tianzi, ed., *Xiangyan congshu* 香豔叢書, Beijing: Renmin wenxue chubanshe, 1992, pp. 3637–3672.

55. For examples, see *Xiaoshuo yuebao* 小說月報 2.4 (April 1910); and *Xiaoshuo shibao* 小說大觀, 1915.

56. *Huaguo baimeitu* 花國百美圖 (Illustration of one hundred beauties of the kingdom of flowers), Shanghai: Sheng sheng meishu gongsi, 1918, p. 18, Judi (no page number in the text).

57. During the period between 1896 to 1910s, there were thirty or so pure entertainment newspapers; for details, see A Ying 阿英, *Wanqing wenyi baokan shulüe* 晚清文藝報刊述略 (A survey of late Qing literary journals and newspapers), Shanghai: Zhonghua shuju, 1959, pp. 49–89; Zhu Junzhou 祝均宙, "Shanghai xiaobao de lishi yange" 上海小報的歷史沿革 (The historical development of Shanghai tabloids), in *Xinwen yanjiu ziliao,* 42:163–179 (1988).

58. *Fengshuang fei* 鳳雙飛 (A pair of phoenixes takes off), serialized in *Youxi bao* from November 1897 on.

59. For details, see A Ying 阿英, "*Gengzi guobian tanci,*" 庚子國變彈詞 in Wei Shaochang, ed., *Li Boyuan yanjiu ziliao,* p. 260, and his note on the *Guanchang xianxing ji* 官場現形記, ibid., p. 72.

60. Wu Woyao 吳沃堯, "Li Boyuan zhuan" 李伯元傳 (A biography of Li Boyuan), in Wei Shaochang, ed., *Li Boyuan yanjiu ziliao,* p.10.

61. Zhu Junzhou, "Shanghai *xiaobao* de lishi yange," 43:137–139 (1988).

62. The *Da shijie* 大世界 (*The Great World Daily News*) was founded in July 1, 1917, and closed in June 1931. After the founding of the Republic in 1911, the *xiaobao* as a genre almost disappeared. Could this be due to a momentary triumph of "serious" talk? It only revived in the late 1910s; for details, see Zhu Junzhou, "Shanghai *xiaobao* de lishi yange," 42:170 (1988).

63. The *Xianshi leyuan ribao* 先施樂園日報 (*The Eden*) was founded in March 19, 1918, and closed in May 1927.

64. The *Jing bao* 晶報 (*Crystal*) was founded on March 3, 1919, and closed on May 23, 1940.

65. See Wei Shaochang, 490–492.

66. For details, see A Ying, "Xiqiu sheng fei Li Boyuan huaming kao" 惜秋生非李伯元化名考 (Xiqiu sheng is not a pseudonym of Li Boyuan), in Wei Shaochang, ed., *Li Boyuan yanjiu ziliao,* pp. 486–489; Wei Shaochang, "Rongyuan Xi Qiusheng qi ren qi shi 茂苑惜秋生其人其事 (On the Loves and Labors of Xi Qiusheng from Maoyuan), ibid., pp. 490–494; Shun Ying 釧影, "Bu Maoyuan Xi Qiusheng shi" 補茂苑惜秋 生事 (Additional notes on the life of Xi Qiusheng from Maoyuan), ibid., pp. 495–498.

67. For details, see Zhu Junzhou, "Shanghai *xiaobao* de lishi yange," 42:171–172 (1988).

68. See Zhu Junzhou, "Shanghai *xiaobao* de lishi yange," in *Xinwen yanjiu ziliao* 42:163–179 (1988), 43:137–153 (1988), 44:211–220 (1988).

69. For details on the Zhangyuan, see Gu Bingquan 顧柄權, *Shanghai fengsu guji kao* 上海風俗 古蹟考 (Investigations of historical sources concerning Shanghai's customs), Shanghai: Huadong shifan daxue, 1993, pp.149–150; Xiong Yuezhi 熊月之, "Zhangyuan: Wan Qing Shanghai yige gonggongkongjian yianjiu" 張園: 晚清上海一個公共空間的研究 (Zhang Gardens: A study on a public sphere in late Qing Shanghai), in Zhang Zhongli, ed., *Zhongguo jindai chengshi qiye, shehui, kongjian,* Shanghai: Shanghai Shehui Kexueyuan chubanshe, 1998, p. 334–359.

Contributors

NATASCHA GENTZ is Chair of Chinese Studies in the School of Asian Studies, Program Director for the Master of Chinese Studies, and Director of the Confucius Institute at the University of Edinburgh, Scotland.

NANNY KIM is a Research Associate at the Institute of Chinese Studies, University of Heidelberg, Germany.

BARBARA MITTLER is Professor of Chinese Studies at the Institute of Chinese Studies, University of Heidelberg, Germany, and Director of the Institute.

RUDOLF G. WAGNER is the Chair of Sinology, Institute for Chinese Studies and the Director of the Center for East Asian Studies at the University of Heidelberg, Germany.

CATHERINE VANCE YEH is a Research Associate at the Institute of Chinese Studies, University of Heidelberg, and now an Associate Professor of Chinese Literature and Culture at Boston University.

Index